# THE
# LICENSING (SCOTLAND)
# ACT 1976

*[Including The Law Reform (Miscellaneous Provisions)
(Scotland) Act 1990, Part III and Schedule 8 and
The Licensing (Amendment) (Scotland) Act 1992.]*

THE PD
LICENSING (SCOTLAND)
ACT 1976

[Including The Law Reform (Miscellaneous Provisions) (Scotland) Act 1990, Part III and Schedule 8 and The Licensing (Amendment) (Scotland) Act 1992]

# ALLAN and CHAPMAN'S

# THE
# LICENSING (SCOTLAND)
# ACT 1976

*[Including The Law Reform (Miscellaneous Provisions)*
*(Scotland) Act 1990, Part III and Schedule 8 and*
*The Licensing (Amendment) (Scotland) Act 1992.]*

THIRD EDITION

by

**Sir Crispin H. Agnew of Lochnaw, Bt,** *Advocate*

and

**Heather M. Baillie,** B.A., LL.B., *Solicitor*

W. GREEN/Sweet & Maxwell
EDINBURGH
1992

First published in 1977
Reprinted in 1984
Second edition 1989

© W. Green & Son Ltd.
1992

ISBN 0 414 01000 0

*Text typeset by LBJ Enterprises Limited*
*of Aldermaston and Chilcompton*
*Printed in Great Britain by*
*Butler and Tanner Ltd.,*
*Frome and London*

# PREFACE TO THIRD EDITION

THIS third edition of the annotations to the Licensing (Scotland) Act 1976 by Allan and Chapman follows hard on the heels of the second edition because of the substantial amendments made to the 1976 Act by the Law Reform (Miscellaneous Provisions) (Scotland) Act 1990, Part III and the additions to the law contained in the 1990 Act itself. The three years since the second edition appeared have also seen a substantial further body of case law develop particulary in the field of judicial review of a licensing board's decisions.

We would like to thank Peter Nicholson and the staff of W. Green for their courteous assistance with the preparation of this edition, and J. Ronald Gardiner, W.S., of Messrs Brodies who made his knowledge and experience of licensing law available to us when we were revising the final draft.

We have tried to state the law as at August 31, 1991

EDINBURGH                                                    C.H.A. of L.
October 1991                                                 H.M.B.

# PREFACE TO SECOND EDITION

DURING the last 13 years, since the passing of the Licensing (Scotland) Act 1976, there have been substantial developments in licensing law and a number of important decisions regarding the interpretation of the Act, which has also undergone some amendment. In part this has been due to the investments made by major companies in licensed premises, who, having the financial resources, are then prepared to test the decisions of a licensing board in the courts. The introduction of the judicial review procedures has opened up a whole new field in licensing litigation. These developments have warranted a new edition of the well loved annotations to the 1976 Act by John Allan and Charles Chapman.

In this revision of the annotations to the Licensing (Scotland) Act 1976 by Allan and Chapman, we have made the minimal revision which we considered necessary to bring the notes up to date. In the original annotations to *Current Law Statutes* the authors included a brief summary of the Clayson proposals and the origins of each section, which we have in general deleted from the notes, because the Act has now been in force for over 11 years and so these notes are, in the main, only of general interest. We have sought to expand the Introduction to give a more general overview of the law and practice of liquor licensing in Scotland. We have tried to state the law as at December 31, 1988.

EDINBURGH
April 1989

C.H.A. of L.
H.M.B.

I should like to acknowledge with thanks the following: Mr A. J. Wilson, W.S., for introducing me to this area of law and encouraging me to practise it; Mr. J. C. Cummins, solicitor, Glasgow, for reading and revising the final drafts, and Mr Peter Nicholson of W. Green & Son for his forbearance and assistance throughout.

EDINBURGH
July 1989

H.M.B.

# PREFACE TO FIRST EDITION

FOLLOWING the coming into force of the Licensing (Scotland) Act 1959, the eighth edition of Purves's *Scottish Licensing Laws* was published, the commentary of which was rewritten and realigned so as to apply to the 1959 Act. A considerable number of the provisions of the 1959 Act have been re-enacted in the 1976 Act, and the annotators have, wherever possible, adapted and followed the commentary in the eeeighth edition of Purves, and acknowledge the debt they owe to the learned author of that edition.

Since the *Current Law Statutes* annotations on the 1976 Act were published, a number of queries have been raised, mainly by local authority staff who will be responsible for the administration of the new licensing boards, and some anomalies in the wording of the Act have come to light. These queries and anomalies are considerd in the Appendix under the heading of the section to which they relate. [*Note.* Not printed in 3rd ed.]

KIRKCALDY
April 1977

J.A.
C.D.C.

# TABLE OF CONTENTS

# TABLE OF CASES

# INTRODUCTION

## (1) Historical background

**1.1.** The roots of the licensing legislation lie in the desire of governments to impose a social control on the drinking habits of the population and to control the manufacture and sale of alcoholic liquor as a source of revenue. The first licensing Act for Scotland is said to be the Act of 1756 (29 Geo. 2, c. 12). The outline of the present system of licensing was introduced by the Act of 1802 (48 Geo. 3, c. 143). The system was established in its present form by the Home Drummond Act 1828 (9 Geo. 4, c. 58), which set up regular meetings of justices in counties and magistrates in royal burghs to grant certificates, without which the Excise could not grant licences. The Act provided for the transfer of licences at those meetings, and for appeals to the quarter sessions. The certificates contained certain conditions, the breach of which was punishable by means of a fine or imprisonment, or forfeiture of certificate or both. This idea of breach of conditions attached to certificates continued until the passing of the Licensing (Scotland) Act 1976 (the 1976 Act), which introduced the concept of licensing offences rather than breaches of certificate.

**1.2.** The Forbes Mackenzie Act 1853 (16 & 17 Vict. c. 67) settled the closing hour at 11.00 p.m. and separated the public house licence from the off-licence (the grocer's certificate), and disqualified blacksmiths from their ancient privileges of supplying spirits. The Public House Amendment Act 1861 (25 & 26 Vict. c. 35) amended the licensing legislation, mainly by introducing policing measures and giving constables rights of entry to premises for the detection of illegal stills. The Act created a number of drink-related offences such as being found in a shebeen, being disorderly in licensed premises or being drunk, and provided that these offences and those of a breach of certificate were to be prosecuted by the procurator fiscal. The Act further provided for a register of applications and regulated the manner in which objections could be made.

**1.3.** The Publicans' Certificate Act 1876 (39 & 40 Vict. c. 26; amended by 40 & 41 Vict. c. 3), placed table-beer licences under the control of the licensing authority and made other changes to the procedures. The Inland Revenue Act 1880 (43 & 44 Vict. c. 20) and the Hours of Closing Act 1887 (50 & 51 Vict. c. 38) altered the times at which premises could be open.

## Licensing (Scotland) Act 1903

**1.4.** By the turn of the century numerous other Acts incidentally affected the licensing legislation and the rights and obligations of certificate holders. As a consolidating and amending Act was by then necessary, a royal commission was appointed in 1896, which held 134 sittings, examined 289 witnesses and in 1899 published nine volumes of evidence with a majority and minority report. As a result of the commission's work the Licensing (Scotland) Act 1903, which incorporated many of the recommendations of both the majority and minority reports, was passed.

**1.5.** The 1903 Act made radical changes in the licensing legislation. It altered the constitution and jurisdiction of the licensing courts; introduced offences in relation to drunkenness and imposed penalties on persons other than the certificate holder; penalised the sale of liquor from non-registered premises and hawking; introduced the code for registering clubs; forbade the sale of liquor on Sundays except to travellers and, most importantly, provided for the deposit of plans for the proposed premises and empowered the licensing courts to enforce certain building or reconstruction works in relation to licensed premises. Further details of the 1903 Act are given in the *Encyclopaedia of the Laws of Scotland (Dunedin Edition)*, Vol. 9, paras. 351 *et seq.*

*Licensing (Scotland) Act 1959*
**1.6.** The 1903 Act remained the basis of the licensing legislation and practice, with amendments (some temporary to deal with the exigencies of the two wars) and with the introduction of ancillary legislation dealing with licensed premises in the New Towns Act 1952 and the Licensing (Seamen's Canteens) Act 1954, until the passing of the Licensing (Scotland) Act 1959, a consolidating Act, which did not radically alter the concepts of licensing introduced by the 1903 Act. The law regarding excise licences and excise duties payable by licensed premises such as hotels, clubs, public houses and licensed grocers was consolidated in the Customs & Excise Act 1952 (amended by the Finance Act 1959).

*The Guest and Clayson reports*
**1.7.** Since the passing of the Licensing (Scotland) Act 1959 there have been two departmental committees on the Scottish licensing laws, the Guest Committee, appointed in 1959, and the Clayson Committee, appointed in 1971. Prior to the Guest Committee, the most recent inquiry into the law regulating the sale and supply of alcoholic liquor was the Royal Commission under the chairmanship of Lord Mackay appointed in 1929. The Mackay Commission were not unanimous in their views, and presented in 1931 a majority and a minority report. Neither the recommendations of the majority or of the minority report were implemented by legislation. The remit of the Guest Committee was to review the law relating to the sale and supply of liquor on Sundays, the permitted hours for the sale and supply of liquor on weekdays, the constitution of licensing courts and courts of appeal, and to the granting of certificates for the sale of liquor in areas of housing development and redevelopment. The committee presented two reports. The first report (1960, Cmnd. 1217), dealt with the sale and supply of liquor on Sundays and the permitted hours. Its principal recommendations were that, instead of varied hours as fixed by local licensing courts, there should be standard permitted hours for the whole of Scotland and that public houses,

restaurants, and hotels should have permitted hours on Sundays. Under the 1959 Act there were no permitted hours on Sundays, but residents and *bona fide* travellers were entitled to obtain liquor in hotels. The first report gave rise to the Licensing (Scotland) Act 1962, which provided for standard permitted hours for the whole of Scotland, and for Sunday opening, which was restricted, however, to hotels and, in certain circumstances, to premises providing meals. The 1962 Act also introduced two new kinds of certificate, *viz.* a restricted hotel certificate, which allowed liquor to be supplied to residents and to persons taking meals, and a restaurant certificate which allowed liquor to be supplied to persons taking meals, and made provision for the extension of licensing hours on premises supplying meals.

**1.8.** The second report of the Guest Committee (1963, Cmnd. 2021), was concerned with those parts of the remit which were not considered in the first report. Its main recommendation was that licensing courts, as then constituted, should continue to carry out the functions entrusted to them but that there should be a right of appeal from the decision of a licensing court to the sheriff. No legislation followed the recommendations of the second Guest Report.

**1.9.** In 1971 the committee under the chairmanship of Dr Christopher W. Clayson was appointed with the broad remit "to review the liquor licensing law of Scotland and to make recommendations on what changes, if any, might be made in the public interest, and to report." The committee's report (1973, Cmnd. 5354) made far-reaching recommendations. It concluded that, since liquor licensing involved the exercise of an administrative discretion in the interests of the community, it was not an appropriate function for a court of law, that the system of licensing courts and courts of appeal, which was continued by the 1959 Act, should be replaced, and that the function of liquor licensing should be carried out by a tribunal composed of local authority district council members. It further proposed that there should be a right of appeal against the decision of a board to the sheriff. As regards types of licences, the committee were of the opinion that two new types of licence should be introduced, a refreshment licence permitting the sale of alcoholic liquor on premises where food and non-alcoholic beverages were available for sale, and an entertainment licence permitting the sale of liquor on premises where entertainment was provided. On the matter of the permitted hours, the report was in favour of their retention, but put forward the proposal that public houses should have permitted hours on Sundays, that such hours should not be confined to hotels as was the case under the 1962 Act, and that a licensing board should have the power to restrict and extend permitted hours where the circumstance in a locality justified it. It was further recommended that the temperance legislation should be repealed. As regards registered clubs, the main proposal was that the police should have the same power of entry into registered clubs as they had into licensed premises, *i.e.* that they should be entitled to

3

enter them without a warrant. The report of the Clayson Committee became the basis of the proposals embodied in the Licensing (Scotland) Act 1976. The major proposals not incorporated into the Act included the proposal that all premises in respect of which public house licences were held should have permitted hours on Sundays, and that clubs should be open to police inspection without a warrant.

### (2.a.) The scheme of the Licensing (Scotland) Act 1976

**2.1.** Part I implements the proposals of Clayson as regards the transference of the functions of licensing courts to boards consisting of district or islands council members (s.1). Instead of half-yearly meetings, as was the case under the 1959 Act, the new boards are to have quarterly meetings in January, March, June and October, for the disposal of business involving applications for the grant of new licences, including provisional grants, applications for renewals where there are competent objections, applications for the extension of permitted hours, the restriction of permitted hours, and the restoration of restricted permitted hours, applications for the Sunday opening of public houses, and the restriction orders relating to the Sunday opening of public houses (ss.4 and 5). Whereas, under the 1959 Act, the clerk of the licensing court was the town clerk in the case of a burgh, and the clerk of the peace in the case of a county, the clerk to a licensing board is to be an advocate or solicitor appointed by the appropriate district or islands council (s.7).

**2.2.** Part II of the Act deals with the general licensing system. It introduces the two new types of licence recommended by Clayson, the refreshment licence and the entertainment licence (s.9). It gives effect to the proposal that legal *personae* other than natural persons, such as limited companies, should be able to hold licences (s.11). Whereas the 1959 Act contained the conditions under which the certificate was held, and also enacted that it was a criminal offence to breach any of the conditions, the 1976 Act provides for the type and not the form of certificate, leaving it to the individual board to decide on the form (s.9 and Sched. 1), and dispenses with the offence of breach of certificate, making, in Pt. VI, separate statutory provisions for offences against the Act.

**2.3.** Part II also makes provision for the procedure for the grant or provisional grant of a new licence, and the transfer or renewal of an existing licence. It regulates the procedure for making objections, and specifies the persons or bodies entitled to object (s.16), and the grounds on which a board may refuse an application (s.17), and provides for an appeal to the sheriff against a board's decision on most matters within their province under the Act (s.39). Such an appeal can only be upheld on the grounds stated in the section, and there is further appeal from the sheriff to the Court of Session on a question of law. As regards applications for new licences (s.23) or provisional grants (s.26), the Act makes it necessary for the applicant to produce certificates from the appropriate authorities as regards planning permission, building control, and food hygiene, and provides for consultation by the board with the fire authority (s.24). The recommendation of Clayson to extend the period of the currency of a licence to three years is accepted (s.30). Consequential to this acceptance, new controls over a licence during its currency are introduced, giving a board the power to suspend a licence (s.31) following a complaint, and to order the closure of premises (s.32) on their own initiative. Part II of the Act also makes provision for occasional licences, entitling a licence holder or a club to sell liquor at a place outwith the licensed premises or the club premises, and introduces the new conception of allowing the granting of an occasional permission for the sale of liquor by a voluntary organisation at an event related to the activities of the organisation (s.34).

**2.4.** Part III substantially repeats the previous legislation as regards the licensing of seamen's canteens and Part IV (now repealed) the special requirements relating to the grant of new licences in new towns.

**2.5.** Part V is concerned with the permitted hours. The principal changes it makes include the extension of the terminal time of the evening permitted hours from 10 p.m. to 11 p.m., and the authorisation of permitted hours in respect of a public house on Sundays where an application for such hours is granted by a licensing board (s.53(2) and Sched. 4). Another principal change made by Pt. V is to provide for occasional and regular extensions of the permitted hours, and for the restriction, including the temporary restriction, of these hours. A licensing board, by virtue of s.64, may grant an occasional extension of the permitted hours to a licence holder or a registered club, whereby the licence holder or the club may sell liquor outwith the permitted hours between the time specified for a period of not longer than one month. Under the 1959 Act, the procedure for obtaining permission to sell liquor outwith permitted hours was to apply for special permission, which permission could only be granted if it was required for a function or an occasion which did not originate from the licence holder applying for the permission. The 1976 Act does not restrict extensions of the permitted hours to functions not originating from the applicant, though certain boards seek to impose such a condition in respect of regular extension. Also in virtue of s.64, a board may grant a regular extension of the permitted hours for a period not exceeding one year, where the board consider it desirable to do so, having regard to the circumstances and activities of the locality. The basis upon which a board assesses the desirability of granting such an extension has been substantially restricted by the terms of s.47 of the 1990 Act. See **2(b)**. By s.65, a board may restrict the permitted hours to end not earlier than 10 p.m. where the sale of liquor is causing a nuisance or a threat to public safety or order. A police officer of the rank of chief inspector or above may request a temporary restriction from a licensing board whereby licensed premises can be closed for a period of up to three hours, where it is desirable in the interests of public order or safety. The rest of Part V re-enacts the previous legislation relating to the prohibition of the sale of liquor outwith the permitted hours (s.54), to the variation of the permitted hours in the case of athletic clubs in winter (s.56), and to the variations of such hours where liquor is supplied with a meal (s.55 and ss.57 to 60).

**2.6.** Part VI specifies the offences under the Act. It is primarily a re-enactment of the offences constituted by the 1959 Act, but includes offences by way of breach of the conditions of a certificate. The penalties for a contravention of the 1976 Act are specified in Sched. 5, including whether the contravention carries the penalty of disqualification of the premises and of the licence holder. The Schedule also specifies whether an offence is one for which the licence holder is vicariously liable. Sections 67 to 73 of Part VI make provision for offences in connection with the presence of and the supply of liquor to young persons and children in licensed premises. The main differences from the legislation which the sections supersede is that persons over 16 years of age can now be supplied with wine with a meal (s.68), that cognisance is taken of the special position of premises operated under a refreshment licence in connection with the presence in and use of them by children and young persons (ss.70 and 73), and that the defence that an accused used due diligence to prevent the commission of an offence is available in connection with offences involving young persons or children (s.71). Sections 74 to 81 substantially re-enact the provisions of the 1959 Act relating to conduct on licensed premises. The prohibition on drinking alcoholic liquor in unlicensed premises and in places of public refreshment is also re-enacted, with the variation that the prohibition is not to apply to private functions related to a particular occasion (ss.82 and 83). Sections 84 to 86 repeat the previous provisions relating to offences in connection with the police, and the powers of the police to enter both licensed and unlicensed premises. The rest of Pt. VI re-enacts miscellaneous offences which were in the 1959 and 1962 Acts (ss.87 to 99), and makes it an offence to sell liquor outwith the conditions specified in Sched. 1 for a refreshment licence (s.100) and an entertainment licence (s.101). As regards restrictions on credit sales, allowance is made for the use of credit tokens as defined by s.14 of the Consumer Credit Act 1974 (s.87).

**2.7.** Part VII substantially repeats the provisions of the 1959 Act on the matter of registered clubs, with adaptations. It does, however, make a number of not insignificant changes. As regards the procedure for applying for a certificate of registration, a list of members need not now be lodged with the application, but any change in the club rules or the officials or committee of the club lodged with the application must be intimated forthwith to the registrar (s.103(3) and (5) as amended). If such intimation is not made forthwith, then the failure to do so becomes a ground of objection to the grant or renewal of a certificate of registration (s.108(g)). Recommendations made by Clayson on the matter of intimation of an application for registration or renewal of a certificate of registration, and the right to object to such an application, are given effect to. Notice of the application has to be given in a local newspaper, and has to be displayed on or near the club premises. The right to object is additionally conferred on local churches and community councils, and is withdrawn from the procurator fiscal (s.105). The presence of a bar on the club premises ceases to be a competent objection. The currency of a certificate is increased to three years (s.106). As regards the cancellation of certificate of registration, in accordance with Clayson, a club cannot now renew its certificate of registration within less than one year after the date of the cancellation (s.109). On the matter of the age of persons permitted to be in clubs, persons under 14 years of age are not permitted to be in the bar of a club during the permitted hours (s.112). A club must keep a list of members on the club premises, which list is to be open to police inspection (s.115(3)). Finally, there are provisions designed to make the committee of management and officials liable for certain offences, for which see the note to s.33 in the Appendix at p. 143.

**2.8.** Part VIII is concerned with miscellaneous, transitional and general provisions. It provides for the trading hours of off-sale premises (s.119), making no substantial changes thereto, and repeats the provisions of the 1959 Act which prohibit the sale of liquor in unregistered clubs (s.120). On the matter of the sufficiency of evidence in certain prosecutions under the Act, the previous legislation on the matter of proof of trafficking without a licence (s.122), and on the matter of proof of drunkenness (s.126), is re-enacted along with a new provision which raises a presumption that a container contains what the label states it contains, in order to obviate unnecessary expense in adducing of expert analysts as witnesses (s.127). Two major repeals are made by this part of the Act, the repeal of s.91(6) of the Local Government (Scotland) Act 1973 which prohibited the granting of a certificate for the sale of liquor to local authorities (s.124), and the repeal of the temperance provisions of the 1959 Act (s.131).

**2.9.** The whole of the Licensing (Scotland) Act 1976 was brought into force by October 1, 1977.

**(2.b.) Part III of the Law Reform (Miscellaneous Provisions) (Scotland) Act 1990**

**2.10.** The 1976 Act was substantially amended by Part III of the Law Reform (Miscellaneous Provisions) (Scotland) Act 1990, which was introduced partly with a view to tightening up the basis upon which licences could be issued, partly to make it more difficult to have long regular extensions, and partly to correct difficulties which had emerged in the 1976 Act. See "Licensing Reform" by J. C. Cummins, 1991 S.L.T. (News) 271.

**2.11.** Section 45 provides the new basic permitted hours for days other than Sunday from 11 a.m. to 11 p.m., thus abolishing the requirement to apply for afternoon extensions. Section 46 introduces new procedure for obtaining opening on a Sunday. Procedurally, many of the requirements of Sched. 4 of the 1976 Act have been simplified; however the reasons for refusal of an application for Sunday opening are more onerous than the grounds for refusal of an extension of permitted hours. Section 47 provides that a regular extension under s.64 of the 1976 Act shall not be granted unless the board are satisfied that "there is a need in the locality" which is a harder test than that which formerly applied.

**2.12.** Sections 49 and 50 introduce a Clayson recommendation that there should be a "Children's Certificate" to allow children under the age of 14 years to be taken to suitable premises.

**2.13.** The major change introduced by s.51 in amending s.25 of the 1976 Act in regard to the transfer of licences, which provides that a temporary transfer has to be granted prior to an application for a permanent transfer, makes for substantial difficulties in the sale and conveyancing of licensed premises; see note to s.25.

**2.14.** The remainder of the Act set out to correct anomalies and difficulties which had arisen under the 1976 Act since its introduction and, which had either been highlighted in practice or in the judicial decisions under the Act.

**(2.c.) Licensing (Amendment) (Scotland) Act 1992**

This amendment which came into force on 15 April 1992 allows an applicant to apply to a quarterly meeting of the licensing board for a permanent transfer of a licence without the need to follow the temporary transfer procedure as a preliminary. Thus reinstating the old s.25 procedure as an option for the transfer of a licence if the new temporary transfer procedure introduced by s.51 of the 1990 Act cannot be used for the reasons anticipated in the Note to s.25 of the 1976 Act and para. 3.44 *infra*.

**(3) The Act in practice**

**3.1.** The transference of the functions of licensing courts in Scotland to boards of local councillors has resulted in a proliferation of "geographical" styles dependent on the particular district in which an application for a licence is made. Individual boards have developed their own style of disposing of applications; both the form in which they expect the application to be made and their treatment of that application at the board meeting can vary, depending on the area, their application of local knowledge and the number of applications being dealt with in their district. In order to ascertain whether an application will be accepted, it is important to find out from the clerk to the board or his/her staff whether all the preliminary requirements laid down by the particular board have been complied with. The licensing board has power to make procedural regulations with respect to the making of applications (s.37) and bye-laws (s.38) in terms of the Act. It is useful, when obtaining the relevant application forms from the clerk to the licensing board, to obtain a list of the regulations and, on the grant of an application, the bye-laws which may regulate the licence, *e.g.* the conditions which may be attached to licences for the improvement of standards of, and conduct in, licensed premises (s.38(*f*)).

**3.2.** Recent discussion of the powers of a clerk to decide whether an application should be considered by a board, where all the statutory requirements have not been complied with, can be found in *Main* v. *City of Glasgow District Licensing Board*, 1987 S.L.T. 305 and *Tait* v. *City of Glasgow District Licensing Board*, 1987 S.L.T. 340. It appears to be accepted after consideration of the point by the courts that the clerk should not usurp the discretion of the board. The clerk must advise the board on matters of procedure, however the board having been properly advised must reach a decision as to whether they can properly deal with an application and how to dispose of it. For discussion of the time at which a "late" application for the grant or renewal of a licence can be lodged see *Purdon* v. *City of Glasgow District Licensing Board*, 1989 S.L.T. 201; *Indpine Ltd.* v. *City of Dundee District Licensing Board*, 1991 G.W.D. 29–1759, and *A. R. Sanders* v. *Birmingham Licensing Justices & Others*, Birmingham Crown Court (January 12, 1990) *Licensing Review*, Vol. 2, p. 20.

**3.3.** In addition to the regulations and bye-laws which may affect the making/granting of an application, certain boards apply their own "guidelines" when considering an application, in particular for regular extension of permitted hours. When considering an application in terms of s.64 of the Act, the board have the discretion to grant an extension of permitted hours "having regard to the social circumstances of the locality," or "to activities taking place in that locality." The basis on which a board may consider an application has been changed by the coming into force of s.47 of the 1990 Act. The "guidelines" to which an applicant may be referred are an expression of the board's policy, in relation to applications of a particular kind, and may set out the hours to which the board is prepared to extend permitted hours, or the extra requirements they impose in granting regular extensions, *i.e.* provision of entertainment, or on the occasion of a function being held on the premises only. Certain boards will grant an extension automatically if it falls within their "guidelines" and will only cite an applicant to speak to an application if it does not fall within the guidelines. The practice is widespread, although the imposition of "guidelines" in certain circumstances, where only an applicant outwith the guidelines is required to speak to the application, may be considered to be prejudging certain applications and "fettering" the board's discretion. Similarly, certain boards will not consider an application for regular extension of permitted hours at all, until a "demand" has been established by the applicant, by

9

way of a series of applications for occasional extension. This is an exercise of discretion which to date remains unchallenged. There is no requirement in terms of the section for "demand" to be established in this way. For discussion of the way in which the courts have dealt with the imposition of "guidelines" and general policy see *Semple* v. *City of Glasgow District Licensing Board*, 1989 G.W.D. 36–1677, 1990 S.C.L.R. and *Elder* v. *Ross & Cromarty District Licensing Board*, 1990 S.L.T. 307, 1990 S.C.L.R. 1. With regard to the renewal of licences and to the regular extension of permitted hours, it is still the practice of some boards to send intimation of the requirement to renew a licence or its extension to the licence holder. The practice should not, however, be relied upon, as there is no statutory requirement to remind the licence holder of the need to renew a licence and many boards, particularly in larger districts, do not intimate or have decided to cease giving such intimation.

**3.4.** The relationship between a licensing board and the various departments from which it obtains reports and recommendations can lead to the development of specific practices at a board meeting. As a result of the changes introduced by para. 5 of Sched. 8 of the 1990 Act and s.53 of Part III of the 1990 Act, comments by the chief constable require to be intimated to the applicant, following the decision in *Centralbite Limited* v. *Kincardine & Deeside District Licensing Board, 1990 S.L.T. 231*, Paragraph 5 of Sched. 8 of the 1990 Act gives the fire authority and the local authority the right to object. Consideration should be given to whether the ratio of the *Centralbite* decision can be applied to comments by the fire authority and the local authority, now that they have a statutory right to make formal objections. See also discussion regarding relevance of observations by the Environmental Health Department in *Bantop Ltd.* v. *City of Glasgow District Licensing Board*, 1990 S.L.T. 366, 1989 S.C.L.R. 731.

*Administration*

**3.5.** A separate licensing board exists for each district and islands area in Scotland who may divide the district or area into separate licensing divisions. The board must consist of not less than one quarter of the members of the district or islands council and in no case can it comprise less than five members. A quorum for any meeting of the licensing board must be half the members of the board, and in no case less than three members (s.1). Addresses, etc., for licensing boards can be found in Section D of the *Scottish Law Directory*.

**3.6.** The board must hold meetings in January, March, June and October of each year and has the power to adjourn any meeting for a maximum of one month (s.4). The board can hold other meetings at its own discretion. Certain applications can be dealt with only at a meeting of the full licensing board, whereas other applications can be dealt with by a committee of the board, a member or members of the board or the clerk. It is advisable to ascertain from the clerk which category a particular application falls into, as some applications can be administered without the appearance of the applicant (s.5).

**3.7.** Generally, procedure at a licensing board is less formal than in court. Few licensing boards require solicitors to wear gowns, and there is no statutory requirement that solicitors should so. The members of the board should be addressed as "your honours," and as a general rule the meeting will be conducted by the chairman.

**3.8.** Applications for new licences are heard after all other cases have been disposed of (s.13(1)). Where more than one application has been made in respect of premises they may be heard together, *i.e.* permanent transfer and regular extension of permitted hours (s.13(1)).

*Types of licence (Sched. 1)*
**3.9.** The types of licence which may be granted are set out in Sched. 1 to the Act.
   (*a*) Public house—for consumption on or off the premises.
   (*b*) Off sales—for consumption off the premises.
   (*c*) Hotel—for consumption on and off the premises.
   (*d*) Restricted hotel—where there is no bar counter and sale of liquor is restricted to diners or guests or friends of guests who are entertained at the expense of the guest.
   (*e*) Restaurant—where there is no bar counter and liquor is sold for consumption with, and ancillary to, a meal.
   (*f*) Refreshment—where there is no bar counter and refreshments (including food and non-alcoholic beverages) are sold. This type of licence allows children under the age of 16 to be present in the premises when accompanied by an individual over the age of 21 and that until 8.00 p.m. each evening.
   (*g*) Entertainment—for places of public entertainment where consumption of liquor is on the premises and ancillary to the entertainment.

*Relevance of Planning Consents & Conditions*
**3.10.** The interrelationship between the type of licence applied for or granted and the planning permission relating to the premises is often confused or forgotten by a board, objectors or the applicant. The type of licence required is specified by the Act, but the uses to which the premises may be put are limited by the planning permission relating to the premises. A board will have to bear in mind that it is the planning committee which requires to take into account planning matters in relation to the premises and that the board's function is different; see *Donald* v. *Stirling District Licensing Board*, 1991 G.W.D. 24–1396 and *Leisure Inns (U.K.) Ltd.* v. *Perth and Kinross District Licensing Board*, 1991 G.W.D. 15–942. While a restaurant with a bar requires a public house licence [because Schedule 1 limits a restaurant licence to a premises which "do not contain a bar counter"], it is the planning permission and

11

conditions which will limit the restaurant's mode of operation to prevent the premises being operated like a conventional public house. Thus an objection to an application by a restaurant for a public house licence, that the premises are to be a "public house" in the full sense, may well be irrelevant if the planning permission conditions restrict the types of use to which the premises may be put.

*Fees*

**3.11.** The Secretary of State for Scotland has fixed fees payable by applicants to all boards in Scotland. Such fees are set by statutory instrument (s.8), at present by the Liquor Licensing (Fees) (Scotland) Order 1990 (S.I. 1990 No. 2458).

(*a*)  Grant of a new licence—£120.00
(*b*)  Provisional grant of a licence—£96.00
(*c*)  Declaration of finality of a provisional grant—£24.00
(*d*)  Renewal of a licence—£60.00
(*e*)  Transer to new tenant or occupier—£71.00
(*f*)  Occasional licence—£12.00
(*g*)  Occasional extension of permitted hours—£12.00
(*h*)  Regular extension of permitted hours—£60.00
(*i*)  Sunday opening (unaccompanied by application for new licence or renewal in which case there is no charge)—£60.00.

*Applications*

**3.12.** Generally applications for consideration by any board must be lodged with the clerk to the board not later than *five* weeks before the meeting at which the application is to be considered (s.10). This includes all forms of application including new grants, provisional grants, transfers, applications for Sunday openings, and regular extension of permitted hours. See the effect of para. 18 of Schedule 8 of the 1990 Act which allows the name of the employee or agent to be published in notices in terms of s.10, care of the agent dealing with the matter in the interests of confidentiality and security.

**3.13.** Adherence to the time scale is essential. Although some boards allow late applications to be considered, this should not be relied upon. Late applications through inadvertence and or misadventure, where the last date for lodging an application has been missed, can be made in respect of applications for a new licence or the renewal of a licence only (s.13). In the case of inadvertence or misadventure the licensing board can decide to hear an application or an objection where the preliminary statutory requirements have not been complied with (*i.e.* lodged late) if they are satisfied that this occurred by reason of inadvertence or misadventure. If the board accepts the reason for late lodging, it will allow the application to be dealt with at an adjourned meeting of the board. See *Purdon* v. *City of Glasgow District Licensing Board*, 1989 S.L.T. 201, 1988 S.C.L.R. 466 and *Indpine Limited* v. *City of Dundee District Licensing Board*, 1991 G.W.D. 29–1759 for discussion of the time at which late application may be made. It is important to note that the regular extension of permitted hours requires to be renewed annually. The principal licence bears a validity date, and requires to be renewed on that date. Should application be made for a temporary transfer on change of manager (s.25(3)), the licence requires to be confirmed at the next meeting of the board (s.25(4)). S.51 of the 1990 Act at subsection (4B) clarifies the validity of a confirmed licence, as being from the date of the original grant or renewal until the quarterly meeting three years later, not withstanding the transfer or subsequent continuation. In the past Board practice varied, however the correct approach is set out in the 1990 Act. It is advisable to lodge the confirmation application at the same time as the application for temporary transfer. A provisional licence (including a former provisional grant which has been declared final) also requires to be renewed within one year of the original grant or renewal (s.26(8)).

**3.14.** Each licensing board uses *pro forma* application forms which can be obtained from the clerk.

**3.15.** *Limited companies.* Where a limited company holds the licence there must be an individual named as having the day-to-day responsibility for the premises (s.11). This person is usually an employee/manager of the limited company. The individual is co-holder of the licence, and in the event of a change of employee/manager application should be made for the temporary transfer of the licence (s.25(3)). A temporary transfer application is dealt with by the clerk: however, the full licence then requires to be confirmed at the next sitting of the licensing board (see para. 3.11). It is important that application for a temporary transfer of the licence in the event of a change of manager be granted within eight weeks of that change, otherwise the licence ceases to have effect. However, see *Argyll Arms (McManus) Ltd.* v. *Lorn, Mid-Argyll, Kintyre and Islay Divisional Licensing Board*, 1988 S.L.T. 290 for discussion of the implications of a licence "ceasing to have effect." See also *Fereneze Leisure Ltd.* v. *Renfrew District Licensing Board*, 1991 S.C.L.R. 751 where it was held that a licensing board, when considering the fitness of a limited company, should consider the fitness of the company as a separate legal persona and not the fitness of the directors of the company as individuals.

*New and provisional grants—preliminary requirements*

**3.16.** An application for the provisional grant of a licence or the grant of a new licence must be accompanied by plans of the premises (s.10(2)(a)). Check the particular board's regulations regarding plans. Some boards require plans for off-sale premises, and the regulations will specify the scale and number of plans to be lodged. A provisional application allows the applicant the opportunity of ascertaining whether a licence will be granted, before incurring the cost of work to the premises, provided thereafter the applicant then completes the premises in compliance with the board's requirements and without deviating materially from the plans lodged. In addition to the application form and plans, the applicant must lodge certificates from each of the following departments: environmental health, building control and planning, confirming that the premises are suitable for the purpose of operating the licence which is being applied for if completed in accordance with the plans lodged (s.23). In many cases a board requires the certificates to be lodged with the application and in *all* cases a certificate must be obtained from planning. However, the wording of the section is that "an application . . . shall not be entertained by the licensing board unless . . . " and accordingly some boards allow the certificates to be submitted after the application has been made but before the board meeting. This is an area where the practice of different boards varies considerably. Check regulations carefully to avoid an application being unsuccessful through a failure to comply with a board's particular requirements. Similarly an applicant may apply provisionally for a licence in respect of the site of premises still to be built, without the need for detailed plans. This is known as a provisional (site only) application (s.26(2)). A site plan and description of the proposed premises must be lodged and a certificate of suitability from the planning department obtained (s.23). A provisional (site only) grant requires to be affirmed within one year of its grant or it becomes "ineffective." Some boards will consider an application to renew a provisional grant in circumstances where it has not been affirmed or declared final within one year. Detailed plans require to be lodged before a provisional (site only) grant can be affirmed. Once affirmed (if necessary) and once the premises are ready for final inspection by the various departments mentioned above, application should be made for a declaration of finality. The various departments will arrange inspection of the premises and report with confirmation that the premises have been completed in accordance with the plans lodged. Notwithstanding the grant of finality, a provisional licence requires to be renewed within one year of its grant (s.26(8)). There is usually no need in the case of a corporate licence holder to name the person to be responsible for the day to day running of the premises when the application is made for a provisional grant. However, if a person is not named in the original application, there may be a delay in the grant of declaration of finality as the board will require to be satisfied that the person is fit and proper to hold a licence which may require a report from the police. A provisional licence is not in force until declared final. Accordingly, it is important to liaise with those working on the premises, the inspecting departments, and the licence holder to make sure that the licence comes into force as soon as possible after completion of the premises, so that liquor can be sold from the time the premises open for business. An application for affirmation must be considered at a meeting of the licensing board, however an application for declaration of finality can be dealt with under delegated powers. A request should be made for consideration under delegated powers in order to make the timing of the bringing into force of the provisional grant of the licence more flexible, where a licensing board is prepared to delegate consideration in terms of s.5(1) of the 1976 Act.

**3.17.** *Off sales licences.* An application for the grant of an off sale licence in terms of the 1976 Act does not require lodging of plans, but some boards require this in terms of their own regulations. Applicants are advised to familiarise themselves with each board's requirements. Provisional grant applications do however require plans (s.10(3)). Certificates under s.23 are not required with applications for off sale licences. See s.52 of the 1990 Act which amends the 1976 Act adding s.90A which introduces controls regarding the premises from which alcoholic liquor can be sold wholesale.

*Attendance*

**3.18.** A licensing board may decline to consider an application if the applicant or his representative does not attend the meeting of the board (s.15) (see *Bury* v. *Kilmarnock and Loudon District Licensing Board*, 1989 S.L.T. 110). In cases where application for renewal or permanent transfer of licence is being considered an applicant or his representative need only attend the meeting if cited to do so (s.15(1)). In practice, many boards do not require attendance unless there are objections, or comments by the environmental health, fire or police departments; however, it is essential to check the particular board's practice, in order to ascertain whether attendance is required. Some boards will wish the applicant, or representative, to be present, but will deal with the application "en bloc" and will not require those in attendance to speak to the application. Some boards, particularly where a new application or application for permanent transfer is being considered, will insist on the attendance of the applicant, and, where the applicant is represented, on the attendance of both the representative and the applicant. Where the applicant or his representative fails to attend, the usual practice is for the application to be continued to the adjourned meeting of the board; however the section provides that the board "may decline to consider the application": it does not provide for refusal. Accordingly an application which is "not considered" by reason of non-appearance, can be reconsidered within two years of the original application.

*Objections*

**3.19.** Competent objectors to the grant, renewal or permanent transfer of a licence are (s.16 as amended by para. 5, Sched. 8 of the 1990 Act):
- (*a*) a neighbouring owner or occupier or an organisation representing such persons;
- (*b*) a community council;
- (*c*) an organised church representing a significant body of opinion in the neighbourhood;
- (*d*) the chief constable;
- (*e*) the fire authority for the area in which the premises are situated;
- (*f*) a local authority for the area in which the premises are situated.

**3.20.** This list has been amended by para. 5 of Sched. 8 to the 1990 Act, which extends the right to object to the fire authority and the local authority. Although it has not been explored judicially in terms of the new legislation, the relevance of comment by local authorities is discussed in *Bantop Ltd.* v. *City of Glasgow District Licensing Board*, 1990 S.L.T. 366.

**3.21.** Objections to an application must be lodged with the clerk to the board within seven days before the meeting of the licensing board; the seven days does not include the date of the board meeting, nor the date of notice of the objection (s.16(2)). Notice of objection requires to be intimated to the applicant seven days before the meeting by delivering a copy of the notice of objection to him, or sending a copy by registered post or recorded delivery to his proper address, or leaving a copy of the notice of objection at his proper address (s.16(3)). The proper address in the case of an individual applicant is his place of abode as specified in the application, and the case of a limited company, is the address specified in the application (normally the registered office of the company). Section 53 of the 1990 Act inserts a new s.16A to the 1976 Act. The requirement to amend the section arose from the decision in *Centralbite Ltd.* v. *Kincardine & Deeside District Licensing Board*, 1990 S.L.T. 231 where the Lord Ordinary held that an "observation" by the chief constable amounted to an objection and therefore required to be intimated to the applicant in the interests of fair notice.

*Grounds for refusal of an application (s.17)*
**3.22.** A licence can be refused on one or more of the following four grounds:

(a) The applicant, or the person on whose behalf or for whose benefit the applicant will manage the premises, is not a fit and proper person to hold a licence. In the case of a licence held by a limited company application, unsuitability applies not only to the actual applicant but also, where the applicant is not an individual person, to the person named in the application as the person responsible for the day to day running of the premises. The board may have regard to any misconduct whether or not the misconduct constitutes a breach of the Act or a bye-law made under it (s.17(3)). (See *Fereneze Leisure Ltd.* v. *Renfrew District Licensing Board*, 1991 S.C.L.R. 751).

(b) The premises are unsuitable or inconvenient for the sale of alcoholic liquor having regard to their location, character and condition, the nature of the proposed use and the persons likely to resort to them. In refusing to grant a licence on the grounds of unsuitability of the premises, the board's discretion is very wide, as it can take into account not only the location, character, conditions and proposed use of the premises but also the type of person liable to frequent them. It is often on this ground that a board will refuse an application where there is local objection in relation to noise, disturbance, unruly behaviour and proximity to residential property. See decision in *Leisure Inns Ltd.* v. *Perth & Kinross District Licensing Board*, 1990 G.W.D. 11–588 where loss of amenity was regarded by the court to be speculative and *Chief Constable*,

*Strathclyde Police* v. *City of Glasgow District Licensing Board*, 1988 S.L.T. 128, which concerned suitability of access to licensed premises.

(c) Where the use of the premises for the sale of alcoholic liquor is likely to cause undue public nuisance, or a threat to public order and safety. The cause of the public nuisance or the threat to public order or safety must arise out of the use of the premises for the sale of alcoholic liquor. However, in practice the scrutiny by the board's designated officials, by virtue of there being a liquor licence in force in respect of the premises, can lead to the refusal, or a condition being imposed where the licence is granted, without there being a great deal of discussion as to whether the nuisance or threat complained of is caused directly by the sale of alcoholic liquor. See *Harpspot* v. *City of Glasgow District Licensing Board*, 1990 G.W.D. 39–2269 and *Surrey Health Council* v. *McDonalds Restaurants Ltd.*, Q.B.Div., June 22, 1990, *Licensing Review*, Vol. 3, p. 21.

(d) Where, having regard to the facilities of the same or similar kind already available in the locality (where in respect of full or provisional grant) the grant of an application would result in the over-provision of such facilities.

This ground of refusal has been changed by para. 6 of Sched. 8 to the 1990 Act, see note to schedule 8 of the 1990 Act, and *Mount Charlotte Investments P.L.C.* v. *City of Glasgow District Licensing Board*, 1992 G.W.D 2–87. The board now require to have regard to the number of licensed premises in the locality at the time they consider the application and the number of provisional grants "in force" at the time of consideration.

The requirement to consider "same or similar facilities" has been removed, however it is felt that in the interest of a proper exercise of discretion it would not be sufficient simply to count the number of licences in a locality, without giving some attention to the type of licences and the facilities provided by the licensed premises which comprised that number.

This ground of refusal often focuses trade objections, where an existing licence holder in the locality fears the competition which will result from the grant of a further licence to a potential competitor. The issue of competition and choice has been considered by the court in the case of *Mecca Bookmakers (Scotland) Ltd.* v. *East Lothian District Licensing Board*, 1988 S.L.T. 520 where it was decided that competition and choice are factors which the licensing board can legitimately consider (albeit the application in that case was for a Betting Office licence). The case of *Augustus Barnett Ltd.* v. *Bute & Cowal Divisional Licensing Board*, 1989 S.L.T. 572, 1989 S.C.L.R. 413 should still be considered to give an indication of the correct approach when considering the question of over provision in the interest of a proper exercise of discretion. The interpretation of that case and *Collins* v. *Hamilton District Licensing Board*, 1984 S.L.T. 230 were approved in *Mohammed* v. *Docherty*, 1991 G.W.D. 25–1449.

Where an objection is made on the ground of over provision, there is a requirement to define the locality and the Board in providing reasons for reaching its decision must define the locality considered. See *Semple* v. *Glasgow District Licensing Board*, 1989 G.W.D. 36–1677, 1990 S.C.L.R. 73; *Bottrills of Blantyre* v. *Hamilton District Licensing Board*, 1986 S.L.T. 14. Given the changes introduced by the 1990 Act, the question of the locality in which the application is made becomes even more important, as the definition of locality will dictate the number of licences to be taken into account. The courts have considered the definition of locality; see *Lazerdale Ltd.* v. *City of Glasgow District Licensing Board*, 1988 G.W.D. 36–1485 and *Loosefoot Entertainments Ltd.* v. *City of Glasgow District Licensing Board*, 1991 G.W.D. 3–166. See also *Mohammed* v. *Docherty*, 1991 G.W.D. 25–1449 and *Leisure Inns (U.K.) Ltd.* v. *Perth & Kinross District Licensing Board*, 1991 G.W.D. 15–942.

**3.23.** Both parties, where an application is objected to, should be given an opportunity to address the board. Where an applicant has not had proper intimation of an objection, the board may refuse to hear the objector. Prior to the amendment introduced by para. 5(c) of Sched. 8 to the 1990 Act some boards refused to consider an objection where the objector failed to appear to speak to his or her written objection, however the board is required by the amendment to consider an objection properly lodged even if the objector does not attend the board in person. Questions may arise however if the applicant alleges that proper intimation of the objection has not been received if the objector is not in attendance to advise the board of steps taken to intimate to the applicant as required. Where both parties are present or represented, the board will usually hear the applicant, then the objector, and then give the applicant the right to reply. Where an objection to an application is by way of petition, the practice of boards differs: many boards consider an objection which bears the signatures of several persons to be an individual objection, unless each signatory has lodged a separate "Notice of Objection" as specified in the Act with the clerk to the licensing board. A proper reading of the legislation would require a separate notice, unless objection is made by a community council or other competent representative body.

**3.24.** *Refusal.* Where an application for a new licence is refused, it should be noted that applications cannot be reconsidered for a period of two years (s.14), unless direction to the contrary is made by the board *at the time of the refusal* of the first application. Accordingly, an *application* for a s.14 declaration *should be made at the time of the refusal.*

**3.25.** There is no statutory requirement to lead evidence when making application to a licensing board, and very few boards make it their practice to require evidence to be led in support of an application or objection. It is within the discretion of the licensing board to hear evidence. A requirement that an applicant should lead evidence would require to be intimated, presumably by way of regulation in terms of s.37. From a practical point of view the time involved in the consideration of evidence would be prohibitive. Where a special hearing for suspension of a licence is being considered, and the facts on which the complaint which has given rise to the hearing for suspension are in dispute, it may be of assistance to the licence holder to suggest that evidence be led at the hearing in order to assist the licensing board in ascertaining the facts upon which the complaint proceeds. At present only one district licensing board (Glasgow) makes arrangements for its proceedings to be recorded by a shorthand-writer. Reference to shorthand notes can be extremely helpful should an application or refusal be appealed. An applicant may consider it prudent to arrange for a shorthand-writer privately, in order to have an accurate recording of the proceedings before the board.

### Reasons for refusal

**3.26.** In terms of s.18, (as amended by para.7, Sched. 8 to the 1990 Act) a licensing board may be required to give reasons for arriving at any decision mentioned in s.5(2) within 21 days of being required to do so. A request for reasons may be made by any party having an interest in the application, including objectors, but the application has to be made in writing to the clerk of the board within 48 hours of the decision. It should be noted that a board cannot be required to give reasons for a decision, which is not a decision under s.5(2) (*Purdon* v. *City of Glasgow District Licensing Board*, 1989 S.L.T. 201).

**3.27.** In giving written reasons for their decision it is not sufficient for the board to reiterate the statutory grounds on which their decision is based; see cases cited in Note to s.18. If a board gives just the statutory ground on which their decision is based they may be required by the sheriff under para. 5 of Act of Sederunt (Appeals under the Licensing (Scotland) Act 1976) 1977 [S.I. 1977 No. 1622] to give their reasons for finding such ground or grounds of refusal to be established. It has been opinioned by the Lord Justice-Clerk (Ross) that, where a board have given inadequate reasons for their decision (see *infra*) the Act of Sederunt cannot be used to request the board to amplify their reasons (*Leisure Inns Ltd.* v. *Perth & Kinross District Licensing Board*, 1991 G.W.D. 15–942 commenting on the observations of Lord Murray in *Augustus Barnett Ltd.* v. *Bute & Cowal District Licensing Board*, 1989 S.L.T. 572 at p. 578B).

**3.28.** Many appeals are taken against the decision of a licensing board on the grounds that the reasons given under s.18 are inadequate. It is therefore important that the board state adequate and sufficient reasons for their decisions. The general principles of what amounts to adequate and sufficient reasons given by an administrative authority have been laid down in a number of cases, two of which are generally cited as setting out the principles to be applied.

**3.29.** In *Albyn Properties Ltd.* v. *Knox*, 1977 S.C. 108 a case relating to rent review, the Lord President (Emslie) said at page 112, "The statutory obligation to give reasons is designed not merely to inform the parties of the result of the committee's deliberations but to make clear to them and to this Court the basis on which their decision was reached, and that they have reached their result in conformity with the requirement of the statutory provisions and the principles of natural justice. In order to make clear the basis of their decision a committee must state (i) what facts they found to be admitted or proved; (ii) whether and to what extent the submissions of parties were accepted as convincing or not; and (iii) by what method or methods of valuation applied to the facts found their determination was arrived at."

**3.30.** In *Wordie Propertie Co. Ltd.* v. *Secretary of State for Scotland*, 1984 S.L.T. 345, a planning case, the Lord President (Emslie) said at page 348 that "The decision must, in short, leave the informed reader and the Court in no real and substantial doubt as to what the reasons for it were and what were the material considerations which were taken into account in reaching it." Note the two requirements to identify the reasons for the decision and the material considerations taken into account.

**3.31.** In considering the adequacy of reasons under the 1976 Act, in *R. W. Cairns Ltd.* v. *Busby East Kirk Session*, 1985 S.C. 110 at pages 118–119 the Lord Justice-Clerk (Wheatley) said in a case where the licensing board granted a Sunday operating licence in the face of objections, that "The provisions of section 18 which provide for reasons being given in writing, when read in conjunction with the provisions of paragraph 7, would seem to call for reasons showing clearly why a decision to grant a licence had been made in face of the objections to it, and why in particular the granting of the licence would not in the circumstances cause undue disturbance or public nuisance in the locality." Absence of reference to certain objections in the statement of reasons was held to warrant the conclusion that the board had not exercised its discretion properly.

**3.32.** It is therefore important that the clerk to the licensing board give detailed consideration to the reasons to be given under s.18, so that they cover all the material points. Inadequate reasons will give good grounds for an appeal. If the statement of reasons fails to mention some particular objection or other relevant material the court will often infer that the board failed to take that material into consideration and so exercised their discretion unreasonably. This may give the sheriff grounds to take it upon himself to overturn the decision and to deal with the application himself under s.39(6)(*b*).

*Permitted hours*

**3.33.** (*a*) The permitted hours for a public house licence or a refreshment licence are (s.53 of the 1976 Act as amended by s.45 of the 1990 Act)

*Monday to Saturday*—11.00 a.m. to 11.00 p.m.

If Sunday opening is granted for either of these two types of licence the premises can open for the sale of liquor from 12.30 p.m. until 2.30 p.m. and 6.30 p.m. until 11.00 p.m. These hours can now be extended in terms of para. 12 of Sched. 8 of the 1990 Act and s.64(4A) of the 1976 Act.

(b) For a hotel, restricted hotel licence, restaurant licence and entertainment licence:

*Monday to Saturday*—11.00 a.m. to 11.00 p.m.
*Sunday*—12.30 p.m. until 2.30 p.m. and 6.30 p.m. until 11.00 p.m.

(c) For an off sales licence:

*Monday to Saturday*—8.00 a.m. until 10.00 p.m.

Off sales premises and off sales parts of hotels and public houses (as defined in s.119) do not have permitted hours on Sundays.

**3.34.** The Licensing (Scotland) Act 1976 does not contain a requirement that premises be open for the sale or supply of alcoholic liquor during the permitted hours. A licence is an entitlement to sell liquor and not an obligation to do so. Individual boards can make bye-laws requiring licensed premises to be closed on New Year's Day and up to a further four days in each year (s.38(1)(a)).

*Extension of permitted hours (s.64)*

**3.35.** There are two methods of extending the permitted hours for licensed premises with the exception of off sales (s.64). Section 64 has been substantially amended by s.47 of the 1990 Act. The amendment extends the criteria to be taken into account by the licensing board when considering an application for extended hours. The new section places the onus on the applicant to satisfy the board that there is a need for an extension and that the extension is likely to be of such benefit to the community as a whole as to outweigh any detriment.

(a) An application can be made to a quarterly board in respect of a public house, hotel, restricted hotel, restaurant, entertainment, refreshment registered club or seamen's canteen licence for regular extension of permitted hours.

(b) Application for occasional extension of permitted hours (in respect of an appropriate event) for not more than one month can be made in respect of the same types of licence as mentioned above (s.64). This application is dealt with by the clerk and can be made at any time. Boards have wide discretion as to the grant of extensions of permitted hours for licensed premises (other than premises with off sales licence) either on a regular or occasional basis. Any applicant for the same must ensure that a copy of the application is sent to the chief constable. These extensions, occasional or regular, are at the discretion of the board. The changes introduced by s.47 of the 1990 Act make the criteria to be satisfied more stringent. Some boards now require more detailed submissions either when applying or when addressing the board in support of the application directed at the requirement to satisfy the board that "there is a need in the locality" and that the extension "is likely to be of such benefit to the community as a whole as to outweigh any detriment" in the locality. The new criteria have been used by some boards to curb late night extensions, often as a matter of board policy. For discussion of the court considerations of a board's policy see *Semple* v. *City of Glasgow District Licensing Board*, 1990 S.C.L.R. 73 and *Elder* v. *Ross & Cromarty District Licensing Board*, 1990 S.L.T. 307. The ratio appears to be that a general policy must still allow each application to be considered on its merits and must not be applied as an absolute bar to the admission of an exception to the general policy where circumstances allow. An occasional extension may be granted in respect of any occasion which the board considers appropriate, but cannot be for more than one month.

**3.36.** It is useful to find out from the clerk to the licensing board what policy or guidelines apply in relation to regular extension of permitted hours in his/her particular district. Different boards have different "guidelines" to which they adhere. For example, some boards require entertainment to be provided after 11.00 p.m., and some boards will not grant an extension beyond a certain hour in the evening. This practice has developed despite the clear requirement of the section that each application be considered on its own merits. This has been reinforced by the term of s.47(2) of the 1990 Act which provides that "In determining whether to grant an application for a regular extension of permitted hours. . . . it shall not be a relevant consideration for the licensing board to have regard to whether any application relating to any other premises in its area has, at any time, been granted or refused or the grounds on which any such application has been granted or refused." Whether a previous decision by a board is distinguishable from their general policy will be a matter of fact in respect of the particular application, however the terms of the subsection clearly underline the ratio of the *Semple* and *Elder* cases (*supra*) that a licensing board requires to consider each application on its own individual merits, must admit exceptions to general policy where circumstances allow and must be seen to be so doing. In terms of s.64(6) of the Act a board may impose conditions to the grant of a regular or occasional extension and breach of such a condition is an offence. It is important to remember that a regular extension of permitted hours can be granted for up to a year only, and accordingly normally requires to be applied for annually. Extensions run independently of the main licence as regards their validity dates. There is no right of appeal if an application for regular extension is refused, though a board's decision can be challenged by way of judicial review (see Introduction, 6.12.). However, even if the court find that the board have not acted reasonably and have not considered the correct criteria, it is very likely the court will remit the application back to the licensing board for reconsideration applying the correct approach, which may not result in the application being granted ultimately. Refusal of an application for regular or occasional extension of permitted hours may result in the applicant being precluded from re-applying for the same extension for a period of one year, if he/she does not obtain a direction in terms of s.64(9) of the 1976 Act, as introduced by para. 12 of Sched. 8 of the 1990 Act. It is to be noted that the subsection applies to both regular and occasional extensions. The direction must be requested and made *at the time of refusal* (similar to a s.14 direction). However, it would appear that consideration of subsequent applications prohibited by the subsection, if a direction is not obtained, relates only to "subsequent application for such an extension in respect of the same premises," thus allowing a subsequent application for different hours, days or a different event or a subsequent application in respect of premises deemed to be different by reason of alteration. (For discussion of different premises see *Kelvinside Community Council* v. *City of Glasgow District Licensing Board*, 1990 S.L.T. 725, 1990 S.C.L.R. 110.) As a result of the amendment introduced by s.51(5) of the 1990 Act adding s.64(3A) of the 1976 Act, extensions now transfer with the main licence, thus removing the difficulties experienced by licensed holders in some areas where the extensions were deemed to have lapsed on transfer. However, despite this sensible and useful amendment, application for extension of hours still requires to be made by the "holder of a licence." The effect of this in respect of a temporary transfer pending the last date for lodging applications for the quarterly meeting at which confirmation of that temporary transfer is to be considered, is that the prospective transferee can not apply to renew the regular extension if it is due to expire at the end of its year's validity. The only pragmatic solution to one of the many difficulties which has come to light with the introduction of the two-tier transfer procedure (s.51 of the 1990 Act) is either to request the existing licence holder/transferor to make application (albeit if the temporary transfer application is granted before the quarterly meeting he/she will not be the applicant at the time the application is considered) or to rely on the good offices of the clerk to accept an application from the transferee in anticipation of the grant of the temporary transfer. The clerk may be more comfortable if he receives an application from both the transferee and the transferor, and it would be in the interest of the transferor to lodge an application anyway as the temporary transfer may be refused. Clearly the amendment by s.51(5) gives an indication that extensions should transfer even where there is an intervening temporary transfer.

A further inconsistency allows a potential licence holder to make application for Sunday opening (at the provisional stage of application for example). However, the same is not available in respect of regular extension of permitted hours, which must be applied for by the holder of a licence. Some boards will consider an application for regular extension at a provisional stage, and then deem the operation of the extension, if granted, to be suspended until the provisional grant is declared final and the licence is in force. However, other boards will not accept an application for the extension of permitted hours until the licence has been declared final and is enforced, thus obliging the applicant to await the quarterly meeting of the licensing board following finalisation.

By virtue of an amendment to s.64(1) of the 1976 Act by para. 12 of Sched. 8 to the 1990 Act, premises with a refreshment licence can apply for regular and occasional extension hours, including any periods on Sunday. The holders of a public house licence can now apply for occasional or regular extension of permitted hours on a Sunday, but only for a period after 2.30 p.m. on Sunday afternoon (s.46(7) of the 1990 Act amending s.64(4) of the 1976 Act). The debate regarding extension of hours on Saturday evening into Sunday morning has been settled by the insertion of s.64(4A) in the 1976 Act by s.46(7) of the 1990 Act, which makes it competent for a board to grant an extension in respect of premises with a public house licence which starts 11 p.m. on Saturday and runs over midnight into Sunday.

**3.37.** *Extension of permitted hours for meals (ss.57–60).* Where licensed premises are structurally adapted and *bona fide* used for the provision of table meals to which the sale of liquor is ancillary, the permitted hours may be extended (other than for off-sale premises) in the afternoon on Sundays (the equivalent period on weekdays is now part of the permitted hours) until 4.00 p.m. (s.57) and in the evening until 1.00 a.m. (s.58). The licensing board must be satisfied that the subjects are structurally adapted for serving meals and notice must be given to the chief constable, and the clerk. In the case of a public house, hotel or registered club, the licensing board must declare itself satisfied that the premises are structurally adapted and *bona fide* used or intended to be used for the purpose of habitually providing the customary main meal at midday or in the evening, which requires a separate application. "Table meal" is defined by s.139(1) of the Act. However what amounts to a "meal" in terms of substance is not defined.

**3.38.** In the case of such an extension the permitted hours are as follows:

> 11.00 a.m. to 4.00 p.m. (from 2.30 p.m. for 1½ hours); (s.57 only applies on Sundays now)
>
> 11.00 p.m. to 1.00 a.m. (from 11.00 p.m. for two hours).

**3.39.** Intimations in respect of restaurant, restricted hotel, refreshment and entertainment licences do not require a declaration from the board: the licence is already subject to the requirement that food or entertainment be provided. Such intimation should be made in writing, giving 14 days' notice of the date on which the extended hours should apply, and be served on the chief constable and intimated to the board as a matter of courtesy.

**3.40.** Where there are no permitted hours on Sunday, premises with a public house licence can apply (by way of intimation as above) in respect of an area declared by the licensing board to be suitable, to open on a Sunday for the purpose of supplying meals to which the provision of alcohol is ancillary, from 12.30 p.m. to 2.30 p.m. and from 6.30 p.m. to 11 p.m. (s.59). The part of the premises to which such permission applies should not contain a bar counter.

Premises with an hotel, restricted hotel, or restaurant licence, or a public house or refreshment licence where there are permitted hours on a Sunday, can apply to extend the permitted hours on a Sunday from 5 p.m. to 6.30 p.m. (s.60). The extension can only be used for the purpose of selling alcohol which is ancillary to the provision of a table meal.

**3.41.** It is emphasised that these additional hours are only for the supply of liquor which is ancillary to the supply of a table meal.

*Sunday opening*

**3.42.** Application for Sunday opening in respect of a public house or refreshment licence requires a separate application. In the case of hotel, restricted hotel, restaurant, entertainment or seamen's canteen licences there is no need for separate application in respect of Sunday opening. [Such premises have permitted hours on a Sunday (see s.53).] There is no provision for Sunday opening in respect of an off sales licence.

**3.43.** Section 46 of the 1990 Act introduces a simplified procedure for applying Sunday opening in respect of premises with public house or refreshment licences. The existing Sched. 4 procedure continues to have effect until existing Sunday openings certificates are renewed or cease to have effect. Thereafter an applicant for the grant or provisional grant or renewal of a public house or refreshment licence need simply state (usually in response to a question on the application form) an intention to open on a Sunday. The new provisions allow for applications for Sunday opening (but not for regular extension; see 3.36 *supra*) by a person who is not yet a licence holder. However, if such Sunday opening application is refused and a subsequent appeal is unsuccessful, it would appear that such a licence holder may not re-apply for Sunday opening until the licence is due for triennial renewal (or annual in the case of a provisional grant) as s.46 of the 1990 Act states that Sched. 4 has effect only "until all [public house and refreshment] licences in force at the commencement of this Act "have been renewed or has ceased to have effect" therefore removing any procedure for applying to a quarterly meeting for Sunday opening independently of an application for a grant, provisional grant and renewal. Where application is made for renewal of a licence there is now no requirement to display or serve notices in respect of the Sunday opening element of the application as before, however, notices for the grant or provisional grant of a new licence require to indicate whether there is an intention to open on a Sunday.

*Transfers*

**3.44.** Transfer—the procedure in terms of s.25 of the 1976 Act for transfer of a licence has been amended by s.51 of the 1990 Act. Application for transfer of a licence to a new or existing tenant or occupier requires to be made to the Licensing Board. As a result of amendment by the 1990 Act and the Licensing Amendment (Scotland)

Act 1992, transfer can be effected in two ways—temporary (at any time) followed by confirmation or permanent (at a quarterly meeting of the Board). A new owner, occupier or tenant must wait until the transfer of the licence either temporarily or permanently before he may legally carry on business under that licence. Deeds of trust and agreements between the transferor and transferee to regulate the sale of liquor until the transfer of the licence by the licensing board, either at a meeting or by delegated powers have no authority as far as the licensing board is concerned, as the board has not had the opportunity to consider whether the transferee is a fit and proper person to hold a licence. In some areas the licensing division of the local police force have indicated that they are not prepared to recognise any such agreement which in their view amounts to trafficking, which is a criminal offence. The main amendment sought to resolve the difficulties which were a result of the restriction that permanent transfer applications could only be dealt with at a quarterly meeting, by introducing a new temporary transfer procedure. However, the new procedure has resulted in further problems and it is hoped that further amending legislation which received Royal Assent on 6 March, 1992 to correct the anomalies which have resulted from the changes was brought into force on 15 April, 1992.

Dealing with the minor amendment first, the insertion in subs. 2 of "new or existing" occupant, allows reorganisation of responsibility in terms of the licence amongst occupants without the requirement that the occupant transferee need be a new occupant. This addresses the previous difficulties highlighted in the case *Chief Constable of Tayside* v. *Angus DLB*, 1980 S.L.T.(Sh.Ct.) 31.

**3.45.** Temporary transfers in terms of subss. (2) and (3) of the Act are now subject to new subss. (4A), (4B) and (4C). The new subsections provide that temporary transfers lodged by executors etc. of deceased licence holders, trustees etc. of bankrupt licence holders and in respect of a change of the person responsible for the day to day running of the premises in terms of s.11 of the 1976 Act, shall have effect until the next meeting of the board (not the appropriate meeting as in new temporary transfers in terms of subs. (1)) and requires the board to be satisfied when considering confirmation of the temporary transfer that the transferee is a fit and proper person to hold a licence.

**3.46.** Subsections (5) and (6) provide that grants of occasional and regular extensions in terms of s.64 of the 1976 Act, transfer with the main licence automatically, thus overruling the decision in *Archyield Ltd.* v. *City of Glasgow District Licensing Board*, 1987 S.L.T. 547 which caused considerable difficulty, and endorsing the interpretation in *C.R.S. Leisure* v. *Dumbarton District Licensing Board*, 1990 S.L.T. 200.

**3.47.** Turning now to the main change, as regards permanent transfer of a licence and the attempt to introduce a procedure whereby a licence could be transferred other than at a quarterly meeting, section 51 of the 1990

Act provides for an initial temporary transfer of a licence, which may be applied for at any time and may be dealt with administratively under delegated powers. The temporary transfer requires to be confirmed by the licensing board at a subsequent meeting, upon application being made for such confirmation by way of permanent transfer. While the amendment allows transfer to take place at times other than quarterly meetings, it makes a mandatory preliminary to a permanent transfer that a temporary transfer has taken place, thus removing the option simply to apply for permanent transfer to a quarterly meeting of the board in terms of the previous procedure, and imposing the temporary transfer step on the potential transferee. Problems are caused by the lapse of time (in terms of subs. (1A) and (1B)) between the grant of the temporary transfer (which effectively transfers the licence) and confirmation by way of permanent transfer at an appropriate meeting of the board. See *Kerr* v. *McAuslin*, 1991 G.W.D. 37–2271. Difficulties have arisen where there is a lender involved in the transaction to buy or sell licensed premises, as it is often the case that the lender will not release funds until permanent transfer has been granted or will insist on a loan being redeemed on grant of temporary transfer, which effectively amounts to entry being taken. Solutions have been suggested (see "Licensing Transfers," 1991 S.L.T. (News) 58 and 1991 S.L.T. (Letters to the Editor) 86) and currently the pragmatic solution which appears to have been adopted by many boards is that suggested as a result of a meeting of clerks, namely, that both temporary and permanent transfer applications be lodged at the same time, and the temporary transfer application granted the day before the quarterly meeting of the board. This reduces the lapse of time between temporary and permanent transfers, but ignores the requirements of subss. (1A) and (1B).

**3.48.** An Act amending s.25 further (the Licensing (Amendment) (Scotland) Act 1992 which received Royal Assent on 6 March 1992 and came into force on 15 April 1992), seeks to reintroduce old style permanent transfers at quarterly meetings, while leaving the new temporary transfer confirmed by permanent transfer procedure in place for those who wish to avail themselves of it, and for whom there are no funding or contractual difficulties in so doing.

**3.49.** A further potential difficulty which may arise as the result of the new temporary transfer procedure in terms of subs. (1) should be noted. The temporary transfer is dealt with in most cases by delegated powers administratively. Most boards liaise with the applicant as regards the date on which the temporary transfer should be granted (though not all) as this effectively dictates the date of entry. However, where an application for temporary transfer has been lodged and there is not close liaison with the clerk regarding the date of the grant of that transfer, the application could be granted (effectively transferring the licence to the purchaser) where the contract between the parties has fallen through, and settlement of the purchase price has not been made. Such a "grant by mistake" could be difficult to undo as there is no procedure in the Act for cancellation of the grant of a temporary transfer, other than by further application for temporary transfer back to the seller. In the meantime, the licence has been transferred to the purchaser who has not paid the price, nor presumably taken entry, and the seller, if he continues to trade from the premises after the grant of the temporary transfer, risks a prosecution in terms of s.90 of the 1976 Act for trafficking without a licence. Great care therefore should be taken when applying for temporary transfer, as at present, much depends on close liaison with board officials and considerable co-operation from all involved in the procedure.

*Consent to Transfer*

**3.50.** Although there is no statutory requirement for the transfer application to be consented to, most boards require the existing licence holder to endorse his/her consent to the transfer in terms of their regulations, either on the principal licence, or by letter of consent, or on the transfer application form. The requirement is made in order to avoid the licence being transferred in error, and consent can usually be lodged a few days before the application is considered. However, as the new temporary transfer can be dealt with administratively there will not be a meeting of the board at which lack of consent can be explained to the board in circumstances where consent is not forthcoming, *i.e.* the existing licence holder has absconded. Further, as consent is often endorsed on the licence prior to application being made, or endorsed on the application form, circumstances may have changed substantially between the parties to the contract by the time the application is considered by the board members. Care should be taken to keep the clerk informed particularly where consent to transfer has been withdrawn.

**3.51.** A temporary transfer in terms of s.25(1) transfers the licence to the applicant. Agreements between the transferor and transferee to regulate the sale of liquor until transfer of the licence is confirmed by permanent transfer have no authority as far as the licensing board is concerned. If the temporary transfer has been granted, the licence has been transferred, albeit that it is not until that transfer is confirmed by way of permanent transfer that the board confirm the transferee as a fit and proper person to hold a licence. The situation is clearly unsatisfactory in circumstances where it is not possible to settle a transaction on the date of the grant of the temporary transfer. Some boards can assist, to the extent that the report from the licensing police regarding the fitness of the transferee will be available at the time of temporary transfer, however this will not cover any gap there may be between that date and confirmation by way of permanent transfer.

**3.52.** The only ground for refusing a permanent transfer application remains that the applicant is not a fit and proper person to hold a licence (s.17(1)).

*Alterations to premises (other than off sales)*

**3.53.** No reconstruction, extension or alteration to licensed premises which affects the public or common part of the premises is permitted without the board's approval (s.35). An application for consent to alteration is normally heard at a quarterly meeting of the board, however the section allows it to be considered at such other time as may be appointed by the board. It is worth checking with the clerk to ascertain the particular board's procedure. Application requires to be made for approval of proposed alterations, before the alterations are carried out. Such alterations cannot be retrospectively approved (except where the board is prepared to exercise its discretion) and if reconstruction, extension or alteration is made without the board's permission, the board may apply to the sheriff for an order for restoration of the premises to their original condition. Consultation with the fire athorities is also required before the consent is granted. The licensing board can require plans to be lodged and if alteration is material (often board regulations will lay down the criteria for assessing what amounts to a "material" change) then an application for a new licence is required. What is "material" and procedures for dealing with alterations, can vary considerably from board to board. It is important that the licence holder is aware of the requirement to obtain the board's consent before altering licensed premises, as there is no statutory vehicle to grant consent retrospectively, and alterations can occur without consent, which only come to light when the licence is inspected at renewal. See: R. v. Chelmsford Crown Court, ex parte George Larkin, Q.B.D., June 13, 1990, Licensing Review, Vol. 2, p. 20 and R. v. Liverpool Crown Court, ex parte Lennon & Hongkins, Q.B.D., July 23, 1990, Licensing Review, Vol. 4, p. 22.

*Suspension of licence (s.31)*

**3.54.** The board may order the suspension of a licence where:
- (a) the licence holder is no longer a fit and proper person to hold a licence; or
- (b) the use of the premises causes undue public nuisance or a threat to public order or safety.

When the board receives a complaint to that effect, it may suspend the licence if it finds such a suspension in the interest of the public. The initial complaint must be considered by the board and if the board decides that there is a case to answer it must order a special hearing to take place, of which the licence holder must be given 21 days' notice. Only then can the board consider whether the licence be suspended. Consideration of suspension is made on receipt by the licensing board of a complaint by any person named in s.16 (those who can competently object), where it is suggested that the licence holder is no longer a fit and proper person to hold a licence, and/or that the use of the premises causes a public nuisance.

**3.55.** Often the application for suspension will be made, in respect of the first ground (fit and proper person), where the licence holder or nominated employee has been convicted of an offence, particularly where the conviction relates to an offence in terms of the Act, *i.e.* under-age drinking, etc. See: *Fereneze Leisure Ltd.* v. *Renfrew District Licensing*

*Board*, 1991 G.W.D. 15–943 for discussion of the correct approach in considering the fitness of a corporate licence holder. See also *Mohammed Anwar v. Clydesdale District Licensing Board*, Lanare Sh.Ct. 17 June 1991, unreported.

**3.56.** It should be noted that a licensing board in considering whether a licence holder is a fit and proper person to hold a licence may have regard to any misconduct on the part of any person mentioned in s.17(1)(*a*) (including any nominated employee or agent) whether or not constituting a breach of the Act or any bye-law, which in the opinion of the board has a bearing on the licensee's fitness to hold a licence (s.17(3)). This provision gives the licensing board a wide power to consider factors which are not directly related to offences under the Act. Further "the person on whose behalf or for whose benefit the applicant manages the premises" is not defined but appears to refer to persons other than those in a "non-individual person" licence holding situation. Any person who derives benefit from the sale of alcoholic liquor for the premises can be considered, though it is suggested that the benefit would have to be substantial. This allows the board to look behind a sham applicant at the person who has put that applicant forward and who will derive benefit from their running of the premises.

**3.57.** In respect of the second ground, the board can consider misconduct of any kind on the part of persons frequenting the premises or misconduct by those persons in the immediate vicinity of the premises, whether or not the said conduct has been the subject of complaint by the licence holder himself (s.31(3)).

*Closure order*

**3.58** A further power to suspend exists where the licensing board itself considers that the premises are no longer suitable or convenient for the sale of alcoholic liquor (s.32). The licensing board in this instance, should have regard to the character and condition of the premises and the nature and extent of the use of the premises. Similarly in terms of this section, the board must hold a hearing and must give the licence holder 21 days' notice thereof.

**3.59.** The licence holder is entitled to be heard at a closure hearing, and the board is obliged to specify the matters by reason of which a closure order has been made. A closure order remains in force until the board is satisfied that the matters by reason of which the order was granted have been satisfactorily remedied. Application can be made by the licence holder for cancellation of the order on the ground that the said matters have been satisfactorily remedied. Clearly considering the case law, a board must have regard to the condition of the premises at the time of the hearing, by which time there may have been considerable improvements.

**(4) Clubs**

**4.1.** The Licensing (Scotland) Act 1903 introduced a code of registration for clubs, borrowed from the English legislation, but which was rendered more rigorous by several new provisions. During the First World War stringent restrictions were placed upon the sale and supply of intoxicating liquor and clubs were brought into line with licensed premises. Although the Licensing (Scotland) Act 1921 repealed most of this legislation, the idea of "permitted hours" for clubs was retained. Clubs required to register by application to the sheriff.

*Certificate of registration*

**4.2.** Clubs, which wish to sell alcohol to their members, do not require a licence, but they are required to have a certificate of registration, renewable triennially (s.106). The sheriff clerk for each sheriff court district, called in the Act "the Registrar," keeps a register of all certificated clubs within the district (s.102). The certificate is granted, renewed or cancelled by the sheriff and not by the licensing board. It is an offence (s.120(1)) to sell or supply alcoholic liquor in a club which is not registered.

**4.3.** An application for a certificate of registration is lodged with the registrar and requires to be signed by the chairman, secretary or solicitor of the club (s.103(1)). While no form is prescribed by the Act, most sheriff clerks have a standard form, which can be obtained from them. It should be noted that an application from a club still to be formally constituted is incompetent (*Scottish Homosexual Rights Group, Petrs.*, 1981 S.L.T.(Sh.Ct.) 18).

*Documentation for certificate of registration*

**4.4.** Section 103 specifies the details and documentation, which have to be provided in or with the application form. Two copies of the club rules have to be lodged. Section 107 sets out the provisions which have to be included in the rules of a club, which seeks certification, although freemasons' lodges constituted under charter from the Grand Lodge of Scotland are exempt. The rules mainly relate to provisions, which have the effect of limiting the sale of alcoholic liquor to persons who could buy it in a public house and ensuring that only *bona fide* members use the club. It has been suggested that the court should have regard to changes in the rules made between the time of application and the hearing (*Scottish Homosexual Rights Group, Petrs., supra*), but not to proposed amendments which have not yet been adopted at the time of the hearing (*British Legion (Scotland) Tiree Branch*, 1947 S.L.T.(Sh.Ct.) 65).

**4.5.** A list containing the names and addresses of the committee of management or governing body of the club has to be lodged (s.103(3)(*b*)), because the Act (as amended) provides that these persons are liable to prosecution if certain offences are committed in or by the club.

*Intimation of application*

**4.6.** When an application for a certificate is lodged, the applicant requires to intimate the application by publishing a notice twice in the seven days immediately following the lodging, in a newspaper circulating in the area and by displaying a notice thereof in a conspicuous place on or near the club premises for 21 days following the lodging (s.105), the precise form of which should be discussed with the registrar. The registrar will intimate the application to the chief constable, the district or islands council and the fire authority (s.105(2)).

*Objections*

**4.7.** Competent objections to the grant or renewal of a certificate of registration, on one of the grounds set out in s.108, may be made by the persons specified in s.105(3), who are required to intimate their objection to the registrar and the applicant within 21 days of the first appearance of the newspaper intimation.

*Renewals*

**4.8.** Applications for renewal of a certificate require to be lodged 21 days before the date of expiry of the certificate (s.104). The provisions of s.103 apply to renewals, with such modifications as are necessary. The sheriff may, on cause shown (s.104(2)), entertain a late application, but it is important to note that this does not include an application lodged after the certificate has expired (*Royal British Legion Club, Petr.*, 1984 S.L.T.(Sh.Ct.) 2). The secretary requires to lodge a certificate to the effect that there have been no changes in the club rules or list of officials, or specifying what changes have taken place. Section 105 applies to renewals, as it does to applications for a grant of a certificate, except that intimation in the newspaper and on the club premises is not required. Intimation is made to the chief constable, the council and the fire authority by the registrar and competent objections may be lodged.

*Cancellation of certificate*

**4.9.** A club's certificate may be cancelled under s.109 if anyone entitled to object to an application (s.105(3)) applies to the sheriff for a finding that the club is being, or has been at any time during the currency of the certificate of registration, managed or carried on in such a way as to give rise to one of the grounds of objection specified in s.108 and the sheriff so finds or the club is convicted under s.95 (sale or supply of alcoholic liquor for consumption outside the club premises). Where a certificate is cancelled, the club may apply for a renewal, but not earlier than 12 months after the cancellation (s.109)4)).

*Finality of sheriff's decision*

**4.10.** The sheriff's decision on an application for a grant of renewal or cancellation of a certificate is final (s.117) on the merits, but a procedural interlocutor may be reviewed. A decision may be subject to reduction, probably by judicial review, if it is *ultra vires*, contrary to natural justice etc. (see heading "Appeals" *infra*, paras. 6.1 *et seq.*).

*Offences*

**4.11.** Sections 111 to 113 establish certain offences, which can be committed by or on the club premises. In terms of each section every member of the committee of management or governing body of the club can be found guilty of the offence. This is a species of vicarious liability, although there is a defence that the offence was committed without the knowledge or consent of the official and that he used due diligence to prevent the offence (see heading "Offences" *infra*, paras. 7.1 *et seq.*).

*Police entry*

**4.12.** Section 114 gives the police powers of entry into a club's premises where there are reasonable grounds for believing that the club is being managed in a way that gives rise to a competent objection or that an offence is being committed. In *Southern Bowling Club Ltd.* v. *Ross* (1902) 4 F. 405, the court held that at common law the police had the power to enter clubs in plain clothes to discover if an offence was being committed.

### (5) The Board's discretion

**5.1.** The licensing boards acting under the 1976 Act are vested with an administrative discretion, which is not as wide as that conferred by the Licensing (Scotland) Acts 1903 and 1959, but nevertheless it is an administrative and not a judicial function that the boards perform. It is clear from s.39(4)(*d*) that the boards are exercising a discretion, because an appeal is allowed if the board exercised its discretion "in an unreasonable manner"; see also *Freeland* v. *City of Glasgow District Licensing Board*, 1979 S.C. 226, Lord Kissen at p. 234.

**5.2.** While s.32 of the 1959 Act gave a licensing court an absolute discretion to grant certificates to "such and so many persons as the court shall think fit," on the recommendation of the Clayson Committee (Report, Chap. VII, para. 7.39), who considered that an absolute discretion "makes it possible for a decision to be reached which may be little better than arbitrary or even biased" and "makes for uncertainty," this discretion has been severely restricted in the 1976 Act. For example, s.17 provides that a board "shall grant the application" for a licence, unless it finds that certain grounds for refusal are established; s.41 provides that a grant of a seamen's canteen licence shall not be refused, unless certain grounds are established, while in contrast the board have an almost unfettered discretion under s.64 in relation to occasional and regular extensions of permitted hours.

**5.3.** When a board exercises its discretion it is required to act lawfully in the broadest sense of the word; it must exercise a real discretion, which it must not fetter; it must take into account relevant considerations and not consider the irrelevant; it must exercise its discretion reasonably; it must not use its discretion for improper purposes or in bad faith; it must not act *ultra vires*; it must not reach a decision based on an error in law; and it must not act contrary to natural justice in its procedures and in reaching its decision.

**5.4.** While the principles can be easily stated, the law is complex. For a fuller consideration of the issues the relevant textbooks should be consulted; *Stair Memorial Encyclopaedia*, Vol. 1, "Administrative Law." paras. 213 to 285; Davidson and St Clair, *Judicial Review*; S. A. de Smith, *Judicial Review of Administrative Action*, 4th Ed. (1980) by J. M. Evans.

**5.5.** A breach of natural justice tends to relate to the conduct of the hearing, rather than to the decision. The principles of natural justice are that both sides must be given an equal opportunity of presenting their case and of knowing the case they have to answer; that the licensing board should not be or even appear to be a judge in a matter in which they have an interest; and that justice must not only be done but be seen to be done. Particular sections of the 1976 Act are designed to prevent breaches of natural justice; *e.g.* s.2 (disqualification of interested persons from the board), s.16 (objections to be lodged and served timeously on all parties), and s.32 (need to hold a hearing before a licence can be suspended), etc.

**5.6.** Cases in which a licensing board's discretion or breaches of natural justice have been considered are given in greater detail in the annotations to the Act—*e.g.* s.2 and s.39.

**(6) Appeals**

**6.1.** The Clayson Report, following the Guest Committee on this point, recommended the replacement of the licensing appeal courts by an appeal to the sheriff principal, but went on to recommend "that the sheriff should not have power to set aside the decision of a licensing board except on the grounds that it was wrong in law, 'ultra vires,' or fundamentally bad or an unreasonable exercise of discretion" (para. 6.16). It was from this recommendation that s.39 of the 1976 Act was drafted, entitling a sheriff to uphold an appeal if he considered that in arriving at their decision, the licensing board (a) erred in law, (b) based its decision on any incorrect material fact, (c) acted contrary to natural justice, or (d) exercised its discretion in an unreasonable manner.

*The Sheriff's remit on appeal*

**6.2.** In considering an appeal the sheriff acts in his judicial capacity and is vested with a wide discretion, which must be exercised reasonably; *Martin v. Ellis*, 1978 S.L.T.(Sh.Ct.) 38 and *Botterills of Blantyre* v. *Hamilton District Licensing Board*, 1986 S.L.T. 14. The scope of a sheriff's remit in considering an appeal and the basis upon which he may overturn a board's decision under s.39 was considered in detail by Sheriff G. H. Gordon, reviewing the authorities, in *Loosefoot Entertainment Ltd.* v. *City of Glasgow District Licensing Board*, 1990 S.C.L.R. 584 [on appeal 1991 G.W.D. 3–166]. The sheriff held that a board's decision should be upheld "unless they acted in the absence of any factual basis for their decision or their decision was so unreasonable that no reasonable licensing board could have reached it or they took into account matters which they should not have taken into account and failed to take relevant matters into account" (at p. 587).

*Sections under which appeals competent*

**6.3.** A difficulty is that the Act does not provide for a general right of appeal under all the sections. Only certain decisions of the licensing board are appealable under s.39. Other sections do not provide for any right of appeal and certain administrative decisions in relation to licensing applications made by, for example, the clerk to the board are not subject to an appeal under the Act. Under certain sections, such as appeals in relation to seamen's canteens (s.44), the right of appeal is limited to particular refusals. No rights of appeal are provided against a sheriff's decision in relation to the registration of clubs, which is final (s.117). The normal criminal rights of appeal apply to offences created under the Act, but it should be noted that certain proceedings instituted by "complaint" (under s.35(4)) are not necessarily criminal proceedings, but are civil proceedings, which can perhaps be appealed under the ordinary rules of court (*City of Glasgow District Licensing Board* v. *MacDonald*, 1978 S.L.T.(Sh.Ct.) 74).

**6.4.** In instituting any proceedings in which it is sought to appeal any decision under the Act, detailed consideration will have to be given to the method by which a review of that decision is sought, because there are a number of potential pitfalls. It should be noted that an appeal lies either to the sheriff or to the sheriff principal, but there is no appeal from the sheriff to the sheriff principal (*Troc Sales Ltd.* v. *Kirkcaldy District Council Licensing Board*, 1982 S.L.T.(Sh.Ct.) 77). An appeal under s.39(8) lies to the Court of Session on a point of law.

**6.5** Where the Act clearly provides for an appeal to the sheriff under s.39, no difficulty should arise. The note to s.39 sets out the sections which provide for a right of appeal. An appeal under a section which does not provide for an appeal in general is incompetent (*Sloan* v. *North East Fife District Licensing Board*, 1978 S.L.T.(Sh.Ct.) 62). Care should be taken, where a section does not provide for a right of appeal, but the effect of a decision under that section is ancillary to a decision under a section, which provides for a right of appeal, because the decision under the former section may be subject to an appeal under s.39, *e.g.* the refusal to attach a condition to a licence under s.62 on a transfer of that licence under s.10 (*Wallace* v. *Kyle and Carrick District Licensing Board*, 1979(Sh.Ct.) 12). In *Kelvinside Community Council* v. *City of Glasgow District Licensing Board*, 1990 S.L.T. 725 it was held that an objector had a right to appeal under s.17(5) where the applicant, whose application was under s.14, might not have such a right.

*Time limits*

**6.6.** There are time limits for appeals to the sheriff under s.39. An appeal has to be lodged with the sheriff clerk within 14 days of the decision, unless written reasons for the decision have been requested under s.18, when the 14 days run from the date of receipt of that letter giving the reasons, which is deemed to be the day after the posting date (s.39(2)).

Under s.39(3), on good cause shown, the sheriff may extend the time limit. An appeal from the sheriff's decision to the Court of Session must be made within 28 days (s.39(8)).

**6.7.** It should be noted that, if a review by petition for judicial review is sought, the court may refuse the petition if there has been a failure to seek review of the decision within a reasonable time (*Hanlon* v. *Traffic Commissioner*, 1988 S.L.T. 802).

**6.8.** Appellants should also bear in mind the provisions of s.130, which imposes a two-month prescription in respect of proceedings raised in regard to anything done in execution of the Act, and is difficult to construe. Certain remedies, beyond the rights of appeal and time limits set by s.39, may be subject to the time limit set in s.130: see D. M. Walker, *Civil Remedies* (1974), Chap. 74; *Boyd* v. *Hislop* (1902) 9 S.L.T. 466.

*Parties to appeal*

**6.9.** It is clear from the Act, as amended by para. 11(2) of Sched. 8 to the 1990 Act, and the decisions that the applicant, the licensing board, and any objector who appeared before the licensing board, may institute and be party to an appeal under s.39. S.16(5) now allows objections to be considered "whether or not the objector appears", but an objector who does not appear, probably has no right of appeal; see s.17(5). In *Kelvinside Community Council* v. *City of Glasgow District Licensing Board*, 1990 S.L.T. 725 it was held that although the applicants had no right of appeal under s.14, that objectors retained their right of appeal under s.17(5).

*Evidence at appeals*

**6.10.** A particular difficulty which arose out of s.39(4) was that evidence could only be led in an appeal against a decision based on an incorrect material fact. This led to a very unsatisfactory position, where a licensing board could deny certain factual averments regarding their actings, which the appellant had no opportunity of disputing (*Tennant Caledonian Breweries* v. *City of Aberdeen District Licensing Board*, 1987 S.L.T.(Sh.Ct.) 2). This difficulty was corrected by amendment of subs. 39(4) by para. 11(3) of Sched. 8 to the 1990 Act, to bring the provision under this Act in line with para. 18(8) of Sched. 1 to the Civic Government (Scotland) Act 1982, where evidence may be led under each head of appeal.

*Judicial review or reduction*

**6.11.** Where the Act provides no right of appeal under s.39, it may still be possible to have the decision of the licensing board or of a board's official reviewed or reduced by way an action of reduction [see *Elantosh Ltd.* v. *City of Edinburgh District Licensing Board*, 1984 S.L.T. 92 (overruled on the merits by *Grainger* v. *City of Edinburgh District Licensing Board*, 1989 G.W.D. 13–568) for attempted action of reduction; *Allied Breweries* (*U.K.*) *Ltd.* v. *City of Glasgow District Licensing Board*, 1985 S.L.T. 302 for an action of reduction on the grounds that decision of board was *ultra* *vires*] or by judicial review. Judicial review, which is a specialised public law procedure for the control by the Court of Session of the acts of inferior tribunals and administrative bodies, such as licensing boards, is only competent in the Court of Session under R.C.S. 260B, which was introduced on April 30, 1985. Judicial review has effectively superseded an action of reduction as a mode of review of a licensing board's actings.

**6.12.** Since its introduction in 1985 judicial review, in a licensing context, has been used to review *inter alia*; (a) the refusal by the clerk of the board to accept a licensing application which was tendered late (*Main* v. *City of Glasgow District Licensing Board*, 1987 S.L.T. 305 and *Tait* v. *City of Glasgow District Licensing Board*, 1987 S.L.T. 340) [see the comments on those cases in *Kelvinside Community Council* v. *City of Glasgow District Licensing Board*, 1990 S.L.T. 725]; (b) the refusal of a direction under s.32 of the Gaming Act 1968 as being unreasonable (*Mecca Leisure Ltd.* v. *City of Glasgow District Licensing Board*, 1987 S.L.T. 483); (c) a board's decision that a regular extension lapsed upon a transfer of a licence and refusal to consider such an application on grounds it had lapsed (*Archyield Ltd.* v. *City of Glasgow District Licensing Board*, 1987 S.L.T. 547 and *C.R.S. Leisure Ltd.* v. *Dumbarton District Licensing Board* 1990 S.L.T. 200; now clarified by s.15(5) of the 1991 Act); (d) a board's grant of gaming licence under the Gaming Act 1968 in the face of objections, sought to be reviewed by an objector on grounds that grant contrary to statutory provision and consideration of irrelevant material (*Patmor Ltd.* v. *City of Edinburgh District Licensing Board*, 1987 S.L.T. 492; 1988 S.L.T. 850 and *Mecca Bookmakers (Scotland) Ltd.* v. *East Lothian District Licensing Board*, 1988 S.L.T. 520); (e) a council's decision to issue more taxi licences, where only the committee's officials had considered all the material and the committee were said to have failed to take into account all relevant material (*City Cabs (Edinburgh) Ltd.* v. *City of Edinburgh District Council*, 1988 S.L.T. 184); (f) a board's decision that a licence had ceased to have effect under s.11(4) of the 1976 Act and accordingly could not be transferred to another employee (*Argyll Arms (McManus) Ltd.* v. *Lorn, Mid-Argyll, Kintyre & Islay Divisional Licensing Board*, 1988 S.L.T. 290); (g) the refusal by a board to exercise their discretion under s.13(2) to accept a late lodging of an application to renew a licence on grounds that board acted unreasonably (*Purdon* v. *City of Glasgow District Licensing Board*, 1989 S.L.T. 201); (h) a board's decision to refuse to entertain an application for a regular extension because the applicant was not present or represented at the meeting on the grounds that the board acted capriciously and failed to take account of the whole circumstances (*Bury* v. *Kilmarnock and Loudon District Licensing Board*, 1989 S.L.T. 110); (i) the grant by the board of an application by the chief constable for a temporary restriction order under s.66(1) on the ground that the decision was *ultra vires* (*Grainger* v. *City of Edinburgh District Licensing Board*, 1989 S.L.T. 633); (j) the refusal of a board to grant a regular extension based upon an adverse environmental health department report (*Bantop* v. *City of Glasgow District Licensing Board*, 1990 S.L.T. 366); (k) the taking into account by a board of a letter of "observations" by a chief constable [now permitted under s.16A.] and a circular by the Scottish Home and Health Department as being irrelevant and the use by the board of a "policy" against regular extensions as a ground for refusing the application (*Centralbite Ltd.* v. *Kincardine and Deeside District Licensing Board*, 1990 S.L.T. 231); (l) a board's refusal of a regular extension on the ground that the refusal was based on a "policy" and was unreasonable in that nothing had occurred to change the *status quo* (*Elder* v. *Ross and Cromarty District Licensing Board*, 1990 S.L.T. 307 and *Semple* v. *Glasgow District Licensing Board*, 1990 S.C.L.R. 73); (m) the continuation of the consideration of an application for a gaming permit under the Gaming Act 1968 to await the outcome of an appeal to the sheriff against the refusal of an entertainment licence (*Noble Developments Ltd.* v. *City of Glasgow District Licensing Board*, 1990 S.L.T. 394); and (n) a board's decision to have a hearing to determine the competency and relevancy of objections to the renewal of a bookmaker's permit (*Cooper* v. *City of Edinburgh District Licensing Board*, 1990 S.L.T. 246; 1991 S.L.T. 47).

**6.13.** A court in reviewing a decision of a licensing board by way of judicial review is not acting as a court of appeal and may not substitute its own view for that of the licensing board. The court cannot usurp the function of the board, by substituting its own decision for that of the board, as the sheriff may on an appeal under s.39(6); see *Tait* v. *City of Glasgow District Licensing Board*, 1987 S.L.T. 340 and *Baillie* v. *Wilson*, 1917 S.C. 55. All the court can therefore do is to reduce the decision or grant an appropriate declarator, while remitting the application to the board for reconsideration. The court can grant *interim* relief, by way of suspension or interdict *ad interim* to preserve the *status quo* and may make such orders as are necessary to require the board to meet again to reconsider the application; see *Tait supra*, at page 343B/C.

**6.14.** Judicial review of a licensing board's decision is becoming a regular feature of licensing actions, but it must be clearly remembered that it cannot be a means of appeal against the decision on its merits, unless the decision is so unreasonable that no board could have reached that decision. There are numerous judicial *dicta* to the effect that practitioners should not use judicial review in an attempt to appeal a decision, where Parliament has specifically excluded a right of appeal against a board's exercise of a discretion.

**6.15.** If a petition for judicial review is to be raised against a decision of the licensing board, usually there will be no difficulty in regard to title and interest to raise the petition if the petitioner was a party to the application, but other parties may find difficulty in this regard. In *Patmor Ltd.* v. *City of Edinburgh District Licensing Board*, 1987 S.L.T. 492 (an application for judicial review brought under the Gaming Act 1968) Lord Jauncey considered the question of title to sue and held that objectors had a title and interest to raise such a petition (see also 1988 S.L.T. 850). In *Tait* v. *City of*

*Glasgow District Licensing Board*, 1987 S.L.T. 340 it was held that an applicant for a licence and a person entitled to apply for a licence had title and interest to seek judicial review of a clerk's decision. The question of title and interest should be considered before a petition is raised.

**6.16.** A board's decision may be reduced if the board acted *ultra vires*, erred in law, or conducted its proceedings contrary to natural justice; see sub-heading "The Board's Discretion" *supra*. For consideration of the authorities regarding the review of a licensing board's discretion in a judicial review of a decision under the Gaming Act 1968 where the considerations will be similar to a review under the 1976 Act, see *Mecca Leisure Ltd.* v. *City of Glasgow District Licensing Board*, 1987 S.L.T. 483. If a decision is reduced on one of these grounds, the proper course would be for the matter to be remitted by the court for a reconsideration by the board, and if they then proceed to exercise their discretion correctly the outcome may be the same.

*Appeals against s.35(4)—forfeiture, etc.*

**6.17.** Under s.35(4), on a complaint by a licensing board, a sheriff may declare a licence forfeit or impose other conditions. No appeal provisions are provided, nor is the decision declared to be final. The complaint is made by way of a summary application (*City of Glasgow District Licensing Board* v. *MacDonald, cit. supra*), and accordingly it is suggested that the sheriff's decision may be appealed in the normal way under rr. 91 *et seq.* of the Sheriff Court Ordinary Cause Rules (*Arcari* v. *Dumbartonshire C.C.*, 1948 S.C. 62). Alternatively the decision would be reducible if the appropriate circumstances were established.

*Registration of clubs—appeals*

**6.18.** With regard to the registration of clubs under Pt. VII of the Act, s.117(2) provides that a sheriff's decision shall be final. It has been held that procedural interlocutors of a sheriff during the course of hearings under this part of the Act, such as treating objections as abandoned, may be appealed: *Chief Constable of Strathclyde* v. *Hamilton and District Bookmakers Club*, 1977 S.L.T.(Sh.Ct.) 78; *Edinburgh North Constituency Association S.N.P. Club* v. *Thomas H. Peck Ltd.* 1978 S.L.T.(Sh.Ct.) 76.

**6.19.** Whether or not the sheriff's final decision is subject to review is more difficult. An action of reduction is certainly competent if the sheriff acted *ultra vires*, contrary to natural justice, erred in law, or proceeded upon irrelevant considerations or failed to take into account material considerations, etc. (D. M. Walker, *Civil Remedies*, at p. 187), but then the application would revert to the sheriff for reconsideration. It is recognised that a sheriff may be acting in an administrative rather than to judicial capacity (*Arcari, supra*), and that some of his acts in regard to licensing may be administrative (*Glasgow Corp.* v. *Glasgow Church Council*, 1944 S.C. 97, Lord President at p. 127). While it has been decided that in dealing with appeals under s.39 a sheriff, although vested with a wide discretion, acts judicially (*Martin* v. *Ellis*, 1977 S.L.T.(Sh.Ct.) 62), it would seem that in considering an application for the registration of a club, he is acting administratively rather than judicially. If this is the case, there would seem to be no reason in principle, why this administrative decision should not be subject to judicial review. The court will not have a power to substitute its own decision for that of the sheriff and will only be able to remit the matter back to the sheriff for reconsideration; see para. 6.13 *supra*.

**6.20.** The certificate of registration remains in force initially for three months pending the final decision of the sheriff (s.106).

### (7) Offences
**7.1.** Under the 1959 Act the majority of offences relating to licensing were breaches of the conditions of a certificate. The standard conditions were set out in Sched. 2 to the Act and s.131 provided that a breach of those conditions was to be an offence.

*Offences and penalties*
**7.2.** The 1976 Act has set out the offences relating to licensing as specific offences in the Act. A summary of the offences created by the Act is set out in Sched. 5 (as amended) to the 1976 Act, which specifies the nature of the offence, whether the licensee can be found vicariously liable, whether the licence holder or the premises can be disqualified and the level of the penalty, which applies to each offence. Section 128 provides that all offences are to be tried in a summary manner, but s.128(2) provides for trial on indictment in appropriate cases. The fixed monetary penalties of the original Act have been replaced by "levels" of fine in terms of ss.289E to 289G of the Criminal Procedure (Scotland) Act 1975 introduced by s.54 of the Criminal Justice Act 1982.

*Vicarious liability*
**7.3.** The doctrine of vicarious responsibility for criminal offences, set out in this Act, does cause difficulty. The Clayson Report considered it essential that the licence holder should be responsible for the acts of his staff and the general conduct of the premises, particularly as provision was to be made in the 1976 Act (s.11) that a licence could be held by companies or other unincorporated *personae*, which had not been allowed under the earlier legislation. The Clayson Report, with a dissenting minority, recommended that the vicarious liability should be absolute (Clayson, paras. 10–10 to 10–24).

**7.4.** Parliament, however, adopted the minority recommendation and by s.67(2) provided: "that it shall be a defence for the licence holder to prove that the offence occurred without his knowledge or connivance and that he exercised all due diligence to prevent its occurrence." This proviso raises the two issues of "knowledge" and "due diligence."

*Knowingly/knowledge*

**7.5.** The English cases dealing with the licensee "knowingly" allowing an offence to be committed need to be approached with caution, because the English have a doctrine of delegation, whereby if the licensee delegates the management of a premises to another person "then the knowledge of the servant or agent becomes that of the master or principal": see *Linnett* v. *Metropolitan Police Commr.* [1946] K.B. 290. For a review of the English authorities on the doctrine of delegation, see *R.* v. *Winson* [1969] 1 Q.B. 371, where Lord Parker C.J. at p. 204 says under reference to *Noble* v. *Heatly*, 1967 J.C. 5, that although the doctrine of delegation applies in England, it does not appear to apply in Scotland.

**7.6.** In *Noble* v. *Heatly*, 1967 S.L.T. 26; 1967 J.C. 5, a Full Bench decision where two persons were found drunk in a public house in which the certificate holder had delegated the management of the premises to an experienced supervisor, who was in sole charge at the time of the offence, of which the certificate holder had no personal knowledge, it was held that in the absence of personal knowledge on the part of the certificate holder, he could not be convicted of knowingly permitting drunkenness, thus excluding from Scots law the English doctrine of "delegation."

**7.7.** Sheriff Gordon (*Criminal Law* (2nd ed.) at para. 8–22) considers that *Noble* implies that a failure to institute a system to ensure observance of the statute would constitute sufficient *mens rea* for an offence of "knowingly permitting," in that it amounted to wilful blindness. While Sheriff Gordon criticises this approach, it is dealt with in the proviso to ss.67(2), with the defences that (a) it occurred without knowledge, but also (b) that the licensee exercised all due diligence to prevent the offence. Failure to institute a system to ensure observance of the statute would amount to a failure to exercise "due diligence."

**7.8.** In *Bunting* v. *Procurator Fiscal, Glasgow*, July 5, 1977, High Court of Justiciary, unreported, the Lord President in considering an appeal against a conviction under the Betting, Gaming Lotteries Act, s.10(1) and Rule 2 of Sched. 4, of admitting to or allowing to remain on the premises an under age boy said: "what must be established in order to lead to a contravention of the section is an act of permission by the person charged, that is to say the person charged must be shown to have permitted the under aged person to enter the betting shop or in the alternative form the person charged must be shown to have permitted an under aged person who had gained entry to the premises to remain there. In the result it is obvious that there is a positive obligation in the rules and that proof of knowledge is necessary. What knowledge is, of course, involves a consideration of cases such as *Mallon* v. *Allan* [1964] 1 Q.B. 385 and the case of *Knox* v. *Boyd*, 1941 J.C. 82. . . . It may be that in certain circumstances where the person charged does not have actual knowledge of the presence of the under aged person on the premises he may be convicted on the basis that he had the means of knowledge and by connivance or wilful blindness to the sources of knowledge he managed to keep the actual knowledge from his mind." This dicta is relevant in considering offences under, *e.g.* sections 68, 69 and 70 of the 1976 Act of allowing under age person into or to remain in licensed premises.

### Defence of "due diligence"

**7.9.** It should be noted in the proviso that the defence is that "he exercised all due diligence" and not that all due diligence was exercised. Had the latter been the defence, then the licensee would have had to prove that he and his servants exercised due diligence. It is therefore important in considering other cases on "due diligence" to see if the statute makes it a personal defence or one in which both master and servant have to exercise the due diligence. In *Tesco Supermarkets Ltd.* v. *Nattrass* [1972] A.C. 153, which is perhaps the leading English authority on vicarious liability in crime and the defence of due diligence, Lord Morris of Borth-y-Gest said at p. 180F., in considering the defence "that he took all reasonable precautions and exercised all due diligence to avoid the commission of such an offence by himself or any other person under his control," that "a system had to be created which could rationally be said to be so designed that the commission of offences would be avoided"; and Lord Diplock said at p. 203C. that "To exercise due diligence to prevent something being done is to take all reasonable steps to prevent it," and went on to say that it was contrary to the statute to hold that the due diligence had not been exercised if the servants failed to carry out instructions which had been given to them.

**7.10.** The issue of "exercised due diligence" was considered in *Byrne* v. *Tudhope*, 1983 S.C.C.R. 337 (in which it was suggested before the magistrate that there were no reported cases on due diligence and none are referred to in the opinion of the High Court), where a licensee was convicted of a failure to exercise due diligence where she had failed to draw an employee's attention to a portfolio of instructions which set out his duties under the Act. The implication of that case is that due diligence would have been exercised if the licensee had drawn the employee's attention specifically to his duties under the Act or the provision of the statute. Probably there would have to be a system of reminder to show continuing due diligence. The defence of due diligence was also considered in *Gorman* v. *Cochrane* (1977) S.C.C.R. Supp. 183.

### Onus of proof of defence

**7.11.** Where the onus of the defence is placed on the accused, as it is in the proviso to s.67(2), the defence need only be proved on a balance of probabilities: *H.M.A.* v. *Mitchell*, 1951 J.C. 53; *Neish* v. *Stevenson*, 1969 S.L.T. 229, and Walker and Walker, *Law of Evidence in Scotland*, p.76.

For a more detailed consideration of each offence, reference is made to the annotations to the statute.

# Licensing (Scotland) Act 1976

## (1976 c. 66)

### ARRANGEMENT OF SECTIONS

### PART I

### LICENSING BOARDS

### PART II

### THE GENERAL LICENSING SYSTEM

# PART III

## SEAMEN'S CANTEENS

# PART IV

## NEW TOWNS

[Repealed.]

# PART V

## THE PERMITTED HOURS

# PART VI

## OFFENCES

## Part VII

### Clubs

## Part VIII

### Miscellaneous, Transitional and General

# PART I

## LICENSING BOARDS

**Licensing boards**

**1.**—(1) For the administration of licensing with respect to alcoholic liquor on and after July 1, 1977, Scotland shall have licensing boards constituted in accordance with the provisions of this section.

(2) There shall be a separate licensing board for—

(*a*) each district and islands area which is not divided into licensing divisions under subsection (8) below, and

(*b*) each licensing division.

(3) The council of any district or islands area may from time to time determine whether the district or area shall be divided (or continue to be divided) into licensing divisions for the purposes of this Act, and such a council shall, on making a determination under this subsection, forthwith notify the Secretary of State of such determination and cause notice thereof to be published in two successive weeks in one or more newspapers circulating in the district or area.

(4) Subject to subsections (9) and (13) below, a licensing board shall consist of not less than one-quarter of the total number of members of the district or islands council and in no case shall consist of less than five such members.

(5) Where a district or islands area is divided into licensing divisions, then unless the Secretary of State otherwise directs, not less than one-

third of the members of the licensing board for a licensing division shall be councillors for a ward or electoral division within the area of the licensing division.

(6) The members of a licensing board for a district or licensing division of a district shall be elected at the first meeting of the district council held after the ordinary election of that council in 1977 and, in the case of subsequent elections, of those members—

(a) except in so far as paragraph (b) below otherwise provides, at the first meeting of the council held after each subsequent ordinary election of the council; and

(b) where a determination under subsection (3) above is made (whether or not at such meeting of the council as is mentioned in paragraph (a) above), either—

(i) at the meeting at which the determination is made; or

(ii) at the first meeting of the council held after such meeting as is mentioned in sub-paragraph (i) above.

(7) The members of a licensing board for an islands area or licensing division of an islands area shall be elected at a meeting of the council of the islands area to be held on a date between May 16, 1977 and June 30, 1977 to be determined by the council, and, in the case of subsequent elections of those members—

(a) except in so far as paragraph (b) below otherwise provides, at the first meeting of the council held after each subsequent ordinary election of the council; and

(b) where a determination under subsection (3) above is made (whether or not at such meeting of the council as is mentioned in paragraph (a) above), either—

(i) at the meeting at which the determination is made; or

(ii) at the first meeting of the council held after such meeting as is mentioned in sub-paragraph (i) above.

(8) The term of office of members of a licensing board shall begin with the day of their election under subsections (6) and (7) above and shall end on the day of the next election of members of the licensing board, but any member of a board shall be eligible for re-election.

(9) A member of a licensing board who has ceased to be a member of the authority by whom he was appointed by reason of an ordinary election to the council of that authority shall continue to be a member of the board until the first meeting of the council after the election.

(10) Any casual vacancy arising in a licensing board from death, resignation, disqualification or other cause may be filled by the election of a duly qualified person at the first meeting of the appointing council following upon the vacancy, and members so elected shall hold office until the date of the next meeting for election to the board.

(11) If a licensing board is not elected at the time at which it ought to be elected, or an insufficient number of members is elected for a board,

the Secretary of State may by order provide for the holding of an election or elections for supplying such fault or deficiency in election at such times and in such manner as he may think expedient.

(12) No election held in pursuance of this Act shall be deemed to be vitiated in consequence of any technical defect in the proceedings which has not been prejudicial to the interests of any party concerned in such election.

(13) For the purposes of any proceedings at the quarterly meeting in March in the final year of office of members of a licensing board which are not finally disposed of before the expiry in that year of the term of office of the members, the members of the licensing board in office at the date of the said meeting shall, notwithstanding such expiry, be deemed to constitute the licensing board.

GENERAL NOTE

Amended, 1981, c. 23, Sched. 3. From July 1, 1977 there are separate boards for each district or island area (or division of such an area) (subss. (2) and (3)). The membership of a licensing board is to consist of not less than one-quarter of the members of the area island or district council with a minimum membership of five (subs. (4)), and, where a licensing area is divided into divisions, one-third of the membership must be divisional councillors unless the Secretary of State directs otherwise (subs. (5)). The section also provides for the election of board members (subss. (6) and (7)), their term of office (subs. (8) and (9)), and the filling of casual vacancies in the membership (subs. (10)). The 1976 Act confers a right of appeal to the sheriff against a determination by a licensing board, and a further right of appeal from the decision of the sheriff to the Court of Session on a question of law. (For appeals from a decision of a licensing board, see. 39.)

*Subs*. (1): "*Alcoholic liquor*." This expression replaces the phrase "excisable liquor" which was used in the 1959 Act, and is defined in s.139(1). In addition to the function of administering liquor licensing, as provided for by the subsection, the boards also have functions in relation to the granting of permits and licences under the Betting, Gaming and Lotteries Act 1963 and the Gaming Act 1968 (see s.133 and Sched. 7, para. 7).

*Subss*. (2) and (3). There is to be a separate board for each district or islands area or division of such an area (subs. (2)). A district or islands area may be divided or continue to be divided by its council into licensing divisions. A decision to make licensing divisions must be intimated forthwith to the Secretary of State and published for two successive weeks in newspapers circulating in the area (subs. (3)). For a list of licensing boards and divisions see *Scottish Law Directory* ("The White Book").

*Subs*. (4). For the number of members required for a quorum, see s.5(3).

*Subs*. (5). The purpose of the subsection is to ensure that there is local representation on the licensing board for a division.

*Subs*. (6). In the case of a licensing board for a district or division of a district, the members were to be elected at the first meeting of the district council after its ordinary election in 1977 and thereafter after every ordinary election. Provision is made for the election of members of a new divisional board, either at the meeting at which it was determined that a new division should be established or at the first meeting thereafter.

*Subs*. (7). In the case of a board for an islands area or division of an islands area, the members were to be elected at a meeting of the islands council to be held between May 16, 1977, and June 30, 1977, and thereafter at the first meeting of the council after every ordinary election. Provision is made for the election of members of a new divisional board, either at the meeting at which it was determined that a new division should be established or at the first meeting thereafter.

*Subs*. (8). For the situation where a member of a board ceases to be a member of the authority which elected him, see subs. (9). For the position as regards proceedings before a board which are not completed before the expiry of the term of office of a member or members, see subs. (13).

*Subs*. (9). Where a member of a board is not re-elected to the authority which appointed him at an ordinary election, he remains a board member until the first meeting of the authority after the election.

*Subs*. (10). Casual vacancies in the membership of a board may be filled by the election of a duly qualified person at the first meeting of the appointing council after the vacancy occurred and the person elected holds office to the next election of the board. The corresponding provision in the 1959 Act was considered to apply only to vacancies arising in the course of the term of office of a member, and not to vacancies caused by the completion of a term of office (*Brown* v. *Cameron*, 1910 1 S.L.T. 181).

*Subs*. (11). The subsection provides a simple method of solving the difficulty created if a licensing board is not timeously or fully elected.

*Subs*. (12). "*any party concerned in such an election.*" This phrase was considered to mean in the identical provision of the 1959 Act (s.8) a contesting and defeated candidate.

*Subs*. (13). But for this provision, the membership of a licensing board dealing with proceedings at the quarterly March meeting in the year when the board is due for re-election might change during the course of the proceedings as a result of members completing their term of office and new members being elected. The subsection provides that, for the purpose of such proceedings, the original board members are to remain in office.

### Disqualification of interested persons

**2.**—(1) A person who is, or who is in partnership with any person as, a brewer, maltster, distiller or dealer in or retailer of alcoholic liquor, shall not act as a member of a licensing board for any purpose under this Act.

(2) A member of a licensing board who holds a disqualifying interest in a company shall not take part in any proceedings before the board in which that company is an applicant or an objector, and in this subsection "disqualifying interest" means a beneficial interest in shares or stocks of a close company within the meaning of section 282 of the Income and Corporation Taxes Act 1970 which have a total nominal value exceeding £50 or which amount to more than one hundredth part of the nominal value of the issued share capital, or stock, as the case may be, of the company or any class of such capital or stock.

(3) A person who is an employee of a holder of a licence under this Act and any other person engaged in a business which deals in alcoholic liquor, including directors, officers and employees of companies so engaged shall not act as a member of licensing board for any purpose under this Act.

(4) A member of a licensing board shall not act in the granting of a licence in respect of premises of which he is the proprietor, tenant or sub-tenant.

(5) If any person knowingly and wilfully contravenes this section, he shall be guilty of an offence.

(6) Anything done by any person in contravention of this section shall be void:

Provided that the grant of a new licence under this Act shall not be liable to objection on the ground that the members of the licensing board, or any of them, were not qualified to grant a licence.

(7) A person shall not be disqualified from acting as a member of a licensing board in relation to any matter by reason only that as a member of a committee constituted under section 47 of this Act he was concerned with the matter in question.

GENERAL NOTE

A. *Disqualification of Members of Courts—General.* This section (1) disqualifies persons in certain trades from acting in any way as a member of a board, (2) disqualifies a person holding a disqualifying interest in a company from taking part in proceedings in which the company is an applicant or an objector, (3) disqualifies an employee of a licence holder under the Act, and any person engaged in a business dealing with alcoholic liquor, including the directors, officers and employees of companies engaged in such businesses from acting as a member of a licensing board, (4) disqualifies a member of a board, who is the owner or tenant of premises, from acting in the granting of a certificate in respect of those premises, (5) makes it an offence to contravene the section, (6) declares, subject to the proviso (that the grant of a new licence is not liable to objection on the ground that one or more of the members of the board who granted it were not qualified to act), anything done in contravention of the section void, and (7) exempts members of a committee to determine the distribution of licences in a new town from disqualification for being members of a board by reason of their membership of the committee (now repealed). It is to be noted that the disqualification prescribed by subs. (1) applies to acting as a member for the discharge of the functions of a board under the Act. S.133 of the Act makes the licensing board the authority in Scotland for the grant or renewal of bookmakers' permits, betting agency permits, and betting office licences under the Betting, Gaming and Lotteries Act 1963, and for the grant, renewal, cancellation, and transfer of licences and for the purposes of Sched. 9 under the Gaming Act 1968. Such a grant or renewal is a purpose under the Act of 1963 or the Act of 1968 and not of the 1976 Act.

B. *Subsections.* (1) This is an absolute disqualification of the persons mentioned from acting as members of a board for any purpose. For the less sweeping disqualifications applicable to the licensing justices in England, see s.193 of the Licensing Act 1964. In England, for example, a brewer is disqualified from acting as a licensing justice only in the county or borough in which he is a brewer. The position of a shareholder in a brewer's business was discussed in *Braithwaite's Trs.* v. *Linlithgow Justices* (*Scotsman*, January 27, 1909), and he was held not to be a partner for the purposes of a similar provision. A trustee in a sequestrated estate, part of which consisted of a public house business, who did not himself hold the certificate or retail exciseable liquor, was held not to be disqualified under the corresponding provision then in force: *Lundie* v. *Magistrates of Falkirk* (1890) 18 R. 60.

(2) S.282 of the Income and Corporation Taxes Act 1970 (now s.414 of the Income and Corporation Taxes Act 1988) defines, with certain exceptions, a close company as a company under the control of five or fewer participators or of participators who are directors.

(3) This provision extends the classes of persons disqualified by the 1959 Act to include employees of licence holders and persons otherwise employed in the liquor trade.

(4) This is a limited disqualification and applies only to the granting of a licence for premises of which the member of the board is owner or tenant. He is not disqualified from taking part in refusing a certificate or in granting a certificate for other premises. A director and shareholder of a limited company which owned the premises was held not, as such, to be a part-proprietor within the meaning of a similar provision: *Blaik* v. *Anderson* (1899) 7 S.L.T. 299.

(5) For a consideration of "knowingly" and "knowledge" see note to s.68. The offence must be tried summarily in the sheriff court: s.128(1)(c). The maximum penalty is a fine of Level 5 (Sched. 5).

(6) The proviso protects the granting of a new licence in respect only of the disqualifications mentioned in the section. It does not protect the grant of a licence against recall on the ground of one or other of the disqualifications mentioned in note C below. *Ower* v. *Crichton* (1902) 10 S.L.T. 271; *Blaik* v. *Anderson* (*supra*).

C. *Common Law Disqualifications.* A common law disqualification will usually amount to a breach of natural justice and give grounds for either an appeal under s.39(4)(c) or other review of the decision by way of judicial review, reduction, etc.; see s.39.

A member of a board, although not affected by one of the statutory disqualifications above mentioned, may be so closely associated with the subject-matter of the proceedings as to make it improper that he should act and vote as a member of the board in connection with them. The principles of the common law invoked in such cases are *nemo judex in causa sua* (no man can be a judge in this own cause); or *auctor in rem suam* (no man should act in his own interest).

On occasions the courts have gone further and disqualified a member of a tribunal or board "if there are circumstances so affecting a person acting in a judicial capacity as to be calculated to create in the mind of a reasonable man a suspicion of that person's impartiality, those circumstances are sufficient to disqualify although in fact no bias exists"; see *Law* v. *Chartered Institute of Patent Agents* [1919] 2 Ch. 276; *Metropolitan Properties Co.* (*F.G.C.*) v. *London Rent Assessment Panel Committee* [1969] 1 Q.B. 577; *Bradford* v. *McLeod*, 1986 S.L.T. 244. This is an extension of the principle discussed above, but has been subject of comment; see P. W. Ferguson, "Nemo Iudex in Sua Causa?" 1987 S.L.T. (News) 149.

This principle may be infringed when a member of a board takes part in the granting or the rejection of an application for a licence in which he has a personal interest. In such a case the proceedings of the board will be reduced if his interest was "such as gives rise to a real likelihood of bias on his part." *McDonald* v. *Finlay*, 1957 S.L.T. 81, Lord Strachan at p. 83. On this ground the proceedings of the licensing court were either reduced, or the pursuer's averments were held relevant, in the following circumstance: when two of the members of the court had been employed by the applicant as part-time barmen for a number of years, without remuneration apart from money gifts at holiday periods: *McDonald* v. *Finlay* (*supra*); when three of the members of the court were shareholders, and one was a director, of the company owning the property for which the certificate was sought, and when that company was closely allied with another company, the officials and directors of both being the same persons, on whose behalf the certificate was applied for: *Blaik* v. *Anderson* (1899) 7 S.L.T. 299; when a member of the court had recently been a shareholder of the company on whose behalf the certificate was applied for, and he had on previous occasions himself been the applicant on the company's behalf, he being an avowed and pledged advocate of the company: *Ower* v. *Crichton* (1902) 10 S.L.T. 271; when members of a court had, in their capacity as members of a local authority, and with a view to street improvement, taken an active part in negotiating the purchase of licensed premises from brewers, who agreed to pay a sum of money to the local authority if a new licence were obtained for other premises, such as the subject of the application: *R.* v. *Sunderland JJ.* [1901] 2 K.B. 357 (*cf. R.* v. *Tempest* (1902) 18 T.L.R. 433, and for another case where members of the court were also city councillors, see *R.* v. *Sheffield Confirming Authority* [1937] 4 All E.R. 114); when a member of the court was a shareholder of the brewery company which owned the premises in question: *R.* v. *Gee* (1901) 17 T.L.R. 374; when three of the members of a compensation tribunal which refused the renewal of a licence had, along with their fellow justices, instructed a solicitor to oppose the renewal before the tribunal: *Frome United Breweries* v. *Bath JJ.* [1926] A.C. 586; when three members of the committee which granted and confirmed a licence had been shareholders and directors of the company on whose behalf the licence was applied for, although they resigned as directors and sold their shares before taking part in the proceedings: *R.* v. *Hain* (1896) 12 T.L.R. 323. The canvassing by a member of other members of the court, for or against a forthcoming application, has been said to be improper: *Macdougal* v. *Miller* (1900) 8 S.L.T. 284; and has led to proceedings being quashed: *R.* v. *Ferguson* (1890) 54 J.P. 101; although a contrary decision was arrived at when the member concerned, although attending the court, took no part in the deliberation: *R.* v. *London JJ.* (1896) 13 T.L.R. 2 (*cf. R* v. *Hertfordshire JJ.* (1845) 6 Q.B. 753). It has been held that a justice who has originated an objection in the lower court is not, on that account alone, disqualified from taking part in the proceedings of the confirmation court or court of appeal: *R.* v. *Leicester JJ.* [1927] 1 K.B. 557.

The principle that no man can be a judge in his own cause may also be infringed if a person has so actively identified himself with the temperance cause, by his actions in campaigning against the granting of certificates, that it would be contrary to elementary justice that he should act as a member of a licensing board. Mere membership of a temperance society, or the taking of a pledge of total abstinence, or an expression of sympathy with the prohibition of the sale of intoxicating liquor (*McGeehan* v. *Knox*, 1913 S.C. 688), or subscription to the funds of a temperance society (*Goodall* v. *Bilsland*, 1909 S.C. 1152), will not result in disqualification for this reason. It has been held, however, that a paid secretary of a temperance society, who prepared and managed objections to the granting of specific licences, was disqualified from acting as a member of a court. *Goodall* v. *Bilsland* (*supra*), at pp. 1177–1178; *McGeehan* v. *Knox* (*supra*), at p. 694. It has also been said that if a member of a court announced that he would give expression to his views by voting against every licence, he would be disqualified: *McGeehan* v. *Knox* (*supra*), Lord Mackenzie at p. 696.

Decisions as to the disqualification of a magistrate or justice of the peace, in his capacity as a judge in a criminal court, are not directly in point, but may be helpful. Since the function of such a court is solely judicial and in no way administrative, the rule which precludes interest or bias on the part of the judge may be expected to be enforced more, rather than less, strictly than in the case of a licensing board, which is primarily an administrative body. With regard to a member of a criminal court it has been said: "(1) As a general rule a pecuniary interest, if direct and individual, will disqualify, however small it may be. (2) An interest although not pecuniary may also disqualify, but the interest in that case must be substantial. (3) Where the interest . . . is not pecuniary, and is neither substantial nor calculated to cause bias in the mind of the judge, it will be disregarded, especially if to disqualify the judge would be productive of grave public inconvenience": *Wildridge* v. *Anderson* (1897) 25 R.(J.) 27, Lord Moncreiff at p. 34. A magistrate, who was *ex-officio* one of the trustees of a public library, was held not to be disqualified from trying a charge, at the instance of the burgh prosecutor, of wilful and malicious damage to the cushion of a seat in the library: *Wildridge* v. *Anderson* (*supra*). A magistrate, who, as a member of a licensing court and court of appeal, had taken part in a decision to grant no certificates for the sale of spirits within the burgh, was held not to be thereby disqualified from trying one of the applicants affected by the decision for trafficking in spirits without a certificate: *Gorman* v. *Wright*, 1916 S.C.(J.) 44.

### Expenses of members of licensing boards

**3.**—(1) Sections 45 to 50 of the Local Government (Scotland) Act 1973 (which provide for payment of allowances to members of local authorities and other bodies) shall apply with any necessary modifications to members of licensing boards as if the licensing boards were local authorities.

(2) Any amounts by way of allowance payable by virtue of subsection (1) above shall be payable by the council of the district or islands area whose area constitutes or includes the area of the licensing board.

GENERAL NOTE
The section replaces s.17 of the 1959 Act.

### Meetings of licensing boards

**4.**—(1) For the purposes of the discharge of its functions under this Act, every licensing board

(*a*) shall hold a meeting in January, March, June and October of each year beginning on a date in each such month fixed by the licensing board at least eight weeks prior to the meeting;

(*b*) may hold such other meetings as appear to the board to be appropriate.

(2) A licensing board may adjourn any meeting held by virtue of subsection (1) above from time to time during the period of one month next following the first day of such meeting, but no longer.

GENERAL NOTE
*Meetings of licensing boards.* A licensing board has to hold quarterly meetings in January, March, June and October each year, the precise date to be fixed by the board at least eight weeks before the meeting. The board is also empowered to hold such other meetings as it considers appropriate. Certain types of proceedings may only be dealt with at a quarterly meeting (s.5(6)). The proceedings are those involving any of the decisions specified in s.5(2)(*a*) to (*i*). In cases where there have been failures to make applications to licensing courts in time for them to be heard at statutory sittings, the Court of Session has been petitioned for directions, in virtue of its *nobile officium*, to licensing courts to hold special sittings to deal with non-timeous applications. Such petitions were granted in *MacDonald Ptr.*, May 8, 1917, and *Walter Ptr.*, October 29, 1917, where the failures were caused by war-time difficulties, and in *Bell's Exr. Ptr.*, 1960 S.L.T. (Notes) 3, where the executor of a deceased licence holder to whom the licence had been transferred failed, through inadvertence, not only to apply for a renewal at the next half-yearly meeting, but also to request a licensing court to deal with the matter at an ajourned meeting. The decision in *Bell* was held to be of doubtful validity in *Maitland Ptr.*, 1961 S.L.T. 384, where a licensing court was directed to hold a special sitting after it had, *per incuriam*, failed to declare a provisional grant final. In the course of his opinion in *Maitland*, the Lord President (Clyde) observed that the *noble officium* should be exercised where a formal step had been *per incuriam*, omitted, and unnecessary delay and expenditure would result if the whole procedure had to be carried out again; but that it was not to be used as a cloak for incompetence to extend a

statutory remedy to a party who had not been given such a remedy, or, by consent of parties, to supplement statutory procedure by what would be an amendment of a statute.

Where an application under the Act for a grant or renewal of a licence or extension of permitted hours, etc., is submitted too late for consideration by a board at a particular meeting, and the applicant has been rejected by the clerk, who has refused to place it before the board for their consideration, that decision may be subject to appeal under either s.39 (see *M. Milne Ltd.* v. *City of Glasgow District Licensing Board*, 1987 S.L.T. (Sh.Ct.) 145) if the particular application was subject to an appeal under s.39 or to a judicial review if the type of application does not allow of an appeal under s.39 (see *Main* v. *City of Glasgow District Licensing Board*, 1987 S.L.T. 305; *Tait* v. *City of Glasgow District Licensing Board*, 1987 S.L.T. 340). In *Tait*, where Lord Clyde considered that the clerk should not have rejected the late application, his Lordship ordered the board to hold a meeting to consider the application under s.31(2).

For meaning of "at a quarterly meeting" see note to s.30.

*Adjournment of meeting of a licensing board.* Subs. (2) re-enacts the provisions of s.18(3) of the 1959 Act relating to adjournment. A meeting of a licensing board cannot be adjourned beyond the period of one month from the first day of the meeting. In *R.* v. *Wandsworth Licensing Justices* [1937] 1 K.B. 144, it was ruled that the somewhat similar provision in the English Act of 1910 against adjourning for over a month struck only at the consideration of new business and that matters before the court at the general or adjourned meeting could be considered at a further adjournment outwith the month. For circumstances where the English court ordered licensing justices to grant a licence when they had adjourned their meeting beyond the statutory times, see *R.* v. *Denbigh Justices* (1895) 59 J.P. 708. In *R.* v. *Woodbury Licensing Justices, ex parte Rouse* [1960] 1 W.L.R. 461, where justices inadvertently adjourned a meeting beyond the one month period and on discovering the mistake refused to entertain the application, the court ordained the justices to hold a meeting to consider the applications.

## Arrangements for discharge of functions of licensing boards

**5.**—(1) Subject to subsection (2) below, a licensing board may arrange for the discharge of any of its functions by a committee of the board, a member or members of the board, the clerk of the board or any other person appointed to assist the clerk.

(2) A licensing board shall not make any arrangements under subsection (1) above for the discharge of any of the following functions—

(a) making a decision on the application for the grant, including the provisional grant, of a new licence;

(b) making a decision on an application for the renewal of a licence where a competent objection has been lodged;

(c) making a decision to refuse to grant the renewal of a licence;

(d) making a decision on the permanent transfer of a licence;

(e) making a decision on an application for a regular extension of permitted hours;

(f) making a decision on the restriction of the terminal permitted hour;

(g) making a decision on an application for restoration of restricted hours;

(h) making a decision on an application for Sunday opening under Part I of Schedule 4 to this Act other than an application under paragraph 13 of that Schedule where no objection is made in relation to the application;

(i) making a decision as regards a Sunday restriction order or the revocation of such an order under Part II of Schedule 4 to this Act;

(j) making a decision on the suspension of a licence;

(k) making a decision on a closure order;

(*l*) making a decision on an application for the grant of a children's certificate under section 49 of the Law Reform (Miscellaneous Provisions) (Scotland) Act 1990;

(*m*) confirming, under section 25(4) of this Act, the transfer of a licence transferred by virtue of subsections (2) or (3) of that section.

(3) One half of the members of a licensing board (and in no case less than three members) shall be a quorum for any meeting of the board to discharge functions mentioned in subsection (2) above.

(4) The chairman of a licensing board or, in his absence, the clerk of the board may, if a quorum is not present for any such meeting of the board, call a further meeting in place of the meeting not held.

(5) A licensing board may, at any such meeting of the board, act notwithstanding any vacancy, if a quorum is present.

(6) A licensing board may only deal with any proceedings relating to matters mentioned in paragraph (*a*) to (*i*) and (*l*) of subsection (2) above at a quarterly meeting of the board held by virtue of section 4(1)(*a*) of this Act.

(7) Proceedings relating to matters mentioned in subsection (2) above, including voting in connection therewith, shall be held in public, but a licensing board may retire to consider its decision in any such matter and the clerk of the board shall accompany the board when it so retires unless the board otherwise directs.

(8) The district or islands council concerned shall provide accommodation for the meetings, and otherwise defray any necessary expenses in respect of the proceedings of the licensing boards for their area.

GENERAL NOTE

A. *General.* A committee of a licensing board, a member or members of a board, its clerk or his assistant may discharge any of the functions of a board except those involving any of the decisions specified in subs. (2). In the case of the excepted functions, a quorum for a meeting to discharge them consists of one-half of the total membership of the board, and, in no case less than three members (subs. (3)). The section also makes provisions for the calling of a further meeting in the absence of a quorum (subs. (4)), meetings where there are vacancies in the membership (subs. (5)), matters which have to be dealt with at a quarterly meeting (subs. (6)), the holding of meetings in public (subs. (7)), and the expenses of meetings (subs. (8)).

B. *Subsections.* (1) For the meaning of "*licence*" and "*licensing board*," see s.139(1). For "*clerk of the board*" and "*person appointed to assist the clerk*," see s.7.

(2)(*a*) For "*provisional grant*," see s.26. For meaning of "*new licence*," see s.139(1).

(*b*) and (*c*) The special provisions relating to the renewal of a licence are contained in s.24. For an application to be an application for the renewal of a licence, it must be in respect of premises where there is a licence already in force and for a further grant in the form of that licence, otherwise the application is an application for a grant of a new licence (see definition of "*new licence*" in s.139(1)). For "*competent objections*," see s.16.

(*d*) For the provisions relating to the permanent transfer of licences, see s.25.

(*e*), (*f*) and (*g*) For the meaning of "*permitted hours*," see s.139(1). For the provisions relating to the extension and restriction of permitted hours, see ss.64 and 65.

(*j*) and (*k*) For "*suspension orders*" and "*closure orders*," see ss.31 and 32, respectively.

(4) The purpose of this provision, which re-enacts the corresponding provision of the 1959 Act, is to deal with the situation which arose in the case of *Buchanan*, 1910 S.C. 685, where, as a result of there being no quorum at a half yearly meeting of a licensing court, the meeting could not be adjourned under the existing legislation and the Court of Session had to intervene by virtue of its *nobile officium* in order to prevent the expiry of certificates due for renewal at the meeting.

For the appointment of a chairman to a board, see s.6.

(5) The provisions of the subsection are in accord with the decision in *Brown* v. *Cameron*, 1910 1 S.L.T. 181 which was concerned with a meeting of a licensing appeal court under the 1903 Act where, though there was a quorum, two members were absent.

(7) A board must not consider an objection made to it in private. In *R.* v. *Merthy Tydvil JJ.* (1885) 14 Q.B.D. 584, it was held that an objection made by a chief constable to an application for a licence to the court in their private room was not one to which the court could give effect. Even if a board retire to consider a decision they must vote in public: *Najafian* v. *Glasgow District Licensing Board*, 1987 S.C.L.R. 679, *McKay* v. *Banff and Buchan Western Division District Licensing Board*, 1991 S.L.T. 18 and *Simpson* v. *Banff and Buchan Western Division District Licensing Board*, 1991 S.L.T. 20.

(8) For the expenses of members of boards as opposed to the expenses of the boards themselves, see s.3.

## Chairman

**6.**—(1) Every licensing board shall elect annually one of its number to be chairman of the board, and until a chairman is elected, or if the chairman is absent from any meeting, the board shall elect one of its number present at the meeting to be chairman of that meeting.

(2) Where on the election of a chairman an equal number of votes is given for two or more persons, the meeting shall determine by lot which of those persons shall be the chairman.

(3) Subject to subsection (2) above, at any meeting of a licensing board the chairman shall, in a case of equality in voting, have a second or casting vote.

GENERAL NOTE

See *Tuzi* v. *City of Edinburgh District Licensing Board*, 1985 S.L.T. 477, which, although concerned with a gaming licence, considers the terms of this section prior to amendment by the 1990 Act.

*Subsections.* (1) Though the membership of a licensing board is appointed for a period of four years (s.1(6)), the subsection desiderates that the chairman is to be elected annually.

(2) Where there is an equality of votes requiring that the election of a chairman is to be determined by lot, the meeting is entitled to determine the form of lot to be used.

(3) The chairman of a licensing board has a second or casting vote when the voting in connection with a decision by the board is equal. Until removed by amendment introduced by para. 4 of Sched. 8 to the 1990 Act, there was a proviso to this section, which precluded the chairman from having a second or casting vote on an application for a grant or provisional grant of a new licence, which caused substantial difficulty; see *Hart* v. *City of Edinburgh District Licensing Board*, 1987 S.L.T.(Sh.Ct.) 54, where the sheriff held that proviso was effectively repealed by s.17 and had been erroneously enacted, a view, which the amendment confirms. An equal vote under s.17 does not "find" that a ground applies and accordingly is not a situation where this subs applies: *Hart, cit.* For *"provisional grant"* see s.26. For the meaning of *"new licence,"* see s.139(1).

*Voting at meetings of licensing boards.* When a member of a board is disqualified from voting in a particular application, he should vacate his seat during the hearing: *R.* v. *London County Council* [1892] 1 Q.B. 90. If a member of a board arrives late at a meeting, and is not present during the whole of a hearing on an application, he must not vote with regard to that application: *Goodall* v. *Bilsland*, 1909 S.C. 1152.

## Clerk of licensing boards

**7.**—(1) Every district and islands council shall appoint and employ, whether on a full-time or part-time basis—

(a) an officer to be the clerk of every licensing board having jurisdiction within their area, and

(b) such other persons as may be necessary to assist that officer or to act on his behalf as clerk or assistant clerk of those boards and the clerk of a licensing board shall be an advocate or a solicitor.

(2) Where under an agreement an officer of a regional council is placed at the disposal of a district council for the purposes of this section, that officer may perform the duties of clerk or assistant clerk of the aforementioned boards.

(3) The clerk of a licensing board shall not, himself or by his partner or clerk, act as solicitor to, or agent for, any person in any proceedings before that board or in any appellate proceedings which may result therefrom and, if any person contravenes this subsection, he shall be guilty of an offence.

GENERAL NOTE

The clerkship of a licensing board is not to be held by the incumbent of a particular office but is to be held by an officer appointed and employed by the appropriate district or islands council. The council may make the appointment full or part time and it may be held by an officer of a regional council but the appointee must be an advocate or a solicitor. The district or islands council must as necessary appoint other persons to act for or assist the clerk.

*Subs.* (3)

The subsection imposes an absolute prohibition on a clerk of a licensing board, his partner, or clerk acting on behalf of any person in proceedings before a licensing board, and makes it an offence to contravene the subsection. The maximum penalty is a fine of level 5 (Sched. 5).

## *Fees payable*

**8.**—(1) The Secretary of State may, by order made by statutory instrument, determine the fees payable by any applicant to a licensing board.

(2) The fees mentioned in subsection (1) above shall not include fees payable under the provisions of the Betting, Gaming and Lotteries Acts 1963 to 1971 or of the Gaming Act 1968.

(3) Fees determined by the Secretary of State under subsection (1) above shall, on being paid by any applicant to the board, be paid over by the clerk of that board to the council which defray the expenses of that board.

GENERAL NOTE

The current order is S.I. 1990 No. 2458: see Introduction, para. 3.11.

## PART II

## THE GENERAL LICENSING SYSTEM

### Grant of licences by licensing boards

**9.**—(1) A licensing board may, in accordance with the provisions of this Part of this Act, grant a licence to any person for the sale by retail or supply of alcoholic liquor by that person.

(2) A licence so granted by a licensing board shall be in respect of premises specified therein, being premises situated within the area of the board.

(3) The types of licence which may be so granted by a licensing board are those specified in Schedule 1 to this Act.

(4) A licence granted by a licensing board shall be in such form as the board may decide.

(5) A licence granted otherwise than at a properly constituted meeting of a licensing board or otherwise than in accordance with the provisions of this Act shall be void.

GENERAL NOTE

A. *General.* Without having obtained a licence under the Act from a licensing board, it is, in general, illegal for any person to sell alcoholic liquor by retail, and such a sale is usually a contravention of s.90 of the Act. There are certain exceptions to the general rule in virtue of the provisions of s.138(1), namely trafficking in liquor in services' canteens, theatres erected before January 1, 1904, or with passengers on vessels, aircraft, or railway passenger vehicles. The section retains the types of licences provided for by the 1959 and 1962 Acts, and introduces two new types recommended by Clayson (paras. 7.16 to 7.21), refreshment licences and entertainment licences. The 1976 Act specifies in Sched. 1 the types of licence which a board may grant, including the nature of the premises in respect of which any particular certificate may be granted and the authorisation conferred on the licence holder by the licence, and provides for specific offences instead of prosecutions for breach of certificate. The 1976 Act also makes a radical change as regards the grounds for granting or refusing an application for a licence. The 1959 Act (s.32) enabled a licensing court to grant licences for the sale of alcoholic liquor to "such and so many persons as the court shall think fit." This discretion has been considerably narrowed by the 1976 Act which limits the grounds of refusal to those specified in s.17. The tenor of the 1976 Act is permissive: a licence should be granted unless good cause is shown justifying refusal.

B. *Subsections.* (1) "*Licensing board,*" "*licence*" and "*alcoholic liquor*" are defined in s.139(1). "*Grant*" includes grant by way of renewal (s.139(1)).

"*Sale by retail*" is not defined in the Act. The Customs and Excise Act 1952, which contained a definition of "sale by retail," was repealed in 1981. In the case of *Wood* v. *Mackenzie*, 1925 J.C. 13, the definition of sale by retail was considered and it was held that the sale was defined by reference to quantity sold, not to the person to whom that quantity was sold. This accords with the dictionary definitions of "retail" and "wholesale." It has also been held that a wholesale sale does not become a retail sale because the goods are delivered over a period in retail quantities: *Hales* v. *Buckley* [1911] W.N. 32. The Alcoholic Liquor Duties Act 1979, as amended, contains a definition of "wholesale." However see s.90A of the 1990 Act which introduces controls regarding the premises from which alcoholic liquor can be sold.

(2) The subsection confers on the licensing board for the area where the premises to which an application relates are situated jurisdiction over the application. "*Licensing area*" is defined in s.139(1).

(3) For the form of a licence, see subs. (4). The types of licence which a board may grant by virtue of Sched. 1 are as follows.

"*Public house licence*" which authorises the sale by retail of alcoholic liquor for consumption on or off the premises. "*Public house*" is defined by s.139(1) as including an inn, ale-house, victualling house or other premises in which liquor is sold for consumption on or off the premises.

"*Off sale licence*" which authorises the sale of liquor for consumption off the premises in respect of which it has been granted only.

"*Hotel licence*" which gives the same authorisation to the holder as a public house licence except that the premises to which it applies are hotels. "*Hotel*" is defined by s.139(1) as meaning (a) in towns and suburbs a house containing at least four apartments set apart exclusively for the sleeping accommodation of travellers, and (b) in rural districts and places of a population of less than 1,000 according to the most recent census a house containing two such apartments.

"*Restricted hotel licence.*" This form of licence is granted to an hotel structurally adapted and bona fide used for providing main meals at mid-day or in the evening, or both, to persons frequenting the premises, and does not contain a bar counter. The holder may supply liquor to persons taking table meals on the premises, to residents or private friends of residents being bona fide entertained by them, to the private friends for their own or the resident's consumption, and to a resident for his own or a private friend's consumption with a meal supplied at the premises but to be consumed off them. "*Table meal,*" is defined by s.139(1) as meaning a meal eaten by a person sitting at a table or other structure which serves the purpose of a table and is not used for the service of refreshments for consumption by persons not seated at a table or structure serving the purpose of a table, which definition repeats the definition given by the 1962 Act.

"*Restaurant licence*" which authorises the supply of alcoholic liquor to persons taking table meals for consumption as an ancillary to the meal in premises which are adapted for habitually providing meals to persons who frequent them, are principally used for providing main meals at mid-day and in the evening, and do not contain a bar counter. For "*table meal,*" see note to "restricted hotel licence."

"*Refreshment licence.*" This is a new type of licence introduced by the Act. It is granted in respect of premises which are adapted and used for the provision of refreshments including food and non-alcoholic beverages for consumption on the premises, and which do not contain a bar counter. The holder is entitled to sell or supply alcoholic liquor for consumption on the premises but not off the premises, when food and non-alcoholic beverages are also on sale.

"*Entertainment licence.*" This is also a new type of licence introduced by the Act. It relates to places of entertainment such as cinemas, theatres, dance halls, and proprietary clubs and permits the sale or supply of liquor for consumption on the premises to persons frequenting them as an ancillary to the entertainment provided. A licensing board may insert conditions in such a licence to insure that the sale or supply is ancillary to the entertainment.

(4) Unlike the 1959 Act, the 1976 Act does not prescribe any particular form of licence. The form must be such, however, as to confer authority for the sale of alcohol in accordance with the type of licence granted with modifications, if any, in accordance with the provisions of the Act.

(5) Where a licence is granted by a board which has not been properly constituted or is otherwise not in accordance with the Act, the licence is void. Under s.1(12), however, the election of a board member is not vitiated by a technical defect in the proceedings which has not prejudiced other interested parties in the election, and, under s.2(6), the grant of a new licence is not to be objected to on the ground that any of the members of the board granting it were not qualified to grant the licence.

### Application for licence

**10.**—(1) An application to a licensing board of any kind mentioned in subsection (6) below in respect of any premises shall be in such form as may be prescribed, shall be completed and signed by the applicant or his agent, and shall be lodged with the clerk of the licensing board within whose area the premises are situated not later than five weeks before the first day of the meeting of the board at which the application is to be considered.

(2) In the case of an application for the grant of a new licence, the applicant shall—

(*a*) along with his application, lodge with the clerk of the board a plan of the premises in respect of which the application is made; and

(*b*) arrange for the display at the premises, in a place and at a height where it can conveniently be read by the public, of a notice in the prescribed form intimating his application and the type of licence for which he applies, for a period of at least 21 days before the first day of the meeting as aforesaid.

Paragraph (*a*) of this subsection shall not apply to an application for the grant of an off-sale licence.

(3) In the case of an application for the provisional grant of a new licence, the applicant shall—

(*a*) along with his application, lodge with the clerk of the board a plan of the premises in respect of which the application is made; and

(*b*) arrange for the display at the site of the premises of a notice all as mentioned in subsection (2)(*b*) above.

(3A) In the case of an application for the grant, the provisional grant or the renewal of a public house licence or a refreshment licence, the application shall state whether the applicant intends the premises to be open for the sale or supply of alcoholic liquor during the permitted hours on a Sunday.

(4) An applicant shall not be treated as having failed to comply with subsection (2)(*b*) or (3)(*b*) above if the notice is, without any fault or intention of his, removed, obscured or defaced before the first day of the meeting of the board at which the application is to be considered, so long as he has taken reasonable steps for its protection and, if need be, replacement.

(5) In the case of an application for the grant or provisional grant of a new licence, the applicant shall, not later than three weeks before the first day of the meeting of the board at which the application is to be considered, give notice in writing of the application to every occupier of premises situated in the same building as the premises to which the application relates.

(6) The applications referred to in subsection (1) above are as follows—

(*a*) an application for the grant or renewal of a licence;

(*b*) an application for the provisional grant of a new licence;

(*c*) an application for a permanent transfer of a licence;

(*d*) an application for a regular extension of permitted hours.

(7) On receipt of an application of a kind referred to in subsection (6) above, and until the first day of the meeting of the board at which the application is to be considered, the clerk of a licensing board shall make the application, together with the documents lodged therewith, available for inspection by members of the public during normal office hours.

(8) A notice as mentioned in subsection (2) above and notice under subsection (5) above shall include a statement as to whether the applicant intends the premises to be open for the sale or supply of alcoholic liquor during the permitted hours on a Sunday.

GENERAL NOTE

A. *General.* The section applies to applications for the grant or renewal of a licence (including the provisional grant of a new licence), for the permanent transfer of a licence, and for the regular extension of permitted hours (subs. (6)). Such applications are to be made in such form as the board may prescribe, by the applicant or his agent, and lodged with the clerk to the licensing board at least five weeks before the first day of the meeting at which the application falls to be considered (subs. (1)). The board to which an application is to be made is the board for the area in which the premises with which the application is concerned are situated (subs. (1)). The clerk is required to make the application available for inspection during normal office hours by members of the public from the date of lodging until the first day of the meeting at which it is to be considered (subs. (7)). There are additional provisions which apply to applications for the grant of a new licence or the provisional grant of a new licence. An applicant for such a grant requires to lodge with his application a plan of the premises to which the application relates and to display a notice intimating his application at the proposed premises (subss. (2) and (3)). He is also required, not later than three weeks before the date of the meeting, to give written notice of his application to all the occupiers of premises situated in the same building as the premises to which the application relates (subs. (5)).

B. *Subsections.* (1) For the areas covered by separate licensing boards, see s.1. For the meetings of licensing boards, see ss.4 and 5.

(2) *"New licence."* For definition, see s.139(1).

For the meaning of *"off-sale licence,"* see Sched. 1.

(3) For the provisions relating to the provisional grant of a new licence, see s.26. Under s.26(2), detailed plans of the premises need not be lodged but only a site plan showing the location of the premises is required until the provisional grant is affirmed.

*New subs.* (*3A*). Inserted by s.46 of the 1990 Act. An applicant for the grant, provisional grant or renewal of a public house or refreshment licence shall state an intention to open on a Sunday for the sale or supply of alcoholic liquor in the context of that application, without the need to make a separate application in terms of Sched. 4. If such an intention is stated then new subs. (8) of s.10 of the Act requires that Notices in terms of ss.10(2) and 10(5) of the 1976 Act shall include a statement as to whether the applicant intends the premises to be opened on Sundays.

(4) The subsection relieves an applicant from the consequences of the failure to exhibit a notice in compliance with subss. (2)(*b*) or (3)(*b*) where the failure has been caused by the removal, obscuring, etc. of the notice through no fault of the applicant and the applicant has taken reasonable steps to protect and replace the notice. For discussion of adequate display of notice, see *Tevan* v. *Motherwell District Licensing Board (No. 1)* 1985 S.L.T.(Sh.Ct.) 14, where it was held that display of a notice within a post office was sufficient. *Obiter*, the display of a notice within a public house would not be regarded as sufficient.

(5) *"Occupier."* The word was considered to mean, where it was used in s.36 of the 1959 Act, an occupier within the meaning of the Lands Valuation (Scotland) Act 1854 (see Purves, p. 44).

*"Building."* The interpretation of the word "building" is a question of fact in relation to the particular structure to be determined by the board, who have to decide, whether or not this particular group of structures is one building or separate buildings. The subsection makes it clear that there can be a number of "premises" within one building.

*Per* Stroud's *Judicial Dictionary, sub nom* "buildings" "what is a 'building' must be a question of degree and circumstances"; its "ordinary and usual meaning is a block of brick or stone covered by a roof" citing *Moir* v. *Williams* [1892] 1 Q.B. 264. The question of whether or not one roof covers the underlying units need not necessarily be the only consideration although it is material.

In *Bell* v. *Edinburgh Workmen's Dwelling-houses Improvement Co. Ltd.*, 1957 S.L.T.(Sh.Ct.) 10 the sheriff held "what is a building must be a question of fact." He held that a row of tenement blocks was not one building but separate buildings. In *Goodchild* v. *Romford BC* [1940] 2 All E.R. 309 it was held that a row of shops in one person's ownership was not a "building." The fact of one ownership was held not to make the row of shops into one building. The court determined the row of shops was not one building because on the facts it could be seen that some shops had been erected separately. Although the gable walls were common between the shops and they all opened into a common arcade, this was held not to be sufficient to make the row of shops into one building.

(6) For the provisions relating to the renewal of a licence, the provisional grant of a licence, the permanent transfer of a licence, and the regular extension of permitted hours, see ss.24, 25, 26 and 64 respectively.

*New subs.* (*8*). Inserted by s.46 of the 1990 Act.

Sched. 4 to the 1976 Act is amended to take account of the new s.10 procedure, namely that an applicant need no longer make a separate application for Sunday opening. Notice does not require to be given in terms of s.10(2)(b) and (5) when renewing a public house or refreshment licence in respect of Sunday opening. New subs. (15A) states that where there is already a Sched. 4 grant of Sunday opening, it continues until the renewal of the licence by the board or if renewal is refused, or renewal of Sunday opening refused, until the time has elapsed for the making of an appeal under s.39 of the 1976 Act, or that appeal is determined. Thereafter a statement of intention to open on a Sunday for the sale or supply of alcoholic liquor will suffice. However no provision has been made for application at times other than grant or renewal if an intention to open on Sunday is missed or refused and the licence holder wishes to apply again.

## Special provisions for application made other than by individual natural persons

**11.**—(1) Where an application is made for a new licence, or for the renewal or permanent transfer of a licence, by an applicant who is not an individual natural person, the following provisions of this section shall apply.

(2) The application shall name both the applicant and the employee or agent of the applicant whom the applicant intends should have the responsibility for the day to day running of the premises to which the application relates.

(3) Where an application is granted, the licensing board shall grant the licence or transfer in the names of both persons mentioned in subsection (2) above, and any reference in this Act to the holder of a licence includes a reference to both of those persons.

(4) Unless a licence is transferred to another employee or agent within eight weeks from the time when the employee or agent named in a licence ceases to be responsible for the day to day running of the premises to which the licence relates, the licence shall cease to have effect.

GENERAL NOTE

A. *General.* In virtue of s.33 of the 1959 Act, a certificate to sell liquor could only be granted under that Act to an individual person. This provision did not take into account the substantial number of businesses in the licensed trade which are owned and operated by bodies corporate or incorporate and not by individual persons, with the result that the licence holder was a company official who exercised little or no control over the day-to-day running of the premises, or was the manager of the premises, and whose employment could be terminated at any time, irrespective of the date of expiry of the licence, either by his own volition or by his employer's. The section provides that a non-individual person may be granted a licence in its own name and that of the person responsible for the day-to-day running of the premises.

B. *Subsections.* (1) The section applies to the grant of a new licence, or the renewal or the permanent transfer of an existing licence, to a non-natural person. In the case of the provisional grant, the name of the person responsible for the day-to-day running is required when the grant is declared final (s.26(6) and (7)).

"*New licence*" is defined in s.139(1) of the Act. For "*renewal*" and "*permanent transfer*" of licences, see ss.24 and 25 respectively.

"*An applicant who is not an individual natural person*" means bodies either corporate or incorporate which the law recognises as having a separate legal persona. For discussion of "partnership" and transfer from individual licence holder to partnership, see *Singh and Kaur* v. *Kirkcaldy District Licensing Board*, 1988 S.L.T. 286, where it was decided that the licence was held by a partnership with a separate legal persona and that the board were not entitled to look behind that persona at the partners as individuals. See also *Fereneze Leisure Ltd.* v. *Renfrew District Licensing Board*, 1991 G.W.D. 15–943, where it was held that the licensing board required to consider the fitness of the company to hold the licence as a separate legal persona and not the fitness of the directors of the company.

(2) The application by a non-natural person must name the person who is to be responsible for the day-to-day running of the premises, and the licence granted or transferred as a result of the application must name both the non-natural person and the person who is to run the premises.

(4) Where there is a change in the employee responsible for the day-to-day running of the premises, the licence must be transferred into the new employee's name within eight weeks of the change, or the licence ceases to be valid. S.25(3) makes special provision for an application by a non-natural person to change the name of the employee named in the licence as responsible for the day-to-day running of the premises. Where an application to transfer a licence on a change of person with day to day responsibility is lodged outwith the eight week time limit, see *Argyll Arms (McManus) Ltd.* v. *Lorn, Mid-Argyll, Kintyre and Islay Divisional Licensing Board*, 1988 S.L.T. 290, where it was held that the board required to hear the application outwith the eight week period despite the provision that the licence ceases to have effect. Distinction is drawn between existence of licence and its ceasing to have effect. For discussion of the meaning of "all competent applications," see *M. Milne Ltd.* v. *City of Glasgow District Licensing Board*, 1987 S.L.T.(Sh.Ct.) 145, where the clerk to the licensing board refused to accept a late application for renewal in terms of s.13(2) of the Act. The clerk argued that it was not a "competent application." It was held that the clerk erred in law in not allowing the question of whether the application was competent to be considered by the licensing board.

**Publication of list of applications**

**12.**—(1) The clerk of a licensing board shall, in accordance with the provisions of this section, not later than three weeks before the first day of the meeting of the board at which the applications are to be considered, cause to be published in one or more newspapers circulating in the area of the board a list of all competent applications made to the board for—

(*a*) the grant, including the provisional grant, of a new licence;

(*b*) the regular extension of permitted hours.

(2) In relation to each application for a new licence, the list mentioned in subsection (1) above shall specify—

(*a*) the name, designation and address of the applicant;

(*b*) in the case of an application to which section 11 of this Act applies, the names, designations and addresses of both persons named in the application;

(*c*) the address of the premises in respect of which the licence is desired;

(*d*) the type of licence for which application is made;

(*e*) the first day of the meeting of the licensing board at which the application is to be considered;

(*f*) in the case of an application for a public house licence or a refreshment licence, whether the applicant intends the premises to be open for the sale or supply of alcoholic liquor during the permitted hours on a Sunday.

(3) In relation to each application for the regular extension of permitted hours, the list mentioned in subsection (1) above shall specify—

(*a*) the name, designation and address of the applicant;

(*b*) the address of the premises in respect of which the application is made and the type of licence held in respect of those premises;

(*c*) the nature of the extension of hours for which application is made;

(*d*) the first day of the meeting of the licensing board at which the application is to be considered.

GENERAL NOTE

A. *General*. The section provides for the newspaper advertisement of applications for a grant (including a provisional grant) of a new licence and for a regular extension of the permitted hours by the clerk of the board to whom application is made (subs. (1)). The specification of the requirements for listing an application for a new licence is contained in subs. (2), and for listing an application for a regular extension is contained in subs. (3). The advertisement is to be made at least three weeks before the first day of the meeting of the board at which the applications are to be considered (subs. (1)).

B. *Subsections*. (1) "*Competent applications*" should be taken as meaning applications made in accordance with ss.10 and 11 for the grant, including the provisional grant, of a new licence or a regular extension of the permitted hours to the licensing board for the area (or division of an area) where the premises in respect of which the application is made are situated. The applicant may also be required to share with other "adjourned" applicants, the cost of the adjourned meeting, in terms of a particular board's regulations.

For the definitions of "*grant*" and "*new licence*," see s.139(1).

For the provisions relating to provisional grant and the regular extension of the permitted hours, see ss.26 and 64 respectively.

(2)(*b*) S.11 requires, in the case of an application by a non-natural person, that both the non-natural person and the person who is to be responsible for the day-to-day running of the premises be named in the application.

2(*f*) Consequential amendment inserted by s.46(3) of the 1990 Act, to the effect that where an application for a public house licence or a refreshment licence is advertised by the Clerk of a licensing board, the intention to be open for the sale or supply of alcoholic liquor should also be advertised.

Note the effect of para. 18, Sched. 8 to the 1990 Act which allows publication of an agent's name and address in the interests of confidentiality and security.

## Consideration of applications

**13.**—(1) A licensing board shall not at any meeting hear the cases of applicants for new licences until all the other cases have been disposed of:

Provided that where more than one application for a licence has been made in respect of any premises, the licensing board may hear and consider such applications together.

(2) Where an applicant for the grant of a licence or an objector thereto—

    (*a*) has, through inadvertence or misadventure, failed to comply with any of the preliminary requirements of this Act; or

    (*b*) having duly lodged his application or objection, has died before the meeting of the board at which such application or objection was to have been heard;

the board may, if it thinks fit, and upon such terms as the board thinks proper, postpone the consideration of the application or objection to an adjourned meeting.

(3) At such adjourned meeting the licensing board may, if it is satisfied that the terms specified by the board have been complied with—

    (*a*) proceed to grant the licence to the applicant or, as the case may be, to his executors, representatives or disponees (being possessed of the premises in respect of which the application has been made);

    (*b*) proceed to consider the objection, whether on the part of the objector or, in the case of a deceased objector, on the part of his representatives; as if the preliminary requirements of this Act had been complied with.

GENERAL NOTE

A. *Procedure for hearing of applications at meetings of licensing boards.* This section has reference to certain points of procedure which must, or which may, be followed by the licensing board at its meetings. Subject to the overriding requirements of the Act, the procedure for dealing with applications may also be governed by regulations made by the licensing board itself under s.37. The individual board regulations may differ and should be checked in relation to particular procedures for application, particularly with reference to Children's Certificates and consent to alteration applications. For the meetings of licensing boards, see ss.4 and 5.

B. *Subsections.* (1) This subsection provides that certain applications shall not be heard until all the others are disposed of. The order in which applications are heard may sometimes be important, particularly if the granting of a licence raises the question of the overprovision of similar facilities, a ground of refusal under s.17(1)(*d*). In *McEwan* v. *Fort William JJ.*, November 18, 1898, a licensing court was ordained by the Court of Session to hear and determine, of new, an application for a certificate which had been disposed of out of its proper order. The applicants, the hearing of whose cases must be postponed until all the others are disposed of, are the applicants for new licences.

"*Applicants for new licences.*" This is a different expression from that used in the 1959 Act which was "new applicants" and was taken to mean not only applicants for new certificates but also applicants for the renewal or transfer of certificates at present in the name of other persons. The phrase "*new licence*" is defined in s.139(1) of the Act as meaning "a licence granted in respect of premises for which, at the time of the application for such grant, either no licence was in force or a licence different from the form of licence so granted was in force." There is a proviso to the definition which excepts a licence granted to premises which have been rebuilt after destruction in the same form as the previous licence from being a new licence.

"*Disposed of*" is not defined in the Act. It is thought that it does not necessarily mean granted or refused. Such an interpretation would create procedural difficulties, particularly if, for example, a long adjournment were allowed of an application for renewal under the powers given by subs. (2) of this section, with the result that no new applicants could be heard until the adjourned meeting or later. (S.4(2): "no longer than one month.") See opinion of Lord Justice-Clerk Ross in *Tarditi* v. *Drummond*, 1989 S.C.L.R. 201 at 204.

Two applications in respect of the same premises may be heard together, even if one is by a new applicant and the other is not. Such a situation arises, for example, when the present licence-holder and a person claiming, with the owner's consent, to be a new tenant or occupant, both lodge conflicting applications for transfer. (See intro. 3.50.)

(2) and (3) These subsections apply only to applications for the grant (including renewal) of a licence and objections to such applications and not to transfers, for which see s.25. They apply in cases of (a) inadvertence, (b) misadventure and (c) death, and empower licences to be granted to the parties in possession of the premises and objections to be considered whereby an objector himself or his representatives if he is deceased in such cases at an adjourned meeting. That adjourned meeting should be so fixed as to allow those who had not timeously lodged their applications or objections to have these applications or objections timeously lodged for the adjourned meeting of the board. An adjourned meeting requires to take place within one month of the first day of the quarterly board meeting in virtue of the provisions of s.4(2) of the Act. For circumstances where an English court ordered licensing justices to grant a licence when they had adjourned their statutory meeting beyond the statutory time, see *R.* v. *Denbigh Justices* (1895) 59 J.P. 708. In *R.* v. *Wandsworth Licensing Justices* [1937] 1 K.B. 144, it was ruled that the somewhat similar prohibition in the English Act of 1910 against adjourning for over a month struck only at consideration of new business, and that matters before the court at the general or adjourned meeting could be considered at a further adjournment outwith the month. If the omission to apply for a licence or lodge and intimate an objection extends beyond the quarterly meeting of the board the court has decided that application may still be made: see *Purdon* v. *City of Glasgow District Licensing Board*, 1989 S.L.T. 201, 1988 S.C.L.R. 466 and *Indpine Ltd.* v. *City of Dundee District Licensing Board*, 1991 G.W.D. 29–1759 and 1992 G.W.D. 8–436. The terms upon which the adjournment is granted will probably provide for intimation by advertisement being given, or publicity being made, at the expense of the applicant or objector. For the preliminary requirements with which the applicant or objector must normally comply, see ss.11 and 16.

It has been held under an equivalent section in England that, an adjournment having once been allowed on the ground that some requirement was not complied with, the justices had no power to adjourn a second time because another irregularity had occurred: *R.* v. *Poole JJ.* [1951] 2 T.L.R. 261. For discussion of the clerk's powers to accept or refuse an application under this section, see *Tait* v. *City of Glasgow District Licensing Board*, 1987 S.L.T. 340 and *Main* v. *City of Glasgow District Licensing Board*, 1987 S.L.T. 305. See also "Late Licensing Applications," 1987 S.L.T. (News) 157, and *Purdon* v. *City of Glasgow District Licensing Board* (*supra*) where it was held that the board did not require to give reasons for refusal to consider an application in terms of the section unless there appeared to be no basis for that refusal.

## Further application for new licence where previous application refused

**14.** Where a licensing board has refused an application for a new licence in respect of any premises, the board shall not, within two years of its refusal, entertain a subsequent application for a new licence in respect of the same premises unless the board, at the time of refusing the first-mentioned application, makes a direction to the contrary.

GENERAL NOTE

The section prohibits a further application for a new licence for premises in respect of which an application for a licence has been refused by a licensing board within two years from the date of the refusal unless the board directs otherwise. *The direction must be given at the time of the refusal.* The purpose of the section is to protect successful objectors from the necessity of having to renew their objections to the same application for a two year period. The power to direct that the prohibition is not to apply to a refused application enables an applicant, whose application has been refused on grounds which are remediable or because of circumstances which are liable to change, to re-apply within a shorter period.

In *Fife and Kinross Motor Auction Ltd.* v. *Perth and Kinross District Licensing Board,* 1981 S.L.T. 106, a petition for the exercise of the *nobile officium* for review of a decision under s.14 was refused. It was held that the intention of Parliament was that a s.14 direction should be final (*Maitland, Ptr.*, 1961 S.L.T. 384, approved).

*"new licence"* is defined in s.139(1). For discussion regarding a subsequent application for the "same premises" see *Kelvinside Community Council* v. *City of Glasgow District Licensing Board,* 1990 S.L.T. 725, 1990 S.C.L.R. 110 which held that the issue of whether an application related to the same premises was a question of fact for the board. See also para. 12 of Sched. 8 to the 1990 Act which introduces similar provision in respect of an application for extension of permitted hours for a period of one year.

## Attendance at meeting of licensing board by applicant or his representative

**15.**—(1) A licensing board may decline to consider an application if the applicant or his representative does not attend the meeting at which the application is to be considered:

Provided that an applicant for the renewal of a licence or for the permanent transfer of a licence need not attend or be represented unless the applicant has been cited by the board to attend the meeting.

(2) A licensing board shall not refuse an application for the renewal or permanent transfer of a licence without hearing the applicant or his representative:

Provided that the board may refuse such an application if the applicant, having been cited by the board to attend the meeting at which his application is to be considered, fails to attend such a meeting.

GENERAL NOTE

Except in the cases of applications for the renewal or permanent transfer of licences, a licensing board may decline to consider an application where the applicant or his representative are not in attendance at the meeting at which the application is to be considered (subs. (1)), see *Bury* v. *Kilmarnock and Loudon District Licensing Board,* 1989 S.L.T. 110. As regards the excepted cases, the applicant need not attend or be represented unless he has been cited to appear (subs. (1)), and a board is not entitled to refuse his application without hearing him or his representative unless he does not attend after being duly cited (subs. (2)). Both subss. (1) and (2) provide that citation is to be by the board. Accordingly, intimation of an objection to an application for a renewal or a permanent transfer to the applicant in pursuance of s.16(2) does not amount to a citation to attend.

The form and time of citation are not prescribed by the Act. The notice given should be reasonable, and the date, time and place at which the applicant's attendance is required should be specified, with a reference to the relevant section of the Act, *viz.* s.15. It was considered that, under the 1959 Act, an informal meeting of the licensing court prior to the statutory meeting to consider and authorise citations was competent, and there is no reason why such consideration under the 1976 Act should not take place under the provisions of s.15(2).

Subs. (1), as regards applications other than the excepted applications, provides that a board *"may decline to consider"* such applications where there is non-appearance. It does not provide that a board may refuse such applications. Accordingly, where a board decline to consider an application for a new licence on the ground that there was not any attendance by the applicant or his representative, such a declinature does not bar the applicant from reapplying within two years in virtue of s.14. See *CRS Leisure Ltd.* v. *Dumbarton District Licensing Board,* 1990 S.L.T. 200; 1959 S.C.L.R. 566, and *Bury* v. *Kilmarnock and Loudon District Licensing Board,* 1989 S.L.T. 110; 1988 S.C.L.R. 436.

For the provisions relating to *"renewal"* and *"permanent transfer,"* see ss.24 and 25 respectively.

See also para. 5 of Sched. 8 to the 1990 Act which states that a board must consider an objection properly lodged, even if the objector does not appear in person to speak to it.

## Objections in relation to applications

**16.**—(1) It shall be competent for any of the following persons to object in relation to any application to a licensing board for the grant (including the provisional grant) renewal or permanent transfer of a licence, namely—

    (*a*) any person owning or occupying property situated in the neighbourhood of the premises to which the application relates or any organisation which in the opinion of the board represents such persons;

    (*b*) a community council, which has been established in accordance with the provisions of the Local Government (Scotland) Act 1973, for the area in which the premises are situated;

    (*c*) any organised church which, in the opinion of the licensing board, represents a significant body of opinion among persons residing in the neighbourhood of the premises;

    (*d*) the chief constable;

    (*e*) the fire authority for the area in which the premises are situated;

    (*f*) a local authority for the area in which the premises are situated.

(2) Where a competent objector disires to object in relation to any application, he shall, not later than seven days before the meeting of the licensing board at which the application is to be considered—

    (*a*) lodge with the clerk of the board a written notice of objection which shall be signed by the objector or his agent and shall specify the grounds of his objection and

    (*b*) intimate his objection to the applicant in the manner provided by subsection (3) below,

and an objection shall not be entertained by the licensing board unless it is proved or admitted that such objection was intimated to the applicant as aforesaid.

(3) An objection shall, for the purposes of paragraph (*b*) of subsection (2) above, be intimated to the applicant

    (*a*) by delivering to him a copy of the notice of objection lodged with the licensing board under paragraph (*a*) of that subsection; or

    (*b*) by sending a copy of the said notice by registered post or by recorded delivery in a letter addressed to him at his proper address; or

    (*c*) by leaving a copy of the said notice for him at his proper address;

and, for the purposes of paragraphs (*b*) and (*c*) of this subsection, the proper address in the case of an applicant being an individual natural person shall be his place of abode as specified in his application or, in the case of such an applicant applying for the renewal of a licence, the premises in respect of which the application is made or, in the case of the agent of the applicant, shall be his place of business, and, in the case of an applicant other than an individual natural person, shall be the address specified in the application.

(4) Notwithstanding anything in the foregoing provisions of this section, it shall be competent for a licensing board to entertain objections

from the chief constable, lodged at any time before the hearing of an application, if the board is satisfied that there is sufficient reason why due notice and intimation of the objection could not be given, and in such a case the chief constable shall cause his objections to be intimated to the applicant before the hearing.

(5) The licensing board may only entertain an objection under this section if the objection is relevant to one or more of the grounds on which, by virtue of section 17 of this Act, an application may be refused, and shall whether or not the objector appears, consider any competent objection before arriving at its decision.

(6) The licensing board, if in its opinion any objection to the renewal of a licence is frivolous or vexatious, may find the objector liable in the expenses caused by such objection to such extent as the board thinks fit, or, if in its opinion any such objection is unauthorised, may find the agent of the objector liable in the expenses as aforesaid; and the amount of any expenses so found due may be recovered in the sheriff court having jurisdiction, and a certified copy of the finding of the licensing board shall be sufficient evidence and authority for decerning for the said amount with expenses.

### Observations by chief constable in relation to applications

**16A.**—(1) Without prejudice to section 16 of this Act, in considering an application—

> (a) for the grant (including the provisional grant), renewal or permanent transfer of a licence;
>
> (b) the regular extension of permitted hours under section 64 of this Act; or
>
> (c) the grant of a children's certificate under section 49 of the Law Reform (Miscellaneous Provisions) (Scotland) Act 1990,

a licensing board shall have regard to any observations on the application submitted by the chief constable in accordance with the following provisions of this section.

(2) Where the chief constable intends to submit observations in relation to any application, he shall, not later than seven days before the meeting of the licensing board at which the application is to be considered—

> (a) lodge with the clerk of the board a written notice of his observations; and
>
> (b) intimate his observations to the applicant in the manner provided by subsection (3) below,

and observations shall not be entertained by the licensing board unless it is proved or admitted that such observations were intimated to the applicant as aforesaid.

(3) Observations shall, for the purposes of paragraph (b) of subsection (2) above, be intimated to the applicant—

> (a) by delivering to him a copy of the observations lodged with the licensing board under paragraph (a) of that subsection; or
>
> (b) by sending him a copy of the said observations by registered post or by recorded delivery in a letter addressed to him at his proper address; or

(c) by leaving a copy of the said observations for him at his proper address;

and, for the purposes of paragraphs (b) and (c) of this subsection, the proper address of an applicant shall be as provided for in subsection (3) of section 16 of this Act.

(4) Notwithstanding anything in the foregoing provisions of this section, it shall be competent for the licensing board to entertain observations from the chief constable, lodged at any time before the hearing of an application, if the board is satisfied that there is sufficient reason why due notice and intimation of the observations could not be given, and in such a case the chief constable shall cause his observations to be intimated to the applicant before the hearing.

(5) The licensing board shall have regard to any observations submitted by the chief constable in accordance with this section whether or not they are relevant to one or more grounds on which, by virtue of section 17 of this Act, an application may be refused.

GENERAL NOTE

A. *Objections—General.* This section gives effect to the recommendations of the Clayson Committee as to who should have the right to object, confers the right on organisations representing owners and occupiers in the neighbourhood, also makes it obligatory on all objectors to lodge objections with the clerk to the licensing board and to intimate them to the applicant. The right of a member of the licensing court to object in the 1959 Act is not retained. Para. 5 of Sched. 8 to the 1990 Act adds the fire authority and the local authority for the area as potential objectors (see note below).

B. *Subsections.* (1)(a) *Owners or occupiers of property in neighbourhood.* The would-be objector must be either an owner or an occupier of heritable property. Mere residence in the neighbourhood is not enough. *"Occupier"* means an occupier within the meaning of the Lands Valuation (Scotland) Act 1854, although the entries in the Valuation Roll are not necessarily conclusive of the matter. A lady who lived in family with her father, whose housekeeper she was, in the house which he owned and occupied, was held not to be an occupier for the purposes of the corresponding provision of the 1959 Act, s.36, and to have no title to object to an application. *McDonald* v. *Chambers*, 1956 S.C. 542. What is or is not *"in the neighbourhood"* of the premises must be a question of degree and of circumstances in each case. The test would seem to be the likelihood or otherwise of the amenity of the objector's property being adversely affected by the grant of any licence, or of a particular form of licence, in respect of the premises, or by the grant of a licence to a particular person. For a refusal to interfere with an arbitrator's interpretation of *"near"* under the Workmen's Compensation Acts, see *McMillan* v. *Barclay, Curle & Co.* (1899) 2 F. 91. For a refusal to accept an arbitrator's definition of *"about a factory,"* see *Bell* v. *Whitton* (1899) 1 F. 942. The objector need not be an individual and may be a corporate body: Interpretation Act 1889, s.19 ("person").

(b) *"Community council"* means a community council established under Part IV of the Local Government (Scotland) Act 1973. The purpose of such a council, as provided for by s.51(2) of that Act is to co-ordinate and express, to local and public authorities for the area which it represents, the views of the community.

(c) *"any organised church representing a significant body of opinion among residents in the neighbourhood of the premises."* *"Church"* means "a religious society of some sort" (see the judgment of Smith L.J. in *S.C.* [1898] 1 Ch. 391). The issue of whether a church represents a significant body of opinion is a matter for the decision of the licensing board. For *'neigbourhood,"* see note to subs. (1)(a).

(d) *"Chief constable"* means the person appointed by the police authority as chief constable under s.4 of the Police (Scotland) Act 1967 for the area or district where the premises in respect of which a licence is sought are situated. If there is a vacancy in the office of chief constable, or if he is absent from duty, the constable responsible for performing his functions may act. Police (Scotland) Act 1967, s.50(d). See *Stephen* v. *City of Aberdeen District Licensing Board*, 1989 S.L.T.(Sh.Ct.) 94 where an objection by the chief constable was signed by his deputy. It was held that the deputy was permitted to sign as the chief constable's agent under s.16(2).

*Subss. (e) and (f)*
This amendment, introduced by para. 5 of Sched. 8 to the 1990 Act, extends the right to the fire authority and the local authority, for the area in which the premises are situated, to make objections to a licensing application. *Kelvinside Community Council* v. *City of Glasgow District Licensing Board*, 1990 S.L.T. 725 raised, but did not decide the issue as to whether a neighbouring community council, which did not qualify as a council "for the area in which the premises were situated," could qualify as an objector under one of the other heads; *e.g.* under s.16(1)(*a*) as persons owning or occupying property situated in the neighbourhood.

Boards were required to consult with the fire authority under s.24 of the 1976 Act. This procedure meant that applicants were disadvantaged in not being able to answer properly the observations made by the fire authority at a board meeting, which amounted to an objection to the grant of the licence. Following the case of *Centralbite* v. *Kincardine and Deeside District Licensing Board*, 1990 S.L.T. 231, such observations by the fire authority, which could be said to amount to an objection, might have been liable to challenge as incompetent objections.

A "local authority" is defined by s.235(1) of the Local Government (Scotland) Act 1973 to mean "a regional, islands or district council." Where the local authority objector is also the district or island council providing the licensing board under s.1 of the 1976 Act, care will have to be taken to ensure that the rules of natural justice are not broken, so that the board members are not represented on the same committee that recommends that an objection be made, or are not involved in the decision to make an objection to the board meeting.

(2)–(3) All classes of objectors must lodge and intimate a written notice of objection. See *Prime* v. *Hardie*, 1978 S.L.T.(Sh.Ct.) 71, where intimation of an objection to the applicant's agent/employer was held to be sufficient intimation in terms of the section. There is provision for the service of objections on an agent, in conformity with the provisions of the new s.139(6) added by para. 18 of Sched. 8 to the 1990 Act. There is an exception in the case of an objection by a chief constable, for which exception see subs. (4).

The objection must be taken on a relevant ground (subs. (5)). The use of the word "hear" in the subsection was interpreted to mean that personal appearance by the objector or his agent was necessary before the objection would be entertained, but the amendment, introduced by para. 5(*c*) of Sched. 8 to the 1990 Act, means that objections can be considered by the board in the absence of the objector. For the specification of relevant grounds, see subs. (5) and s.17. See also *Chief Constable of Grampian* v. *Aberdeen District Licensing Board*, 1979 S.L.T.(Sh.Ct.) 2, where it was held that mere reiteration of the wording of s.17(1)(*b*) of the Act was insufficient. Proper specification of the grounds of objection was required. The objection here was held to be irrelevant

The objection may be signed by an agent who, for his own protection, ought to obtain a written mandate from those whom he represents: see subs. (6). It is considered that only a solicitor can act for reward as an agent, as was thought was the position under the 1959 Act.

The notice of objection must be lodged and intimated "*not later than seven days before*" the first day of the meeting. This would seem to mean seven clear days from the day of the notice, so that the day of the notice and the day of the meeting are excluded: *Wilson* (1891) 19 R. 219; *Re Railway Sleepers Supply Co.* (1885) 29 Ch.D. 204; *Mercantile Investment Co.* v. *International Company of Mexico* [1893] 1 Ch. 484n.; see also Codifying Act of Sederunt, 1913, F. IV. 3. But a different rule in the computation of time may prevail in Scotland: Lord President Inglis in *Ashley and Others* v. *The Magistrates of Rothesay* (1873) 11 M. 708. In *Frew* v. *Morris* (1897) 24 R.(J.) 50, a prosecution under the Food and Drugs Act, the days counted from midnight of the day the sample was bought. For discussion of "not later than," see article " 'Not Later Than' Defined," 1987 S.L.T. (News) 353. The Interpretation Act 1978, s.7, provides that service by post shall be deemed to be effected by properly addressing, prepaying and posting a letter containing the document sent, and unless the contrary is proved, to have been effected at the time at which the letter would be delivered in the ordinary course of post.

*S.16A*
This section, inserted by s.53 of the 1990 Act, provides that licensing boards are to have regard to any observations (as distinct from objections made under s.16 of the 1976 Act) made by the Chief Constable and provides for the procedure for lodging and intimation of such observations by the Chief Constable. It had become commonplace for Chief Const-

ables to make "observations" upon applications at board meetings, which were said not to amount to an objection. The board would take those observations into account, while the applicant or his agent might have been prejudiced by the lack of notice. The requirement for this section arose from the decision in *Centralbite* v. *Kincardine and Deeside District Licensing Board*, 1990 S.L.T. 231, where the Lord Ordinary held that an "observation" by the Chief Constable amounted to an objection and that as it had not been intimated in terms of s.16 it could not be taken into account.

*Subs. (1)*

The new s.16A provides (16A(1)) that a licensing board shall have regard to any observations made by the Chief Constable in relation to an application made to the board for (a) the grant (including the provisional grant), renewal or permanent transfer of a licence; (b) the regular extension of permitted hours (but not an application for an occasional extension); or (c) the grant of a children's certificate.

*New subss. (2) and (3)*

The terms of these subsections, which are identical to the provisions on lodging and intimation in s.16(2) and (3) of the 1976 Act, provide that observations have to be lodged with the Clerk and intimated to the applicant in terms of subs. (3), not later than seven days before the board meeting. "Not later than" means at least seven clear days before the meeting and would exclude the day of the notice and the day on which the board met: see *Main* v. *City of Glasgow District Licensing Board*, 1987 S.L.T. 305.

*New subs. (4)*

Subs. (4), which is in the same terms as s.16(4) of the 1976 Act, gives the board a limited discretion to dispense with timeous lodging and intimation, provided that the observations are in fact intimated before the hearing. See in general the notes to s.16 in Allan and Chapman, *The Licensing (Scotland) Act 1976* (2nd ed.), p. 49.

*New subs. (5)*

This subsection provides that the board are to have regard to the observations, whether or not they are relevant to one of the grounds on which the application may be refused under s.17 of the 1976 Act. This provision is bound to lead to difficulty in that, if the board take into account an observation which is not relevant to one of the grounds upon which they may refuse the licence, and refuse the application on that ground, then it might be said that they have reached their decision on irrelevant grounds and so it should be reduced. It is suggested that such observations, which are not relevant to a ground of refusal, might be relevant in considering what conditions might be attached to a licence, when the application is granted.

## Grounds for refusal of application

**17.**—(1) A licensing board shall refuse an application of the type described in subsection (2) below if it finds that one or more of the following grounds for refusal, being competent grounds, applies to it—

    (*a*) that the applicant, or the person on whose behalf or for whose benefit the applicant will manage the premises or, in the case of an application to which section 11 of this Act applies, the applicant or the employee or agent named in the application is not a fit and proper person to be the holder of a licence;

    (*b*) that the premises to which an application relates are not suitable or convenient for the sale of alcoholic liquor, having regard to their location, their character and condition, the nature and extent of the proposed use of the premises, and the persons likely to resort to the premises;

    (*c*) that the use of the premises for the sale of alcoholic liquor is likely to cause undue public nuisance, or a threat to public order and safety;

(*d*) that, having regard to—

    (i) the number of licensed premises in the locality at the time the application is considered; and

    (ii) the number of premises in respect of which the provisional grant of a new licence is in force,

the board is satisfied that the grant of the application would result in the over provision of licensed premises in the locality, and otherwise shall grant the application.

(2) The grounds on which different types of application may competently be refused by a licensing board are those mentioned opposite the respective types of application set out below—

| *Type of application* | *Competent grounds* |
|---|---|
| new licence, including the provisional grant of such a licence | those set out in subsection (1) above. |
| renewal of licence | those set out in paragraphs (*a*) to (*c*) of subsection (1) above. |
| permanent transfer of a licence | that set out in paragraph (*a*) of subsection (1) above. |

(2A) A licensing board shall refuse to grant or renew a public house or a refreshment licence in respect of the permitted hours on a Sunday if it finds that the opening and use on a Sunday of the premises to which the application relates would cause undue disturbance or public nuisance in the locality, but the refusal of an application on the ground alone shall not prevent the licensing board from granting the application in respect of days other than Sundays.

(3) In considering the grounds for refusal mentioned in paragraph (*a*) of subsection (1) above, the licensing board may have regard to any misconduct on the part of any person mentioned in that paragraph, whether or not constituting a breach of this Act or any byelaw made thereunder, which in the opinion of the board has a bearing on his fitness to hold a licence.

(4) An applicant for the grant of a new licence, including the provisional grant of such a licence, or for the renewal or permanent transfer of a licence may appeal to the sheriff against a refusal of a licensing board to grant, renew or transfer the licence or to grant the licence in respect of the permitted hours on Sunday, as the case may be.

(5) Any competent objector who appeared at the hearing of any application mentioned in subsection (4) above may appeal to the sheriff against the decision of the licensing board to grant, renew or transfer a licence, as the case may be.

(6) Any person entitled under this section to appeal to the sheriff against the grant or refusal of a licence may appeal to the sheriff against a decision of a licensing board to attach or not to attach a condition to a

licence, being a condition mentioned in section 38(3) or 101(2) of this Act.

GENERAL NOTE

A. *General*. The absolute discretion conferred by the 1959 Act is restricted by the 1976 Act to matters of suitability of the applicant and the premises and implications of public order and the environment in relation to immediate locality and the type of licence sought. No numerical restriction on the number of licences in any particular area is allowed, however the section makes it a ground of refusal that the grant of the licence applied for would result in over provision of facilities of the kind to be provided under the licence. See amendment by para. 6 of Sched. 8 to the 1990 Act (below note to (*d*)). A licence can only be refused when a ground of refusal under s.17 of the Act is present. See *D. & A. Haddow Ltd.* v. *City of Glasgow District Licensing Board*, 1983 S.L.T.(Sh.Ct.) 5, where refusal to grant a licence on the ground that the grant would disturb the distribution of licences within a "limitation area" was held to be incompetent. See note to s.6 regarding majority votes.

B. *Subsections*. (1) The subsection prescribes the grounds on which a board is entitled to refuse an application. The applicability of the grounds to the types of application is specified in subs. (2). Unless the board find that one or more of the prescribed grounds of refusal apply to an application, they must grant it.

(*a*) The ground of the unsuitability of the applicant applies not only to the actual applicant but also, where the applicant is not an individual person, to the person named in the application as the person to be responsible for the day-to-day running of the premises under the provisions of s.11 and to the person on whose behalf or for whose benefit the premises are run. See *Tominey* v. *City of Glasgow District Licensing Board*, 1984 S.L.T.(Sh.Ct.) 2 at p. 4. In virtue of subs. (3), the board are to have regard to any misconduct by the applicant and (where applicable) the person responsible for the running of the premises irrespective of whether the misconduct constitutes a breach of the Act or a byelaw made under it. See *Fereneze Leisure Ltd.* v. *Renfrew District Licensing Board*, 1991 G.W.D. 15–943 and note to s.11 *supra*. The board must have information before it other than the mere fact of a conviction before it can exercise its discretion. The board must give an indication as to why it saw fit to disregard all the points made in the licence holder's favour. The mere existence of a conviction is not sufficient grounds for finding that an applicant is not fit and proper, the nature of the conviction, its gravity and the background to it should all be taken into account by the board when exercising its discretion. See: *Anwar* v. *Clydesdale District Licensing Board* (Lanark Sheriff Court June 11, 1991, unreported).

(*b*) This ground is very wide. In refusing to grant a licence on the ground of the unsuitability of the premises, a board can take into account not only the location, character and proposed use of the premises, but also the type of person liable to frequent them. See *Chief Constable, Strathclyde Police* v. *City of Glasgow District Licensing Board*, 1988 S.L.T. 128; *Leisure Inns Ltd.* v. *Perth & Kinross Licensing Board*, 1990 G.W.D. 11–588 and 1991 G.W.D. 15–942 where "loss of amenity" by owners of residential flats above the application site was regarded as speculative and did not justify refusal of the application and *Loosefoot Entertainments Ltd.* v. *Glasgow District Licensing Board*, 1991 G.W.D. 3–166, 1991 S.L.T. 843.

(*c*) The causation of the public nuisance or the threat to public order must arise out of the use of the premises for the sale of alcoholic liquor. For discussion of use of premises for sale of alcoholic liquor, see *Leisure Inns Ltd.* v. *Perth & Kinross Licensing Board* (*supra*.) "*Alcoholic liquor*" is defined in s.139(1).

(*d*) It is the overprovision of the specific facilities of the kind to be provided and not of the types of licence with which this ground is concerned. See *Khan* v. *City of Glasgow District Licensing Board*, 1980 S.L.T.(Sh.Ct.) 49 for consideration of the same or similar facilities in the locality. The board, in refusing an application for a restaurant licence, took into account the number of public house licences in the locality where the public houses provided food. The application was remitted back to the board for reconsideration by the sheriff, who held that the food being provided in the public houses was not similar to the facilities to be provided by the applicant for the restaurant licence. For further discussion of "facilities of the same or similar kind," see *Collins* v. *Hamilton District Licensing Board*, 1984 S.L.T. 230, where it was held that it is the facilities which have to be the same or similar, not the type of licence. The board took four off-sale licences in the locality into account when considering an application for a public house licence. It was held that they were entitled to do so on the basis that a public house licence authorises the holder to sell by retail alcoholic liquor for consumption on or off the premises and an off-sale licence authorises the holder to sell by retail alcoholic liquor for consumption off the premises. Section 17(1)(d) is amended quite radically by para. 6 of Sched. 8 to the 1990 Act. The old section had been construed to mean that it was the over provision of specific facilities of same or similar kind to be provided which had to be considered: see *Augustus Barnett Ltd.* v. *Bute & Cowal Divisional Licensing Board*, 1989 S.L.T. 572, 1989 SCLR 413. The amendment has the effect of providing that it is the number of licensed premises as a whole, including premises in respect of which there is a provisional grant, which have to be considered, when determining whether or not the grant will result in over-provision. Reference to provision of facilities has been removed by the amendment, the test appears to be the number of licensed premises in the locality at the time of the application, however it is felt that in the interest of a proper exercise of discretion it would not be sufficient to simply count the number of licenses in the locality without giving some attention to the type of licence and the facilities provided by the licensed premises which comprise that number. See introduction, 3.22, and *Mecca Bookmakers (Scotland) Ltd.* v. *East Lothian District Licensing Board*, 1988 S.L.T. 520; *Mohammed* v. *Docherty*, 1991 G.W.D. 25–1449; *Lazerdale Ltd.* v. *City of Glasgow District Licensing Board*, 1988 G.W.D. 36–1485; *Loosefoot Entertainments Ltd.* v. *Glasgow District Licensing Board*, 1991 G.W.D. 3–166, 1991 S.L.T. 843 and *Leisure Inns (U.K.) Ltd.* v. *Perth & Kinross District Licensing Board*, 1991 G.W.D. 15–942, *Scott Catering & Offshore Services Ltd.* v. *Aberdeen District Licensing Board*, 1987 G.W.D. 22–823. . As a result of the amendment introduced here, the question of locality will become a very important basis for consideration of over-provision.

(2) *"New licence"* is defined in s.139(1). *"Permanent transfer"* is defined in s.25(7). For *"renewal of licence,"* see s.24.

The addition of subs. (2A) by s.46(4) of the 1990 Act, requires the licensing board to refuse to grant permitted hours on a Sunday in circumstances where it considers that the grant of permitted hours on a Sunday to premises operating a public house or refreshment licence, would cause undue disturbance or public nuisance in the locality. However, the refusal to grant or renew the permitted hours on a Sunday alone shall not prevent the licensing board from granting the application in respect of days other than Sundays. Section 17(4) is amended to allow the refusal of permitted hours on a Sunday to be appealed to the sheriff.

(3) For a list of offences under the Act, see Sched. 5. For bye-laws under the Act, see s.58.

(4) (5) and (6) An unsuccessful applicant for the grant (including provisional grant) of a new licence, renewal of a licence, or permanent transfer of a licence and an unsuccessful objector may appeal to the sheriff against the licensing board's decision. For the procedure and grounds of appeal, see s.39. See *Wolfson* v. *Glasgow District Licensing Board*, 1981 S.L.T. 17, where an application for a new off-sale licence was granted in restricted form in terms of s.29(1) of the Act. It was held that such a grant where the application was for a full new licence constitutes a refusal and can be competently the subject of an appeal under s.17(4). "Competent objector" will now include the fire authority and the local authority, see *Bantop Ltd.* v. *City of Glasgow District Licensing Board*, 1990 S.L.T. 366, 1989 S.C.L.R. 731.

### Giving of reasons for decisions of a licensing board

**18.**—(1) A licensing board shall within 21 days of being required to do so under subsection (2) below give reasons for arriving at any decisions mentioned in section 5(2) of this Act.

(2) Reasons for decisions referred to in subsection (1) above may be required to be given by the board in writing on a request being made to the clerk of the board, not more than 48 hours after the decision is made, by the applicant or, as the case may be, by the holder of the licence, or by any objector, or by any complainer who appeared at the hearing.

(3) Where a licensing board gives reasons in writing at the request of a party to the hearing, the board shall give copies of those reasons to all other parties to the hearing.

(4) The period of 21 days referred to in subsection (1) above and the period of 48 hours referred to in subsection (2) above shall not include a day which is a Sunday, Christmas Day, New Year's Day, Good Friday, a

bank holiday, or a public holiday, or a day appointed for public thanksgiving or mourning.

GENERAL NOTE

In virtue of subs. (1) a board can only be required to give reasons in connection with the types of decision specified in s.5(2) where the request for a decision is made in accordance with subs. (2); see *Purdon* v. *City of Glasgow District Licensing Board*, 1989 S.L.T. 201, where it was held that a board were not required to give reasons for a decision reached under s.13(2) as this was not a section to which s.5(2) applied. Where the clerk has been required to give reasons under subs. (2) he is required to give the reasons within 21 days (amended Sched. 8 para. 7 of The 1990 Act). Whether this time limit will be treated as mandatory, so that reasons issued after that date will not be considered at an appeal under s.39 to the effect that the court will deal with the appeal on the basis that there are no reasons for the decision before the court remains to be seen, but as other time limits have been treated as mandatory, there is no good reason why this time limit should not also be treated as mandatory. In *H.D. Wines (Inverness) Ltd.* v. *Inverness District Licensing Board*, 1982 S.L.T. 73, it was held that a request for written reasons for the board's decision required to be in the hands of the clerk within the specified 48 hour period, and that the time limit is mandatory. See also s.39(2). The time limit for appeal can only be extended under this section if the reasons stated by the board for its decision are reasons requested in terms of s.18(2). Subs. (3) provides that copies of reasons in writing are to be given by the board to all the parties to the hearing in respect of which they have been requested, and subs. (1) defines the time limit for the requesting and the giving of reasons laid down by subs. (2).

In giving written reasons for their decision it is not sufficient for the board to reiterate the statutory grounds on which their decision is based: *Martin* v. *Ellis*, 1978 S.L.T.(Sh.Ct.) 38 at p. 40; *Chief Constable of Grampian* v. *City of Aberdeen District Licensing Board*, 1979 S.L.T.(Sh.Ct.) 2, and *Troc Sales Ltd.* v. *Kirkcaldy District Licensing Board*, 1982 S.L.T.(Sh.Ct.) 77. If a board give just the statutory ground on which their decision is based they may be required by the sheriff under para. 5 of the Act of Sederunt (Appeals under the Licensing (Scotland) Act 1976) 1977 [S.I. 1977 No. 1622] to give their reasons for finding such ground or grounds of refusal to be established. Where a board have given inadequate reasons for their decision (see *infra*) the Act of Sederunt probably cannot be used to request the board to amplify their reasons (*Leisure Inns Ltd.* v. *Perth & Kinross District Licensing Board*, 1991 G.W.D. 15–942.

In giving written reasons under s.18 the board are required to give adequate and sufficient reasons. The principle was laid down in *Wordie Properties Co. Ltd.* v. *Secretary of State for Scotland*, 1984 S.L.T. 345, a planning case, where the Lord President (Emslie) said at page 348 that "The decision must, in short, leave the informed reader in no real and substantial doubt as to what the reasons for it were and what were the material considerations which were taken into account in reaching it." Note the two requirements to identify the reasons for the decision and the material considerations taken into account. See also *Albyn Properties Ltd.* v. *Knox*, 1977 S.C. 108 at page 112; *R.W. Cairns Ltd.* v. *Busby East Church Kirk Session*, 1985 S.C. 110 at page 119 and Introduction, paras. 3.26 to 3.32.

## Canvassing

**19.**—(1) If any applicant for the grant, renewal, permanent transfer, temporary transfer under section 25(1A) of this Act or confirmation of transfer under subsection (4) of that section of a licence or for a regular extension of permitted hours, either by himself or by another person at the instigation of the applicant, attempts to influence a member of a licensing board to support his application at any time before its consideration by the board, he shall be guilty of an offence.

(2) If proceedings are pending under subsection (1) above, the licensing board may adjourn consideration of an application to which the proceedings relate until the proceedings are concluded.

(3) If an applicant is convicted of an offence under subsection (1) above in relation to an application before the board, the board may refuse to consider the application.

GENERAL NOTE

The section prohibits canvassing in the sense of the attempt of an applicant or of another person at his instigation to influence a member of a licensing board to support his application for a grant, renewal or permanent transfer of a licence, or for a regular extension of permitted hours before the application is considered by the board (subs. (1)). Where a prosecution for a contravention of subs. (1) is pending, a board may adjourn the application with which the proceedings are concerned until the proceedings are concluded (subs. (2)). Such a prosecution must be taken in the sheriff court (s.128(1)) and the maximum penalty for a contravention of subs. (1) is a fine of level 3 (Sched. 5) with both the convicted licence-holder and the premises liable to disqualification. Where an applicant is convicted, the licensing board may refuse to consider the application with which the conviction was concerned.

For meanings of "*permanent transfer*" and "*regular extension of permitted hours*," see ss.25(7) and 64 respectively.

## Register of applications and decisions

**20.** The clerk of each licensing board shall keep a register of applications for licences and shall, at the end of each day's meeting of the board enter in the register the decisions taken on the applications.

This register shall be available to any member of the public at times and places to be determined by the clerk.

GENERAL NOTE

The section does not prescribe the form in which the register is to be kept.

## Issue of licences

**21.**—(1) The clerk of each licensing board shall make out and deliver a licence to every person to whom a licence is granted by the board, and shall do so within 28 days of the grant of the licence.

(2) The clerk of a licensing board shall, on application, make out a duplicate of any licence issued by him under this section and shall certify such duplicate to be a true copy of the original licence, and any such duplicate, duly certified as aforesaid, shall be sufficient evidence of the facts therein contained and of the terms of the original licence.

(3) The period of 28 days referred to in subsection (1) above shall not include a day which is a Sunday, Christmas Day, New Year's Day, Good Friday, a bank holiday, or a public holiday, or a day appointed for public thanksgiving or mourning.

GENERAL NOTE

No form of licence is prescribed in this section.

The amendment, by virtue of para. 8 of Sched. 8 to the 1990 Act, introduces a time limit of 28 days within which the clerk shall make out and deliver a licence, and is designed to deal with cases where a clerk had been dilatory in giving out a licence. The words "lawfully required" which had given rise to some difficulty, are now replaced with the requirement "on application" to give out a duplicate. The new subs. (3) excludes Sunday, etc. from the calculation of days; see note to s.18 *supra*.

## List of licence holders to be sent to Customs and Excise

**22.**

GENERAL NOTE

Repealed 1983, c. 28, s.9, Sched. 10.

## Special provisions relating to applications for new licence

**23.**—(1) Subject to subsection (6) of this section, an application for the grant or provisional grant of a new licence (other than an off-sale licence) shall not be entertained by a licensing board unless there are produced to the board, in accordance with the provisions of this section, certificates from the appropriate authority as to the suitability of the premises for which the licence is sought in relation to planning, building control and food hygiene.

(2) In relation to planning, the certificate from the appropriate authority should state that the applicant has obtained in respect of the premises planning permission under the Town and Country Planning (Scotland) Act 1972 or, in the case of an application for the provisional grant of a licence, outline planning permission under sections 39 and 40 of that Act, or, in either case, a determination under section 51 of that Act that planning permission is not required.

(3) In relation to building control, the certificate from the appropriate authority—

(a) in the case of an application for a new licence, should state—

(i) either that a warrant for the construction of the premises has been granted under section 6 of the Building (Scotland) Act 1959 and a certificate of completion has been granted under section 9 of that Act, or that no warrant for construction of the premises is required; and

(ii) either that a warrant for the change of use of the premises has been granted under the said section 6 or that no such warrant is required; and

(b) in the case of an application for the provisional grant of a licence, should state—

(i) that a warrant for the construction of the premises has been granted under section 6 of the said Act of 1959; and

(ii) either that a warrant for the change of use of the premises has been granted under the said section 6, or that on completion of the construction of the premises in accordance with the warrant a warrant for the change of use will be granted, or that no such warrant is required.

Expressions used in this subsection and in the said Act of 1959 have the same meanings in this subsection as they have in that Act.

(4) In relation to food hygiene, the certificate from the appropriate authority should, in the case of an application for a new licence, state that the premises to which the application relates comply, or, in the case of an application for the provisional grant of a licence, would comply, with the requirements of regulations made under section 13 of the Food and Drugs (Scotland) Act 1956 relating to construction, layout, drainage, ventilation, lighting and water supply or concerned with the provision of sanitary and washing facilities.

(5) Before granting or making the provisional grant of a new licence, the licensing board shall consult the fire authority for the area.

(6) In relation to building control, food hygiene and consultation with the fire authority, subsections (1), (3), (4) and (5) of this section shall not apply to the application for or the making of a provisional grant of a

licence under section 26(2) of this Act but shall apply to the application for affirmation and to the affirmation of such a grant.

(7) In this section, in relation to planning and building control, the appropriate authority in the case of the Highland, Borders and Dumfries and Galloway Regions is the regional council and, in any other case, is the district or islands council, and in relation to food hygiene, the appropriate authority is the district or islands council.

GENERAL NOTE

A. *General.* An application for the grant of a new licence or the affirmation of a provisional grant of a licence is not to be considered by a licensing board, unless there are produced with the application certificates from the appropriate authorities relating to planning, building control, and food hygiene (subs. (1)). Further, in the case of such an application, the licensing board must consult with the fire authority (subs. (5)). As regards an application for a provisional (site only) grant, in terms of s.26(2) of the 1976 Act a certificate from the appropriate planning authority has to be produced (subs. (6)).

B. *Subsections.* (1) *"new licence"* is defined in s.139(1). For *"provisional grant"* see s.26. For *"appropriate authority . . . in relation to planning, building control, and food hygiene,"* see subs. (7).

(2) *"outline planning permission"* means planning permission granted in accordance with the provisions of a development order with the reservation for subsequent approval by the local planning authority or the Secretary of State of matters (referred to in the section as reserved matters) not particularised in the application (s.39(1) of the Town and Country Planning (Scotland) Act 1972). S.39 of the Town and Country Planning (Scotland) Act 1972 provides for the grant of outline planning permission and s.40 of the Act makes supplementary provisions in that connection. S.51 enables a person who intends to carry out operations on land to apply to the local authority for a determination as to whether planning permission is required. S.51 repealed 1991 Ch. 34 Sched. 13, para. 17 but not in force as at 31 December 1991.

(3) The Building (Scotland) Act 1959 defines *"warrant"* as meaning a warrant under s.6 of the Act, including (in the case of a warrant which has been granted) any conditions to which it is subject, and any amendment which has been made to it. S.6 makes it obligatory (with certain exceptions) for a person conducting building operations or changing the use of a building to apply to the buildings authority for a warrant authorising the proposed works. The warrant is not granted unless the proposed works are in accordance with the appropriate building regulations. S.6 amended 1974, c. 37, Sched. 7, and repealed in part 1973, c. 65, Scheds. 15, 29.

*"certificate of completion"* has the meaning assigned to it by s.9 of the Building (Scotland) Act 1959 (s.29(1) of the Act). S.9 provides for application being made for a certificate of completion, which application is to be granted if the works as completed comply with the warrant under which they were executed. S.9 amended 1974, c. 37, Sched. 7; 1986, c. 65, s.19; repealed in part 1973, c. 65, Scheds. 15, 29.

(4) The relevant regulations are the Food Hygiene (Scotland) Regulations 1959 to 1978, which comprise the original regulations (S.I. 1959 No. 413) and the Food Hygiene (Scotland) Amendment Regulations 1961, 1966 and 1978 (S.I. 1961 No. 622, 1966 No. 967 and 1978 No. 173). The 1966 amendments are not of importance since they are concerned with stalls and vehicles. As regards sanitary facilities, the British Standard Code of Practice (CP3, Chap. VII (1950)), tables 8 and 10, give the scale on which such facilities should be provided in the cases of hotels and restaurants.

(5) The general practice of a fire authority, a practice which is followed in relation to their being consulted by a licensing board under the subsection, in considering the safety of a building and its likely occupants from the risk of fire may be summarised as follows. The authority examine the building for the purpose of determining whether the structure or the use of the building creates undue risk. It considers whether the building has adequate structural means of escape whereby persons could make their way safely from it by their own unaided efforts, recommending, if necessary, structural alterations should the means be inadequate. It also considers the sufficiency of the fire warning and alarm system, including the question of whether automatic detectors should be installed, the sufficiency of the routine to be followed in the event of fire, the sufficiency of the fire fighting equipment to be provided, and, since licensed premises are in use during the hours of darkness, the question of whether emergency lighting should be provided.

(6) For affirmation of a provisional grant, see s.26(3).

77

See: *Donald* v. *Stirling District Licensing Board*, 1991 G.W.D. 24–1396 which held that not board's function to purport to deal with planning matters, terms of s.23(2) mandatory.

## Special provisions relating to applications for renewal of a licence

**24.**—(1) Before granting the renewal of a licence, the licensing board shall consult the fire authority for the area.

(2) On any application for the renewal of a licence, the licensing board may require a plan of the premises to which the application relates to be produced to it and lodged with the clerk.

GENERAL NOTE

For the position as regards the attendance of an applicant for a renewal at the meeting of the licensing board at which his application is to be considered, see s.15. For the period of currency of a licence, see s.30. An application is an application for a renewal where it relates to premises in respect of which the applicant has been granted a licence which is due to expire and is for the same type of licence as that previously granted.

*Subsections.* (1) For consultation with the fire authority, see s.23(5).

(2) Applies to any licence. Although a licensing board may resolve to call for the production of plans under the subsection in respect of a number of existing licences, a separate requirement must be recorded and intimated to the licence holder in respect of each licence separately. An adjournment of each application will normally be necessary in order to allow time for the plan to be produced.

## Transfer of licences

**25.**—(1) A licensing board may, on an application made to the board in that behalf transfer to a new tenant or to a new or existing occupant of any licensed premises the licence then subsisting in respect of those premises.

(1A) At any time, a licensing board may make such a transfer on a temporary basis and the licence so transferred shall have effect until the appropriate meeting of the board, which shall be—

(a) the next meeting of the board; or

(b) where the temporary transfer has been made within the period of six weeks before the first day of the next meeting, the next following meeting of the board.

(1B) At the appropriate meeting and on an application for a permanent transfer, the licensing board shall make a decision on the permanent transfer of the licence transferred temporarily under subsection (1A) above.

(1C) Where a board refuses to make a permanent transfer of a licence which has been temporarily transferred under subsection (1A) above, the licence so transferred shall have effect until the time within which an appeal may be made has elapsed or, if an appeal has been lodged, until the appeal has been abandoned or determined.

(2) A licensing board may, on an application made to it in that behalf by—

(a) the executors, representatives or disponees of any person who held a licence in respect of premises situated within the area of the board and who has died before the expiry of the licence; or

# PRG

## Paterson Robertson & Graham
*Solicitors and Notaries Public*

F.A.O. Mr. H. Leyland

Enclosed, copies of Lease & Assignation as requested.

## With Compliments

1 KILBOWIE ROAD, CLYDEBANK G81 1TL   Tel: 041-952 0019
Rutland Exchange Box 491   Fax No. 041-952 4957

(b) the trustee, judicial factor or curator bonis of any person holding such a licence who has become bankrupt, insolvent or incapable before the expiry of the licence;

transfer the licence to the applicant if the applicant is in possession of the premises.

(3) A licensing board may, on an application made to it in that behalf by a person other than an individual natural person, substitute another employee or agent of the applicant for the employee or agent mentioned in section 11 or 26 of this Act.

(4) A licence transferred by virtue of subsection (2) or (3) above shall have effect until the next meeting of the licensing board, which, on an application for confirmation of the transfer of the licence, shall consider whether it is satisfied that the person to whom the licence has been transferred is a fit and proper person to be the holder of a licence and—

(a) if it is so satisfied, it shall confirm the transfer of the licence, and;

(b) if it is not so satisfied, it shall refuse to confirm the transfer.

(4A) In considering the fitness of the person to whom the licence has been transferred, the licensing board may have regard to any misconduct on his part, whether or not constituting a breach of this Act or any byelaw made thereunder, which in its opinion has a bearing on his fitness to hold a licence.

(4B) If the transfer of a licence has been confirmed under subsection (4) above, the licence shall have effect, in accordance with subsections (4) and (5) of section 30 of this Act, until the quarterly meeting of the licensing board three years after the meeting at which the licence was originally granted or renewed by a licensing board.

(4C) If a licensing board refuses to confirm the transfer of a licence under subsection (4) above, the person to whom the licence had been transferred may appeal to the sheriff against that refusal and the licence shall have effect until the time within which an appeal may be made has elapsed or, if an appeal has been lodged, until the appeal has been abandoned or determined.

(5) Where a licence is transferred under this section to any person, the clerk of the licensing board shall, on payment of the appropriate fee, endorse on the licence a note of the transfer.

(6) Any licence transferred under this section shall be held subject to the conditions on which it was originally granted.

(7) References in this Act to the permanent transfer of a licence shall be construed as references to the transfer of a licence by virtue of subsection (1) or (1B) above.

GENERAL NOTE

A. *Transfer of licences—general.* A transfer of a licence can only take place during its currency (for which see s.30). Section 25 of the 1976 Act, as amended by s.51 of the 1990 Act, and further amended by the Licensing (Amendment) (Scotland) Act 1992, provides for an initial temporary transfer of the licence, which may be applied for at any time between board meetings. Such a temporary transfer will be effected administratively under the delegated powers given by s.5(1) of the 1976 Act a temporary transfer then needs to be confirmed by the licensing board at a subsequent meeting, upon an application being made to the board for a permanent transfer. The section makes consequential amendments to other sections of the 1976 Act. This amendment attempts to remedy the lacuna in s.25, where the permanent transfer of a licence could only be effected at a quarterly board meeting, which put purchasers or new tenants in difficulty if their date of entry was at a date between board meetings. The amendment by the 1992 Act reintroduces permanent transfer at a quarterly meeting as an option for applicants for whom temporary transfer followed by confirmation is not practicable.

Subs. (5) amends s.64 of the 1976 Act, so that grants of occasional and regular extensions automatically go with the temporary or permanent transfer of the licence, which clarifies the conflicting decisions in *Archyield* v. *City of Glasgow District Licensing Board* 1987 S.L.T. 547 and *CRS Leisure* v. *Dumbarton District Licensing Board* 1990 S.L.T. 200 and corrects an obvious injustice if *Archyield* was correctly decided. The temporary transfer of a licence may be effected to a representative of the licence holder where the licence holder has died, become bankrupt, insolvent, or incapable during the currency of the licence (subs. (2)). Some boards have made it a procedural requirement in their regulations that evidence of title to a property be produced in support of the application for temporary or permanent transfer, where the existing licence holder's consent is not forthcoming, or where there are conflicting applications by prospective transferees. The consent of the existing licensee is not a statutory requirement, however most boards insist that consent is endorsed on the principal licence or is indicated to the clerk in writing, in order to ensure no dispute arises after the application is considered as to who the correct licence holder should be. An application for a permanent transfer is an application under Part II of the Act, and it follows that there has to be compliance with the relevant provisions on the part of an applicant making such an application and the licensing board in considering it. In particular, it is to be noted in that connection that ss.10(1) and (6) (form and time for lodging of application), 11 (applications by non-natural persons), 13 (order in which applications are to be considered by a board), 15 (attendance of applicant), 16 (objections to applications), 17 (grounds for refusing an application), 18 (the giving of reasons by a licensing board), 19 (canvassing), 20 (register of applications and decisions) and 21 apply. Where an application for a permanent transfer is refused, or granted where the grant involves the repelling of an objection by a competent objector who appeared at the hearing, the unsuccessful applicant or objector may appeal to the sheriff (s.17(4) and (5)), and from the sheriff to the Court of Session on a point of law (s.39(8)). (For the procedure in appeals, see s.39.)

As regards the transfer of a licence to the representatives of a dead, bankrupt, or incapable licence holder, the application can be heard at any meeting of a licensing board or under an arrangement under s.5(1).

When a licence has been transferred, either under subs. (1) or under subs. (2), the transferee holds the licence subject to the conditions on which it was originally granted: subs. (6); and the original licence-holder may never again sell alcoholic liquor under its authority. Where a certificate was transferred during the first half-year of its currency, and renewal of the transfer was refused at the October meeting, so that for its second half-year the certificate was in abeyance, the original holder, who resumed occupation of the premises and recommenced business, was held to have been rightly convicted of trafficking without a certificate: *Miller* v. *Linton* (1885) 15 R.(J.) 37. In *Campbell* v. *Neilson* (1897) 24 R.(J.) 28, where the circumstances were similar, it was said by Lord Justice-General Robertson at p. 30: "It is the transferee alone who can lawfully carry on business in the premises under the certificate. The transfer may become null and void, as here, or the certificate may not be renewed, as in *Miller*, but nothing that can happen to the transfer or transferee will ever revive the right of a man who, *ex hypothesi*, has removed or yielded up possession of the premises to which the certificate relates."

*Licensing (Amendment) (Scotland) Act 1992*

This amendment which came into force on 15 April 1992 allows an applicant to apply to a quarterly meeting of the licensing board for a permanent transfer of a licence without the need to follow the temporary transfer procedure as a preliminary. Thus reinstating the old s.25 procedure as an option for the transfer of a licence if the new temporary transfer procedure introduced by s.51 of the 1990 Act cannot be used for the reasons anticipated in the Note above and Introduction 3.44.

B. *Subsections*. (1) This subsection is amended by the Licensing (Amendment) (Scotland) Act 1992, to the effect that the initial transfer can be a temporary transfer. The insertion of "to a new or existing" occupant, corrects a difficulty focused upon in *Chief Constable of Tayside* v. *Angus District Licensing Board*, 1980 S.L.T.(Sh.Ct.) 31, which held that in a reorganisation of responsibility between a husband and wife, the wife could not take a transfer, as "new" qualified both tenant and occupant and she was neither a new tenant nor a new occupant.

New subss. (1A), (1B) and (1C) to s.25 of the 1976 Act. Subs. (1A) provides that the temporary transfer granted under s.25(1) as amended is only effective "until the appropriate meeting" of the board, which is either (a) the next meeting of the board or (b) if the temporary transfer was made within the period of six weeks before the first day of the next meeting, to the next following meeting of the board. Subs. (1B) requires the temporary transferee to make an application in terms of s.10 of the 1976 Act to the appropriate board meeting for a permanent transfer. At the appropriate meeting, the board are required to make a decision on the application for a permanent transfer in terms of s.17(1)(a) of the 1979 Act. Subs. (1C) provides that where a board refuse a permanent transfer, the person to whom the temporary transfer has been made may appeal to the sheriff (under s.39 of the 1976 Act) against that refusal and that the licence will continue in force until the time for an appeal has lapsed or, if an appeal has been lodged, it has been abandoned or determined. See *Kerr* v. *McAuslin*, 1991 G.W.D. 37–2272 which confirms the statutory requirement that there be six weeks between the grant of temporary transfer and subsequent confirmation thereof.

(2) *Transfer to representative of dead, bankrupt or incapable licence-holder.* This subsection makes provision for the death, bankruptcy or incapacity of a licence-holder during the currency of a licence. In the case of death the licence is transferred to an executor, representative or disponee, in the case of bankruptcy to the trustee, and in the case of incapacity to the judicial factor or *curator bonis*, provided, in each case, that the applicant is in possession of the premises and is a fit person to hold a licence. The question of who is an "occupant" is discussed in *Paterson* v. *City of Glasgow District Licensing Board*, 1982 S.L.T.(Sh.Ct.) 37, where a new manager who applied for a permanent transfer of an off sale licence was held not to be an "occupant" where he had no interest in the premises other than as an employee. However, a distinction is drawn between the position where premises are owned by a company and managed by an employee (*Paterson*) and a case involving premises owned by an individual and managed by another. It was decided in the case of *Tominey* v. *City of Glasgow District Licensing Board*, 1984 S.L.T.(Sh.Ct.) 2 that the latter could be said to be an "occupant."

If so desired, there seems no reason why the applicant, instead of applying under this subsection, should not, as an "occupant," apply for a temporary and subsequent permanent transfer from the licensing board at a quarterly meeting under subs. (1).

The transfer can be granted through an arrangement under s.5(1). There is no provision for publication or notice to interested persons.

The two prerequisites for a transfer, apart from the representative relationship with the licence-holder, are possession of the premises and fitness for holding a licence. The subsection says that the board "*may*" transfer, but this has been interpreted as meaning *shall* transfer, if they are satisfied as to fitness. "The representatives should as soon as possible furnish themselves with a licence, and they can go to any magistrate at hand without any formality requiring a day's delay" (*Cook* v. *Gray* (1891) 29 S.L.R. 249 *per* Lord President Robertson). This dictum was followed by the opinion of the Lord Advocate (Mr. Graham Murray) and the Dean of Faculty (Mr. Asher) on November 2, 1893, that "the fitness of the applicant seems to us to be the only question upon which, on an application for a transfer, the magistrates may exercise their discretion"; and by the opinion of the town clerk of Glasgow (December 18, 1894), that, if satisfied that the applicant is a suitable person, "all usual and more general considerations must be reserved till the annual licensing period."

(3) In virtue of the provisions referred to in the subsection, where a licence is granted to or a provisional grant confirmed in the name of a non-natural person, the name of the person responsible for the day-to-day running of the premises must be included. See *Argyll Arms (McManus) Ltd.* v. *Lorn Mid-Argyll, Kintyre & Islay Divisional Licensing Board*, 1988 S.L.T. 290, 1988 S.C.L.R. 421, for discussion regarding failure to lodge temporary transfer application within eight weeks, where new person responsible for day to day running substituted. See note to s.11.

New subss. (4), (4A), (4B), and (4C) are substituted for subs. (4), making new provisions for the former temporary transfers, which could be effected by executors, etc. of deceased persons and trustees, etc. of persons who had become bankrupt or incapable during the currency of the licence. New subs. (4) provides that the temporary transfer under subss. (2) and (3) shall have effect until the next board meeting (and not the appropriate board meeting as in a temporary transfer under subs. (1)) and spells out the requirement, which was considered to be implied in the former subs. (4), that the board, on an application for confirmation of the temporary transfer, shall consider whether it is satisfied that the person to whom the licence has been transferred is a fit and proper person to be the holder of the licence and, if so satisfied, (a) shall confirm it, or (b) if not so satisfied, shall refuse to confirm the transfer. In considering whether a transferee is a "fit and proper person" the board are to take account of the factors set out in subs. (4B), which echoes s.17(3) of the

1976 Act. Subs. 4(C) provides for an appeal to the sheriff against a refusal to confirm the temporary transfer and that the licence shall continue in force until the time for an appeal has lapsed, or, if an appeal has been lodged, it has been abandoned or determined.

*(5) and (6)* These subsections provide that grants of occasional or regular extensions under s.64 of the 1976 Act follow the transfer automatically, which overrules the decision in *Archyield* v. *City of Glasgow District Licensing Board*, 1987 S.L.T. 547 that a grant of a regular extension fell on the transfer of a licence under s.25. The correctness of that decision was questioned in *CRS Leisure* v. *Dumbarton District Licensing Board*, 1990 S.L.T. 200.

C. *Purchase and sale of licensed premises.* Where a seller was not in possession of a licence which could be transferred to the buyer at the date of completion of the contract it was decided that, the seller having failed to execute the contract, the purchaser could repudiate it: *Day* v. *Kuhke* (1868) L.R. 5 Eq. 336; *Cowles* v. *Gale* (1871) L.R. 7 Ch. 12. But the seller is not bound, unless by special contract, to procure to the purchaser a transfer of the licence: *Tadcaster Tower Brewery Co.* v. *Wilson* [1897] 1 Ch. 705.

Where a contract is made on the footing of the existence of a licence, and it appears that the licence is subject to qualifications, the contract cannot be enforced: *Modlen* v. *Snowball* (1861) 4 De G.F. & J. 143. So where public house premises in England were sold as "fully licensed" whereas the licence was a six-day licence, the court held that the vendor could not enforce specific performance: *Fraser* v. *Pugsley* (1920) 37 T.L.R. 87. Where a purchase of licensed premises was made subject to the purchaser obtaining a transfer of the certificate, and the purchaser undertook to do all in his power to obtain a transfer, and the transfer was refused by the licensing court, and the purchaser refused to appeal or to concur in an appeal against the refusal, it was held that he had failed to do all in his power to obtain a transfer, and was found liable in damages to the seller: *Skinner* v. *Breslin* (1905) 13 S.L.T. 91; *cf.* *M'Cormick* v. *Dalrymple* (1904) 41 S.L.R. 578. The position of a trustee for a bankrupt certificate-holder is dealt with in note D below. The goodwill carries the right to apply for the transfer: *Rutter* v. *Daniel* (1882) 30 W.R. 801. Under the Revenue Acts goodwill is situated locally with the business: *Inland Revenue* v. *Muller & Co.* [1901] A.C. 217. See also *Tarditi* v. *Drummond* 1989 S.C.L.R. 201.

Under the previous statutory provisions it was suggested that offers should be conditional on the licences being permanently transferred by the licensing board. A temporary transfer, which appears to be a mandatory preliminary to a permanent transfer, makes difficulties for such a condition, because the new acquirer has to take entry, before or at the time of a temporary transfer. As the decision on whether or not the temporary transfer will be made permanent might not be made for four and a half months after the temporary transfer, if that was made less than six weeks from the next board (new subs. (1A)(*b*)) it might be difficult, at that stage, to undo a contract.

Any seller would be wise to insist that the buyer, who has to satisfy the board on applying for a permanent transfer under the terms of s.17(1)(*a*) of the 1976 Act, that he is a fit and proper person to hold a licence, takes the risk of failing to get a permanent transfer after taking entry upon a temporary transfer. This may well make for difficulties with lenders, who may be unwilling to release funds until a temporary transfer has been made permanent. It may be possible to devise a contract whereby the intended purchaser takes entry as under a licence to occupy, upon which he obtains a temporary transfer, with the contract being purified, when the permanent transfer is granted. Such a scheme would have dangers for the seller, who would be bound to cede occupation, at least in part, to the intended purchaser. As the issue of a temporary transfer is an administrative act under the delegated powers, careful liaison will be required with the clerk of the board, to ensure that the temporary transfer takes place at the same date as entry. See "Licensing Nightmare" 1990 S.L.T. (News) 374 and "Licensing Transfers" 1991 S.L.T. (News) 58. See also *Tarditi* v. *Drummond* 1989 S.C.L.R. 201.

D. *Bankrupt licence-holders and their trustees.* Where a licence-holder became bankrupt, and thereafter, with the approval of his trustee under the Bankruptcy Acts, applied for, and obtained, an hotel licence from the licensing court, and the goodwill of the business was thereupon sold by the trustee, the bankrupt was ordered to deliver to the trustee his hotel certificate as an accessory to the hotel. The alleged right of lien pled by the bankrupt's solicitor was repelled: *Selkirk* v. *Coupland* (1886) 23 S.L.R. 456. On a certificate-holder becoming bankrupt, the certificate, the permit book, and other documents must be delivered up to the trustee as the property of the creditors: *Fraser's Tr.* v. *Fraser* (1896) 23 R. 978. Delivery and not assignation is the proper mode of divesting one of a certificate: *Clift* v. *Portobello Pier Co.* (1877) 4 R. 462. Where, in competition with the liquidator of an insolvent company, a creditor of the company was successful in obtaining a renewal of the certificate (though he had neither right to, nor possession of, the premises in respect of which the certificate was granted) and admitted that he held it in trust for the company's creditors, he was ordered to deliver up the certificate to the liquidator: *Wm. Forbes Ltd. (in liquidation)* v. *Paterson*, 1926 S.L.T. 654.

The trustee in bankruptcy can sell the goodwill of a business and its trade so as to exclude the bankrupt, when discharged, from commencing a similar business under the same name, nor issuing the same or similar trade mark: *Melrose-Drover* v. *Heddle* (1901) 4 F. 1120. An hotel-keeper became bankrupt, the yearly lease terminated and the trustee did not offer himself as a tenant, and the bankrupt's wife became tenant. Thereafter the trustee applied for the certificate, but the opinion was expressed that the justices could not grant a renewal or transfer of a certificate to a person who, not being in possession, could not carry on the business: *Budge* v. *Goudie* (1895) 2 S.L.T. 406.

As to whether a trustee under a trust deed is an assignee of, or manager for, an insolvent certificate-holder, in a question with the landlord, see *Dewar* v. *Ainslie* (1892) 20 R. 203.

An insolvent certificate-holder does not by his declared bankruptcy, nor by signing a trust deed for behoof of his creditors, divest himself of his certificate. He is not contravening the Act in carrying on his business either by himself, by a manager, or by his trustee. "It is not open to question that a licence-holder may lawfully carry on his business through a manager," and "a trust deed is not a matter with which the public authorities are concerned": *per* Lord M'Laren, *Wylie* v. *Thom* (1889) 16 R.(J.) 90. In that case a conviction of a manager for an insolvent certificate-holder, who had granted a trust deed, of having trafficked "without having a certificate" was suspended. A similar opinion was expressed *obiter* in *Rattray* v. *White* (1891) 19 R.(J.) 23.

A judicial factor was appointed on the sequestrated estate of a partner in a licensed business, his share in the partnership property being part of his sequestrated estate. In the course of the sequestration proceedings in the sheriff court he was sentenced to 30 days' imprisonment for contempt of court, because he had entered the licensed premises and interfered with the management thereof after giving an undertaking that he would not do so. The sentence was held by the High Court of Justiciary to be competent: *Graham* v. *Robert Younger Ltd.*, 1955 J.C. 28.

The purchaser of a licensed business from the trustee of a bankrupt certificate-holder must with reasonable dispatch get the bankrupt's certificate transferred to him. If that be not done, he is guilty of a technical offence: *Brunfaut* v. *Neilson* (1893) 20 R.(J.) 68. An opinion was expressed that such a purchaser under a suspensory condition (that the money be only handed over on the certificate being got by the purchaser) is not necessarily committing a violation of the Act, "assuming that he shows proper diligence in endeavouring to obtain the certificate, and is acting throughout in bona fide": *per* Lord Trayner, *ibid*. See also a similar opinion in a civil matter by Lord President Robertson, in *Cook and Mearns* v. *Gray* (1891) 29 S.L.R. 247.

In a civil question between the creditors of a deceased and insolvent certificate-holder and his widow, who, without objection by the creditors, obtained the certificate and thereafter carried on the business without any agreement being made regarding her paying her husband's debts, or the application of the profits during her tenancy, it was decided that she was not bound to account to the creditors for the profits earned by her under her own certificate: *Stewart's Trs.* v. *Stewart's Executrix* (1896) 23 R. 739. But she was bound to account to the trustee for the estate received by her, including the goodwill, as at her husband's death.

## Provisional grant of licence

**26.**—(1) A licensing board may, on an application in that behalf made to the board by any person interested in premises about to be constructed or in course of construction for use as licensed premises, make a provisional grant of a licence in respect of those premises if the board is satisfied—

(*a*) that the premises will be fit and convenient for their purpose, and

(*b*) that, if the premises had been completed in accordance with the plan thereof lodged with the board in pursuance of section 10 of this Act, the board would on application have granted such a licence in respect thereof.

(2) If on an application under this section the applicant lodges with the board, instead of the plan mentioned in paragraph (*b*) of subsection (1)

above, a plan sufficient to identify the site of the premises, together with such description of the premises as will give a general indication of their proposed size and character (with reference in particular to the sale of alcoholic liquor), then—

    (a) the licensing board shall deal with the application as if made under subsection (1) above; but

    (b) any provisional grant of a licence made on an application under this subsection shall become ineffective unless affirmed by the licensing board on application made to the board to that effect within 12 months of the provisional grant of the licence, any such application being accompanied by a plan of the premises.

(3) A licensing board may consider any application made to it under paragraph (b) of subsection (2) above at any meeting of the board held not earlier than 14 days after the making of the application and shall affirm the provisional grant if the board is satisfied that the premises, if completed in accordance with the plan mentioned in that paragraph, will be fit and convenient for their purpose and that the said plan does not deviate materially from the site plan and description of the premises lodged under the said subsection (2).

(4) A licence of which a provisional grant has been made as aforesaid shall not come into force until such grant is declared final by the licensing board, and subject to subsection (6) below, the board shall, on being so requested, declare the grant final if it is satisfied either—

    (a) that the premises in respect of which the grant was made have been completed in accordance with the plan thereof lodged with the board, or

    (b) that the premises have been completed and that such deviations from the said plan as exist are of minor importance and have not materially altered the character of the premises or the facilities for the supply of alcoholic liquor thereat.

(5) A licensing board shall not entertain a request to declare the provisional grant of a licence final unless the person to whom the grant was made has given to the board such notice of his intention to make the request as may be prescribed.

(6) in the case of a request by a person other than an individual natural person that the licensing board shall declare the provisional grant of a licence final, that person shall include in the notice in subsection (5) above the name of the employee or agent whom it is intended should have the day to day running of the premises, and the board shall not declare the provisional grant final if it finds that the employee or agent so named in the notice is not a fit and proper person to be the holder of a licence.

(7) Where a licensing board declares a provisional grant final in such a case as is described in subsection (6) above the licence shall be in the names of both persons mentioned in that subsection, and any reference in this Act to the holder of a licence includes a reference to both of those persons.

(8) Until the date of the first renewal of licences provisionally granted under subsection (1) or (2) above after those licences have been declared

final, subsections (2) to (5) of section 30 of this Act shall have effect in relation to those licences with the substitution in subsection (3) of section 30 of a reference to one year instead of the reference to three years.

(9) A licensing board may refuse to renew a licence provisionally granted under subsection (1) or (2) above if the board considers that there has been unreasonable delay on the part of the applicant in completing the premises.

(10) An applicant may appeal to the sheriff against a decision of a licensing board to refuse to affirm a licence under subsection (2) above or to refuse to declare a provisional grant of a licence final under subsection (4) above.

GENERAL NOTE
A person wishing to build, or in the course of building licensed premises, may apply to the licensing board for the grant of a provisional licence. The applicant can lodge with the board either a full plan of the premises in accordance with s.10 (subs. (1)) or a site plan together with a description (subs. (2)). The matters about which the board have to be satisfied before making a provisional grant are specified in subs. (1) and subs. (2)(*a*). Where an applicant proceeds under subs. (2), he must apply within 12 months of the making of the provisional grant to have the grant affirmed, which application has to be accompanied by a full plan of the premises (subs. (2)(*b*)). This application is not to be confused with an application to have a provisional grant to be declared final under subs. (4). The matter of declaring a provisional grant final is dealt with in subss. (4) and (5) with additional provisions for persons other than natural persons in subss. (6) and (7). The name of such a person may be changed under s.25(3). The currency of a provisional grant where it is not declared final is to be a period of one year (subs. (8)), and unreasonable delay in completing the premises is to be a ground for refusing to renew such a grant (subs. (9)).

A board can only refuse a provisional grant for the reasons specified in s.17(2), and there is a right of appeal against such a refusal to the sheriff in virtue of s.17(4), and also against the refusal of a board to affirm a licence under subs. (2) and the refusal of a board to declare a licence final under subs. (4) (subs. (10)). For appeals see s.39.

It should be borne in mind that an application for the grant of a provisional licence is an application under Part II of the 1976 Act, and must conform with its provisions, in particular with ss.5, 10(1), (3), (5), (7), 12, 17 and 23. It is to be noted that the provisions contained in s.13(2) (relief from the consequences of failure to comply with the Act), s.15(1) (attendance at the meeting of a board by an applicant or his representative), s.16 (objections to an application), and s.18 (giving reasons by a board for its decision) apply to applications for a provisional grant. It is to be noted that subs. (8) makes it necessary for an application for renewal of a provisional licence, whether granted in terms of subs. (1) or subs. (2) to be made at intervals of one year after the provisional grant was made. A provisional grant of a licence cannot be transferred under s.25 of the Act. See *Baljaffray Residents Association* v. *Milngavie & Bearsden District Council Licensing Board*, 1981 S.L.T.(Sh.Ct.) 106 where it is held that a provisional grant of a licence is not "in force" until declared final. A transfer can only be effected in respect of a new tenant or new or existing occupant of "licensed premises" and licensed premises are premises in respect of which a licence is in force. See changes introduced by s.46 of the 1990 Act which allows the holder of a provisional licence to state that he/she intends to open on a Sunday thus overruling the decision in *Ginera* v. *City of Glasgow District Licensing Board*, 1982 S.L.T. 136.

## Grant of provisional licence

**27.** A licensing board may grant a provisional licence to the holder of any licence to enable him to carry on business in temporary premises during the reconstruction of his premises.

GENERAL NOTE
A provisional licence may be granted to the holder of any form of licence. It authorises the carrying on of the licence-holder's business temporarily in other premises, whilst the premises to which his licence applies are being reconstructed.

### Licence not to be granted for premises on special roads

**28.**—(1) Premises shall be disqualified for receiving a licence if they are situated on land acquired or appropriated by a special road authority, and for the time being used, for the provision of facilities to be used in connection with the use of a special road provided for the use of traffic of class 1 (with or without other classes).

(2) For the purposes of this section—

(*a*) "special road" and "special road authority" have the same meanings as in the Roads (Scotland) Act 1984 and

(*b*) "class 1" means class 1 in Schedule 3 to the Act, as varied from time to time by any order under section 8 of that Act, but, if that Schedule is amended by such an order so as to add to it a further class of traffic, the order may adapt the reference in this section to traffic of class 1 so as to take account of the additional class.

GENERAL NOTE
This section amended; 1984, c. 54, Sched. 9.

### Alcoholic liquor which may be sold under licence

**29.**—(1) A licence granted under this Act by a licensing board shall authorise the holder thereof to sell by retail spirits, wine, made-wine, porter, ale, beer, cider, perry, and any other alcoholic liquor:

Provided that the licensing board may, when granting a licence or an application for an extension of the permitted hours, restrict the alcoholic liquor which may be sold thereunder to wine, made-wine, porter, ale, beer, cider and perry.

(2) Where by virtue of a decision of a licensing board under the proviso to subsection (1) above only alcoholic liquor other than spirits may be sold, it shall be an offence for the licence-holder or his employee or agent to sell spirits.

GENERAL NOTE
*Subsections.* (1) For the meaning of *"alcoholic liquor,"* see s.139(1). The kinds of alcoholic liquor which may be sold under a full licence are enumerated in the main clause of the section. The group of alcoholic liquors which may be sold under a restricted licence are enumerated in the proviso. The subsection applies to any type of licence.

The substitution of a restricted licence for a full licence on an application for renewal is a refusal of the application within the meaning of s.15(2), and is incompetent unless the applicant has been heard by the licensing board on the matter, or, having been cited to attend the board meeting, fails to attend: *Baillie* v. *Wilson*, 1917 S.C. 55; *Wolfson* v. *City of Glasgow District Licensing Board*, 1981 S.L.T. 17 and *Bury* v. *Kilmarnock & Loudon District Licensing Board* 1989 S.L.T. 110, 1988 S.C.L.R. 436. Moreover, it also follows from such a substitution amounting to a refusal that the provisions relating to the grounds on which an application for a renewal of a licence can be refused (s.17(2)), and the right of appeal against such a refusal are applicable (s.17(4)).

(2) The maximum penalty is a fine of level 5 with both the premises and the licence-holder liable to disqualification (Sched. 5).

### Currency of licence

**30.**—(1) A new licence shall come into effect on being granted by a licensing board, except that where there were objections at the hearing the licence shall not come into effect until—

(a) the time within which an appeal may be made has elapsed, or

(b) where an appeal has been lodged, the appeal has been abandoned or determined in favour of the applicant for the licence.

(2) A renewed licence shall come into effect on being renewed by a licensing board.

(3) A licence shall have effect in accordance with the following provisions of this section until the quarterly meeting of the licensing board three years after the meeting at which the licence was granted or renewed by a licensing board.

(4) Subject to section 13(2) of this Act, if no application is made for the renewal of a licence at the quarterly meeting mentioned in subsection (3) above, the licence shall expire on the first day of that meeting.

(5) If an application is made for the renewal of a licence, the licence in respect of which the application is made shall continue to have effect—

(a) until the application for renewal is granted by the board;

(b) if the application for renewal is refused, until the time within which an appeal may be made has elapsed or, if an appeal has been lodged, until the appeal has been abandoned or determined.

GENERAL NOTE

A. *General.* The section dispenses with the fixed date provisions of the previous legislation, by enacting that a licence is to come into effect on the day it is granted or renewed (subss. (1) and (2)). The section makes special provision for the position where an unsuccessful objector appeals against the grant of a licence (subss. (1) and (5)(b)), for the expiry of a licence where there is no application to renew (subs. (4)), and the continuing of the validity of a licence where an application for a renewal has been made but not determined by the licensing board (subs. (5)(a)). For the provisions relating to the currency of the final certificate granted under the 1959 Act, see s. 132.

B. *Subsections.* (1) For "*new licence*," see s.139(1). An appeal must be taken within 14 days of the decision complained against, or, where a board are required to state reasons under s.18(2), within 14 days of the receipt of the reasons in writing (s.39(2)).

(3) For the quarterly meetings of a licensing board, see s.4(1). S.13(2) enables a board, if it thinks fit, to adjourn an application where there has been a failure to comply with the requirements of the Act, or where an applicant has died.

(4) For discussion re "at a quarterly meeting" see *Purdon* v. *City of Glasgow District Licensing Board*, 1989 S.L.T. 201; 1988 S.C.L.R. 466; *Indpine Ltd.* v. *City of Dundee District Licensing Board*, 1991 G.W.D. 29–1759 and *Tarditi* v. *Drummond*, 1989 S.C.L.R. 201.

(5) For the time within which an appeal has to be lodged, see note to subs. (1).

## Suspension of licence on receipt of complaint

**31.**—(1) Where on a complaint being made to a licensing board by any person or body mentioned in section 16(1) of this Act the board is satisfied that it is in the public interest to do so, it may, in accordance with the provisions of this section, suspend a licence.

(2) A licensing board may order the suspension of a licence on one or both of the following grounds—

(a) that the licence-holder is no longer a fit and proper person to be the holder of a licence;

(b) that the use of the premises in respect of which the licence is held has caused undue public nuisance or a threat to public order or safety.

, in considering a complaint under this section, the licensing board may have regard to—

    (a) any misconduct on the part of the holder of the licence, whether or not constituting a breach of this Act or any byelaw made thereunder, which in the opinion of the board has a bearing on his fitness to hold a licence;

    (b) any misconduct on the part of persons frequenting licensed premises occurring in those premises or any misconduct in the immediate vicinity of licensed premises which is attributable to persons frequenting those premises.

(4) On receipt of a complaint under this section, the licensing board shall decide whether or not to hold a hearing on the issue and shall inform the complainer of the board's decision in the matter.

(5) Where the licensing board decides to hold a hearing as mentioned in subsection (4) above—

    (a) the clerk of the board shall serve on the holder of the licence, not less than 21 days before the hearing, a notice that the board proposes to hold a hearing, specifying the complaint and the grounds upon which suspension of the licence is sought;

    (b) the clerk of the board shall give notice of the hearing to the complainer;

    (c) any person or body mentioned in section 16(1) of this Act may, not less than seven days before the hearing, lodge notice with the clerk of the board that he or it wishes to be heard in support of suspension of the licence specifying the grounds on which he or it seeks such suspension, and any such notice shall be intimated by such person to the holder of the licence;

    (d) the board shall not order suspension of a licence without hearing the holder thereof unless after receiving due notice of the hearing the holder fails to appear.

(5A) Where the licensing board decides to hold a hearing as mentioned in subsection (4) above in respect of a complaint under this section which was made by a person or body other than the chief constable, the chief constable may, not less than seven days before the hearing, lodge with the clerk of the board observations in respect of the proposed suspension of the licence, and any such observations shall be intimated by the chief constable to the holder of the licence.

(6) Where a licensing board decides to order the suspension of a licence, the suspension shall not take effect until the expiry of the time within which the holder of the licence may appeal to the sheriff, or, if the holder appeals to the sheriff or thereafter to the Court of Session, until the appeal has been determined in favour of the suspension or has been abandoned.

(7) The period of the suspension of a licence under this section shall be a fixed period not exceeding one year or the unexpired portion of the duration of the licence, whichever is the less, and the effect of the suspension is that the licence shall cease to have effect during the period of the suspension.

(8) The holder of the licence may appeal to the sheriff against any order of a licensing board under this section, including the period of suspension mentioned in the order.

GENERAL NOTE

A. *General.* Clayson considered (paras. 8.38 to 8.40), that, should (as the Act has done by the previous section) the currency of a licence be extended to three years, it was desirable that a licensing board should have some form of sanction against the licence-holder where the premises were being misconducted, or where their suitability had deteriorated, and that such a sanction should be the power to suspend a licence. The section enables a licensing board to suspend a licence on the ground that the licence-holder is no longer a fit and proper person, or that the premises cause undue public nuisance or are a threat to public order or safety (subs. (2)). The procedure is that any person or body entitled under s.16(1) to object to the grant of a licence may make a complaint about that licence to the licensing board (subs. (1)). The board decide whether the complaint merits a hearing and notify the complainer of their decision (subs. (4)). Where the board decides to hold a hearing, notice must be given to the licence-holder and the complainer in accordance with subs. (5)(*a*) and (5)(*b*) respectively. Any person entitled under s.16(1) to object may support the suspension in accordance with subs. (5)(*c*). In considering a complaint under the section, the board may have regard to the factors specified in subs. (3), and are not entitled to suspend the licence without hearing the holder unless the holder fails to appeal after receiving notice (subs. (5)(*d*)). The maximum period of suspension is one year or the unexpired period of the licence whichever is the less (subs. (7)). The holder of a licence may appeal against a suspension order (subs. (8)), and on an appeal being taken, the suspension remains ineffective until the appeal is finally determined or abandoned (subs. (6)). See note below concerning changes introduced by s.53(2) of the 1990 Act—observations by chief constable.

B. *Subsections.* (1) "*licence*" means any licence granted under the Act other than a seamen's canteen licence (see s.139(1)). Seamen's canteens are included, however, in virtue of the provisions of s.45.

(2) and (3) The two subsections should be read together, subs. (2) specifying the grounds on which a licence may be suspended, and subs. (3) misconduct to which the board may have regard in considering whether grounds for suspension have been substantiated. For byelaws generally, see s.38. Subsection (3) makes it clear that a licence may be suspended not only on the grounds of the actings of the licence-holder but also on grounds attributable to the actings of persons frequenting the premises or the vicinity of the premises.

(4) The purpose of the preliminary decision on the question of whether or not a hearing is to be held is to prevent the licence-holder from being harassed by frivolous or vexatious complaints. The hearing may be under an arrangement under s.5(1).

(5A) New subsection (5A) inserted by s.53(2) of the 1990 Act. The new subsection allows the chief constable, where he is not the complainant under s.31(4) seeking the suspension of the licence, to make observations in respect of the proposed suspension, for consideration by the board. The observations have to be lodged not less than seven days before the hearing with the clerk of the board. Although "not later than" is not used, the effect of the wording is the same. Such observations have to be intimated to the holder of the licence. No timetable is given for intimation to the holder of the licence, but the intimation would have to be before the hearing.

(8) For appeals, see s.39 and *Lightheart* v. *City of Edinburgh District Licensing Board*, 1978 S.L.T.(Sh.Ct.) 41.

## Other power to suspend licence

**32.**—(1) Where a licensing board considers that licensed premises are no longer suitable or convenient for the sale of alcoholic liquor, having regard to their character and condition, and the nature and extent of the use of the premises, the board may decide to hold a hearing with a view to making a closure order under this section, and the effect of a closure order is that the licence held in respect of the premises shall cease to have effect while the closure order is in force.

(2) Where the licensing board decides to hold a hearing as mentioned in subsection (1) above—

(*a*) the clerk of the board shall serve on the holder of the licence, not less than 21 days before the hearing, a notice that the board proposes to hold the hearing specifying the grounds on which the board proposes to hold the hearing;

(*b*) the board shall not make a closure order without hearing the holder of the licence unless, after receiving due notice of the hearing, the holder fails to appear.

(3) Where after a hearing under this section a licensing board is satisfied as to any one or more of the matters mentioned in subsection (1) above, the board may order the closure of the licensed premises and any such order shall specify the matters on which the order is based.

(4) The closure order shall remain in force until such time as the board is satisfied that the matters which led to the closure order have been satisfactorily remedied.

(5) The licence-holder may apply to the board for the cancellation of the closure order on the ground that the matters which led to the closure order have been satisfactorily remedied.

(6) Where a licensing board decides to make a closure order under this section, the order shall not take effect until the expiry of the time within which the holder of the licence may appeal to the sheriff, or, if the holder appeals to the sheriff or thereafter to the Court of Session, until the appeal has been determined in favour of the closure order or has been abandoned.

(7) The holder of the licence may appeal to the sheriff against the closure order or against a refusal of a licensing board to cancel a closure order.

GENERAL NOTE

A. *General.* As in the case of the previous section, the purpose of the section is to give a licensing board a measure of control over licensed premises during the currency of a three-year licence. The section entitles a board to make a closure order where they consider that the licensed premises are no longer suitable for the sale of liquor. The effect of the order is that the licence for the premises ceases to have effect. The procedure for making a closure order is contained in subss. (1), (2) and (3). The matters giving rise to the order must be specified in the order (subs. (3)) and the order remains in force until these matters are remedied (subs. (4)). Where a closure order has been made, the licence-holder has the right to apply to the board for cancellation of the order, on the ground that the cause of the order has been rectified (subs. (5)). There is a right of appeal against the making of a closure order (subs. (7)) with provision for suspending the order where an appeal is taken until the appeal has been determined or abandoned (subss. (6) and (7)).

B. *Subsections.* (1) The section differs from the previous section in that it is concerned with the suitability of the premises and not with the fitness of the licence-holder or the orderliness of persons frequenting the premises. It also differs in that the decision to hold a hearing with a view to making a closure order is initiated by the board itself and not as a result of a complaint to them.

(2) and (3) A closure order hearing must be before a full board meeting, but not necessarily before a quarterly meeting (s.5).

(5) The requirements for a meeting of a board to consider the cancellation of a closure order are the same as those for the making of an order (see note to subss. (2) and (3)).

(6) and (7) For appeals, see s.39.

## Occasional licence for premises other than licensed premises or clubs

**33.**—(1) A licensing board may grant an occasional licence to the holder of a licence authorising him to sell alcoholic liquor, during such hours and for such period of not more than 14 days as the board may determine, in the course of catering for an event taking place outwith the licensed premises in respect of which he is the holder of a licence.

(2) A licensing board may grant an occasional licence to a registered club authorising the club to sell alcoholic liquor, during such hours and for such period of not more than 14 days as the board may determine, at an event held outwith the premises of the club if the event arises from or relates to the functions of the club.

(3) In granting an occasional licence under this section, which shall be in writing, the licensing board may impose such conditions as it thinks fit including a condition as to the type of alcoholic liquor which may be sold under the licence, and an occasional licence granted to the holder of a restricted hotel licence or a restaurant licence shall be subject to a condition that the sale of alcoholic liquor under the authority of the licence shall be ancillary to the provision of substantial refreshment.

(4) If the holder of the licence or his employee or agent contravenes a condition attached to an occasional licence, he shall be guilty of an offence.

(5) If a condition attached to an occasional licence is contravened as regards any club, every person whose name is, at the time of the contravention, contained in the list lodged under subsection (3)(b) of section 103 of this Act, or as the case may be in the new list last lodged under subsection (5) or (5A) of that section, in respect of that club, shall be guilty of an offence:

Provided that a person shall not be convicted of such an offence if he proves that the contravention in question took place without his knowledge or consent.

(6) The provisions of this Act and of any byelaws or regulations made thereunder, other than provisions relating to permitted hours, shall apply to the sale of alcoholic liquor under subsection (1) above as if the sale took place on licensed premises and to the sale of alcoholic liquor under subsection (2) above as if the sale took place in the registered club.

(7) An application for an occasional licence under this section shall be made in writing to the clerk of the licensing board and shall specify the name and address of the applicant, the premises or place and occasion for which the licence is required, and the hours and period for which the licence is requested.

(8) At the same time as the application is made under subsection (7) above the applicant shall send a copy of the application to the chief constable, and if an occasional licence is granted under this section the clerk of the licensing board shall send a copy of the licence to the chief constable not less than 24 hours before the beginning of the event to which it relates.

(9) A licensing board shall make such arrangements as it thinks fit as respects the consideration of applications under this section or any objection made thereto but the board shall not cause to be published the address of the applicant if the applicant provides the name and address of an agent through whom he may have intimated to him any objections.

(10) In subsection (1) above, "the holder of a licence" includes the holder of an off-sale licence but does not include the holder of a refreshment licence or of an entertainment licence.

GENERAL NOTE

Subs. (5) amended, 1980, c. 55, s.21(2).

A. *General.* S.60 of the 1959 Act was concerned with the granting of special permission to sell exciseable liquor both on the certificate-holder's premises and in other premises or places. The two purposes of s.60 have been separated in the 1976 Act, s.33 being concerned with the sale of liquor outwith the licence-holder's premises, and s.64 with the occasional extension of permitted hours on the premises. Under the 1959 Act, only the holder of a public house or an hotel certificate could apply for a special permission, whereas, under s.33, any licence-holder, other than the holder of a seamen's canteen, refreshment or entertainment licence, may apply for an occasional licence. In the case of an application by a licence-holder the occasional licence allows the sale of liquor "in the course of catering for an event taking place outwith the licensed premises" (subs. (1)), and, in the case of a registered club, the occasional licence allows the sale of liquor outwith the club premises at an event arising from the club functions (subs. (2)). In both cases, the conditions under which liquor may be sold are subject to the provisions of subs. (6). Where an occasional licence is granted to the holder of a restricted hotel licence or a restaurant licence, it is subject to the restriction contained in subs. (3). Subss. (7) and (8) deal with the procedure for applying. A board can make its own arrangements for considering such applications (subs. (9)) and they may be heard under an arrangement under s.5(1). A board may restrict the type of liquor which may be sold under an occasional licence (subs. (3)). Subss. (4) and (5) make it an offence to contravene any of the conditions of an occasional licence.

B. *Subsections.* (1) "*licence*" does not include a seamen's canteen licence (see s.139(1)), nor a refreshment licence or an entertainment licence (see subs. (10)).

"*licensed premises*" does not include the premises of a seamen's canteen (s.139(1)).

(2) For the meaning of "*registered club*," see s.139(1).

(4) and (5) The maximum penalty for a contravention of either of the subsections is a fine of level 3, with both the licence-holder and the premises liable to disqualification, and with vicarious liability on the part of the licence-holder (Sched. 5).

(6) For "*byelaws*," see s.38 and "*regulations*," see s.37.

Subsections (1) and (2) amended by para. 9 of Sched. 8 to the 1990 Act to overcome the difficulty caused by the restriction of an occasional licence and permission to "on such day" in the singular. Events which lasted two or more days required a separate occasional licence or permission for each day. The amendment allows for intimation of objections to be made to an agent in conformity with the new s.139(6) added by para. 18. See *Hollywood Bowl (Scotland) Ltd.* v. *Horsburgh,* 1991 G.W.D. 27–1627 for discussion which explains the amendment by para. 9 of Sched. 8 to the 1990 Act, notwithstanding that the judgment postdates the coming into force of that Act—but see note to Sched. 8 to the 1990 Act.

## Occasional permissions

**34.**—(1) A licensing board may grant an occasional permission to a person representing a voluntary organisation or a branch of a voluntary organisation authorising him to sell alcoholic liquor during such hours and for such period of not more than 14 days as the board may determine, in the course of catering for an event, arising from or related to the acivities of the organisation, taking place outwith licensed premises.

(2) Not more than four occasional permissions may be granted by a licensing board in any one year on behalf of the same voluntary organisation or the same branch of a voluntary organisation.

(3) In granting an occasional permission under this section, which shall be in writing, the licensing board may impose such conditions as it thinks fit including a condition as to the type of alcoholic liquor which may be sold under the permission, and if the person to whom the permission is granted contravenes such a condition he shall be guilty of an offence.

(4) The provisions of section 68 of this Act shall apply to any premises or place in respect of which an occasional permission is granted as they apply to licensed premises, with the substitution of references to the holder of the permission for the references to the holder of a licence.

(5) The provisions of section 85 of this Act shall apply to any premises or place in respect of which an occasional permission is granted as they apply to premises in respect of which a licence (other than an off-sale licence) is in force.

(6) The person to whom an occasional permission is granted shall ensure that the provisions of this Act or any byelaws or regulations made thereunder relating to the conduct of licensed premises are observed in the premises or place in respect of which the permission was granted as if he were the holder of a public house licence, and if he contravenes this subsection he shall be guilty of an offence:

Provided that it shall be a defence for any person charged with an offence under this subsection if he proves that he used due diligence to prevent the occurrence of the offence.

(7) Subsections (7) to (9) of section 33 of this Act shall apply in relation to applications for occasional permissions as they apply in relation to applications for occasional licences.

GENERAL NOTE

A. *General.* Clayson (para. 15.05) was of the view that small voluntary organisations should be able to supply alcoholic liquor at functions without having to find a willing certificate-holder, and should be able to gain some financial benefit from the sale of liquor to members. The section allows a licensing board to grant an occasional permission to a representative of a voluntary organisation whereby liquor may be sold during specified hours in the course of catering for a function outwith licensed premises, which function arises from the activities of the organisation (subs. (1)). No more than four special permissions may be granted to any one organisation or branch of any organisation in the same year (subs. (2)). Application for a special permission is to be made in the same manner as for an occasional licence (subs. (7)). The permission is subject to the conditions set out in subss. (3) to (6).

B. *Subsections.* (1) See note above to s.33—amendment para. 10 of Sched. 8 to the 1990 Act.

(3) The maximum penalty for a contravention of the subsection is a fine of level 3 (Sched. 5).

(4) S.68 is concerned with the prohibition of the sale of liquor to persons under 18 years of age.

(5) S.85 gives the police power of entry into licensed premises, and makes it an offence to refuse or obstruct such entry.

(6) For "*byelaws*" and "*regulations,*" see ss.38 and 37 respectively. For the maximum penalty, see subs. (3). The defence contained in the proviso applies only to a contravention of subs. (6) and not to a contravention of subs. (3).

## Consent of licensing board required for reconstruction, etc. of certain licensed premises

**35.**—(1) No reconstruction or extension of or alteration in any premises in respect of which a licence (other than an off-sale licence) is in force, being a reconstruction, extension or alteration which will affect a public or common part of such premises or any communication with such part, shall be made unless the licensing board within whose area such premises are situated has consented to such reconstruction, extension or alteration at a quarterly meeting of the board or at such other time as may be appointed by the board, or unless such reconstruction, extension or alteration is required by order of some lawful authority.

(2) A licensing board shall not give its consent under this section to any reconstruction, extension or alteration which will materially alter the character of the premises in question or materially alter the external appearance, shape or size of the premises and may, before considering an application for the board's consent under this section, require plans of the proposed reconstruction, extension or alteration to be lodged with the clerk of the board at such time as the board may appoint.

(3) Before giving its consent under this section, the licensing board shall consult the fire authority for the area.

(4) If subsection (1) above is contravened, the sheriff may on a complaint at the instance of the licensing board, by order declare the licence which is in force for the premises in respect of which the contravention took place to be forfeited, or may direct that, within a time fixed by the order, the premises shall be restored to their original condition.

(5) For the purposes of this section—

(a) "public part" means a part open to customers who are not residents or guests of residents; and

(b) "common part" means a part open generally to all residents or to a particular class of them.

GENERAL NOTE

A. *General.* The section provides the procedure whereby the holder of a licence (other than an off-sale licence) may obtain the consent of the licensing board to the reconstruction or alteration of the public or common part of the premises where the reconstruction or alteration is not so material as to be excluded by subs. (2). For the meaning of public or common part, see subs. (5). Reconstruction or alteration of the premises without this consent may lead to forfeiture of the licence (subs. (4)). The licensing board may itself order structural alterations to be executed under s.36.

B. *Subsections.* (1) "*licence*" is defined in s.139(1) as being any licence granted under the Act other than a seamen's canteen licence. The section does, however, apply to seamen's canteens in virtue of the provisions of s.45.

"*Alterations in any premises.*" For a discussion of the meaning of these words in a similar English provision, see *R.* v. *Weston-super-Mare JJ.* [1939] 1 K.B. 700 and *R.* v. *Chelmsford Crown Court, ex parte George Larkin,* Q.B., June 13, 1990, Licensing Review, Vol. 2, p. 20; *R.* v. *Liverpool Crown Court, ex parte Lennon and Hongkins,* Q.B., July 23, 1990, Licensing Review, Vol. 4, p. 22.

As to how far a licensing board is entitled to impose conditions before sanctioning an alteration, see *R.* v. *Wandsworth Licensing JJ.* [1921] 3 K.B. 487.

(2) Where there is such a material alteration, the proper procedure is to apply for a fresh grant.

(3) For consultation with the fire authority, see note to s.23(5).

For appeal, see *City of Glasgow District Licensing Board* v. *MacDonald,* 1978 S.L.T.(Sh.Ct.) 74, which confirmed the competent procedure to be a summary application to the sheriff where the alteration had been carried out without consent.

See also Introduction 3.54.

## Power of licensing board to order structural alterations on renewal of certain licences

**36.**—(1) On any application for the renewal of a licence in respect of any premises (other than off-sale premises), a licensing board may require a plan of the licensed premises to be produced to the board and lodged with the clerk, and on renewing such licence the board may order that, within a time fixed by the order, such structural alterations as the board thinks reasonably necessary to secure the proper conduct of the business shall be made in that part of the licensed premises in which alcoholic liquor is sold or consumed.

(2) Where an order made under this section is complied with, the licensing board shall not make a further order in respect of those premises within the six years following the date of the first-mentioned order unless during that time the board has refused to renew the licence in force in respect of the premises.

(3) If the holder of a licence makes default in complying with an order made under this section, he shall be guilty of an offence, and he shall be guilty of a further offence for every day on which the default continues after the expiry of the time fixed by the order.

(4) If the holder of a licence makes default in complying with an order made under this section, the licensing board may order the suspension of his licence and any such order shall specify the matters on which the order is based.

(5) An order under subsection (4) above shall remain in force until such time as the board is satisfied that the matters which led to the order have been satisfactorily remedied.

(6) The licence-holder may apply to the board for the cancellation of the order on the ground that the matters which led to the order have been satisfactorily remedied.

(7) Where a licensing board decides to order the suspension of a licence the suspension shall not take effect until the expiry of the time within which the holder of the licence may appeal to the sheriff, or, if the holder appeals to the sheriff or thereafter to the Court of Session, until the appeal has been determined in favour of the suspension or has been abandoned.

(8) The holder of the licence may appeal to the sheriff against an order made under subsection (4) above or against a refusal of a licensing board to cancel such an order.

GENERAL NOTE

A. *Power of licensing court to order structural alterations of hotels and public houses.* The licence-holder may not reconstruct or alter premises without the consent of the licensing board: s.35(1). Under this section he may be *ordered* by the licensing board to make alterations, and failure to comply with such an order is an offence. The board may suspend a licence where there is default in carrying out the order. The section does not apply to off-sale licences or to seamen's canteens, seamen's canteens being outwith the definition of licensed premises in s.139(1).

B. *Subsections.* (1) For the meaning of *"licence,"* see s.139(1).

Although the licensing board may resolve to call for the production of plans under this section in respect of a number of existing licences, a separate *requirement* must be recorded, and intimated to the licence-holder, in respect of each licence separately. An adjournment of each application will normally be necessary in order to allow time for the plan to be produced.

As to the extent of the structural alterations which the licensing board may *order* under this subsection, see *Bushell* v. *Hammond* [1904] 2 K.B. 563, where it was held that it included alterations to passages and means of access. It has been held, however, that the licensing board is not entitled to make it a condition of the renewal of a licence that the applicant *use* his premises in a particular way, as, for example, by keeping a door locked: *Smith* v. *Portsmouth JJ.* [1906] 2 K.B. 229. See also *R.* v. *Shann* [1910] 2 K.B. 418; *R.* v. *Watford Licensing JJ.* [1929] 1 K.B. 313. The order, when made, should be formally intimated to the licence holder.

There is a right of appeal against the making of an order under this subsection: subs. (8).

In his own interests the licence-holder, when structural alterations have been completed in compliance with an order, should intimate that fact to the clerk to the licensing board.

A provisional licence may be granted to enable a licence-holder to carry on business in temporary premises during reconstruction of the licensed premises: s.27.

(2) The period has been increased from the five years prescribed by the 1959 Act.

(3) The maximum penalty is a fine of level 3 with an additional fine of £5 for every day the licence-holder is in detail, with both the licence-holder and the premises liable to disqualification (Sched. 5).

(8) For appeals, see s.39.

## Power of licensing board to make regulations

**37.** A licensing board may make regulations with respect to the making of applications for licences (including occasional licences and occasional permissions), extension of permitted hours and restriction of the terminal permitted hours and the procedure following thereon, and such regulations may include provisions designed to assist the board in determining the fitness of applicants to hold licences and the expediency of granting licences for the premises in respect of which application is made; and the board may also make regulations with respect to the procedure to be followed in transferring licences under this Act and with respect to any matters which, by virtue of this Act, may be prescribed.

GENERAL NOTE

A. *Subject-matter of regulations made by licensing board.* The regulations which a licensing board may make are concerned with procedure only. They may be compared in this respect with the wider legislative powers delegated to the licensing board by s.38, in connection with the making of bye-laws. Regulations may deal only with the making of the types of application specified in the section and the procedure following thereon. They may include provisions which will assist the licensing board to determine the fitness of applicants and the suitability (in its widest sense) of premises.

Regulations made by a licensing court must be *intra vires*. See, on this matter, note A to s.38. See also note B below.

Regulations may be made at any meeting. They should state how they are to be published or intimated to persons interested.

B. *Regulations must not conflict with provisions of the Act.* Regulations made under this section must not be inconsistent with the provisions of the Act. The broad principle that "where a power to make regulations is given to a public body by statute, no regulations made under it can abridge a right conferred by the statute itself" is too clear to need justification: *R.* v. *Bird* [1898] 2 Q.B. 340, *per* Wills J. at p. 345. *R.* v. *Bird* dealt with an English provision regarding the procedure for confirmation of a new licence by a confirming authority which gave the justices power to make rules as to the proceedings to be adopted for confirmation. The justices made a rule which directed that every person intending to oppose the confirmation of a new licence should, within seven days after the grant of the licence, give notice of his intention to the applicant and to the clerk of the peace, and that no person who had failed to comply with the rule might appear to oppose confirmation. An objector, who had not given the notice required by the rule, was not allowed to oppose confirmation when he sought to appear before the confirming authority, and the licence was confirmed. It was held that the rule was *ultra vires*. Wills J., at p. 344, said: "Parliament has . . . given to a person desirous of opposing . . . power to appear and to be heard. . . . The right of the justices to make rules . . . cannot affect [this] privilege. . . . These rules . . . impose fresh conditions upon the exercise of the objector's right . . . as a necessary preliminary of the right to oppose: something which is not in the statute." Kennedy J., at p. 346, said: "To make a . . . rule which has the effect of debarring a man from the exercise of an absolute statutory right, unless he complies with a number of requirements is . . . clearly *ultra vires*." The confirming authority was directed to hold an adjourned session, to hear and determine the application, and to hear the objector thereon.

Regulations made under this section must not delegate to one or more members of the licensing board, or to officials or other persons, except as authorised by the Act, any responsibility which must be exercised by the licensing board at any of their meetings. They must not, moreover, limit in advance the discretion entrusted by the Act to any meeting of the licensing board at which applications are heard and disposed of.

## Power of licensing board to make byelaws

**38.**—(1) Without prejudice to its other powers under this Act, a licensing board may make byelaws for any of the following purposes—

(a) for closing licensed premises wholly or partially on New Year's Day, and on such other days not being more than four in any one year as the board may think expedient for special reasons;

(b) for prohibiting holders of licences from residing in their licensed premises, or for requiring the dwellinghouses of holders of licences to be separate from their licensed premises;

(c) for requiring all wines, made-wines and spirits sold by the holder of an off-sale licence to be sold in corked, stoppered or sealed vessels, cans, jars or casks;

(d) for requiring every holder of a hotel or public house licence to keep in his licensed premises and to renew from day to day a sufficient supply of drinking water, and such eatables as may be specified in the byelaw, and to display, offer and supply the same as may be required by the byelaw;

(e) for printing a list of all applications coming before any meeting of the licensing board, with such other information as may be considered necessary by the board;

(f) for the setting out of conditions which may be attached to licences for the improvement of standards of, and conduct in, licensed premises;

(g) for the granting of a licence of a type other than that applied for; provided that a byelaw made under paragraph (c) above shall not apply to licensed premises where no groceries are kept or sold and where a bona fide wholesale business in alcoholic liquor is carried on.

(2) Byelaws made under subsection (1) above shall not have effect until they are confirmed by the Secretary of State, and the provisions of subsections (4) to (12) and (15) of section 202 of the Local Government (Scotland) Act 1973 and of section 204 of that Act shall, with any necessary modifications, apply in relation to byelaws to be made or made under this section as they apply in relation to byelaws to be made or made under that Act.

(3) When granting a licence, a licensing board may attach to the licence any condition set out in a byelaw by virtue of paragraph (f) of subsection (1) above.

(4) The holder of any licence or any employee or agent of his shall be guilty of an offence if he commits a breach of any byelaw or any condition attached to a licence by virtue of a byelaw.

GENERAL NOTE

A. *Bye-laws made by licensing board—general.* A bye-law made by a licensing board under this section must be *intra vires*, *i.e.* the scope of the bye-law must not exceed the power given by the section. For examples of bye-laws which were held to be *ultra vires*, see *Scottish General Transport Co.* v. *Glasgow Corporation*, 1928 S.C. 248; *Malloch* v. *Aberdeen Corporation*, 1973 S.C. 227. It must be reasonable, and it must not be repugnant to the general law of the country. For the subject generally, see Gloag and Henderson, *Introduction to the Law of Scotland*, 9th ed., p. 5, D. M. Walker, *Scottish Legal System*, 5th ed., pp. 238–245 and *Halsbury's Laws of England*, 4th ed., Vol. 28, paras. 1323–1338 and cases there cited. See also s.37, note B.

As to evidence of the terms of a bye-law, and of the fact that all the formalities relating to it have been complied with, see note B(2) below.

Any condition that a board may seek to attach to a licence can only be attached by a valid bye-law: *Allied Breweries (U.K.) Ltd.* v. *City of Glasgow District Licensing Board*, 1985 S.L.T. 302. S.140(6) provides that bye-laws made under the 1959 Act continue in force.

B. *Subsections.* (1) *Subject-matter of bye-laws.* (*a*) For an example of a prosecution for breach of a bye-law made under this paragraph in respect of sale or supply of alcoholic liquor on New Year's Day, after the hour appointed by the bye-law for the closing of licensed premises on that day, see *Herkes* v. *Dickie*, 1958 J.C. 51. For an unusual case in which, on an interpretation of a bye-law, Monday, January 2, was held to be properly treated as a Sunday for the purposes of supplying travellers, see *Henderson* v. *Ross*, 1928 J.C. 74.

(*b*) A bye-law made under this paragraph clearly cannot be made to apply to hotel or restricted hotel licences.

(*c*) For the meaning of *"off-sale licence,"* see Sched. 1.

A bye-law made under this paragraph shall not apply to licensed premises where a *bona fide* wholesale business in alcoholic liquor is carried on and no groceries are kept or sold (see proviso). *"Dealing wholesale"* means the sale at any one time to any one person of quantities not less than (a) in the case of spirits, wine or made-wine, two gallons or one case; or (b) in the case of beer, four and a half gallons or two cases: Alcoholic Duties Act 1979, ss.65(8) and 4(1).

(*e*) As to the list of applications of new applicants which the clerk to the licensing court is required by the Act to publish, see s.12.

(*g*) The granting of a licence other than of the type applied for amounts to a refusal of an application.

(2) S.202 (as amended) of the Local Government (Scotland) Act 1973 prescribes the procedure for the making of bye-laws by a local authority. S.202B, introduced by s.110 of the Civic Government (Scotland) Act 1982, provides for a register of bye-laws to be kept available for inspection. S.204 makes provision for the sufficiency of evidence as regards bye-laws.

(4) The maximum penalty for an offence under the subsection is a fine of level 3 with both the licence-holder and the premises liable to disqualification. The offence is one in respect of which there is vicarious liability on the part of the licence-holder (Sched. 5).

## Appeals to sheriff

**39.**—(1) An appeal which may be made by virtue of any provision of this Act against any decision of a licensing board shall be to the sheriff, and the decision of the sheriff on any such appeal may include such order as to the expenses of the appeal as he thinks proper.

(2) An appeal under this section shall be lodged with the sheriff clerk within 14 days from the date of the decision appealed against or in a case where reasons for a decision have been given under section 18(2) of this Act, within 14 days from the date of receipt of those reasons, which shall be presumed to have been received on the day after the date on which they were posted, except that in the case of reasons posted on a Friday or Saturday, they shall be presumed to have been received on the Monday next following.

(2A) A licensing board may be a party to any appeal under this section.

(3) On good cause being shown, the sheriff may hear an appeal under this section notwithstanding that it was not lodged within the time mentioned in subsection (2) above.

(4) The sheriff may uphold an appeal under this section only if he considers that the licensing board in arriving at its decision—

(a) erred in law;

(b) based its decision on any incorrect material fact;

(c) acted contrary to natural justice; or

(d) exercised its discretion in an unreasonable manner.

(5) In considering an appeal under this section, the sheriff may hear evidence by or on behalf of any party to the appeal.

(6) On upholding an appeal under this section the sheriff may—

      (a) remit the case with the reason for his decision to the licensing board for reconsideration of its decision; or

      (b) reverse or modify the decision of the licensing board.

(7) On remitting a case to a licensing board under subsection (6) above, the sheriff may—

(a) specify a date by which the rehearing by the board must take place;

(b) modify any procedural steps which otherwise would be required in relation to the matter by or under any enactment;

and any decision of a licensing board on any such case shall be valid as if reached at a quarterly meeting as mentioned in section 4(1)(a) of this Act.

(8) If any party to an appeal to the sheriff under any provision of this Act (other than Part VII) is dissatisfied in point of law with a decision of the sheriff, he may appeal therefrom to the Court of Session within 28 days from the date of that decision.

(9) The Court of Session may, by act of sederunt, make rules for the conduct of proceedings under this section.

GENERAL NOTE

A. *General*. The section provides, under certain sections of the Act, for a right of appeal against a decision of the licensing authority to the sheriff, and a further right of appeal from the sheriff to the Court of Session on a point of law. Unless an appeal under the Act is provided for by the particular section, or a right of appeal is available derivatively from another section, any appeal is incompetent; *e.g.* s.64, extension of permitted hours; *Sloan* v. *North East Fife District Council Licensing Board*, 1978 S.L.T.(Sh.Ct.) 62. Care should, however, be taken where a section appears to confer no right of appeal, but that section is in fact linked to another section where a right of appeal exists; *e.g.* under s.62 a licensing board may attach conditions to a grant or transfer of a licence and apparently there is no right of appeal against that section, but in *Wallace* v. *Kyle and Carrick Licensing Board*, 1979 S.L.T.(Sh.Ct.) 12, it was held that as s.62 was ancillary to s.10 under which licences were granted, an appeal was competent; see *M. Milne* v. *City of Glasgow District Licensing Board*, 1987 S.L.T.(Sh.Ct.) 145 where an appeal against a decision by the clerk under s.10(1) refusing to accept a late application for renewal was allowed in respect that the application related to a renewal of a licence under s.17(4); and *Kelvinside Community Council* v. *City of Glasgow District Licensing Board*, 1990 S.L.T. 725, where it was held that an objector had a right of appeal against a decision under s.14, even though the applicant himself had no right of appeal. Where no right of appeal exists a review of the licensing board's decision will have to be by way of a petition for judicial review; see Introduction paras. 6.10 to 6.15. An appeal to the *nobile officium* is not competent (*Fife & Kinross Motor*

*Auctions Ltd.* v. *Perth and Kinross District Licensing Board*, 1981 S.L.T. 106). It is competent to appeal to either the sheriff or the sheriff principal, but no appeal lies from the sheriff to the sheriff principal (*Troc Sales Ltd.* v. *Kirkcaldy District Licensing Board*, 1982 S.L.T.(Sh.Ct.) 77). A grant of a licence in a restricted form, when a full licence has been applied for constitutes a refusal and may be appealed (*Wolfson* v. *Glasgow District Licensing Board*, 1981 S.L.T. 17).

The right of appeal to the Court of Session does not apply to the decision of a sheriff in an application relating to registered clubs under Part VII of the Act (subs. (8)). The decisions which may be appealed are a refusal to grant, renew, transfer or provisionally grant a licence (s.17(4)), the right of appeal being conferred on the applicant, a grant of a new licence, or a grant of a renewal, permanent transfer, or provisional grant of a licence (s.17(5)), the right of appeal being restricted to competent objectors who appeared at the hearing of the application, the attaching or refusal to attach a condition under s.38(3) or s.101(2) of the Act, the right of appeal being conferred on applicants and unsuccessful competent objectors who appeared [N.B. an objection can be considered without an appearance (s.16(5))] at the hearing (s.17(6)), a refusal to affirm or declare final a provisional grant (s.26(10)), the right of appeal being limited to the applicant, the making of a suspension order (s.31(8)) or a closure order (s.32(7), the right of appeal being limited to the licence-holder), the suspending of a licence under s.36 where the licence-holder fails to execute structural alterations, the refusal to cancel such a suspension (s.36(8), the right of appeal being limited to the licence-holder), the decisions referred to in s.44 relating to seamen's canteens (the right of appeal being limited to the licence-holder or the applicant), the making of a restriction order (s.65(8)), the right of appeal being limited to the registered club, or licence-holder concerned and any complainer who appeared at the hearing, the granting or refusal of an application by a public house licence-holder for Sunday opening of the premises (the right of appeal being conferred on both an unsuccessful applicant and an unsuccessful objector (Sched. 4, Part I, paras. 8 and 9)), and the making of a Sunday restriction order, by the same parties as entitled to appeal under s.65(8) (Sched. 4, Part II, para. 22).

The appeal procedure is regulated by the Act of Sederunt (Appeals under the Licensing (Scotland) Act 1976) 1977 (S.I. 1977 No. 1622), as amended by S.I. 1979 No. 1520 (see Appendix). An appeal is made by initial writ, which is disposed of as a summary application under the Sheriff Courts (Scotland) Act 1907 and 1913 (Dobie, *Sheriff Court Practice*, p. 101; Macphail, *Sheriff Court Practice*, para. 27–189; *Hutcheon* v. *Hamilton District Licensing Board*, 1978 S.L.T.(Sh.Ct.) 44). A copy of the initial writ requires to be served on (1) the clerk of the licensing board and (2) all parties who appeared or were represented at the hearing including the applicant if the appeal is by an objector, at the same time as the initial writ is lodged with the sheriff clerk or as soon as may be thereafter (para. 3, S.I. 1977/1622. This includes the board and the chief constable; *Padda* v. *Strathkelvin District Licensing Board*, 1988 S.C.L.R. 349). Failure to serve or to serve "as soon as may be thereafter" is fatal to the appeal (*Binnie* v. *Glasgow District Licensing Board*, 1979 S.L.T. 286 and *Padda, cit.*). It is not clear whether the S.I. is authority for the service or whether a warrant is required from the sheriff clerk. It is considered prudent to seek warrant for the initial writ.

Contrary to some earlier decisions (*viz. Hutcheon, cit.*) it was held competent for the licensing board to be a party to the appeal (*Joe Coral (Racing) Ltd.* v. *Hamilton District Council*, 1981 S.L.T. (Notes) 106), now regularised by the introduction of subs. (2A). The chief constable cannot be a party to the appeal, unless he formerly objected to the original application (*Hutcheon, cit.*).

The chief constable's objections require to be intimated in terms of the Act and require fuller specification beyond a recital of the statutory wording of the grounds of objection (*Chief Constable of Grampian* v. *City of Aberdeen District Licensing Board*, 1979 S.L.T.(Sh.Ct.) 2). The initial writ requires to identify the licensing board's failures and specify the circumstances which are relied on to show that the board erred; it is not sufficient to recite without specification all the statutory grounds of appeal (*Sutherland* v. *City of Edinburgh District Licensing Board*, 1984 S.L.T. 241). Subss. (2) and (3) prescribe the time within which an appeal may be taken, subs. (4) the grounds in respect of which an appeal may be sustained, subs. (5) permits evidence to be adduced, subss. (6) and (7) deal with the courses a sheriff may take in sustaining an appeal, and subs. (8) with an appeal to the Court of Session on a point of law, which must be taken within 28 days of the sheriff's decision.

B. *Subsections.* (1) In considering the appeal, the sheriff acts in his judicial capacity and is vested with a wide discretion, which must be exercised reasonably (*Martin* v. *Ellis*, 1978

S.L.T.(Sh.Ct.) 38; *Botterills of Blantyre* v. *Hamilton District Licensing Board*, 1986 S.L.T. 14). The scope of a sheriff's remit in considering an appeal and the basis upon which he may overturn a board's decision under s.39 was considered in detail by Sheriff G. H. Gordon in *Loosefoot Entertainment Ltd.* v. *Glasgow District Licensing Board*, 1990 S.C.L.R. 584 [on appeal, 1991 G.W.D. 3–166].

(2) S.18(2) confers the right on an applicant, licence-holder, objector or complainer who appeared at the hearing to request that the board give their reasons for their decision in writing. The licensing board require to give reasonably full reasons for their decision. A mere repetition of the statutory wording of the grounds for refusal is insufficient (*Martin* v. *Ellis*, *cit.*). A licensing board will be held to have failed to exercise its discretion in a reasonable manner; if it gives reasons, which are held to be inadequate: see Note to s.18 and Introduction paras. 3.26 to 3.31. A failure by the clerk of the Board to give reasons within the 21 days time limit set in s.18 (*q.v.*) may give a good ground of appeal. Where a board merely give a statutory ground as the reason for its decision the sheriff may, under para. 5 of the Act of Sederunt, request the board to give reasons, but the paragraph probably cannot be used to request a board to amplify inadequate reasons; *Leisure Inns Ltd.* v. *Perth & Kinross District Licensing Board*, 1991 G.W.D. 15–942 and Introduction para. 3.27.

(3) A sheriff may hear the appeal, notwithstanding that the request of reasons under s.18(2) was not made timeously (*H.D. Wines (Inverness) Ltd.* v. *Inverness District Licensing Board*, 1982 S.L.T. 73).

(4)(*a*) For error in law, see Walker, *Civil Remedies*, pp. 166 to 169. Error in law includes acting *ultra vires* (*Allied Breweries (U.K.) Ltd.* v. *City of Glasgow District Licensing Board*, cit., incompetence (*D. & A. Haddow* v. *City of Glasgow District Licensing Board*, 1983 S.L.T.(Sh.Ct.) 5).

(*c*) For natural justice, see Walker, *Civil Remedies*, pp. 165 to 166. There have been appeals under the Betting and Gaming Acts where the question of a breach of the rules of natural justice was raised. In *Prise* v. *Aberdeen Licensing Court*, 1974 S.L.T.(Sh.Ct.) 48 and *Hunt* v. *City of Glasgow District Licensing Board*, 1987 S.C.L.R. 244, an appeal was sustained on the ground that the court proceeded on a consideration which was unknown to the applicant. In *Low* v. *Kincardine Licensing Court*, 1974 S.L.T.(Sh.Ct.) 54, it was held to be a relevant ground of appeal that a rule of natural justice that no interested party should have an opportunity to confer with the licensing court outwith the presence of another party to the cause was broken. In *Cigaro (Glasgow) Ltd.* v. *City of Glasgow District Licensing Board*, 1983 S.L.T. 549 it was held not to be a breach of natural justice to hear only submissions and not to allow evidence to be led, where this was the practice of the licensing board. In cases under this Act, *e.g. Coppola* v. *Midlothian District Council Licensing Board*, 1983 S.L.T.(Sh.Ct.) 95, it was held to be a breach of natural justice, where a licensing board consulted with the director of environmental health at their deliberations, where he had put in a report objecting to the grant of a licence. In *Moughal* v. *Motherwell District Licensing Board*, 1983 S.L.T.(Sh.Ct.) 84 and *Roberston* v. *Inverclyde Licensing Board*, 1979 S.L.T.(Sh.Ct.) 16 it was held that the licensing board were not entitled to proceed on local knowledge of the members, where the parties were not give an opportunity to comment thereon. Whether an obviously biased intervention by a board member and the introduction of new material by an objector, which had not been previously intimated to the applicant, amounted to breaches of natural justice was considered in *Tennent Caledonian Breweries Ltd.* v. *City of Aberdeen District Licensing Board*, 1987 S.L.T.(Sh.Ct.) 2. In *Mecca Ltd.* v. *Kirkcaldy Burgh Licensing Court*, 1975 S.L.T.(Sh.Ct.) 50, it was held that a licensing court was not entitled to found on information neither adduced in evidence, nor within judicial knowledge. In *Stephen* v. *City of Aberdeen District Licensing Board*, 1989 S.L.T.(Sh.Ct.) 94, it was held not to be a breach of natural justice that the board refused to listen to a plea in mitigation after it had issued its decision on a suspension under s.31. The court held that the agent should have submitted all his arguments, including his arguments in mitigation, prior to the board retiring to consider its decision. The *ratio* is applicable to any decision under the Act which a board might have to make on the grant or refusal of a licence.

(*d*) Whether or not a board had exercised its discretion reasonably or not is a matter of law; see Introduction paras. 5.3 and 5.4 and the texts there cited. The question has arisen whether a refusal on general grounds constitutes a valid exercise of discretion; see *Re Findlay* [1985] A.C. 318, *Holt* v. *Watson*, 1983 S.L.T. 588 and *Elder* v. *Ross and Cromarty District Licensing Board*, 1990 S.L.T. 307 for a discussion on the extent to which an administrative body such as a board may give effect to a policy. In *Aitken* v. *Motherwell and Wishaw Licensing Court*, 1971 S.L.T.(Sh.Ct.) 25, it was held that a licensing court had no powers to make policy or blanket decisions (see *Re Findlay* [1985] A.C. 318), and in *Keith* v. *Dunfermline Town Council*, 1968 S.L.T.(Sh.Ct.) 51, the refusal of a permit for amusements with prizes on general grounds was found to be unreasonable. On the other hand, in *Patullo* v. *Dundee Corporation*, 1969 S.L.T. 31, *MacIntyre* v. *Elie and Earlsferry Town Council*, 1967 S.L.T.(Sh.Ct.) 78, and *MacGregor* v. *Berwickshire County Council*, 1967 S.L.T.(Sh.Ct.) 13, appeals were refused where the decision appealed against proceeded on general policy. For decisions where a licensing court was held not to have validly exercised its discretion, see *Mecca Ltd.* v. *Edinburgh Corporation*, 1967 S.L.T.(Sh.Ct.) 43; *Atherlay* v. *Lanark County Council*, 1968 S.L.T.(Sh.Ct.) 71 and *Augustus Barnett Ltd.* v. *Bute and Cowal Divisional Licensing Board*, 1989 S.L.T. 572; over-provision, failure to compare like with like, *Crolla* v. *City of Edinburgh District Licensing Board*, 1983 S.L.T.(Sh.Ct.) 11; *Lazerdale Ltd.* v. *City of Glasgow Licensing Board*, 1988 G.W.D. 36–1484 (1st Div.) where it was held that a radius of 200 metres was a reasonable "locality" under s.17(1)(*d*) within Glasgow, [it should be noted that the ground rules relating to over provision considered in the foregoing cases have been changed by the amendment to s.17(1)(*d*) introduced by the para. 6 of Sched. 8 to 1990 Act; see Note to s.17], and *Bury* v. *Kilmarnock and Loudon District Licensing Board*, 1989 S.L.T. 110, where it was held that the board had exercised its discretion unreasonably in refusing to consider an application for an extension on the basis of non-representation without asking whether that non-representation was material as they had all the facts before them.

(5) Evidence now may be led in respect of a decision based on any of the grounds of appeal. (5) Prior to amendment by para. 11 of Sched. 8 to the 1990 Act it was incompetent to lead evidence regarding any ground of appeal except an appeal arising under s.39(4)(*b*) [decision based on incorrect material fact]; see Introduction para. 6.9. This has now been amended by para. 11 of Sched. 8 to the 1990 Act and it is competent to lead evidence in regard to any of the grounds of appeal.

(6) In *Jack* v. *Edinburgh Corporation*, 1973 S.L.T.(Sh.Ct.) 64, it was held that where an appeal was considered in circumstances substantially different from those considered by the licensing authority, the proper course was to remit back to the authority for reconsideration. Where a decision is made to remit back to the licensing board, the interlocutor should include any specification or modification required under subs. (7).

(8) Appeal lies only to the Court of Session on a point of law. The licensing board have an interest to maintain an appeal to the Court of Session (*Wolfson* v. *Glasgow District Licensing Board*, 1981 S.L.T. 17 confirmed by the introduction of subs. (2A)). It is not competent to appeal from the sheriff to the sheriff principal (*Troc Sales Ltd.* v. *Kirkcaldy District Licensing Board*, *cit.*). The court can remit the case back to the sheriff with a direction that he should remit it to the licensing board to reconsider their decision (*R. W. Cairns Ltd.* v. *Busby East Church Kirk Session*, *cit.*) or remit the case to the sheriff to proceed as accords (*Collins* v. *Hamilton District Licensing Board*, 1984 S.L.T. 230).

PART III

SEAMEN'S CANTEENS

**Power to authorise grant of licences for seamen's canteens**

**40.** If a body approved by the Secretary of State have provided or propose to provide a seamen's canteen the need for which has been certified by him after consultation with the Merchant Navy Welfare Board, the licensing board within whose jurisdiction the said canteen is or will be situated may grant a licence under this Part of this Act authorising the person who is the manager of the canteen to sell alcoholic liquor in the canteen.

GENERAL NOTE

"*Alcoholic liquor*" is defined in s.139(1). As to the meaning of "*canteen*," see s.46 and s.139(1).

*Seamen's canteens—general.* This Part of the Act imposes certain duties upon licensing boards in respect of seamen's canteens. If a seamen's canteen is certified as necessary by the Secretary of State, the licensing board *may*, and in certain circumstances (see s.41(1)), *must*, grant a licence. This licence plays the same part in relation to seamen's canteens as a licence granted under Part II of the Act in relation to licensed premises. A seamen's canteen licence only permits the sale of alcoholic liquor for consumption in the canteen, and it is an offence to supply in or take from a seamen's canteen liquor for consumption off the premises (see s.96).

## Procedure for grant of licences

**41.**—(1) A licensing board shall not refuse to grant a licence under this Part of this Act except under subsection (2) below or on one or more of the following grounds—

(a) that the applicant is disqualified by or under this or any other enactment for holding a licence or is in other respects not a fit and proper person to hold a licence under this Part of this Act; or

(b) that the premises to which an application relates are not fit and convenient for the purposes of the canteen; or

(c) in a case where objection has been made to the situation of the canteen, on the ground specified in the objection; or

(d) that the applicant or body providing the canteen has entered into an agreement limiting the sources from which the alcoholic liquor or the mineral waters to be sold in the canteen may be obtained;

but nothing in this subsection shall prevent a licensing board from specifying in the licence granted by it the types of liquor (including if the board thinks fit types of liquor other than those in respect of which the application for the licence was made) which may be sold under the licence, and the holder of the licence or his employee or agent shall be guilty of an offence, if he sells alcoholic liquor of a type other than that specified in the licence.

(2) Before application is made for the grant of a licence under this Part of this Act, draft rules as to the persons entitled to use the canteen shall be prepared for submission with the application, and the licensing board shall refuse to grant the licence unless the body providing the canteen undertake to make rules for the canteen in the form of the draft, with the modifications, if any, required by the licensing board, and not to vary those rules without the consent of the licensing board.

(3) Any licence granted under this Part of this Act shall provide that at all times at which alcoholic liquor is sold, food and beverages other than alcoholic liquor shall also be provided for sale, and if such food and beverages are not so provided, the holder of the licence or his employee or agent, as the case may be, shall be guilty of an offence.

(4) Part I of Schedule 2 to this Act shall have effect as respects the notices to be given and the documents to be served on an application for the grant of a licence under this Part of this Act.

(5) A licence under this Part of this Act may, in a case where it is proposed to construct or convert premises for a seamen's canteen, be a provisional licence to be made final after the proposal has been carried out; and Part II of the said Schedule 2 shall have effect as respects such licences.

(6) Where any person desires to oppose an application for the grant of a licence under this Part of this Act, he shall, not later than seven days before the meeting of the licensing board at which the application is to be considered, give to the licensing board and to the applicant written notice

of his objection specifying the ground of his objection in the manner mentioned in section 16(2) and (3) of this Act.

(7) Notwithstanding the foregoing provisions of this section, it shall be competent for a licensing board to entertain objections from the chief constable, lodged at any time before the hearing of an application, if the licensing board is satisfied that there is sufficient reason why due notice and intimation of the objection could not be given, and in such case the chief constable shall, where practicable, cause his objections to be intimated to the applicant before the hearing.

GENERAL NOTE

A. *Power of licensing board to grant or refuse seamen's canteen licence*. The discretion of the licensing board to refuse to grant a seamen's canteen licence is limited by this section. If the necessary certification from the Secretary of State has been obtained (see s.40), the licensing board must grant the licence except on one or other of the grounds mentioned in subss. (1) and (2). The licensing board may, however, specify the types of alcoholic liquor which may be sold and these may be other than those in respect of which the application for a canteen licence was made (subs. (1)). It is an offence to sell liquors other than of the types specified in the licence. It must be a condition of all seamen's canteen licences that food and non-intoxicating drinks are always available while alcoholic liquor is being sold: subs. (3). Special procedure is provided for provisional licences where building or reconstruction has yet to be done: subs. (5), Sched. 2, Part I. For the period of currency of a seamen's canteen licence, see s.42.

The special procedure for the making of applications is prescribed in Sched. 2, Part I. As to the right to object to the grant of a licence, see note B (1)(*c*), below.

B. *Subsections*. (1) This subsection specifies the only grounds upon which a seamen's canteen licence may be refused.

(*a*) As to the persons "*disqualified by . . . this or any other enactment*" for holding a licence, see Sched. 5 for list of offences carrying disqualification under the Act.

(*b*) The applicant is bound to lodge with his application a plan of the canteen and particulars of the means of access, and of the sanitary accommodation: Sched. 2, Part I, para. 1(1)(iii).

(*c*) Where objection has been made to the situation of the canteen, it may be sustained and the application refused on that ground.

(2) A licence must be refused if the body providing the canteen fails to undertake to make rules in terms of a draft approved by the board, and to refrain from altering them without the consent of the board. Draft rules regarding the persons who are to be entitled to use the canteen must be submitted to the licensing board along with the application: subs. (2), Sched. 2, Part I, para. 1(1)(ii). See note to s.103 for rules, relating to clubs, which may have some relevance to rules for seamen's canteens. The hours for canteens are prescribed by Part V of the Act.

(3) See note to s.98 regarding the requirement to provide meals with the sale of alcohol and what constitutes a "meal."

### Renewal of licences

**42.**—(1) Section 30 of this Act shall have effect in relation to licences under this Part of this Act.

(2) If the Secretary of State has, in the calendar year in which the licence would otherwise expire, certified that the canteen is still needed, the licensing board may renew the licence.

(3) A licensing board shall not refuse an application for the renewal of a licence under this Part of this Act except under subsection (4) below or on one or more of the following grounds—

(*a*) that the manager is disqualified by or under this or any other enactment for holding a licence or is in other respects not a fit and proper person to be the holder of a licence under this Part of this Act; or

(b) that the rules as to the persons entitled to use the canteen have not been observed or that the canteen has in other respects been improperly conducted; or

(c) that the manager or the body providing the canteen has entered into an agreement of the kind mentioned in paragraph (d) of section 41(1) of this Act.

(4) On renewing a licence under this Part of this Act a licensing board may by order, to be served on the holder, direct that, within a time fixed by the order, such structural alterations shall he made in the premises comprising the canteen as the board thinks reasonably necessary to secure the proper conduct of the canteen; and if, when application for renewal of the licence is next made after the time fixed by the order has expired, it is not shown to the satisfaction of the licensing board that the order has been complied with, the licensing board may refuse to renew the licence.

If an order under this subsection is complied with, the licensing board shall not make a further order within the six years following the first-mentioned order.

(5) Any person intending to oppose an application for renewal of a licence under this Part of this Act shall, not later than seven days before the hearing of the application, give to the holder of the licence and to the licensing board notice in writing of his intention, specifying the ground of his objection in the manner mentioned in section 16(2) and (3) of this Act.

(6) Notwithstanding the foregoing provisions of this subsection, it shall be competent for the licensing board to entertain objections from the chief constable, lodged at any time before the hearing of the application if the board is satisfied that there is sufficient reason why due notice and intimation of the objection could not be given, and in such a case the chief constable shall, where practicable, cause his objections to be intimated to the applicant before the hearing.

GENERAL NOTE

*Renewal of seamen's canteen licences.* The power to renew a seamen's canteen licence is exercisable at the quarterly meeting three years after the meeting at which the licence was first granted (subs. (1), applying s.30 to seamen's canteen licences).

For the corresponding provisions regarding renewal of licences, see ss.5, 24 and 30. The corresponding provision for licensed premises with regard to structural alterations directed by the licensing board will be found in s.36. It will be noted that failure to comply with a direction regarding structural alterations to a seamen's canteen may result in a refusal to renew the licence at the next application, and not to a fine as under s.36.

The licensing board must renew a licence if, during the calendar year in which, but for renewal, it would expire, the Secretary of State certifies that the canteen is still needed, except on one or more of the four grounds mentioned in subss. (3) and (4). Intending objectors to a renewal, other than the chief constable, must give notice specifying the grounds of objection, both to the licence-holder and to the board, not later than seven days before the hearing: subs. (6). For a consideration of the law applicable to (1) objections, see notes to ss.16 and 39, and (2) a case where rules were habitually broken, see *Madin* v. *McLean* (1894) 21 R.(J.) 40; 1 Adam 376.

## Transfer of licences

**43.**—(1) Where the holder of a licence under this Part of this Act subsequently ceases to be the manager of the canteen, the person for the time being in charge of the canteen may, during the period of 14 days from the date on which the holder of the licence ceased to be the manager, sell alcoholic liquor in the canteen as if that licence had been transferred to him.

(2) A transfer of a licence under this Part of this Act shall not be refused except on the ground that the applicant is disqualified by or under this or any other enactment for holding a licence or is in other respects not a fit and proper person to hold a licence under this Part of this Act.

(3) An applicant under this section shall give the notices required by Part III of Schedule 2 to this Act.

GENERAL NOTE

*Transfer of a seamen's canteen licence.* Where the holder of a canteen licence ceases to manage the canteen, the person who is in charge for the time being can, for a period of 14 days from the date when the holder ceased to be manager, sell liquor as if the licence had been transferred to him. The procedure for applying for a transfer is prescribed by Sched. 2, Part III. The only ground of refusal (against which there is a right of appeal under s.45) is that the transferee is disqualified from holding a licence or is not a fit and proper person to hold a canteen licence (subs. (2)). For a consideration of "*fit and proper*," see note to s.17. An application for a transfer does not require to be heard by a quarterly meeting of a board but can be heard by a meeting convened under s.5(1).

## Rights of appeal

**44.** Where a licensing board—

(*a*) refuses to grant, renew or transfer a licence under this Part of this Act, or

(*b*) on an application for the grant of a licence under this Part of this Act, specifies, as types of liquor which may be sold under the licence, types other than those in respect of which the application for the licence was made, or

(*c*) on an application for renewal of a licence under this Part of this Act, does not comply with any request duly made by the applicant for a change in the specification of the types of liquor which may be sold under the licence, or

(*d*) requires modifications in the rules proposed to be made as to the persons entitled to use the canteen, or withholds its consent to a variation of those rules, or

(*e*) makes an order under section 42(4) of this Act,

the applicant, or as the case may be, the licence-holder may appeal to the sheriff from such a decision of the licensing board.

GENERAL NOTE

*Appeals against the decision of a licensing board in an application relating to a seamen's canteen licence.* The only persons who may appeal against such a decision are the applicant and the licence-holder. The decisions which may be appealed against are specified under headings (a) to (e) of the section.

(*b*) and (*c*). S.41(1) enables a licensing board to specify the types of liquor which may be sold under a seamen's canteen licence.

(*e*) In virtue of s.42(4), a licensing board may order structural alterations to a canteen.

(*d*) S.41(2) gives a licensing board power to require modifications of the draft rules desiderated by para. 1(1)(ii) of Part I of Sched. 2.

For appeals, see s.39.

## Provisions of this Act which apply to licensed canteens

**45.**—(1) The provisions of this Act mentioned in subsection (2) below shall apply to licensed canteens, to the holders of licences under this Part of this Act and to their employees and agents as if a licensed canteen were a public house and as if the licence-holder of a canteen were the licence-holder of a public house.

(2) The provisions of this Act referred to in subsection (1) above are sections 31, 35, 65, 66, 71, 76, 77, 78, 84, 85, 87, 88 and 126.

GENERAL NOTE
The definitions of licence and licence-holder in s.139(1) exclude a canteen licence and its holder. The purpose of the section is to include, for the provisions specified, seamen's canteen licences and their holders within the meaning of the definitions.

## Interpretation of Part III

**46.** In this Part of this Act, "canteen" includes a part of a hostel where food or drink is supplied, whether or not the food or drink is separately paid for.

## PART IV

## NEW TOWNS

GENERAL NOTE
Pt. IV, ss.47–52, repealed: 1981, c. 23, s.8, Sched. 4.

## PART V

## THE PERMITTED HOURS

## Permitted hours in licenced premises and registered clubs

**53.**—(1) Subject to the provisions of this Act, the permitted hours in licensed premises, licensed canteens and registered clubs shall be—

(a) for days other than Sundays, the period between eleven in the morning and eleven in the evening; and

(b) for Sundays, the period between half-past twelve and half-past two in the afternoon and the period between half-past six and eleven in the evening.

(2) Nothing in this section shall authorise the sale or supply of alcoholic liquor of consumption off the premises, being premises in respect of which a refreshment licence, an entertainment licence, a restricted hotel licence, a restaurant licence or a licence under Part III of this Act is in force.

DEFINITIONS
"entertainment licence": s.9 and Sched. 1 of the 1976 Act.
"licensed canteens": s.139(1) of the 1976 Act.
"licensed premises": s.139(1) of the 1976 Act.
"permitted hours": s.139(1) of the 1976 Act.
"refreshment licence": s.139(1) of the 1976 Act.
"registered clubs": s.139(1) of the 1976 Act.
"restaurant licence": s.9 and Sched. 1 of the 1976 Act.
"restricted hotel": s.9 and Sched. 1 of the 1976 Act.

GENERAL NOTE
This section replaces s.53 of the Licensing (Scotland) Act 1976 (inserted by s.45 of the 1990 Act) and provides new basic permitted hours in licensed premises, licensed canteens

and registered clubs. The hours for days other than Sundays are 11 a.m. to 11 p.m., thus abolishing the requirement to apply for an extension of hours on weekday afternoons. On Sunday the permitted hours remain 12.30 p.m. to 2.30 p.m. and 6.30 p.m. to 11 p.m. Premises operated under a public house or refreshment licence may have permitted hours on Sundays only where applications for Sunday opening have been granted in terms of Sched. 4 to the 1976 Act or s.46 of the 1990 Act. In cases of premises operated under hotel, restricted hotel, restaurant or entertainment licences or a registered club, basic permitted hours are the same, *i.e.* 12.30 p.m. to 2.30 p.m. and 6.30 p.m. to 11 p.m., but no application is required for Sunday opening. The new section repeats the express prohibition of Off-Sales on premises where a refreshment, entertainment, restricted hotel, or restaurant licence or a licence under Pt. III of the 1976 Act (Seamen's Canteen) is in force.

Consequent amendment is made to s.56 of the 1976 Act to allow application to the sheriff for alternative permitted hours for athletic clubs on Sundays. The alternative hours are 12.30 p.m. to 2 p.m. and 4 p.m. to 9 p.m.

### Prohibition of sale and consumption of alcoholic liquor except during permitted hours

**54.**—(1) Subject to the provisions of this Act, no person shall, except during the permitted hours—

(*a*) sell or supply to any person in any licensed premises, or licensed canteen, or in the premises of a registered club any alcoholic liquor to be consumed either on or off the premises, or

(*b*) consume in, or take from, any such premises any alcoholic liquor.

(2) Subsection (1) above shall not apply to off-sale premises or to the off-sale part of premises (within the meaning of section 119 of this Act) in respect of which a public house licence or hotel licence is held.

(3) Nothing in subsection (1) above shall prohibit or restrict—

(*a*) the consumption of alcoholic liquor in any premises at any time within 15 minutes after the conclusion of the permitted hours in the afternoon or evening, as the case may be, if such liquor was supplied in those premises during the permitted hours;

(*b*) the taking of alcoholic liquor from any premises within 15 minutes after the conclusion of the permitted hours in the afternoon or evening, as the case may be, if such liquor was supplied in those premises during the permitted hours and was not supplied or taken away in an open vessel;

(*c*) the sale or supply to, or consumption by, any person of alcoholic liquor in any premises where he is residing;

(*d*) the taking of alcoholic liquor from any premises by a person residing there;

(*e*) the supply of alcoholic liquor in any premises, for consumption on those premises, to any private friends of a person residing there who are bona fide entertained by, and at the expense of, that person, or the consumption by such friends of alcoholic liquor so supplied to them;

(*f*) the ordering of alcoholic liquor to be consumed off the premises or the despatch by the vendor of liquor so ordered;

(*g*) the supply of alcoholic liquor for consumption on licensed premises to any private friends of the holder of the licence bona fide entertained by him at his own expense, or the consumption of alcoholic liquor by persons so supplied;

(*h*) the consumption of alcoholic liquor at a meal by any person at any time within half an hour after the conclusion of the permitted hours in the afternoon or evening, as the case may be, if the liquor was supplied during the permitted hours and served at the same time as the meal and for consumption at the meal;

(i) the sale of alcoholic liquor to a trader for the purposes of his trade, or to a registered club for the purposes of the club; or

(j) the sale or supply of alcoholic liquor to any canteen in which the sale or supply of alcoholic liquor is carried on under the authority of the Secretary of State or to any authorised mess of members of Her Majesty's naval, military or air forces.

(4) If any person contravenes this section he shall be guilty of an offence.

(5) Nothing in this Act shall be taken to require any premises to be open for the sale or supply of alcoholic liquor during the permitted hours.

GENERAL NOTE

A. *General*. This section prohibits the sale or supply of alcoholic liquor in licensed premises and in the premises of registered clubs, or the consumption in, or the taking away from such premises of alcoholic liquor except during the permitted hours. It also provides certain exceptions to the general prohibition.

Certain premises such as services canteens, and passenger aircraft, vessels and railway trains, although retailer's excises licences are granted in respect of them, are not licensed premises within the meaning of the section because no licences under the Act are first obtained. To these premises, the permitted hours and the prohibition against the sale, supply and consumption outwith these hours do not apply with the exception of the restrictions on the sale of liquor on passenger vessels on Sundays imposed by s.93.

For the meaning of *"permitted hours,"* see. s.139(1).

B. *Subsections*. (1) The subsection imposes the general prohibition.

*"licensed premises,"* *"licensed canteen"* and *"registered club"* are defined in s.139(1).

For the meaning of *"alcoholic liquor,"* see s.139(1).

(2) For the meaning of *"off-sale premises,"* see s.139(1). S.119 provides for the setting off of part of public house or hotel premises for off-sales only, the part to be known as the *"off-sale part."* S.119 also lays down the permitted hours for off-sale premises.

(3) *Exemptions from prohibition*. In addition to the exemptions specified in the subsection, there is an exemption in the case of an international airport (see s.63).

(a) and (b) preserve the additional period for consuming alcoholic liquor or taking away alcoholic liquor supplied in a closed vessel purchased during the permitted hours introduced by s.3 of the 1962 Act. The period is increased to 15 minutes.

(c), (d) and (e) *"Residents at any premises."* Such persons are exempted from the provisions of subs. (1) as regards the sale or supply to, consumption of or the taking away by them of alcoholic liquor at or from the premises where they are residing ((c) and (d)). There is also an exemption in the case of the supply of alcoholic liquor for the consumption of friends of a resident who are being bona fide entertained by him at his expense at the premises where he is residing (e).

(f) *Ordering or despatching outwith permitted hours*. Although sale or supply outwith permitted hours is prohibited, liquor may be ordered outwith permitted hours for consumption off the premises, or, having been ordered for consumption off the premises, it may be despatched by the vendor outwith permitted hours. But while the certificate-holder may take the order outwith permitted hours, he must not complete the sale outwith permitted hours, by accepting payment, or handing the liquor to the customer, or delivering the liquor to the customer's house. In the same way he may only despatch the liquor to the customer outwith permitted hours, if the contract of sale has already been completed during permitted hours: *Valentine* v. *Bell*, 1930 J.C. 51; *Sinclair* v. *Beattie*, 1934 J.C. 24. To complete the sale outwith permitted hours is a contravention of subs. (1)(a) of this section, and a breach of certificate. Reference may also be made to the Sale of Goods Act 1893, s.1(3); *Titmus* v. *Littlewood* [1916] 1 K.B. 732; *Mizen* v. *Old Florida Ltd.* (1934) 50 T.L.R. 348.

(g) *Private friends of the certificate-holder*. In *Jack* v. *Thom*, 1952 J.C. 41, a party of police constables, who were celebrating the wedding of one of their number, was supplied by the certificate-holder gratuitously on his premises outwith permitted hours. The constables were known to the certificate-holder personally. The magistrates were held entitled to find that the constables were not private friends of the certificate-holder bona fide entertained by him, and to convict him of a contravention of subs. (1)(*a*) of this section. For an English decision, see *Schofield* v. *Jones* [1955] 1 W.L.R. 1133.

The earlier decisions, such as *Smith* v. *Stirling* (1879) 5 R.(J.) 24; *Boyd* v. *McJannet* (1879) 6 R.(J.) 43; *White* v. *Neilson* (1904) 6 F.(J.) 51, which supported the view that the supply of liquor during prohibited hours was not a breach of the licensing laws if it was gratuitous, must now be regarded as of little assistance.

(*h*) *Extra half-hour for consumption only*. "*Meal*" is not defined in the Act. However, the High Court of Justiciary considered the supply of exciseable liquor outwith the permitted hours where an extension of the permitted hours had been granted for the sale or supply of alcoholic liquor to persons taking a table meal, and the liquor had been supplied to persons who had not requested or been provided with a meal. See *Stewart* v. *Dunphy*, 1980 S.L.T. (Notes) 93 in which it was decided such persons were guilty of an offence. "*Half an hour after the conclusion of the permitted hours*" means half an hour after the end of the period, in the afternoon or evening as the case may be, during which the consumption of alcoholic liquor is permitted under this Part of the Act.

(*i*) *Sale to a trader or registered club*. The purpose and application of this exemption are not clear. It should be noted that it is only the sale, and not the supply, of alcoholic liquor outside permitted hours which is authorised by this provision.

(*j*) *Service canteens*. Such canteens are not licensed premises within the meaning of the Act.

(4) The maximum penalty for the sale or supply of liquor outside the permitted hours (subs. (1)(*a*)) is a fine of level 3 and disqualification of the premises and the licence-holder. The holder is vicariously liable for a contravention. The maximum penalty for the consumption of liquor outwith the permitted hours is a fine of level 3 (Sched. 5).

## Additional provisions regarding restricted hotel and restaurant licences

**55.** Section 55 repealed by 1990 (c. 40), Sched. 9.

GENERAL NOTE

*Restriction of permitted hours for restaurant or restricted hotel licence*. Where a restaurant certificate or a restricted hotel licence is being granted or transferred, if it appears to the licensing board that only a mid-day meal or an evening meal is being provided, it can restrict the permitted hours to the mid-day period, if only a mid-day meal is being provided, or to the evening period, if only an evening meal is being provided. The restriction is made effective by inserting a condition that there shall be no permitted hours in the evening or only permitted hours in the evening.

## Alternative permitted hours in certain athletic clubs during winter

**56.**—(1) A registered club may apply to the sheriff for an order providing that during the winter period the permitted hours in the club on Sundays shall not be those set out in section 53 of this Act, but shall instead be the period between half-past twelve and two in the afternoon and the period between four and nine in the evening; and the sheriff shall, if in his opinion the conditions set out in subsection (2) below are satisfied, make the order applied for.

(2) The conditions referred to in subsection (1) above are—

(*a*) that the premises of the club are structurally adapted and bona fide used, or intended to be used, wholly or mainly for the purpose of providing facilities in connection with the carrying on by members of the club and their guests of athletic sports or athletic games;

(*b*) that one or more of such sports or games is or are usually carried on out of doors and, when so carried on, can (unless artificial lighting is used) only be carried on during hours of daylight;

(*c*) that the said premises are regularly used, or are intended regularly to be used, during the winter period, for providing facilities in connection with the carrying on by members of the club and their guests, during the hours of daylight, of such a sport or game as is mentioned in paragraph (*b*) above;

(*d*) that having regard to the time at which the said sport or game is usually carried on by members of the club and their guests, the permitted hours set out in section 53 of this Act are not suitable for the supply of alcoholic liquor in the said premises to persons who participate in that sport or game.

(3) On an application for an order being made under subsection (1) above by any club, the sheriff clerk shall forthwith give notice thereof to the chief constable who may, within 21 days of the date of the receipt by him of such notice, lodge with the sheriff clerk objections to the making of such order on the ground that one or more of the conditions set out in subsection (2) above has not or have not been satisfied in relation to the club, and shall, on lodging any such objections, send a copy thereof to the secretary of the club; and if any such objections are lodged and not withdrawn, the sheriff shall, as soon as may be, hear parties upon the application and objections and may order such enquiry as he thinks fit, and shall thereafter make or refuse to make the order applied for, and may award expenses against the unsuccessful party.

(4) An order made under this section by the sheriff in respect of any club shall expire on the date on which the certificate of registration which is in force in respect of the club expires.

(5) In this section, the expression "the winter period" means the period beginning with October 1, and ending with March 31.

GENERAL NOTE
*Alternative permitted hours for athletic clubs.* This section permits sports clubs to have alternative permitted hours in the winter where the sport is played out of doors. The alternative permitted hours are, on Sundays 12.30 p.m. to 2 p.m. and 4 p.m. to 9 p.m. Amended to refer to Sundays only, as there is no longer a requirement to apply in respect of weekday afternoons, by virtue of s.45(2) of the 1990 Act. This takes account of the change in weekday permitted hours, and allows sports clubs to have alternative permitted hours on a Sunday. In order to qualify for alternative permitted hours, the club must fulfil the following conditions (subss. (1) and (2)), *viz.*: (*a*) that the club premises are adapted and used by members and their guests for carrying on athletic sports or games; (*b*) that at least one of the sports or games is carried on out of doors, and in daylight (unless artificial light is used); (*c*) that the premises are regularly used during winter and the hours of daylight for a sport specified in (*b*); (*d*) that the usual permitted hours are not suitable for the time at which the game or sport is usually played by members and their guests for the supply of liquor to those participating in the game.

The procedure is by application to the sheriff for an order granting the alternative permitted hours on Sundays. The sheriff-clerk gives notice of the application to the chief constable who can lodge objections on the ground that one or more of the conditions specified above have not been fulfilled. The chief constable must make his objections within 21 days of the receipt by him of the notice, and must, on lodging objections, send a copy of them to the secretary of the club.

Where no objections are lodged, the sheriff is bound, if he is satisfied that the conditions have been fulfilled, to grant the order (subs. (1)). Where objections are lodged, the sheriff hears parties on the application and objections, orders such inquiry as he thinks fit, and thereafter grants or refuses the order. He can award expenses against the unsuccessful party (subs. (3)). Any order made expires when the certificate of registration of the club expires.

"*Registered club*" is defined by s.139(1) of the Act as meaning a club in respect of which a certificate of registration under Part VII of the Act has been granted and is in force.

"*Winter period*" means the period October 1 to March 31 (subs. (5)).

111

**Extension of permitted hours in the afternoon in certain licensed premises and clubs**

**57.**—(1) This section shall apply to any premises for which a licence (other than an off-sale licence) is held or to the premises of a registered club—

(a) if the holder of the licence or, as the case may be, the club gives notice of the application of the section to the premises in accordance with subsection (6) below, and

(b) as from such date as may be specified in the said notice:

Provided that, in the case of premises for which a public house or a hotel licence is held or the premises of a club, the licence-holder or the club, as the case may be, shall not give notice of application as aforesaid, and this section shall not apply to such premises, unless the licensing board for the area within which the premises are situated is satisfied that the premises are structurally adapted and bona fide used, or intended to be used, for the purpose of habitually providing the customary main meal at midday for the accommodation of persons frequenting the premises.

(2) While this section applies to any premises, the effect shall be that, for the purposes mentioned in subsection (3) below, the permitted hours in those premises in the afternoon on Sundays shall be increased by the addition of one and a half hours at the end thereof.

(3) The purposes referred to in subsection (2) above are—

(a) the sale or supply to persons taking table meals in the premises of alcoholic liquor supplied in a part of the premises usually set apart for the service of such persons, and supplied for consumption by such a person in that part of the premises as an ancillary to his meal; and

(b) the consumption of alcoholic liquor so supplied.

(4) While this section applies to any premises, then for purposes other than those mentioned in subsection (3) above, or in parts of the premises other than the part so mentioned, the permitted hours shall be the same as if this section did not apply to the premises.

(5) This section shall cease to apply to any premises on such day as may be specified in the notice, if the holder of the licence or the club, as the case may be, gives notice of the disapplication of the section from the premises in accordance with subsection (6) below:

Provided that this section shall cease to apply to premises for which a public house or a hotel licence is held, or to the premises of a club, at any time on the licensing board ceasing to be satisfied as mentioned in the proviso to subsection (1) above.

(6) A notice of the application of this section to, or of the disapplication of this section from, any premises—

(a) shall be in writing;

(b) shall, in the case of a club, be given by the secretary of the club on its behalf;

(c) shall, in the case of a notice of application, specify the date from which the section is to apply to the premises and, in the case of a notice of disapplication, state that the section is to cease to apply to the premises on the date specified in the notice;

(*d*) shall be served on the chief constable not later than 14 days before the date specified as aforesaid.

(7) The secretary of any club to the premises of which this section applies shall notify the licensing board for the area within which such premises are situated of any reconstruction or extension of, or alteration in, the premises which affects the facilities available in the premises for the provision of the customary main meal at midday, and if the secretary of any club contravenes this subsection he shall be guilty of an offence.

(8) The holder of the licence for premises to which this section applies shall keep posted in some conspicuous place in the premises a notice stating that this section applies thereto and setting out the effect of its application, and if any person contravenes this subsection he shall be guilty of an offence.

GENERAL NOTE

A. *Extension of permitted hours in the afternoon in licensed premises and clubs.* Licensed premises (other than off-sale premises) and clubs may obtain an extension of the permitted hours in the afternoon on Sundays in order to supply alcoholic liquor for consumption, as an ancillary to a table meal, in a part of the premises set aside and adapted for meals. The procedure is by the holder of the licence or the club giving notice of application of the section to the premises, the notice specifying the date it is intended to apply the section to the premises (subs. (1)(*a*) and (b)). Before, however, notice is given in respect of premises for which a hotel or public house licence is held or in respect of the premises of a registered club, a declaration of the licensing board's satisfaction that the premises are constructed and used (or intended to be used) for providing for the accommodation of persons frequenting the premises the customary main meal at mid-day must be obtained. For discussion of "usually set apart" see *McAlpine v. Heatly*, 1967 J.C. 537.

Notice of application of the section must (i) be in writing (subs. (6)(*a*)); (ii) specify the date from which the section is to apply (subs. (6)(*c*)); and (iii) be served on the chief constable more than 14 days before the date of application of the section (subs. (6)(*d*)). Once the section has been applied to premises the afternoon permitted hours are extended on Sundays by one and a half hours for the sale and supply of liquor for the purposes specified in subs. (3). The licence-holder of premises to which the section applies must exhibit in a conspicuous place a notice stating that the section applies and the effect of its application (subs. (8)). Where a club has supplied the section, the secretary must notify the licensing board for the area of any alteration to, reconstruction of or extension to, that part of the premises where the main meal is provided.

*Disapplication of section to premises.* The holder of a licence or a club can disapply the section to premises by giving notice specifying the date of disapplication which fulfils the requirements of subs. (6). A licensing board may disapply the section to premises at any time if they cease to be satisfied that the requirements of the proviso to subs. (1) have been met.

B. *Subsections.* (1) For the meaning of "*licence*" and "*registered club*," see s.139(1). For the meaning of "*off-sale licence*," see Sched. 1.

(2) "*Permitted hours*" are defined in s.139(1). The effect of the application of the section to premises is to extend the permitted hours in the afternoon to 4 p.m.

(3) For the meaning of "*table meal*," see s.139(1).

(4) The purpose of the subsection is to make it clear that the extension of the permitted hours on Sundays only applies to the part of the premises set apart for the consumption of main meals by a person having a table meal there.

(7) The maximum penalty for a contravention of the section is a fine of level 3 (Sched. 5).

(8) The maximum penalty for a contravention of the subsection is a fine of level 1 (Sched. 5).

## Extension of permitted hours in the evening in certain licensed premises and clubs

**58.**—(1) This section shall apply to any premises for which a licence (other than an off-sale licence) is held or to the premises of a registered club—

(a) if the holder of the licence or, as the case may be, the club gives notice of the application of the section to the premises in accordance with subsection (6) below, and

(b) as from such date as may be specified in the said notice:

Provided that, in the case of premises for which a public house or a hotel licence is held or the premises of a club, the licence-holder or the club, as the case may be, shall not give notice of application as aforesaid and this section shall not apply to such premises, unless the licensing board for the area within which the premises are situated is satisfied that the premises are structurally adapted and bona fide used, or intended to be used, for the purpose of habitually providing, for the accommodation of persons frequenting the premises, substantial refreshment to which the sale and supply of alcoholic liquor is ancillary.

(2) While this section applies to any premises, the effect shall be that for the purposes mentioned in subsection (3) below the permitted hours in those premises in the evening shall be increased by the addition of two hours at the end thereof.

(3) The purposes referred to in subsection (2) above are—

(a) the sale or supply to persons taking table meals in the premises of alcoholic liquor supplied in a part of the premises usually set apart for the service of such persons, and supplied for consumption by such a person in that part of the premises as an ancillary to his meal; and

(b) the consumption of alcoholic liquor so supplied.

(4) While this section applies to any premises, then for purposes other than those mentioned in subsection (3) above, or in parts of the premises other than the part so mentioned, the permitted hours shall be the same as if this section did not apply to the premises.

(5) This section shall cease to apply to any premises on such day as may be specified in the notice if the holder of the licence or the club, as the case may be, gives notice of the disapplication of the section from the premises in accordance with subsection (6) below:

Provided that this section shall cease to apply to premises for which a public house or a hotel licence is held, or to the premises of a club, at any time on the licensing board ceasing to be satisfied as mentioned in the proviso to subsection (1) above.

(6) A notice of the application of this section to, or of the disapplication of this section from, any premises—

(a) shall be in writing;

(b) shall, in the case of a club, be given by the secretary of the club on its behalf;

(c) shall, in the case of a notice of application, specify the date from which the section is to apply to the premises and, in the case of a notice of disapplication, state that the section is to cease to apply to the premises on the date specified in the notice;

(d) shall be served on the chief constable not later than 14 days before the date specified as aforesaid.

(7) The secretary of any club to the premises of which this section applies shall notify the licensing board for the area within which such

premises are situated of any reconstruction or extension of, or alteration in, the premises which affects the facilities available in the premises for the provision of substantial refreshment, and if the secretary of any club contravenes this subsection he shall be guilty of an offence.

(8) The holder of the licence for premises to which this section applies shall keep posted in some conspicuous place in the premises a notice stating that this section applies thereto and setting out the effect of its application, and if any person contravenes this subsection he shall be guilty of an offence.

GENERAL NOTE

*Extension of permitted hours in the evening.* The section enacts similar provisions to the previous section for the purpose of enabling the extension of the permitted hours by two hours in the evening. In the case of such an extension, the premises have to be adapted and used for providing substantial refreshment to which the sale and supply of liquor is ancillary (subs. (1)), whereas, in the case of an afternoon extension, the premises have to be adapted and used for providing the customary main meal at mid-day.

## Restaurants in public houses may have permitted hours on Sundays in certain cases

**59.**—(1) This section shall apply to any premises for which a public house licence is held and in respect of which there are no permitted hours on a Sunday—

(*a*) if the holder of the licence gives notice of the application of the section to the premises in accordance with subsection (6) below, and

(*b*) as from such date as may be specified in the said notice:

Provided that a licence-holder shall not give notice of application as aforesaid, and this section shall not apply to the premises for which he holds his licence, unless—

(i) the licensing board for the area within which the premises are situated is satisfied that the premises are structurally adapted and bona fide used, or intended to be used, for the purpose of habitually providing the customary main meal at midday or in the evening, or both, for the accommodation of persons frequenting the premises, and that the part of the premises mentioned in subsection (3) below does not contain a bar counter.

(ii) [repealed 1981 c. 23, Sched. 4.]

(2) While this section applies to any premises, the effect shall be that for the purposes mentioned in subsection (3) below there shall be permitted hours in those premises on Sundays, such permitted hours being the period between half-past twelve and half-past two in the afternoon and the period between half-past six and eleven in the evening.

(3) The purposes referred to in subsection (2) above are—

(*a*) the sale or supply to persons taking table meals in the premises of alcoholic liquor supplied in a part of the premises usually set apart for the service of such persons, and supplied for consumption by such a person in that part of the premises as an ancillary to his meal; and

(*b*) the consumption of alcoholic liquor so supplied.

(4) While this section applies to any premises, then for purposes other than those mentioned in subsection (3) above, or in parts of the premises other than the part so mentioned, or except as otherwise provided by this Act, there shall be no permitted hours on Sundays.

(5) This section shall cease to apply to premises on such day as may be specified in the notice if the holder of the licence gives notice of the disapplication of the section from the premises in accordance with subsection (6) below:

Provided that this section shall cease to apply to premises at any time on the licensing board ceasing to be satisfied as mentioned in paragraph (i) of the proviso to subsection (1) above.

(6) A notice of the application of this section to, or of the disapplication of this section from, any premises—

(a) shall be in writing;

(b) shall, in the case of a notice of application, specify the date from which the section is to apply to the premises and, in the case of a notice of disapplication, state that the section is to cease to apply to the premises on the date specified in the notice;

(c) shall be served on the chief constable not later than 14 days before the date specified as aforesaid.

(7) The holder of the licence for premises to which this section applies shall keep posted in some conspicuous place in the premises a notice stating that this section applies thereto and setting out the effect of its application, and if any licence-holder contravenes this subsection he shall be guilty of an offence.

GENERAL NOTE

*Permitted hours for restaurants in public houses on Sundays.* The section only applies to public houses (for meaning of *"public house,"* see s.139(1)) in respect of which applications for permitted hours on a Sunday have not been granted, and, in respect of which, part of the premises have been adapted and set aside for the provision of the customary main meal at mid-day or in the evening or both. The wording of s.59 is amended by s.45(5) of the 1990 Act to include reference to permitted hours on a Sunday granted other than in terms of an application under Sched. 4 of the 1976 Act. The procedure for applying the section to the premises is similar to the procedure under s.57. Before a licence-holder can apply the section to his premises, he has to obtain a declaration of satisfaction from the licensing board that part of his premises are adapted and used or intended to be used for habitually providing the customary main meal at mid-day or in the evening and that the adapted part does not contain a bar counter (subs. (1)). (For the meaning of *"bar,"* see s.139(1). For the requirements excluding places at which meals are served or places at which alcoholic liquor is dispensed from being within the meaning of *"bar counter,"* see s.139(2)).

Once the section has been applied to premises, liquor can be supplied for consumption at a table meal (for the meaning of *"table meal,"* see s.139(1)) as an ancillary to the meal in that part of the premises set aside for meals between 12.30 p.m. and 2.30 p.m. and 6.30 p.m. and 11 p.m. on Sundays (subss. (2) and (3)). A notice stating the application of the section to premises and its effects must be exhibited, otherwise the licence-holder commits an offence (subs. (7)), the maximum penalty for which is a fine of level 1 (Sched. 5). The mode of disapplication of the section to premises is the same as that prescribed by s.57.

## Other provisions as respect extension of permitted hours on Sundays

**60.**—(1) This section shall apply to any premises for which a hotel licence, restricted hotel licence, or restaurant licence is held and to any premises for which a public house licence or refreshment licence is held and in respect of which there are permitted hours on Sundays in accordance with section 53 of this Act if the licence-holder gives notice of the application of the section to the premises in accordance with the provisions of section 58(1) of this Act, and the effect of the application of this section to those premises shall be that, for the purposes mentioned in section 58(3) of this Act, the permitted hours on Sundays shall be extended by the addition to them of the hours between five and half-past six in the evening, and subsections (4), (5), (6) and (8) of that section shall apply accordingly.

(2) This section shall apply to any premises for which a public house licence is held and to which section 59 of this Act applies if the licence-holder gives notice of the application of the section to the premises in accordance with the provisions of subsection (1) of section 59 of this Act, and the effect of the application of this section to those premises shall be that, for the purposes mentioned in subsection (3) of section 59 of this Act, the permitted hours on Sundays shall be extended by the addition to them of the hours between five and half-past six in the evening, and subsections (5) to (7) of that section shall apply accordingly.

GENERAL NOTE
*Extension of permitted hours on Sundays.* The section prescribes the procedure under which premises operated under an hotel licence, a restricted hotel licence, a restaurant licence, a public house licence, or a refreshment licence (where, as regards premises operated under the latter two types of licence, there are permitted hours on a Sunday—amended by s.46(6) of the 1990 Act) may have permitted hours on a Sunday which commence at 5 p.m. (subs. (1)). The section also makes similar provisions for premises operated under a public house licence to which s.59 applies (subs. (2)).

## Six-day licences

**61.**—(1) [ . . . ]

GENERAL NOTE
Section 61 repealed by 1990 (c. 40), Sched. 9.

## Seasonal licences

**62.**—(1) On granting or transferring a licence in respect of any premises, a licensing board may, if the applicant so requests and if the board is satisfied that the requirements of the area for which the board is constituted make it desirable, insert in the licence a condition that, during such part or parts of the year as may be specified in the condition (being a part which is not longer, or parts which taken together are not longer, than 180 days),—

(*a*) in the case of premises other than off-sale premises, there shall be no permitted hours in the premises; or

(*b*) in the case of hotel premises, there shall be no permitted hours in the premises except in that part or those parts of the premises which consist of a bar or a restaurant which is open to the public; or

(*c*) in the case of off-sale premises, the licence-holder shall not open the premises for the serving of customers with alcoholic liquor.

(2) A licence in which such a condition has been inserted is in this Act referred to as a seasonal licence.

GENERAL NOTE

*Seasonal certificates.* Under the 1959 Act, a certificate-holder could not obtain a certificate which allowed him to open his premises for a part of the year only. This section repeats the provision introduced by the 1962 Act for the insertion of a condition in a licence which permits the licence-holder to close for part or parts of the year only, such part or parts not to be longer than 180 days. In addition, the section permits a licensing board to allow the holder of a hotel licence to operate his bar or restaurant during a period when the residential parts of the hotel are closed. Where such a condition is inserted into a licence, the licence is to be known as a "seasonal licence." There is no restriction on the type of licence which can be made a seasonal licence.

When a certificate is being granted or transferred, the applicant may request a seasonal certificate. The licensing board, before granting the request, must be satisfied that the requirements of the licensing area make a seasonal certificate desirable. They may then insert a condition in the certificate that for part or parts of the year (totalling not more than 180 days), in the case of off-sales premises, the certificate-holder shall not supply customers with alcoholic liquor, and in the case of all other premises that there shall be no permitted hours. In the case of the additional provision, the condition is that there shall be no permitted hours except in a bar or restaurant open to the public.

"*Grant*" includes grant by way of renewal. For the meaning of "*off-sale premises*," see s.139(1).

As to appeals, see *Wallace* v. *Kyle and Carrick Licensing Board*, 1979 S.L.T.(Sh.Ct.) 12.

## Exemption of international airports from restrictions on times at which alcoholic liquor may be sold or supplied

**63.**—(1) The Secretary of State may by order bring this section into operation at any airport which appears to him to be an airport at which there is a substantial amount of international passenger traffic.

(2) At an airport where this section is in operation, neither section 54 nor section 119 of this Act nor any provision or rule of law prohibiting or restricting the sale or supply of alcoholic liquor on Sunday shall apply to licensed premises which are within the examination station approved for the airport under section 22 of the Customs and Excise Management Act 1979.

(3) Before the Secretary of State makes an order bringing this section into operation at an airport, he shall satisfy himself that arrangements have been made for affording reasonable facilities in licensed premises within the said examination station on the airport for obtaining hot and cold beverages other than alcoholic liquor at all times when alcoholic liquor is obtainable for consumption in those premises, and if it appears to him that at any airport where this section is in operation such arrangements are not being maintained he shall revoke the order in force as respects that airport; but this subsection shall be without prejudice to his power of making a further order with respect to that airport.

(4) The power of making orders under this section shall include power to revoke a previous order and shall be exercisable by statutory instrument.

GENERAL NOTE

Subs. (2) amended, 1979, c. 2, Sched. 4, para. 12.

*Subsections.* (2) S.54 prescribes the permitted hours for all premises with the exception of off-sale premises. S.119 prescribes the permitted hours for the excepted premises.

(2) and (3) For the meanings of "*alcoholic liquor*" and "*licensed premises,*" see s.139(1). "*Examination station*" is the part of, or the place at, a custom airport approved by the Commissioners of Customs and Excise, in terms of the Customs and Excise Act 1979, s.22(1) for the loading and unloading of goods, and the embarkation and disembarkation of passengers.

### Occasional and regular extensions of permitted hours

**64.**—(1) Any person holding a public house licence, a hotel licence, a restricted hotel licence, a restaurant licence, an entertainment licence, a refreshment licence or a licence under Part III of this Act, in respect of any premises, may apply to the licensing board within whose area the premises are situated for the grant of an occasional or regular extension of permitted hours, and at the same time as he makes the applcation he shall send a copy of the application to the chief constable.

(2) A licensing board may grant an application for an occasional extension of permitted hours in connection with any occasion which the board considers appropriate, and such a grant shall authorise the person to whom it was granted to sell or supply alcoholic liquor in the premises to which the application relates during such period not exceeding one month and between such hours and on such day as may be specified in the grant.

(3) After considering the application and any objections made thereto, a licensing board may grant an application for the regular extension of permitted hours if, having regard to the social circumstances of the locality in which the premises in respect of which the application is made are situated or to activities taking place in that locality, the board considers it is desirable to do so, and such a grant shall authorise the person to whom it was granted to sell or supply alcoholic liquor in the premises to which the application relates during such period in the year succeeding the date of the grant and between such hours and on such days as may be specified in the grant.

(3A) Where a licence has been transferred by virtue of section 25 of this Act and an application under subsection (1) above has been granted under subsection (2) or (3) above to the previous holder of the licence, the reference in subsections (2) and (3) above to the person whose application has been granted shall include a reference to the person to whom the licence has been transferred.

(4) A licensing board shall not grant an application from the holder of a public house licence for an occasional or regular extension of permitted hours on Sundays except—

    (*a*) as respects premises to which section 59 of this Act applies and for the purposes of that section; and

    (*b*) in the case of other premises, as respects any period or periods after half-past two in the afternoon,

and the board shall refuse to grant such an application if it finds that the extension of permitted hours would cause undue disturbance or public nuisance in the locality.

(4A) Nothing in subsection (4) above shall prevent the granting of an application for an occasional or regular extension of permitted hours on a Saturday for a period which continues into Sunday morning.

(5) The secretary of a registered club may apply to the licensing board within whose area the premises of the club are situated for the grant of an occasional or regular extension of permitted hours under this section, and the licensing board may grant such an extension if it is satisfied as to the matters mentioned in subsection (2) or (3) above or, in the case of an application for an occasional extension of permitted hours, consider that the occasion or circumstances in respect of which the application is made arise out of or are related to the functions of the club or a private function organised by an individual member or group of members of the club.

(6) A licensing board may attach such conditions as it thinks fit to the grant of an occasional or regular extension of permitted hours under this section, and if—

(a) the holder of a licence or his enployee or agent contravenes such a condition he shall be guilty of an offence; or

(b) such a condition is contravened as regards any club, every person whose name is, at the time of the contravention, contained in the list lodged under subsection (3)(b) of section 103 of this Act, or as the case may be in the new list last lodged under subsection (5) or (5A) of that section, in respect of that club shall be guilty of an offence:

Provided that a person shall not be convicted of an offence under this paragraph if he proves that the contravention in question took place without his knowledge or consent.

(7) Any person mentioned in section 16(1) of this Act may object to an application for the regular extension of permitted hours, and any such objection shall be made in writing and lodged with the clerk of the licensing board and a copy thereof sent to the applicant not less than seven days before the quarterly meeting at which the application is to be considered.

(8) A licensing board shall not grant an extension of permitted hours under this section if it considers that the extension of permitted hours under this section is likely to cause undue public nuisance or to be a threat to public order or safety.

(9) Where a licensing board has refused an application under subsection (1) above for the grant of an occasional or regular extension of permitted hours in respect of any premises, the board shall not, within one year of its refusal, entertain a subsequent application for such an extension in respect of the same premises unless the board, at the time of refusing the first-mentioned application, makes a direction to the contrary.

GENERAL NOTE

Subs. (6) amended, 1980, c. 55, s.21.

New subs. (3A) inserted by s.51(5) of the 1990 Act.

New subs. (4) inserted by s.46(7) of the 1990 Act.

New subs. (9) inserted by para. 12 of Sched. 8 of the 1990 Act.

A. *General.* The section provides for the occasional and regular extensions of the permitted hours. The Act enables a board to grant an occasional extension of the permitted hours in connection with any occasion the board considers appropriate (subs. (2)). A copy of the application for an extension has to be sent to the chief constable (subs. (1)). In the case of an application for a regular extension, any person or body entitled to object to the grant, renewal or transfer of a licence under s.16(1) may object (subs. (7)), and a board are only to grant such an extension if they consider it desirable to do so having regard to the social circumstances or the activities in the locality in which the premises in respect of which the application is made are situated (subs. (3)). New criteria for consideration of an application for an extension of permitted hours inserted by s.47 of the 1990 Act (see below). An application for the extension of the permitted hours is to be refused if it is likely to cause nuisance or to threaten public order or safety (subs. 8)). Public houses can only obtain an extension for a Sunday inserted by s.46(7) of the 1990 Act (subs. (4)). The section provides for a registered club applying for an extension (subs. (5)) and for the insertion of conditions in the grant of an extension (subs. (6)).

B. *Subsections.* (1) For *"public house licence," "hotel licence," "restricted hotel licence," "restaurant licence"* and *"entertainment licence,"* see Sched. 1. *"A licence under Part III of this Act"* means a licence for a seamen's canteen.

(1) Amended by para. 12 of Sched. 8 of the 1990 Act to allow the holder of a refreshment licence to apply for an extension.

(2) An occasional extension cannot be for a longer period than one month.

(4) S.64(4) of the 1976 Act is replaced by a new subsection which allows a holder of a public house licence to apply for an occasional or regular extension of permitted hours on a Sunday but only in respect of premises to which s.59 of the 1976 Act applies, namely premises permitted to open on a Sunday during permitted hours of which all or part is structurally adapted and bona fide used for providing meals at midday or in the evening and which do not have a bar counter; or in respect of other premises to which s.59 does not apply, only for periods after 2.30 p.m. A licensing board must refuse the application if it finds that such an extension of hours would cause undue disturbance or public nuisance in the locality. The new s.64(4) applies a stricter test than that which applies to other applications under the section. This subsection applies a different test from that which applies to the other applications under the section, where the test in terms of s.64(8) of the 1976 Act requires the licensing board to refuse if it *considers* the extension is *likely* to cause undue public nuisance or to be a threat to public order or safety.

*New subs. (4A).* This clarifies the position as regards an extension granted on Saturday evening which extends into Sunday morning. In the past certain boards have interpreted s.64(4) as a prohibition of the extended hours on a Sunday altogether in public houses and have not allowed a Saturday evening extension to go beyond midnight. The addition of the new subsection confirms that a Saturday evening extension granted in respect of premises with a public house licence can continue into the Sunday following.

(6)(*a*) The maximum penalty for a contravention of the subsection is a fine of level 3 with both the licence-holder and the premises liable to disqualification. The offence is one for which the licence-holder is vicariously liable (Sched. 5).

(6)(*b*) The intention of the Act that all the members of the governing body of the club should be liable for certain offences was frustrated by the fact that only the secretary's name appeared in the Register of Clubs. Section 103 as amended provides for a list of members and officials to be lodged and kept up to date.

(9) Amended by para. 12 of Sched. 8 of the 1990 Act to introduce to applicants for occasional and regular extensions a similar prohibition to that which applies under s.14 of the 1976 Act to applications for a new licence which have been refused to the effect that a further application cannot be made for two years without a direction made at the time of refusal that such an application could be made. The amendment provides that where an applicant for an occasional or regular extension is refused, a further application cannot be made within one year of the refusal unless the board at the time of the refusal makes a contrary direction. Where a refusal is intimated at a board meeting, it is important that the party or agent appearing makes an immediate application for such a direction, because *the direction must be given at the time of the refusal*; see note to s.14.

It was decided in the case of *Sloan* v. *North East Fife District Licensing Board*, 1978 S.L.T.(Sh.Ct.) 62 that an appeal against the refusal of a s.64 application was incompetent. However see introduction 6.12, judicial review. See Lord Jauncey's comments in respect of judicial review in *Mecca Bookmakers (Scotland) Ltd.* v. *East Lothian District Licensing Board*, 1988 S.L.T. 520. See also *Bantop Ltd.* v. *City of Glasgow District Licensing Board*, 1990 S.L.T. 366, 1989 S.C.L.R. 731, where the board refused an application for regular extension stating that although the social circumstances of the locality made it desirable to grant the application (which was a renewal of extended hours enjoyed by the premises previously) an adverse environmental health report made it undesirable that large numbers of people should be permitted to consume alcohol in the premises late at night. The applicant argued that the premises should have been inspected at the date of the hearing and also that the reasons for refusal were an irrelevant consideration in terms of s.64(3). It was held that the test under s.64(3) was whether, having regard to social circumstances, the board considered it desirable to grant the extension. The Act provided procedure for dealing with unsatisfactory conditions and the board should have used the alternative procedures open to them. *Elder* v. *Ross & Cromarty District Licensing Board*, 1990 S.L.T. 307, 1990 S.C.L.R. 1 where it was held that there was no objection to a statutory body with discretionary power announcing a general policy when examining applications, provided that it was based on proper grounds, did not override discretion and still permitted individual consideration of the application on its merits. Obiter, to apply such a policy might be desirable to achieve consistency. *Semple* v. *Glasgow District Licensing Board*, 1990 S.C.L.R. 73, where it was argued that the board policy was so rigidly formulated that it disabled the board from exercising their discretion properly. Held, nothing in the policy which excluded applications being considered on their individual merits, therefore not inconsistent with the terms of the Act.

*Sangha* v. *Bute & Cowal Divisional Licensing Board* 1990 S.C.L.R. 409, refusal of a regular extension following an objection by the chief constable based on various offences within and near the premises. Argued that no distinction had been made between instants arising from the use of the premises for entertainment and these from the use of the premises for the sale of alcohol. Held, the two uses of the premises were related and the board addressed the correct question whether the use of the premises for the sale of alcohol had led to undue public nuisance and disturbance of public order. Observed, the board were entitled to take into account incidents previously founded on in an unsuccessful application to suspend the licence by the chief constable and no distinction can be drawn between offences connected with public order and other offences such as theft or misuse of drugs. *Harpspot Ltd*. v. *City of Glasgow District Licensing Board*, 1990 G.W.D. 39–2269, refusal of a provisional entertainment licence with regular extension of permitted hours. Over provision objection rejected, and it was accepted that any noise nuisance could be dealt with by the Environmental Health Department. Refused on the grounds that it was inevitable that on closing there would be noise amounting to undue public nuisance in the early hours. Held the legislator enacted that such licences could be issued, and therefore presume that such licences would not inevitably cause public nuisance.

LAW REFORM (MISCELLANEOUS PROVISIONS) (SCOTLAND) ACT 1990 s.47.

S. 47 of the 1990 Act and Note thereto provides:

**Regular extensions of permitted hours**

**47.**—(1) A licensing board shall not grant an application under section 64 of the principal Act for an extension of permitted hours unless it is satisfied by the applicant, taking account of the factors mentioned in subsection (3) of that section—

(a) that there is a need in the locality in which the premises in respect of which the application is made are situated for a regular extension of the permitted hours; and

(b) that such an extension is likely to be of such benefit to the community as a whole as to outweigh any detriment to that locality.

(2) In determining whether to grant an application for a regular extension to permitted hours in respect of any premises it shall not be a relevant consideration for the licensing board to have regard to whether any application relating to any other premises in its area has, at any time, been granted or refused or the grounds on which any such application has been granted or refused.

(3) Expressions used in this section and in the principal Act shall have the same meaning as in the Act.

GENERAL NOTE
This section extends the criteria to be taken into account by the licensing board when considering an extension of permitted hours in terms of s.64 of the 1976 Act. The wide discretion given to licensing boards in respect of their consideration of occasional and regular extensions has been restricted by the new wording, which states that a Board "shall not" grant an application unless satisfied, by the applicant, having regard to the social circumstances of the locality and to activities taking place in that locality (s.64(3)) that there is a need for an extension of permitted hours *and* that an extension is likely to be of such benefit to the community as a whole as to outweigh any detriment.

*Subs. (1)*
This places the onus on the applicant to place before the board sufficient material upon which it may be satisfied with regard to the requirements set out in the 1976 Act.

*Subs. (2)*
This reinforces the requirement that each application for regular extension of permitted hours be considered on its own individual merits, and makes it irrelevant to consider that (1) other premises in the board's area may have been granted or refused extended hours or (2) the grounds upon which an application in respect of other premises was granted or refused. (For refusal see s.64(8) and Sched. 8, para. 12, to this Act.)

## Restriction orders

**65.**—(1) Where, on a complaint being made to a licensing board by any person mentioned in section 16(1) of this Act in respect of any licensed premises or registered club, the board is satisfied that—

(*a*) the sale or supply of alcoholic liquor in the afternoon or in the evening in licensed premises or in a registered club is the cause of undue public nuisance or constitutes a threat to public order or safety; or

(*b*) the use of licensed premises is the cause of undue disturbance or public nuisance having regard to the way of life in the locality on a Sunday,

the board may make an order, in this section referred to as an "afternoon restriction order" or "evening restriction order" in the case of the grounds mentioned in paragraph (*a*) above or as a "Sunday restriction order" in the case of the grounds mentioned in paragraph (*b*) above; and, in this section, "restriction order" includes any such order.

(1A) The effect of an afternoon restriction order is that the permitted hours between half-past two and five in the afternoon shall be reduced by such a time and for such a period as may be specified in the order.

(1B) The effect of an evening restriction order is that the permitted hours in the evening shall be reduced by such a time and for such a period as may be specified in the order but no such order shall restrict the permitted hours before 10 in the evening.

(1C) The effect of a Sunday restriction order is that there shall be no permitted hours on Sunday for such period as may be specified in the order or that the permitted hours on Sunday shall be reduced by such a time and for such a period as may be so specified.

(2) The provisions of subsections (4) to (6) of section 31 of this Act shall, with any necessary modifications, apply in relation to a restriction order as they apply in relation to the suspension of a licence.

(3) The licensing board may make a restriction order in relation to individual premises or in relation to a group of premises in respect of

which the same type of licence is held provided that no restriction order shall be made in respect of premises in respect of which no complaint has been made.

(4) An application for the revocation of a restriction order may only be made after the expiry of two-thirds of the period for which the restriction order is in force.

(5) An application for the revocation of a restriction order shall be made in writing by the licence-holder of the premises or by the secretary of the registered club to which the order relates and lodged with the clerk of the licensing board not less than 21 days before the quarterly meeting at which the application is to be considered, and the licence-holder or secretary shall, at the same time, send a copy of the application to the persons whose complaint led to the making of the restriction order.

(6) Any person competent to make a complaint under this section may object to the revocation of a restriction order, and any such objection shall be made in writing and lodged with the clerk of the licensing board and a copy thereof sent to the licence-holder or to the registered club not less than seven days before the quarterly meeting at which the application for revocation is to be considered.

(7) After considering the application and any objections made thereto, the licensing board may take such decision in the matter as it thinks fit and any such decision may relate to all or any of the premises which are the subject of the restriction order.

(8) The holder of the licence or a registered club may appeal to the sheriff against a decision of a licensing board to make a restriction order or against the period specified in a restriction order or against a refusal of the board to revoke the order, and any complainer who appeared at the hearing of an application for the revocation of a restriction order may appeal to the sheriff against a decision of the board to revoke the order.

GENERAL NOTE

A. *Restriction order.* Clayson considered that an extension of the duration of the permitted hours might have an effect on the amenity of an area where licensed premises are situated and that, where such an effect occurred, there should be a procedure available for cutting back the terminal permitted hour (para. 9.71). The section makes provision for the restriction of the permitted hours where the sale of liquor in premises or registered clubs causes disturbance or threats to safety. The procedure is initiated by complaint to the appropriate licensing board. The complaint may be made by any person or body entitled to object to the grant of a licence in virtue of s.16(1), *viz.* any person owning or occupying property in the neighbourhood of the premises to which the complaint relates or organisation representing such persons, a community council, an organised church representing a significant body of opinion in that neighbourhood, and the chief constable (s.16(1)). On receipt of the complaint, the board decide whether to have a hearing on the matter and inform the complainant of their decision (subs. (2) and s.31(4)). Such a decision may be taken at an arrangement convened under s.5(1) as well as a full meeting of the board convened under s.4. Where the board decide to hold a hearing, the provisions of s.31(5) have to be followed (subs. (2)). Following the hearing, the board, if they are satisfied that the sale of liquor on the premises to which the complaint relates, is the cause of "undue public nuisance, or constitutes a threat to public order or safety" may make a restriction order restricting the permitted hours in the evening to such time as is specified in the order but not to a time earlier than 10 p.m. (subs. (1)). The holder of a licence in respect of which a restriction order has been made may appeal against the order to the sheriff (subs. (8)), and the order is not to come into effect until the time within which an appeal may be taken (14 days from the date of the decision complained against) (s.39(1)), or until the appeal has been determined or abandoned (subs. (2) and s.31(6)). An unsuccessful complainant can also appeal. A restriction order may be made in relation to a group of premises operated under the same type of licence or to individual premises (subs. (3)). The provisions of s.65 of the 1976 Act have been extended by s.48 of the 1990 Act to take account of the new and extended permitted hours on weekdays and Sunday (see ss.45, 46 and para. 12 of Sched. 8 to the 1990 Act) for the restriction of permitted hours for the sale of liquor in premises or registered clubs where such sale is the cause of undue public nuisance or constitutes a threat to public safety or order or the use of the premises is the cause of disturbance or a threat to public order or safety, on a Sunday. The phrase "any person entitled to object to the grant of a licence" in terms of s.16(1) of the 1976 Act, is amended by para. 5 of Sched. 8 to the 1990 Act. The section distinguishes between difficulties arising as a result of a sale or supply of alcoholic liquor in the afternoon, in the evening and on Sundays. The restriction order which the board is authorised to make must now relate to the particular part of the day in which the board considers that undue nuisance or threat to public order or safety occurs. Previously the only restriction order which could be made related to permitted hours in the evening and such an order could restrict to a time not earlier than 10 p.m. The same restriction now relates to an "evening restriction order" only. A board may also impose an "afternoon restriction order," reducing the permitted hours from 2.30 p.m. to 5 p.m. as they see fit, if they are satisfied that the sale or supply of alcoholic liquor in the afternoon is the cause of undue public nuisance, etc. Further, the board may impose a "Sunday restriction order" if satisfied that "the use of licensed premises" (more general than sale or supply of alcoholic liquor in afternoon and evening restrictions) is the cause of undue disturbance or public nuisance having regard to the "way of life" in the locality, a further distinction in respect of Sunday, charging the licensing board to consider the particular locality in which the premises are situated and the habits of those who live there.

*Subs. (3)*

Subs. (3) of s.65 is amended by s.48(3) of the 1990 Act with the addition of a proviso that a restriction order can only be made in respect of premises which are the subject of a complaint. S.65(3) of the 1976 Act allows the board to make a restriction order in relation to individual premises or in relation to a group of premises in respect of which the same type of licence is held. The subsection makes it clear, in respect of a group of premises, that only those premises specifically complained of may be the subject of a restriction order.

*Revocation of a restriction order.* A licence-holder or the secretary of a registered club in respect of which a restriction order has been made can apply for the revocation of a restriction order where two-thirds of the period of the order has expired (subss. (4) and (5)). The application has to be in writing and lodged with the clerk to the board not less than 21 days before the quarterly meeting at which it is to be considered, with copies being sent at the same time as it is lodged to the person or persons whose complaint or complaints led to the making of the order (subs. (5)). Objection can be taken to the revocation by any person entitled to complain under subs. (1), but the objection must be made in writing with copies to the licence-holder or club concerned not later than seven days before the meeting at which the application falls to be considered (subs. (6)). After considering the application, the board may make such decision as they think fit. There is a right of appeal to the sheriff against the decision of a board to revoke or to refuse to revoke a restriction order (subs. (8)).

## Temporary restriction of permitted hours

**66.**—(1) On an application made to a licensing board by a constable of the rank of chief inspector or above for an order making a temporary restriction of permitted hours the board may, if it considers it desirable in the interests of public order or safety, order that the premises to which the application relates be closed to the public for such time of up to three hours and on such day or days as may be specified in the order.

(2) The licensing board may make an order under subsection (1) above in relation to individual premises or in relation to a group of premises in respect of which the same type of licence is held.

(3) The licence-holder of premises to which an application under subsection (1) above relates or the registered club concerned shall have no right to object to the application.

(4) An order under this section may be made in relation to any licensed premises or registered club.

GENERAL NOTE

The purpose of the section is to give effect to the recommendation of Clayson (para. 9.72) that, where there is the possibility of disorder arising out of a given event on a given day, *e.g.* a football match, a board should have the power to close premises for a period or periods of up to three hours if they are satisfied that it is necessary in the interests of public order or safety. The application for a temporary restriction order is to be made by an officer of the rank of chief inspector or above (subs. (1)), and the order applied for may relate to licensed premises or registered clubs (subs. (4)), and to premises or groups of premises operated under the same type of licence (subs. (2)). The licence-holder or club to which the application relates has no right of objection to the application (subs. (3)).

For discussion of the distinction between a s.65 restriction order and a temporary restriction order under s.66, see *Grainger* v. *City of Edinburgh District Licensing Board*, 1989 G.W.D. 13–568, overruling *Elantosh Ltd.* v. *City of Edinburgh District Licensing Board*, 1984 S.L.T. 92.

## PART VI

### OFFENCES

### Penalties for offences against provisions of this Act and Prevention of Corruption Acts

**67.**—(1) Schedule 5 to this Act shall have effect in accordance with the provisions of this section with respect to the penalties for offences against the provisions of this Act specified in column 1 of that Schedule, of which a rough description is given in column 2 thereof, and in that Schedule—

> (*a*) column 3 shows whether the licence-holder has vicarious responsibility in relation to offences in accordance with subsection (2) below;
>
> (*b*) column 4 shows whether the licence-holder and his premises are liable to disqualification under subsection (3) below; and
>
> (*c*) column 5 shows the maximum penalty by way of fine or imprisonment which may be imposed.

(2) Where an employee or agent of a licence-holder commits an offence in respect of which column 3 of Schedule 5 to this Act indicates that the licence-holder has vicarious responsibility, proceedings may be instituted against the licence-holder in respect of that offence whether or not proceedings have been instituted against the person who committed the offence:

Provided that it shall be a defence for the licence-holder to prove that the offence occurred without his knowledge or connivance and that he exercised all due diligence to prevent its occurrence.

(3) Where a licence-holder is convicted of an offence in respect of which column 4 of Schedule 5 to this Act indicates that the licence-holder and the premises in respect of which the licence is held may be disqualified, or of an offence under section 19 of this Act, the court by which he is convicted may make an order in accordance with either or both of the following paragraphs, that is to say—

> (*a*) that the licence-holder shall be disqualified from holding a licence in respect of the premises concerned for a period not exceeding five years;

(b) that the premises in respect of which the licence is held shall be disqualified from being used as licensed premises for a period not exceeding five years.

(4) Where a licence-holder is convicted of an offence under the Prevention of Corruption Acts 1889 to 1916 in connection with an application to a licensing board under this Act, the court by which he is convicted may, in addition to any other penalty which the court may impose, make an order in accordance with either or both of the following paragraphs, that is to say—

(a) that the licence-holder shall be disqualified from holding a licence for a period not exceeding five years in respect of the premises to which the application relates or related;

(b) that the premises to which the application relates or related shall be disqualified from being used as licensed premises for a period not exceeding five years.

(5) Where an offence against this Act which has been committed by a body corporate is proved to have been committed with the consent or connivance of, or to be attributable to any neglect on the part of, any director, manager, secretary or other similar officer of the body corporate, or any person purporting to act in such capacity, he as well as the body corporate shall be deemed to be guilty of that offence and shall be liable to be proceeded against and punished accordingly.

In this subsection, the expression "director," in relation to any body corporate established by or under any enactment for the purpose of carrying on under national ownership any industry or part of an industry or undertaking, being a body corporate whose affairs are managed by the members thereof, means a member of that body corporate.

(6) In this section, "licence-holders" includes the holder of a licence under Part II of this Act.

GENERAL NOTE

A. *General.* All offences created by this Act are to be tried in a summary manner: s.128. The section gives effect to Sched. 5, which prescribes for each offence created by the Act the maximum penalty by way of a fine or imprisonment, whether the licence-holder is vicariously liable, and whether the licence-holder in respect of the premises to which the application related or the premises are liable to disqualification. Sched. 5, as enacted, specified particular monetary penalties for each offence created by the Act, but ss.289E to 289G of the Criminal Procedure (Scotland) Act 1975, as inserted by s.53 of the Criminal Justice (Scotland) Act 1982, have replaced those monetary penalties by reference to fines at a level of 1 to 5, the amounts of which are subject to variation by the Secretary of State for Scotland in line with the changes in the value of money (see Renton and Brown, *Criminal Procedure*, 5th ed., paras. 17–22 to 17–23).

The section also makes special provisions for the case of vicarious liability (subs. (2)), disqualification of licence-holder or premises (subs. (3)), the position where a licence-holder is convicted of an offence under the Prevention of Corruption Acts 1889 to 1916 in relation to an application to a licensing board (subs. (4)) and the commission of an offence by a body corporate in respect of which responsibility to some extent is proved to rest with an officer of the company (subs. (5)).

For a general discussion of "vicarious responsibility" in statutory crimes, with reference to this Act, see G. H. Gordon, *Criminal Law of Scotland*, 2nd ed., pp. 295 *et seq.*

B. *Subsections.* (2) The subsection makes it clear that a licence-holder can be prosecuted for an offence for which he is vicariously liable irrespective of whether the person who actually committed the offence is prosecuted. In virtue of the proviso, the defence is open to a licence-holder where he is vicariously liable that the offence took place without his knowledge or connivance and that he exercised all due diligence to prevent its occurrence; see *Byrne* v. *Tudhope*, 1983 S.C.C.R. 337; *Gorman* v. *Cochrane* (1977) S.C.C.R. (Supp.) 183 and *Tesco Supermarkets Ltd.* v. *Nattrass* [1972] A.C. 153 which is the leading English authority. For a fuller discussion of the defence of "due diligence," see introduction, para. 7.8. For a discussion of "knowledge," see note to s.68.

(3) S.19 makes it an offence to canvass a licensing board member in connection with an application. The subsection includes such an offence in the offences for which a licence-holder or premises may be disqualified. It also provides that the maximum period of disqualification in the cases of both licence-holders and premises is five years. In *Canavan* v. *Carmichael*, 1989 S.C.C.R. 480, the High Court considered the circumstances in which a disqualification was appropriate. In *Deveaux* v. *MacPhail*, 1991 G.W.D. 7–396, the High Court of Justiciary held that disqualification *simpliciter* of a licence-holder was incompetent, because disqualification related to a disqualification in respect of the particular premises concerned.

(4) The Prevention of Corruption Acts 1889 to 1916 in general make it an offence to induce a decision by the offering of a reward. Where a licence-holder is convicted of a contravention of the Acts in relation to an application to a licensing board, the court in which he is convicted may impose disqualification as provided for by the subsection. See G. H. Gordon, *Criminal Law of Scotland*, 2nd ed., pp. 706 and 1010. In *Barr* v. *Crawford*, 1983 S.L.T. 481 the court held that averments seeking to recover a bribe paid for a licence which was then not granted were irrelevant.

(5) It is to be noted that, in defining "director," the Act has taken cognisance of the position of the managing members of a nationalised industry.

(6) The holder of a seamen's canteen licence under Part III of the Act is not included in the definition of licence-holder (see s.139(1)). The purpose of the subsection is to put the holder of a canteen licence in the same position as other licence-holders in relation to the provisions of the section.

### Protection of young persons

**68.**—(1) Subject to subsection (6) below, the holder of a licence or his employee or agent shall not in licensed premises sell alcoholic liquor to a person under 18, or allow a person under 18 to consume alcoholic liquor in a bar, nor shall the holder of the licence allow any person to sell alcoholic liquor to a person under 18.

(2) A person under 18 shall not in licensed premises buy or attempt to buy alcoholic liquor nor consume alcoholic liquor in a bar.

(3) A person shall not knowingly act as agent for a person under 18 in the purchase of alcoholic liquor, nor shall any person knowingly buy or attempt to buy alcoholic liquor for consumption in a bar in licensed premises by a person under 18.

(4) In subsections (1) to (3) above and in sections 69 and 72 of this Act, references to a bar shall not apply to a bar at any time when it is, as is usual in the premises in question, set apart for the service of table meals and not used for the sale or supply of alcoholic liquor otherwise than to persons having table meals there and for consumption by such a person as an ancillary to his meal; and nothing in subsection (1) or (2) above shall prohibit the sale to or purchase by a person who has attained the age of 16, of beer, wine, made-wine, porter, cider or perry for consumption at a meal in a part of the premises usually set apart for the service of meals which is not a bar, or in a bar at any such time as aforesaid, and nothing in subsection (3) above shall prohibit the acting by any person as agent for a person who has attained the age of 16 in the purchase of beer, wine, made-wine, porter, cider or perry for consumption as aforesaid:

Provided that nothing in this subsection shall authorise a person who has attained the age of 16 to purchase alcoholic liquor for consumption by a person under that age.

(5) The holder of a licence or his employee or agent shall not deliver, nor shall the holder of a licence allow any person to deliver, to a person under 18, alcoholic liquor sold in licensed premises for consumption off the premises, except where the delivery is made at the residence or working place of the purchaser, nor shall any person knowingly send a person under 18 for the purpose of obtaining alcoholic liquor sold or to be sold as aforesaid from the licensed premises or other premises from which the liquor is delivered in pursuance of the sale:

Provided that this subsection shall not apply where the person under 18 is a member of the licence-holder's family or his servant or apprentice and is employed as a messenger to deliver alcoholic liquor.

(6) Subsections (1) to (3) of this section shall apply in relation to any licensed canteen as if the canteen were licensed premises, but with the substitution for any reference to a bar of a reference to the canteen.

(7) If any person contravenes this section he shall be guilty of an offence.

GENERAL NOTE

A. *General.* The section makes it an offence for the holder of a licence or his employee or agent to sell alcoholic liquor to a person under 18 years of age, to allow such a person to consume liquor in a bar, or to allow any person to sell liquor to a person under 18 (subs. (1)), and (subs. (5)) to deliver liquor to a person under 18 for consumption off the premises except where permitted by the subsection. A company may be charged with an offence under this section, where the sale is libelled as done "by the hand of an employee or agent or other person, whose identity is meantime to the complainer unknown"; *Wilson* v. *Allied Breweries Ltd.*, 1986 S.L.T. 549. It was observed that if the person is under 18, while the charge might be relevant, proof might be difficult. Normally the company and the nominated holder (see s.11) are both charged. The section also makes it an offence for a person under 18 to buy or attempt to buy or to consume alcoholic liquor in a bar (subs. (2)), and an offence for any person to act as agent for the purchase of liquor for a person under 18, or to buy or attempt to buy knowingly liquor for consumption at a bar by a person under 18 (subs. (3)). Subs. (4) makes an exception in the case of a person over 16 years of age who purchases for consumption at a meal in the part of the premises set apart for the service of meals beer, wine, porter, cider or perry. The prosecution require to prove the child's age by corroborated evidence; *Lockwood* v. *Walker*, 1909 2 S.L.T. 400. Evidence of impression that a person is under 18 is not corroboration of a young person's admission of their age; *Paton* v. *Wilson*, 1988 S.L.T. 634.

"*alcoholic liquor.*" For the meaning, see s.139(1).

"*bar*" is defined in s.139(1). In virtue of subs. (4), references to a bar in subss. (1) to (3) do not include a bar which is set aside at the usual time for the service of table meals and not used for other than the supply of liquor for consumption as an ancillary to the meal.

Subs. (6) extends the premises in respect of which subss. (1) to (3) can be contravened to seamen's canteens.

For the penalties for contravening the section, see Sched. 5.

B. *Subsections.* (1) See s.71 and note for the defence to a contravention of this subsection that the accused used due diligence to prevent the occurrence of the offence, and the defence that the accused had no reason to suspect that the person in relation to whom the charge was brought was under 18. See *Tudhope* v. *McDonald*, 1986 S.C.C.R. 32 for a prosecution under this section, which turned on the statutory presumptions in ss.127(2) [prior to amendment by the 1990 Act] and 139(1), *q.v.*

(3) "*knowingly.*" For a consideration of "knowingly" and "knowledge," see G. H. Gordon, *Criminal Law of Scotland*, 2nd ed., p. 281 and index *sub nom.* "knowingly"; see *Noble* v. *Heatly*, 1967 J.C. 5, where a Full Bench held that a licence-holder, in the absence of personal knowledge, could not be convicted of "knowingly permitting" drunkenness in the premises. In order that a contravention may be established, it must be proved either that the accused knew that the person in relation to whom the charge was brought was under 18 years of age, or that he wilfully shut his eyes to that person's age: see *Knox* v. *Boyd*, 1941

J.C. 82 and *Groom* v. *Grimes* (1903) 89 L.T. 129. "Knowingly" has been considered under the English Licensing Acts in *Linnett* v. *Commissioners of Police for Metropolis* [1946] K.B. 290 (knowingly permitting disorderly conduct, co-licensees); *Vane* v. *Yiannopoullos* [1965] A.C. 486 (imputation of knowledge to licensee where waitress selling liquor); *Ross* v. *Moss* [1965] 2 Q.B. 396 (whether licensee of club had knowledge of breach of conditions in his absence); *Hall* v. *Hyder* [1966] 1 W.L.R. 410 (knowingly allowing a person under age to consume liquor); *R.* v. *Winson* [1969] 1 Q.B. 371 (whether licensee of club liable for sale of liquor by his manager knowingly in breach of condition of licence), a case in which the authorities are reviewed; *Howker* v. *Robinson* [1973] Q.B. 178 (imputation of knowledge to licensee, when barman selling liquor to person under age). The English cases should be treated with caution, because of the English doctrine, which does not apply in Scotland (*Noble, cit.*) that where a licensee delegates his functions to a manager, he is liable for all the manager's acts, whether or not he had knowledge. The corresponding provision in the 1959 Act (s.146(5)) did not include the word "knowingly." See Introduction, para. 7.5.

(4) "*Table meal*" is defined in s.139(1).

A person over 16 years of age can be sold beer, wine, porter, cider or perry provided the sale is in a part of a premises set apart for the service of meals and the liquor is consumed at a meal.

(5) Where liquor is sold for consumption off the premises, it may not be delivered to a person under 18 years of age unless the delivery is effected either at the residence or place of work of the purchaser. The offence can be committed by a licence-holder, his employee, or his agent. The holder can commit the offence by allowing the delivery in respect of which the charge is brought. It is also an offence to send a person under 18 years of age to obtain, be sold or take delivery of liquor from licensed or other premises. The proviso to the section excepts from its provisions a person under 18 who is a member of the licence-holder's family, or is employed as his messenger. The defences open to a licence-holder under s.71 apply to a contravention of the subsection.

"*knowingly*": see note to subs. (3).

(6) "*licensed canteen*" is defined in s.139 of the Act.

### Children prohibited from bars and licensed canteens

**69.**—(1) Subject to section 49 of the Law Reform (Miscellaneous Provisions) (Scotland) Act 1990 the holder of a licence in respect of any premises or his employee or agent shall not allow a person under 14 to be in the bar of those premises during the permitted hours, and the holder of a licence under Part III of this Act in respect of any canteen or his employee or agent shall not allow such a person to be in that canteen during the permitted hours.

(2) Subject to section 49 of the Law Reform (Miscellaneous Provisions) (Scotland) Act 1990 no person shall cause or procure, or attempt to cause or procure, any person under 14 to go to, or to be in, the bar of any licensed premises or in any licensed canteen during the permitted hours.

(3) No offence shall be committed under this section if the person under 14—

(a) is a child of the holder of the licence, or

(b) resides in the licensed premises but is not employed there, or

(c) is in the bar of the licensed premises solely for the purpose of passing to or from some other part of the premises, not a bar, being a part to or from which there is no other convenient means of access or egress, or

(d) is in the licensed canteen solely for the purpose of passing to or from some other part of premises in which the canteen is comprised, not a bar, being a part to or from which there is no other convenient means of access or egress.

(4) No offence shall be committed under this section in respect of a bar which is in any railway refreshment room or other premises constructed,

fitted and intended to be used bona fide for any purpose to which the holding of a licence is merely ancillary.

(5) If any person contravenes this section he shall be guilty of an offence.

(6) Where in any proceedings under this section it is alleged that a person was at any time under 14 and he appears to the court then to have been under that age, for the purpose of the proceedings he shall be deemed to have been then under that age unless the contrary is shown.

GENERAL NOTE

A. *General.* "*Bar*" includes any place exclusively or mainly used for the sale and consumption of alcoholic liquor: s.139(1). For a decision on the corresponding provision of an earlier Act, where the statutory definition included "any open drinking bar" as an alternative to the above definition, and where it was held that a small box in a corner of the bar and separated from it by wooden partitions seven feet in height, containing a table and chairs, used for serving food and drink, was not a bar, see *Donaghue* v. *McIntyre*, 1911 S.C.(J.) 61.

Where a licensed premises holds a "children's certificate" granted under s.49 of the 1990 Act, this section is modified by s.49(3) of the 1990 Act to the extent that it is lawful for a person under the age of 14 years to be present in such part of the premises as is covered by the children's certificate when accompanied by a person over the age of 18 years between the hours of 11.00 a.m. and 8.00 p.m. for the purposes of the consumption of a meal sold or supplied on the premises.

"*Licensed premises*" means premises in respect of which a licence under this Act is in force other than under Part III of the Act: s.139(1).

"*Licensed canteen*" means a seamen's canteen in respect of which a licence under Part III of the Act is in force: s.139(1).

A person shall be deemed to have been "*under 14*" unless the contrary is shown, at any time, where in proceedings under this section, he appears to the court to have been under 14 at the time (subs. (6)). *Per contra*, see note to s.68.

B. *Subsections.* (1) "*Permitted hours*" means the hours during which by virtue of the Act alcoholic liquor may be sold, supplied or consumed in licensed premises: s.139(1).

For the defence open to a licence-holder charged with contravening subs. (1) that he used all due diligence to prevent the occurrence of the offence or that he had no reason to suspect that the person in relation to whom the charge was brought was under 14, see s.71. See note to s.67 *re* "due diligence."

No offence is committed if the child to whom the charge relates comes within the categories specified in subs. (3) or is on that part of the premises to which a children's certificate relates.

(2) Subs. (3) applies to the offence provided for by the subsection.

(5) The maximum penalty for a contravention of subs. (1) is a fine of level 3 with the licence-holder vicariously responsible and both the holder and the premises liable to disqualification, [see Note to s.67 B. Subsection (3)] and for a contravention of subs. (2) the maximum penalty is a fine of level 3.

### Children on premises in respect of which refreshment licence held

**70.**—(1) The holder of a refreshment licence in respect of any premises or his employee or agent shall not allow a person under 14 who is not accompanied by a person of 18 or over to be in the premises during the permitted hours, nor shall he allow a person under 14 to remain on the premises after eight in the evening, and if any person contravenes this section he shall be guilty of an offence.

(2) No offence shall be committed under this section if the person under 14—

(*a*) is a child of the holder of the licence, or

(*b*) resides in the premises but is not employed there.

GENERAL NOTE

The section makes special provisions relating to the presence of persons under 14 years of age on premises operated under a refreshment licence. It is not an offence for the holder of a refreshment licence, his employee, or agent to permit a person under 14 years of age to be present on premises in respect of which a refreshment licence is held unless that person is not accompanied by a person over 18 (the age was reduced from 21 to 18 by para. 14 of Sched. 8 to the 1990 Act) years of age or is present on the premises after 8 p.m. The offence is not committed if the child is the child of the licence-holder or resides in the premises.

For the meaning of "*refreshment licence,*" see s.9 and Sched. 1 and for the meaning of "*permitted hours,*" see s.139(1).

The defences provided for by s.71 apply to a contravention of the section. The maximum penalty for a contravention is a fine of level 3, with the licence-holder vicariously liable and both the licence-holder and the premises liable to disqualification [see Note to s.67 B. Subsection (3)].

### Defence in relation to offences under section 68(1), (5), 69(1), 70 or 97A of this Act

**71.** Without prejudice to any defence available to a licence-holder by virtue of the proviso to section 67(2) of this Act, it shall be a defence for any person charged with an offence under section 68(1), 68(5), 69(1), 70 or 97A of this Act if he proves—

(a) that he used due diligence to prevent the occurrence of the offence, or

(b) that he had no reason to suspect that the person in relation to who the charge was brought was under 18 or under 14, as the case may be.

GENERAL NOTE

S.67(2) makes available to a licence-holder, where Sched. 5 places vicarious responsibility on him, the defence that the offence occurred outwith his knowledge or connivance, and the defence that he exercised all due diligence to prevent the commission of the offence. Without prejudice to these defences, the section makes available to any person charged with selling liquor to a person under 18 or allowing such a person to consume liquor at a bar (s.68(1)), offences in connection with the delivery of liquor to a person under 18 (s.68(5)), the offence of allowing a person under 14 years of age into a bar or licensed canteen (s.69(1)), or offences in connection with the presence of persons under 14 in premises operated under a refreshment licence (s.70), the defence that he used all due diligence and the defence that he had no reason to suspect that a person was under age. See note to s.67, re "*due diligence.*" The defence need only be proved on a balance of probabilities; see Introduction, para. 7.11.

### Persons under 18 not to be employed in bars or licensed canteens

**72.**—(1) If any person under 18 is employed in any bar of licensed premises, or in a licensed canteen, at a time when the bar or canteen is open for the sale or consumption of alcoholic liquor, the holder of the licence or the employee or agent who employed the person under 18 shall be guilty of an offence.

(2) For the purposes of this section—

(a) a person shall not be deemed to be employed in a bar of licensed premises by reason only that in the course of his employment in some other part of the premises he enters the bar for the purpose of giving or receiving any message or of passing to or from some other part of the premises, not a bar, being a part to or from which there is no other convenient means of access or egress;

(b) a person shall not be deemed to be employed in a licensed canteen by reason only that in the course of his employment in some other part of the premises in which the canteen is comprised he enters the canteen for the purpose of giving or receiving any message or of passing to or from some other part of such premises, not a bar, being a part to or from which there is no other convenient means of access or egress.

(3) For the purposes of his section, a person shall be deemed to be employed by the person for whom he works notwithstanding that he receives no wages for his work.

(4) Where in any proceedings under this section it is alleged that a person was at any time under 18, and he appears to the court then to have been under that age, for the purposes of the proceedings he shall be deemed to have been then under that age unless the contrary is shown.

GENERAL NOTE
*Prohibition from employing persons under 18 years of age in bars and licensed canteens.* The section imposes an absolute prohibition on the employment of persons under 18 in bars and licensed canteens. The offence of employing such a person can be committed by the holder of a licence, his employee, or his agent (subs. (1)). A person is not to be deemed to be employed if he is present in the bar for the purpose specified in subs. (2), but is to be deemed employed even if he is not in receipt of wages (subs. (3)). In a prosecution for a contravention of the section, the onus is on the accused to show that the person in respect of whom the charge was brought was over 18 if he appears to the court to be under 18 (subs. (4)). This is a contradiction of the position at common law: see note to s.68. "*licensed premises,*" "*licensed canteen,*" are defined in s.139(1).

## Persons under 18 not to be employed to serve alcoholic liquor in premises for which refreshment licence is held

**73.**—(1) A person under 18 shall not be employed in premises in respect of which a refreshment licence is held if the purpose, or one of the purposes, of his employment is to serve alcoholic liquor to persons in those premises.

(2) For the purposes of this section a person shall be deemed to be employed in the premises where he works notwithstanding that he receives no wages for his work.

(3) Any person who contravenes this section shall be guilty of an offence.

(4) Where in any proceedings under this section it is alleged that a person was at any time under 18, and he appears to the court then to have been under that age, for the purposes of the proceedings he shall be deemed to have been then under that age unless the contrary is shown.

GENERAL NOTE
*Employment of persons under 18 years of age in premises in respect of which a refreshment licence is held.* The section adapts the provisions of s.72 to the conditions of a refreshment licence by making the offence enacted by s.72, as far as premises operated under a refreshment licence are concerned, that of employing persons under 18 to serve liquor in such premises. S.72(3) and (4) are re-enacted in subss. (2) and (4) so as to apply to the offence which is constituted by subss. (1) and (3). The maximum penalty for the offence is a fine of level 3 with the licence-holder vicariously responsible and both he and the premises liable to disqualification (Sched. 5). For "*vicariously responsible,*" see note to s.67.

For the meaning of "*refreshment licence,*" see s.9 and Sched. 1.

## Drunk persons entering or in licensed premises

**74.**—(1) If any person attempts to enter any licensed premises (not being premises where he is residing) while drunk he shall be guilty of an offence.

(2) If any person is in licensed premises while drunk and incapable of taking care of himself, he shall unless he is under the care or protection of a suitable person, be guilty of an offence.

(3) A constable may arrest without warrant any person committing an offence under this section.

GENERAL NOTE

For a consideration of what is meant by "*drunk*," see *Dunning* v. *Cardle*, 1981 S.L.T. (Notes) 107, where it was suggested that the test was for the judge to ask, was this man "sufficiently inebriated as to justify the description of '*drunk*.'" In the English case of *Neale* v. *RMJE* (*a minor*) (1984) 80 Cr.App.Rep. 20, it was said that "drunk" means "having taken intoxicating liquor to an extent which affected steady self-control"; see also *Lanham* v. *Rickwood* (1984) 148 J.P. 737.

"*Licensed premises*" and "*constable*" are defined in s.139(1).

The maximum penalty is a fine of level 1 (Sched. 5).

## Procuring or aiding a drunken person to procure alcoholic liquor

**75.**—(1) If a person in any licensed premises procures or attempts to procure any alcoholic liquor for consumption by a drunken person, he shall be guilty of an offence.

(2) If any person in any licensed premises aids a drunken person in obtaining or consuming any alcoholic liquor in the premises, he shall be guilty of an offence.

GENERAL NOTE

For a consideration of what is meant by "*drunk*," see note to s.74.

"*Licensed premises*" are defined by s.139(1).

For the meaning of "*alcoholic liquor*," see s.139(1).

The maximum penalty is a fine of level 3 (Sched. 5) in respect of a contravention of either subsection.

## Sale or supply of alcoholic liquor to drunken persons

**76.** A licence-holder or his employee or agent shall be guilty of an offence if he sells or supplies in licensed premises any alcoholic liquor to a drunken person.

GENERAL NOTE

The section makes a sale of alcoholic liquor to persons in an intoxicated condition a specific offence. The section applies to licensed canteens (s.45). For a consideration of what is meant by "*drunk*," see note to s.74.

For the meaning of "*alcoholic liquor*," "*licence-holder*" and "*licensed premises*," see s.139(1).

The maximum penalty is a fine of level 5 with the licence-holder vicariously liable for the offence and both the holder and the premises liable to disqualification (Sched. 5). For a consideration of "*vicariously liable*," see note to s.67.

## Licence-holder and employees and agents not to be drunk

**77.** It shall be an offence for the licence-holder of premises or his employee or agent to be in the premises while drunk.

GENERAL NOTE

This section makes it an offence for the licence-holder, his employee or agent to be in a state of intoxication on the licence-holder's premises.

For a consideration of what is meant by "*drunk*," see note to s.74.

For the meaning of "*licence-holder*" and "*licensed premises*," see s.139(1).

The section applies to the holder of a seamen's canteen licence (s.45).

The maximum penalty is a fine of level 3 with the licence-holder vicariously liable and both the holder and the premises liable to disqualification (Sched. 5). For consideration of "*vicariously liable*," see note to s.67.

## Riotous behaviour, etc. in licensed premises

**78.**—(1) If any person in licensed premises—

(*a*) behaves while drunk in a riotous or disorderly manner, or

(*b*) while drunk uses obscene or indecent language to the annoyance of any person,

he shall be guilty of an offence.

(2) A licence-holder or his employee or agent shall be guilty of an offence if he permits any breach of the peace, drunkenness or riotous or disorderly conduct in the premises in respect of which the licence is held.

GENERAL NOTE

S.78(2), which had no equivalent in the 1959 Act, makes it an offence for a licence-holder, his employee, or agent to permit disorderly conduct on licensed premises. The section applies to a seamen's canteen (s.45). See s.126 regarding burden of proof.

For a consideration of what is meant by "*drunk*," see note to s.74.

"*licensed premises*" and "*licence-holder*" are defined in s.139(1).

The maximum penalty for a contravention of s.78(1)(*a*) is a fine of level 3 and/or 60 days' imprisonment, of s.78(1)(*b*) a fine of level 3, and of s.78(2) a fine of level 3 with the licence-holder vicariously liable and both the holder and the premises liable to disqualification (Sched. 5). For consideration of "*vicariously liable*," see note to s.67.

## Refusal to leave licensed premises

**79.**—(1) If a person in any licensed premises—

(*a*) being riotous, quarrelsome or disorderly, refuses or neglects to leave such premises on being requested so to do by the occupier or manager thereof, or his employee or agent, or by any constable, or

(*b*) refuses to leave such premises at the conclusion of the permitted hours in the afternoon or evening, as the case may be, on being requested so to do as aforesaid,

he shall be guilty of an offence.

(2) A constable may assist in expelling from any such premises any person who refuses or neglects to leave the premises on being requested so to do as aforesaid.

(3) A constable may arrest without warrant any person committing an offence under this section.

GENERAL NOTE

"*licensed premises*" and "*constable*" are defined in s.139(1). For the purposes of the section, premises include a licensed canteen (s.45).

*Subs. (1)*. "*Permitted hours*" means the hours during which by virtue of the Act alcoholic liquor may be sold, supplied or consumed in licensed premises: s.139(1). "*Disorderly*" in *Campbell* v. *Adair*, 1945 J.C. 29 was held to indicate less aggressive conduct than would be required to constitute a breach of the peace. In *Ritchie* v. *McPhee* (1882) 10 R.(J.) 9 a charge of being "riotous and disorderly in his behaviour by shouting aloud" was held irrelevant for want of specification.

A licence-holder is under no obligation to supply any member of the public with liquor. He can select his customers, and his reason for his refusal need not be given and cannot be questioned: *per* Holmes J. in *R.* v. *Armagh Justices* (1897) 2 L.R.Ir. 57; *Sealey* v. *Tandy*

135

[1902] 1 K.B. 296. Where a chimney sweep in his working dress came to a public-house bar and refused to leave, it was held that he could be excluded by force, even though the premises were an inn: *Pidgeon* v. *Legge* (1857) 5 W.R. 89. The same principle was upheld where a person accompanied by a large and undesirable dog was held to have been lawfully excluded: *R.* v. *Rymer* (1877) 2 Q.B.D. 136. A man who is drunk or who behaves indecently or improperly has no right to entertainment, even at an inn: *R.* v. *Ivens* (1835) 7 C. & P. 213. As to circumstances where a licence-holder was not held responsible for his servant's act of forcible ejection, see *Gillespie* v. *Hunter* (1898) 25 R. 916.

The maximum penalty for contravening subs. (1) is a fine of level 1 (Sched. 5).

### Penalty for permitting thieves, prostitutes, etc., or stolen goods in licensed premises

**80.** If any person who occupies or keeps any premises in respect of which a licence is held—

(a) knowingly suffers thieves or reputed thieves or prostitutes or reputed prostitutes or persons convicted of an offence under section 4 or 5(3) of the Misuse of Drugs Act 1971 to remain in those premises, or knowingly permits thieves or reputed thieves, or prostitutes or reputed prostitutes or persons convicted of an offence under section 4 or 5(3) of the Misuse of Drugs Act 1971 to meet or assemble in the premises; or

(b) knowingly permits to be deposited in the premises goods which he has reasonable grounds for believing to be stolen goods;

he shall be guilty of an offence.

GENERAL NOTE

The section makes it an offence for the person who occupies or keeps premises in respect of which a licence is held knowingly to suffer thieves or reputed thieves or prostitutes or reputed prostitutes or persons convicted under section 4 or 5(3) of the Misuse of Drugs Act 1971, to remain or to meet on the premises, or knowingly to permit goods, which he has reasonable grounds to believe stolen, to be deposited there. For a consideration of "*knowingly*," see note to s.68. For a consideration of "*reputed thieves*," etc. see G. H. Gordon, *Criminal Law of Scotland*, 2nd ed., pp. 546 and 914.

"*licence*" is defined in s.139(1) of the Act.

The maximum penalty is a fine of level 3, with both the premises and the licence-holder liable to disqualification. The offence is one for which the licence-holder is vicariously liable (Sched. 5); see note to s.67.

### Prohibition of betting and gaming offences

**81.** A licence-holder or his employee or agent shall be guilty of an offence if he permits the playing of any game in the premises in respect of which the licence is held in such circumstances that an offence under the Betting, Gaming and Lotteries Acts 1963 to 1971 is committed.

GENERAL NOTE

The section makes it an offence to permit the playing of a game which, in the circumstances, constitutes an offence under the Betting and Lotteries Acts 1963 to 1971; see G. H. Gordon, *Criminal Law of Scotland*, 2nd ed., Chap. 46—"Betting, Gaming and Lotteries."

For the meaning of "*licence*," see s.139(1).

The maximum penalty is a fine of level 3 with both the licence-holder and the premises liable to disqualification. The licence-holder is vicariously liable for the offence (Sched. 5). For a consideration of "*vicariously liable*," see note to s.67.

### Persons found drinking in unlicensed premises

**82.** If a person is found drunk or drinking in premises in which alcoholic liquor is sold without a licence he shall be guilty of an offence, and a constable may arrest without warrant any person committing such an offence.

GENERAL NOTE
For a consideration of what is meant by "*drunk*," see note to s.74.
"*constable*" is defined in s.139(1).
The maximum penalty is a fine of level 1 (Sched. 5).

### Drinking in places of public refreshment, etc., when public house is closed

**83.**—(1) Subject to the provisions of this Act, alcoholic liquor shall not be consumed in any premises used for the sale to, or consumption by, the public of provisions, refreshments, confectionery or tobacco, during any time when the consumption of such liquor in public houses in the licensing area within which such premises are situated is prohibited by or under this Act, and any person who so consumes alcoholic liquor shall be guilty of an offence.

(2) If any person keeping or occupying any such premises permits alcoholic liquor to be consumed therein in contravention of subsection (1) above, he shall be guilty of an offence, but such a person shall not be guilty of an offence under this section if he proves that the liquor in question was consumed without his knowledge or consent.

(3) This section does not apply to the consumption of alcoholic liquor at a private function held on premises used as mentioned in subsection (1) above, being a private function which is related to a particular occasion.

GENERAL NOTE
A. *General.* The section prohibits the consumption and not just the sale of alcoholic liquor by any person, outwith the permitted hours for public-houses in the area, in premises used for the sale to, or consumption by, the public of provisions, refreshments, confectionery or tobacco.

"*Premises used for the sale to, or consumption by, the public*" means what it says, and the section applies to such premises whatever may be the primary purpose for which they are used: *Adair* v. *Delworth*, 1934 J.C. 83 at pp. 87–88, 91. They may be used for a sale to, or consumption by, *the public*, although their primary purpose is to provide facilities for dancing, and members of public, who are invited by advertisement in the press to attend, have to fill up application forms for club membership (usually with fictitious names), before they are allowed to enter: *Adair* v. *Delworth* (*supra*).

"*Provisions*" and "*refreshments*" are exegetical of each other, and must each be given the ordinary dictionary meaning of food, eatables and drinkables: *M'Intyre* v. *Wilson*, 1915 S.C.(J.) 1, Lord Justice-General Strathclyde at pp. 3–4.

The maximum penalty for a contravention of the section is a fine of level 3 (Sched. 5).

B. *Subsections.* (1) "*Alcoholic liquor*" is defined in s.139(1). As to "*premises*," see note A, above. As to the "*time when . . . consumption . . . in public-houses . . . is prohibited*," see Part V of the Act, s.139(1). "*Licensing area*" is defined in s.139(1).

(2) The subsection provides for a breach of the prohibition imposed by subs. (1) being an offence. The offence can only be committed by the keeper or occupier of the premises to which the charge relates. Similar phraseology to the subsection was used in the 1959 Act (see s.162(1)) and was not considered to constitute an offence (see Purves, 8th ed., pp. 174 and 175). Subs. (2) makes it a defence to a charge under the subsection for the accused to prove that the liquor to which the charge relates was consumed without his knowledge or consent; see note to s.68. The defence need only be proved on a balance of probabilities; see *H.M.A.* v. *Mitchell*, 1951 J.C. 53; *Neish* v. *Stevenson*, 1969 S.L.T. 229 and Walker and Walker, *Law of Evidence in Scotland*, p. 76.

(3) It is also a defence open to a person charged under subs. (2) that the liquor to which the charge relates was being consumed at a private function on a particular occasion.

**Offences in relation to constables**

**84.** If a licence-holder or his employee or agent—

(a) knowingly suffers to remain in his premises any constable during any part of the time appointed for the constable's being on duty, except for the purpose of the execution of the constable's duty; or

(b) knowingly supplies any liquor or refreshment, whether by way of a gift or sale to any constable on duty, except by authority of a superior officer of the constable;

the licence-holder, employee or agent, as the case may be, shall be guilty of an offence.

GENERAL NOTE

For a consideration of "*knowingly*," see note to s.68.
"*licence-holder*" and "*constable*" are defined in s.139(1).
"*refreshment*" must be given its ordinary dictionary meaning: *M'Intyre* v. *Wilson*, 1915 S.C.(J.) 1, *per* the Lord Justice-General (Strathclyde) at pp. 3–4.
The maximum penalty is a fine of level 3 with both the premises and the licence-holder liable to disqualification. The licence-holder is vicariously liable for the offence (Sched. 5); see note to s.67 for "*vicariously liable.*"
This section applies to licensed canteens (s.45).

**Power of police to enter licensed premises**

**85.**—(1) A constable may at any time enter and inspect any premises in respect of which a licence (other than an off-sale licence) is in force, and may also at any time enter and inspect premises in respect of which an off-sale licence is in force if he has reasonable grounds for believing that an offence has been or is being committed on those premises.

(2) If any person fails to admit a constable who demands entry to such premises in pursuance of this section or obstructs the entry to the premises of such a constable, he shall be guilty of an offence.

GENERAL NOTE

*Power of police to enter licensed premises.* "*Constable*" and "*licence*" are defined in s.139(1). For the meaning of "*off-sale licence*," see s.9 and Sched. 1. This section applies to licensed canteens (s.45).
The right of entry conferred on a police constable by this section may be exercised at any time and is not restricted to permitted hours. If, however, a constable merely knocks at the door of the premises at a time when they are closed to the public, without indicating to the persons inside that he is a police officer, the licence-holder is not guilty of the offence in subs. (2) if, because he is unaware of the officer's official status, he refuses to admit him: *Alexander* v. *Rankin* (1899) 1 F.(J.) 58; *Duncan* v. *Dowding* [1897] 1 Q.B. 575. In *Southern Bowling Club Ltd.* v. *Ross* (1902) 4 F. 405 it was held that the police were entitled to enter a club in disguise for the purpose of detecting whether illegal trafficking in liquor was being carried on therein.
The right of entry and inspection of *licensed* premises is given by this section to a police officer of any rank. For the more restricted right given to police officers to enter and inspect *unlicensed* premises, see s.86. The power of the police to enter registered and unregistered clubs is dealt with in ss.114 and 120, respectively.
Evidence of purchase of liquor made by constables who enter licensed premises in plain clothes is admissible on a subsequent prosecution of the certificate-holder for contravention of this Act: *Marsh* v. *Johnston*, 1959 S.L.T.(Notes) 28.
The son of a licensee returning home after permitted hours found the licensed premises surrounded by police officers, and warned his parents of their presence. He was held by a Divisional Court in England to have been rightly convicted of obstructing the police in the execution of their duty, contrary to s.2 of the Prevention of Crimes Amendment Act 1885: *Hinchcliffe* v. *Sheldon* [1955] Crim.L.R. 189. In *Chief Constable, Strathclyde Police* v. *City*

*of Glasgow District Licensing Board*, 1988 S.L.T. 128, the First Division held that a licensing board were entitled to conclude that a chief constable's objection to a grant of a provisional licence on the ground that the premises were unsuitable, as access to the premises could only be gained through private unlicensed premises (a shopping mall) was unfounded and that constables would be able to exercise their rights of access and that the board were therefore bound to grant the application.

The maximum penalty for a contravention of the section is a fine of level 3 with both the licence-holder and the premises liable to disqualification. The holder can be vicariously liable for the offence (Sched. 5); for *"vicariously liable"* see note to s.67.

### Power of police to enter unlicensed premises

**86.**—(1) A constable may at any time enter and inspect any temperance hotel, restaurant, shop, vessel or other place where food or drink is sold for consumption on the premises or in which he has reasonable grounds for believing that alcoholic liquor is being trafficked in unlawfully:

Provided that a constable below the rank of inspector shall not exercise any power of entry conferred by this section unless he has previously obtained the authority in writing of a justice of the peace or of a constable of or above the said rank, and shall not exercise such power later than eight days from the date of such authority and shall exercise it on such time or times only as may be specified in the authority.

(2) If any person fails to admit a constable who demands entry to any premises or place in pursuance of this section or obstructs the entry to the premises or place of such constable, he shall be guilty of an offence.

GENERAL NOTE

*Power of police to enter unlicensed premises.* *"Constable"* and *"trafficking"* are defined in s.139(1), and for *"by retail,"* see s.9 note.

The premises affected by this section are any unlicensed premises where food or drink is sold for consumption on the premises, such as temperance hotels and unlicensed restaurants or cafés, and any unlicensed premises in which trafficking unlawfully in alcoholic liquor is reasonably believed to be carried on.

If the police officer concerned is of or above the rank of inspector he may enter such premises at his own discretion and without warrant or special authorisation from any other person. If the police officer concerned is below the rank of inspector he may not enter such premises without the written authority referred to in subs. (1), and he must act in accordance with its terms. For the right of a police officer of any rank to enter and inspect *licenced* premises, see s.85.

*"Temperance hotel, restaurant, shop, vessel or other place"* is sufficiently wide to cover anything on land or sea where the food is sold for consumption on the premises or where alcoholic liquor is being illegally sold. A railway carriage: *Langrish* v. *Archer* (1882) 10 Q.B.D. 44; a platform of a railway station: *Re Davis* (1857) 2 H. & N. 149; a private house in which a sale by public auction is being held: *Sewell* v. *Taylor* (1859) 7 C.B.(N.S.) 160, have all been held to be "places." The same has been held under the English Betting Acts of a palisade: *Shaw* v. *Morley* (1868) L.R. 3 Ex. 137; a stool covered with an umbrella on raised ground: *Bows* v. *Fenwick* (1874) L.R. 9 C.P. 339; a field wherein a pigeon-shooting match and afterwards a foot-race took place: *Eastwood* v. *Miller* (1874) L.R. 9 Q.B. 440; and a box in a grandstand at a race meeting: *Gallaway* v. *Maries* (1881) 8 Q.B.D. 275. See *Powell* v. *Kempton Park Racecourse Company Ltd.* [1899] A.C. 143.

As to the position when the persons in the premises are unaware that it is a police officer who seeks admission, see s.85, note.

The maximum penalty for a contravention of subs. (2) is a fine of level 3 (Sched. 5).

### Restriction on credit sales

**87.**—(1) A person shall not—

(*a*) sell or supply in licensed premises, or in the premises of a registered club, alcoholic liquor to be consumed on the premises, (*b*) consume alcoholic liquor on any such premises,

unless it is paid for before or at the time when it is supplied or sold:

    Provided that an offence shall not be committed under this section if—

    (*a*) the liquor is sold or supplied for consumption at a meal, supplied at the same time and is consumed with the meal, and the licence-holder is paid for with the meal, or

    (*b*) the liquor is sold or supplied for consumption by a person residing in the premises or by a private friend of such a person who is bona fide entertained by, and at the expense of, that person, and if it is paid for with that person's accommodation, or

    (*c*) the liquor is sold or supplied in premises in respect of which a hotel licence, restricted hotel licence, restaurant licence or entertainment licence is held (other than in a public bar of such premises) in response to the production of a credit token within the meaning of section 14 of the Consumer Credit Act 1974.

    (2) If any person contravenes this section he shall be guilty of an offence.

    (3) Nothing in this section shall prohibit or restrict the sale or supply of alcoholic liquor to any canteen in which the sale or supply of alcoholic liquor is carried on under the authority of the Secretary of State or to any authorised mess of the members of Her Majesty's naval, military or air forces.

GENERAL NOTE

*Restriction on credit sales.* The section prohibits the sale or supply of alcoholic liquor in licensed premises, in the premises of a registered club, and, in virtue of s.45, in the premises of a licensed canteen unless the liquor is paid for at the time of the sale or supply (subs. (1)(*a*)). It also prohibits the consumption of liquor on such premises unless it is paid for at the time it is supplied or sold (subs. (1)(*b*)). Subs. (2) makes it an offence to contravene the prohibitions. The maximum penalty for a contravention of either prohibition is a fine of level 3 with, in the case of a contravention of the prohibition constituted by subs. (1)(*a*) (for which the licence-holder can be vicariously liable—for "*vicariously liable,*" see note to s.67) both the licence-holder and the premises liable to disqualification (Sched. 5). The prohibition is not absolute, certain exceptions being provided for by the proviso to subs. (1). These are (a) in the case of liquor supplied at a meal and paid for with it, (b) in the case of liquor sold to a resident of the premises for his own or a friend's consumption and paid for by the resident when he pays for his accommodation, and (c) in the case of liquor sold in hotel, restricted hotel, or restaurant premises (but not in the public bar of such premises) on the production of a credit token within the meaning of s.14 of the Consumer Credit Act 1974. By subs. (3) service canteens and messes are also excluded from the provisions of the section.

    "*licensed premises*" and "*registered club*" are defined in s.139(1).

    For the meaning of "*alcoholic liquor,*" see s.139(1) and s.9, note.

    For the meanings of "*hotel,*" "*restricted hotel*" and "*restaurant licence,*" see s.9 and Sched. 1.

    For the meaning of "*authorised mess*" see Queen's Regulations, for the Navy Chaps. 14 and 15, for the Army paras. 5.701 to 5.773, and the Air Force Chaps. 20 and 21.

## Fraudulent adulteration of food and drink

    **88.** A licence-holder or his employee or agent shall not fraudulently adulterate the food or alcoholic liquor sold by him or sell the same knowing them to have been fraudulently adulterated, and if he does so the licence-holder, employee or agent, as the case may be, shall be guilty of an offence.

GENERAL NOTE

*Fraudulent adulteration of food or alcoholic liquor.* The section makes it an offence for the licence-holder, his employee or agent fraudulently to adulterate the food or alcoholic liquor sold by him, or to sell them knowing them to have been fraudulently adulterated. For a consideration of *"knowingly,"* see note to s.68. Under the corresponding provision of the Food and Drugs (Scotland) Act 1956 [now repealed], s.2(1), it was an offence to sell for human consumption to the prejudice of the purchaser any food (which includes drink other than water) which was not of the nature, or not of the substance, or not of the quality of the food demanded by the purchaser.

*Adulteration of liquor.* At common law no standard has ever been fixed below which it is fraudulent to adulterate liquor. Under the Food and Drugs (Scotland) Act 1956 [now repealed], however, when a person was charged with the offence mentioned in the immediately preceding paragraph in relation to the sale of diluted whisky, brandy, rum or gin, it was a defence to prove that the spirit was diluted with water only, and that its strength was not lower than 35 degrees under proof: s.3(4).

Ss.2(1) and 3(4) of the Food and Drugs (Scotland) Act 1956 [now repealed by the Food Safety Act 1990] took the place of similar provisions in a series of statutes, all now repealed. It has been held to be the effect of s.3(4) that any spirit diluted to a strength lower than 35 degrees under proof is not in fact whisky. (The same reasoning would no doubt apply to the other spirits mentioned in the subsection.) The sale of spirit so diluted is a sale to the prejudice of the purchaser, within the meaning of s.2(1), unless the customer understands that he is buying, and agrees to buy, something which is not whisky. A notice behind the bar "All spirits sold in this establishment are diluted. No strength guaranteed" is not sufficient to give notice to the customer that any spirit which he buys is diluted beyond the statutory maximum: *Brander* v. *Kinnear*, 1923 J.C. 42. If a publican wishes to show that a customer agreed to accept spirit so diluted instead of the whisky which he ordered, he must be prepared to prove that he informed the customer of the sort of liquor he proposed to supply. The exhibition of a notice "Sale of Food and Drugs Act—Diluted Spirits—Weaker than 35 U.P. . . . . 40," which the customer was not proved to have read, was held not to establish a defence to a prosecution under this provision: *Patterson* v. *Findlay*, 1925 J.C. 54.

It was a defence to any charge under the 1956 Act to prove to the satisfaction of the court that the accused has used all diligence to see that the statute was complied with, and that the contravention was due to the act or default of another person. The extent of the burden of proof resting on the defence in such a case was discussed in *Barclay* v. *Clark*, 1957 S.L.T.(Notes) 33, where the adulteration of whisky with water, which was the burden of the charge, could have been performed either by a manager employed by the certificate-holder or by one or other of two barmen. In these circumstances it was held that the defence had not been established and that the certificate-holder was rightly convicted.

For a statutory definition of spirits, beer, wine, made-wine and cider see Alcoholic Liquor Duties Act 1979, s.1. Ss.2 and 3 define how the strength, weight, volume and gravity of spirits and liquors should be ascertained for the purposes of the Act. For a statutory definition of "*Scotch Whisky*," see the Customs and Excise Act 1952, s.243(1)(*b*), now repealed. It has been held that "*Scots Whisky*" must in its entirety be distilled in Scotland: *Henderson and Turnbull Ltd.* v. *Adair*, 1939 J.C. 83; *Lang Bros.* v. *Goldwell*, 1980 S.C. 237, 1982 S.L.T. 309.

For a successful prosecution for selling adulterated brandy in which there was too much grain spirit and too little grape spirit, see *Wilson and McPhee* v. *Wilson* (1903) 6 F.(J.) 10. It was held in *Reekie* v. *Davidson* (1951) 67 Sh.Ct.Rep. 68 that if the seller is charged with having adulterated whisky with water, and it was in fact adulterated with wine, a conviction is not justified.

The maximum penalty for a contravention of the section is a fine of level 3 with both the premises and the licence-holder liable to disqualification. The licence-holder is vicariously liable for the offence (Sched. 5); for *"vicariously liable,"* see note to s.67.

## Order to close licensed premises

**89.**—(1) A sheriff may, if riot or tumult happens or is expected to happen, order the holder of a licence in respect of premises situated in or near the place where a riot or tumult happens or is expected to happen to close those premises during such time as may be specified in the order.

(2) If the holder of any licence or his employee or agent keeps premises open for the sale of alcoholic liquor during any time at which, by virtue of an order made under subsection (1) above or of an order made by a

141

licensing board under any provision of this Act, they are required to be closed, the licence-holder, employee or agent, as the case may be, shall be guilty of an offence.

GENERAL NOTE

See G. H. Gordon, *Criminal Law of Scotland*, 2nd ed., p. 748, paras. 23–24, for a definition of "*riot*."

The offence can be tried in both the sheriff and the district court. The maximum penalty for the offence is a fine of level 3 with both the premises and the licence-holder subject to disqualification. The offence is one for which the licence-holder is vicariously liable (Sched. 5). For "*vicariously liable*" see note to s.67. Where the offender is the holder of a wholesale licence, his wholesale licence is forfeited and he is disqualified from holding such a licence for two years (s.94).

## Trafficking or bartering without licence or hawking of liquor

**90.** Subject to the provisions of this Act, if any person—

(*a*) traffics in any alcoholic liquor in any premises or place without holding a licence in that behalf, or

(*b*) barters or sells spirits by retail without holding a licence in that behalf, or

(*c*) hawks alcoholic liquor,

he shall be guilty of an offence, and a constable or any other person may arrest without warrant a person committing an offence under paragraph (*c*) above.

GENERAL NOTE

For the meanings of "*trafficking*," "*licence*," "*hawking*" and "*constable*," see s.139(1). For the meaning of "*alcoholic liquor*," see s.139(1). For proof of trafficking, see s.122.

(*a*) *Trafficking without a licence in premises or place*. No offence is committed under this section if the quantity of liquor sold is in excess of the statutory maximum for a retail sale with the result that the transaction is wholesale: *Wood* v. *Mackenzie*, 1925 J.C. 13; or if the transaction takes place elsewhere than in premises which are capable of being certificated, as, for example, in the public street: *Hamilton* v. *Inglis* (1879) 6 R.(J.) 45; *Hutcheon* v. *Cadenhead* (1892) 19 R.(J.) 32. For a consideration of what amounts to "*trafficking*," see *MacDonald* v. *Skinner*, 1978 S.L.T.(Notes) 52.

The supply of excisable liquor by a registered club to its members in a marquee which was not on the club premises, the members paying for the liquor when it was served, was held not to be trafficking, because the liquor was not sold: *Crossgates British Legion Club* v. *Davidson*, 1954 J.C. 35. Offences regarding the sale or supply of liquor in unregistered clubs are separately mentioned in s.120.

For the proof required in a charge of trafficking without a licence, see s.122.

(*b*) *Bartering or sale of spirits without a licence*. "*Barters or sells*" have been held not to be true alternatives, and a finding of guilty as libelled on a charge containing these words has been upheld: *Fitzsimmons* v. *Linton* (1861) 23 D. 1301: *Bruce* v. *Linton* (1861) 24 D. 184. The reason for the inclusion of "barter" is given by Lord Justice-Clerk Inglis in the last-mentioned case at pp. 190–191.

Bartering or selling any kind of alcoholic liquor without holding a licence in that behalf is an offence under (*a*), provided, at least, that it takes place in premises or in a place. The principal distinction between (*a*) and (*b*) is that (*b*) relates only to spirits. For a statutory definition of "*spirits*," etc. see note to s.88.

(*c*) *Hawking*. One act of sale may constitute hawking: *Russell* v. *Paton* (1902) 4 F.(J.) 77; *Hutcheon* v. *Cadenhead* (1892) 19 R.(J.) 32 at p. 35; *Hamilton* v. *Inglis* (1879) 6 R.(J.) 45. "Hawking is a trade carried on irrespective of trade premises. A hawker is an itinerant trader who brings the goods to his customers where they may be. I doubt if the language of this clause can be construed apart altogether from the ordinary meaning of the word which it is intended to define; and I am disposed to think that it means nothing more than that a single act of sale shall be held to be hawking, though that word in its ordinary sense signifies a trade or practice": *Hutcheon* v. *Cadenhead* (*supra*), Lord Rutherfurd Clark at p. 35.

When the alcoholic liquor is hawked by a servant, it is a question of circumstances as to whether his employer is also guilty of the offence created by this section. For circumstances where both the master and the servant were held to be rightly convicted of this offence, see *Hogg* v. *Davidson* (1901) 3 F.(J.) 49. Where a brewer's servant, who had no authority at all from his master to sell beer, was sent with his master's horse and cart to deliver beer to his master's customers in execution of orders previously left at the brewery, and sold beer from the cart on the highway without the knowledge and contrary to the instructions of his master, it was held that his doing so was not an act for which the master was responsible, because the sale was without his knowledge, and not within the scope of the servant's employment: *The Queen* v. *Gilroys* (1866) 4 M. 656; see also *Boyle* v. *Smith* [1906] 1 K.B. 432.

It was held to be a clear case of hawking where the accused, a member of a club, received money in the street from a man, entered the club, procured there, and returned with, a bottle of whisky, and handed it to the man who had paid the money. This was done on three different occasions on the same day for different persons, who were not members of the club, and the accused made a profit on each transaction: *Neilson* v. *Dunsmore* (1900) 3 F.(J.) 6.

It was not hawking for a member of a club on Sunday to take money from a man outside the club premises, and for the member to enter the club and purchase drink there, and thereafter on the street to hand it to his friend, who consumed it: *Dewart* v. *Neilson* (1900) 2 F.(J.) 57. Nor for a certificate-holder to call, some miles distant, and solicit and obtain orders for spirits, executed by delivery next day, even upon the public road. "I cannot say that any definition of hawking that I ever heard of should lead to this result, that where people are living scattered all over a countryside, they are never to obtain a supply by sending an order for it unless they send that order in writing, and have the liquor delivered to them absolutely inside licensed premises": *per* Lord Justice-Clerk Macdonald, *Cameron* v. *Buchan* (1896) 23 R.(J.) at p. 48. See also *Pletts* v. *Beattie* [1896] 1 Q.B. 519, approved in *Mizen* v. *Old Florida Ltd.* (1934) 50 T.L.R. 348. Nor is it hawking, although a breach of certificate, for the holder of a public-house certificate on Sunday, outside his premises, to receive a bottle from a person, hereafter to enter his premises, fill the bottle with liquor, and deliver it outside the premises to the person: *Muir* v. *Campbell* (1888) 16 R.(J.) 20 at p. 23.

The maximum penalty for a contravention of (*a*) and (*b*) is a fine of level 5, and for a contravention of (*c*), a fine of level 3. Also, in the case of (*c*), a licence-holder is vicariously liable (see note to s.67) and both he and the premises are liable to disqualification. Further, in virtue of s.94, if a person convicted under the section is the holder of a wholesale licence, his licence is forfeited and he is disqualified from obtaining one for two years.

### Wholesale selling of alcoholic liquor

**90A.**—(1) A wholesaler or his employee or agent who barters, sells, or exposes or offers for sale alcoholic liquor shall be guilty of an offence unless—

(*a*) he does so from premises which are used exclusively for wholesale trading (whether solely of alcoholic liquor or not); or

(*b*) he does so from licensed premises, a licensed canteen or a registered club during the hours in respect of which it is lawful to sell alcohol by retail from or in these premises, that canteen or that club.

(2) A wholesaler or his employee or agent who sells alcoholic liquor to a person under 18 shall be guilty of an offence.

(3) A wholesaler or his employee or agent who causes or permits a person under 18 to sell alcoholic liquor without that sale having been specifically approved by a person of or over 18 shall be guilty of an offence.

(4) Section 67 of this Act (penalties for offences) shall apply in respect of offences under this section as if references in that section to a licence-holder were references to a wholesaler.

(5) Section 71 of this Act (defence of due diligence) shall apply to any person charged with an offence under this section as if the reference in that section to a licence-holder were a reference to a wholesaler.

(6) In this section—

"licence-holder" includes the holder of a licence under Part III of this Act; and

"wholesale" and "wholesaler," insofar as they relate to the sale of alcoholic liquor, have the meaning given in section 4(1) of the Alcoholic Liquor Duties Act 1979 in relation to dealing in alcoholic liquor.

DEFINITIONS
    "licensed canteen": s.139(1).
    "licensed premises": s.139(1).
    "registered club": s.139(1).

GENERAL NOTE

This section was introduced by s.52 of the 1990 Act to remedy the anomaly which arose from the repeal by the Finance Act 1981 of the excise licence requirements for wholesalers of alcohol and s.94 of the 1976 Act, which had the effect that wholesalers of alcohol were no longer subject to any controls. Concern had been expressed that anyone could set up as a "wholesaler" and, provided that they sold alcoholic liquor in wholesale quantities, they could sell from any premises to any age group: see *Hansard*, H.C. Vol. 177, col. 1143.

The section makes it an offence for a wholesaler or his employee or agent to barter, sell or expose or offer for sale alcoholic liquor unless he does so from (a) premises which are used exclusively for wholesale trading, whether solely of alcoholic liquor or not, or (b) he does so from licensed premises, a licensed canteen or registered club during the hours in which it is lawful to sell alcohol in those premises. The section also makes it an offence for a wholesaler to sell alcohol to a person under the age of 18 or for a person under the age of 18 to sell alcohol unless the sale is specifically approved. The defence of "due diligence" is made available by subs. (5).

*Subsections.* (1) This subsection makes the wholesaler or his employee or agent guilty of an offence if they barter, sell, or expose or offer for sale alcoholic liquor unless (a) they do so from premises which are exclusively used for wholesale trading (whether solely of alcoholic liquor or not), or (b) they do so from licensed premises, a licensed canteen or a registered club during the hours in respect of which it is lawful to sell alcohol by retail from those premises. For a general discussion of the "vicarious liability" of the licence-holder in statutory crimes, see Introduction, para. 7.13 and G. H. Gordon, *Criminal Law of Scotland* (2nd ed.), p. 295 *et seq.*, and in relation to vicarious liability for a "sale" see p. 299. In *British Car Auctions* v. *Wright* [1972] 1 W.L.R. 1519 (*q.v.*, and the cases there cited) a distinction was drawn between an "offer to sell," which was an offence, and an "invitation to treat," which was not an offence. A flick-knife exposed in a shop window with a price tag on it was not "an offer to sell," but an "invitation to treat" and accordingly not an offence: *Fisher* v. *Bell* [1961] 1 Q.B. 394.

(2) The sale by the wholesaler or his employee or agent of alcoholic liquor to a person under the age of 18 is an offence. The prosecution will need to prove that the person is under the age of 18 by corroborated evidence: *Lockwood* v. *Walker* 1909 2 S.L.T. 400. Evidence of impression that a person is under 18 is not corroboration of a young person's admission of their age: *Paton* v. *Wilson*, 1988 S.L.T. 634.

(3) The subsection makes provisions similar to those of the new s.97A apply to wholesalers, so that a sale by a person under the age of 18 years, unless specifically approved, is an offence: see note to s.97A.

(4) This subsection makes wholesalers liable to the same penalties which apply to any licence-holder under the 1976 Act. See note to s.67.

(5) This subsection provides that s.71 shall apply in respect of offences under this section. The defence of "due diligence" is available to a person accused under this section. For a general discussion of that defence, see Introduction, para. 7.9. The defence need only be proved on a balance of probabilities: *H.M.A.* v. *Mitchell*, 1951 J.C. 53; *Neish* v. *Stevenson*, 1969 S.L.T. 229.

(6) By making "licence-holder" include the holder of a licence under Pt. III, the section expands the definition of licence-holder given in s.139(1) to include the holder of a licence for a Seamen's Canteen to take account of permitted sales from licensed canteens under subs. (1)(b).

*Wholesale.* This is defined by ss.4(1) and 65(8) of the Alcoholic Liquor Duties Act 1979 (c. 4) in the terms: "dealing wholesale means the sale at any one time to any one person of quantities not less than the following, namely—(a) in the case of spirits, wine or made-wine, two gallons or one case; or (b) in the case of beer, four and a half gallons or two cases." Words including "case," "spirits," "wine," "made-wine" and "beer" are defined by ss.1 and 4 of the 1979 Act.

A penalty of level 5 applies to an offence under subs. (1), level 3 applies to an offence under subs. (2) and level 1 to an offence under subs. (3).

## Delivery of alcoholic liquor by vehicles, etc.

**91.**—(1) A person shall not, in pursuance of a sale by him of alcoholic liquor, deliver that liquor from any vehicle or receptacle unless—

(a) before the liquor was despatched, the quantity, description and price of the liquor and the name and address of the person to whom it was to be supplied had been entered in a day book kept in the premises from which the liquor was despatched, and

(b) the person delivering the liquor carries a delivery book or invoice in which there had been entered, before the liquor was despatched, the quantity, description and price of the liquor and the name and address of the person to whom it was to be supplied.

(2) A person shall not, himself or by his employee or agent,—

(a) carry in any vehicle or receptacle, while in use for the delivery of alcoholic liquor in pursuance of a sale by that person, any alcoholic liquor that is not entered in a day book and delivery book or invoice under subsection (1) above;

(b) deliver, in pursuance of a sale, any alcoholic liquor at any address not entered as aforesaid.

(3) A person shall not, himself or by his employee or agent, refuse to allow a constable to examine any vehicle or receptacle while in use for the delivery of alcoholic liquor or to examine a delivery book or invoice carried, or day book kept, under subsection (1) above.

(4) Nothing in this section shall prohibit or restrict the delivery of alcoholic liquor to a trader for the purposes of his trade or to a registered club for the purposes of the club.

(5) If any person contravenes the provisions of this section he shall be guilty of an offence.

GENERAL NOTE

"*Alcoholic liquor,*" "*constable,*" "*licence,*" "*registered club*" and "*contravene*" are defined in s.139(1).

A. *Delivery of alcoholic liquor from vehicles—general.* This section applies to all deliveries of alcoholic liquor "*in pursuance of a sale*" by the person delivering or carrying, or instructing the delivery of carriage. The words "in pursuance of a sale by him" make it clear that only deliveries in the course of trade are affected, and that a person delivering a gift of liquor to a friend in his motor car is not guilty of an offence because he has failed to record his gift in a day book or delivery book.

It would seem, however, that the words quoted have the effect of relieving any employee of the seller, such as manager or foreman or carrier, from criminal responsibility, with the exception of the obligation to allow a constable to examine the vehicle and documents (subs. (3)), which applies to the actual carrier, as well as to his employer, and with the possible exception of the obligation to deliver at the addresses entered in the delivery book or invoice (subs. (2)(*b*)). In the last-mentioned provision the words used are "in pursuance of a sale," and not, as in the other provisions of the section, "in pursuance of a sale *by that person,*" *i.e.* by the deliverer or carrier.

B. *Responsibility of seller.* The section applies to all deliveries by vehicle of alcoholic liquor in pursuance of a sale, whether the sale be by wholesale or by retail.

The duty of the seller is to satisfy himself that (a) the orders are entered in the delivery book, that the quantity, description and price of the liquor, and the name and address of each person ordering it, are entered, and that no liquor is sent out that is not ordered; (b) similar entries are written in the day book retained in the licensed premises, and the written-up delivery book is given to the carrier; (c) no fictitious entries are made in the delivery or day books, and that the books be on demand exhibited to any constable; (d) the carrier does not receive or take out any liquor other than that entered in the delivery book; and also (e) to instruct the carrier not to deliver liquor to persons and addresses other than those entered.

The seller, as the person instructing the delivery and the carriage of the liquor, is responsible for any contravention of the section by his *"employee or agent."*

C. *Responsibility of carrier.* The carrier of alcoholic liquor, who is not himself the seller, is guilty of contravention of subs. (3) if he refuses to allow a constable to examine his vehicle and any delivery book, day book or invoice. He is possibly also guilty if he delivers alcoholic liquor at any address not entered in the day book and delivery book or invoice: subs. (2)(b). This seems to depend upon whether "in pursuance of a sale" is to be construed literally, or whether it is to be construed as a shorthand repetition of the words used in the immediately preceding provision, *viz.*: "in pursuance of a sale by that person."

D. *Penalties.* The maximum penalty for a contravention of any of the offences is a fine of level 3 with both the licence-holder and the premises subject to disqualification. The offence is one for which the licence-holder is vicariously liable (Sched. 5); see note to s.67 for *"vicariously liable."*

## Restriction on carriage of alcoholic liquor in crates, etc., on contract carriages

**92.**—(1) If the holder of a P.S.V. operator's licence in respect of any vehicle, either himself or by his employee or agent, or if the employee or agent of such holder permits any alcoholic liquor to be carried on the said vehicle in such a container or other device as is mentioned in subsection (4) below at any time when that vehicle is being used for the carriage of passengers otherwise than at separate fares, he shall be guilty of an offence.

(2) If any person procures or attempts to procure a contravention of subsection (1) above he shall be guilty of an offence.

(3) Where the holder of a P.S.V. operator's licence is charged with an offence under this section by reason only of a contravention of subsection (1) above committed by an employee or agent of his, it shall be a defence for him to prove that the contravention took place without his consent or connivance and that he exercised all due diligence to prevent it.

(4) This section applies to any container or other device (including a container or device fixed to, or forming part of, a vehicle) constructed or adapted for the purpose of holding two or more bottles or cans or of holding liquid in excess of six pints.

(5) In this section "P.S.V. operator's licence" and "contract carriage" have the like meanings as in Part II of the Public Passenger Vehicles Act 1981.

GENERAL NOTE

Amended, 1985, c. 67, Sched. 7.

*Restriction on carriage of liquor in contract carriages.* The purpose of this section is to prevent persons travelling in a party on a hired public service vehicle from carrying quantities of alcoholic liquor with them. The section makes it an offence for the holder of a public service vehicle licence, his servant or his agent to permit more than six pints of liquor to be carried by such a party on the vehicle. The offence is also committed by any person who procures or attempts to procure the contravention. Where the offence is committed by a servant or agent of the public service vehicle licence-holder, it is a defence for the licence-holder to establish that the offence occurred outwith his control, and that he exercised all due diligence to prevent it; see note to s.67 for a discussion *re "due diligence."* The offence is not committed if the party carry the liquor in a separate vehicle other than a public service vehicle.

The maximum penalty for a contravention of subs. (1) is a fine of level 3 as regards a public service vehicle licence-holder and level 1 as regards any other person, and for a contravention of subs. (2) a fine of level 1.

*Subs.* (1). For a definition of *"public service vehicle,"* see Public Passenger Vehicles Act 1981, s.1. A *"P.S.V. Operator's Licence"* means a P.S.V. operator's licence granted under the provisions of Pt. II of the Public Passenger Vehicles Act 1981: see s.82 of the 1981 Act.

## Sale of alcoholic liquor on passenger vessels on Sundays

**93.**—(1) No person shall, except during the period between half-past 12 and half-past two in the afternoon, or the period between half-past six and 11 in the evening, himself, or by his employee or agent, sell or supply alcoholic liquor on a passenger vessel during any voyage commencing on a Sunday and terminating on the same day, being—

(*a*) a voyage between any two places in Scotland; or

(*b*) a voyage in a vessel going from and returning on the same day to the same place in Scotland;

and if any person contravenes this section he shall be guilty of an offence.

(2) In this section, the expression "passenger vessel" means a vessel of any description employed for the carriage of passengers which goes from any place in the United Kingdom to any other such place, or goes from and returns to the same place in the United Kingdom on the same day.

GENERAL NOTE

*Sale of alcoholic liquor on passenger vessels on Sundays.* Passenger vessels do not require a licence under the Act to sell alcoholic liquor (s.138(1)). Subs. (1) under the Act makes it an offence, however, for a person on a passenger vessel on a voyage starting on a Sunday and finishing on the same day between any two places in Scotland or going from and returning to the same place in Scotland on the same day to sell or supply alcoholic liquor outwith the hours of 12.30 p.m. to 2.30 p.m. and 6.30 p.m. to 11 p.m. The maximum penalty for a contravention of the section is a fine of level 3.

For the meaning of *"contravene,"* see s.139(1).

*"Passenger vessel"* is defined in subs. (2).

## Forfeiture or wholesaler's excise licence in certain cases

**94.**

GENERAL NOTE

This section, which replaced s.167 of the 1959 Act, was repealed by the Finance Act 1981, Sched. 19.

## Sale or supply of alcoholic liquor for consumption outside registered club

**95.**—(1) If any person sells or supplies alcoholic liquor in the premises of a registered club for consumption off the premises, or authorises such sale or supply of alcoholic liquor, or pays for alcoholic liquor so sold or supplied, he shall, unless such liquor was sold or supplied to a member of the club in person for consumption by him or to a person holding a licence for the sale of such liquor, be guilty of an offence.

(2) If subsection (1) above is contravened as regards any club, every person whose name is, at the time of the contravention, contained in the list lodged under subs. (3)(*b*) of section 103 of the Act, or as the case may be in the new list lodged under subsection (5) or (5A) of that section, in respect of that club shall be guilty of an offence under subsection (1) above:

Provided that a person shall not be convicted of such an offence if he proves that the contravention in question took place without his knowledge or consent.

(3) Where in any proceedings under this section it is proved that any alcoholic liquor has been received or delivered in the premises of a registered club and taken outside those premises, for the purposes of the proceedings such liquor shall, unless the contrary is shown, be deemed to have been taken for consumption off the premises.

GENERAL NOTE

Amended, 1989, c. 55, s.21(1).

"*Alcoholic liquor*" and "*registered club*" are defined in s.139(1).

*Sale of liquor for consumption outside registered club.* The only persons to whom liquor may be sold on the premises of a registered club for consumption off the premises are members of the club who purchase the liquor in person (a messenger, for example, sent by a club member may not be supplied) and holders of licences for the sale of liquor. The 1959 Act desiderated the holders of an excise licence. The deletion of the word "excise" in the 1976 Act has the effect of restricting the licence-holders who may purchase liquor for consumption outside registered clubs to the holders of licences within the meaning of the 1976 Act, *i.e.* of licences granted under the Act other than under Part III of the Act (see s.139(1)). The licence must cover the type of liquor purchased. It is an offence for a person to sell liquor in a registered club for consumption off the premises other than to a club member in person or to a licence-holder. If, in the course of the trial it is proved the alcoholic liquor changed hands in the club premises and was taken outside the premises, the liquor is deemed to have been taken for consumption off the premises. The maximum penalty for the offence is a fine of level 3 (Sched. 5).

Where there is a contravention of subs. (1), then every member of the committee of management or governing body of the club, whose name is on the list lodged in accordance with s.103 (as amended) is guilty of the offence unless he can prove that the contravention took place without his knowledge or consent (subs. (2)). The defence need only be proved on a balance of probabilities: see note to s.83. For a consideration of "*knowingly*," see note to s.68.

A conviction under the section has to be laid before the sheriff for consideration as to whether it merits cancellation of the convicted club's certificate of registration.

## Prohibition of sale or supply of alcoholic liquor in licensed canteens for consumption off the premises

**96.** If any person—

(*a*) sells or supplies alcoholic liquor in a licensed canteen for consumption outside the canteen, or

(*b*) takes alcoholic liquor from any such canteen for consumption outside the canteen,

he shall be guilty of an offence.

GENERAL NOTE

For the meanings of "*licensed canteen*" and "*alcoholic liquor*," see s.130(1). The maximum penalty for a contravention of (*a*) is a fine of level 3 with both the licence-holder and the premises liable to disqualification, the holder being vicariously liable for the offence, and for a contravention of (*b*) a fine of level 3 (Sched. 5); for "*vicariously liable*," see note to s.67; for "causes or permits" see note to s.97A

## Consumption in, taking away of, and selling liquor from, off-sale premises

**97.**—(1) If the holder of an off-sale licence or his employee or agent sells to any person, alcoholic liquor to be consumed on the premises in respect of which the licence is held, the licence-holder, employee or agent, as the case may be, shall be guilty of an offence.

(2) If any person induces the holder of an off-sale licence in respect of any premises, or the employee or agent of the licence-holder, to sell to him any alcoholic liquor, and consumes such liquor or any part thereof in those premises, he shall be guilty of an offence.

(3) If the holder of an off-sale licence, or his employee or agent takes, or causes or permits any other person to take, any alcoholic liquor from the premises in respect of which he holds such licence, either—

(a) for the purposes of its being sold or hawked on his account or for his benefit or profit, or

(b) for the purpose of its being consumed for his benefit or profit in any house or other premises belonging to him, or hired, used or occupied by him, or in which he may be interested, the licence-holder, employee or agent, as the case may be, shall be guilty of an offence.

(4) A holder of an off-sale licence or his employee or agent shall be guilty of an offence if he sells wine (including made-wine) in an open vessel.

GENERAL NOTE

For the meaning of "*off-sale licence,*" see s.9 and Sched. 1, and of "*alcoholic liquor,*" see s.139(1).

*Subsections.* (1) The condition of an off-sale certificate which the subsection supersedes prohibited the trafficking in or supply of liquor for consumption on the premises (1959 Act, Sched. 2). The subsection makes it an offence for the licence-holder, his employee or agent to sell liquor for consumption on the premises. Prior to amendment by para. 15 of Sched. 8 to the 1990 Act the section prohibited the supply gratuitously or otherwise of liquor for consumption on the premises, but the section was amended to make only the sale an offence. The maximum penalty for a contravention of the subsection is a fine of level 3 with both the licence-holder and the premises liable to disqualification, and with the holder vicariously liable for the offence (Sched. 5).

(2) The maximum penalty is a fine of level 3 (Sched. 5).

(3) For the meaning of "*hawk,*" see note to s.90. The maximum penalty is a fine of level 1 with both the premises and the licence-holder liable to disqualification, and with the licence-holder vicariously liable; for "*vicariously liable,*" see note to s.67; for "causes or permits" see note to s.97A.

(4) The maximum penalty is the same as for a contravention of subs. (1) (Sched. 5).

## Supervision of sales of liquor in off-sale premises

**97A.** A holder of a licence in respect of—

(a) any off-sale premises; or

(b) the off-sale part of any other premises,

or any employee or agent of his, who causes or permits a person under 18 to sell on these premises alcoholic liquor without that sale having been specifically approved by the licence holder or by a person of or over 18 acting on his behalf shall be guilty of an offence.

DEFINITIONS
"alcoholic liquor": s.139(1).
"off-sale premises": s.139(1).

GENERAL NOTE
This section, introduced by s.54 of the 1990 Act, makes provision for the sale of alcoholic liquor in off-sale premises to be supervised by the licence-holder or a person over the age of 18 years acting on his behalf, by making it an offence for a licence-holder, his employee or agent to cause or permit the sale of alcoholic liquor by a person under the age of 18 years, without the sale having been specifically approved by the licence-holder or a person over the age of 18 years acting on his behalf. The provision is a watered-down version of the Licensing Amendment (Scotland) Bill introduced in 1989. The section has been introduced upon a promise that if the Bill was dropped it would be included in this Act. There was public concern that persons under the legal age were able to buy alcohol without difficulty in off-sale premises from other under-18-year-olds working in the shop, particularly in a general store, with an off-sales part, which was not properly supervised.

For a general discussion of the "vicarious liability" of the licence-holder in statutory crimes, see Introduction, para. 7.3 and G. H. Gordon, *Criminal Law of Scotland* (2nd ed.), p. 295 *et seq.* For a discussion of the meaning of "causes or permits" in statutory offences, see Gordon, *op. cit.*, p. 311 *et seq.* The prosecution will need to prove that the person is under the age of 18 by corroborated evidence: *Lockwood* v. *Walker*, 1909 2 S.L.T. 400. Evidence of impression that a person is under 18 is not corroboration of a young person's admission of their age; *Paton* v. *Wilson*, 1988 S.L.T. 634.

Section 71 has been amended to provide that the defence of "due diligence" is available; see Introduction, para. 7.8. The defence need only be proved on a balance of probabilities: *H.M.A.* v. *Mitchell*, 1951 J.C. 53; *Neish* v. *Stevenson*, 1969 S.L.T. 229.

The fine is level 3.

### Restriction on sale or supply of liquor in premises subject to restricted hotel licence

**98.**—(1) The holder of a restricted hotel licence or his employee or agent shall be guilty of an offence if he sells or supplies any alcoholic liquor for consumption on the premises in respect of which a licence is held, except as follows, that is to say—

 (*a*) the licence-holder or employee or agent may sell or supply such liquor to persons taking table meals in the premises for consumption by such a person as an ancillary to his meal;

 (*b*) the licence-holder or employee or agent may sell or supply such liquor to persons residing in the premises, for consumption by such a person or by a private friend of such a person who is bona fide entertained by, and at the expense of, that person;

 (*c*) the licence-holder or employee or agent may supply such liquor to any private friend of a person residing in the premises who is bona fide entertained by, and at the expense of, that person, for consumption by such a friend entertained as aforesaid.

(2) The holder of a restricted hotel licence or his employee or agent shall be guilty of an offence if he trafficks in or supplies any alcoholic liquor for consumption off the premises in respect of which the licence is held, except to persons residing in the premises, for consumption by such a person or by a private friend of such a person who is bona fide entertained by, and at the expense of, that person as an ancillary to a meal supplied at, but to be consumed off, the premises.

GENERAL NOTE
This section and s.99 relate respectively to restricted hotel licences and restaurant licences, forms of licence which were introduced by the 1962 Act. The 1976 Act makes

specific offences of what were formerly breaches of certificate. In accordance with this change, ss.98 and 99 make specific offences sales outwith those permitted by the types of certificate with which the sections are concerned.

For "*restricted hotel licence,*" see s.9 and Sched. 1.

For "*table meal,*" see s.139(1).

For "*traffick,*" see note to s.90.

The maximum penalty for a contravention of the section is a fine of level 3 with both the premises and the licence-holder liable to disqualification. For circumstances in which it was held that sandwiches consumed were subservient to drink and that there was no genuine taking of a meal, see *Robertson* v. *Mackenzie,* 1975 S.L.T. 222; *R.* v. *Liverpool Licensing Justices, ex p. Tynan* [1961] 2 All E.R. 363 and *Stainton* v. *McNaughton,* 1991 G.W.D. 9–548.

### Restriction on sale or supply of liquor in premises subject to restaurant licence

**99.** The holder of a restaurant licence or his employee or agent shall be guilty of an offence if—

 (*a*) he sells or supplies any alcoholic liquor for consumption on the premises, except to persons taking meals in the premises, for consumption by such a person as an ancillary to his meal; or

 (*b*) he trafficks in or supplies any alcoholic liquor for consumption off the premises in respect of which the licence is held.

GENERAL NOTE

See note to s.98.

For "*restaurant licence,*" see s.9 and Sched. 1.

For "*table meal,*" see s.139(1).

For "*person taking meals,*" see note on *Robertson,* s.98.

For "*traffick,*" see note to s.90.

See *Stainton* v. *McNaughtan* 1991 G.W.D. 9–548 for a conviction for selling alcohol not ancillary to a meal. The court held that the word "or" in the subsection was conjunctive and not disjunctive. See Note to s.101 regarding "ancillary to" a meal.

The maximum penalty is a fine of level 3.

### Restriction on sale or supply of liquor in premises subject to a refreshment licence

**100.** The holder of a refreshment licence or his employee or agent shall be guilty of an offence if—

 (*a*) he trafficks in or sells any alcoholic liquor for consumption off the premises in respect of which the licence is held, or

 (*b*) he sells or supplies alcoholic liquor at any time when other refreshments, including food and non-alcoholic beverages, are not available for sale.

GENERAL NOTE

The section makes it an offence to sell under a refreshment licence alcoholic liquor for consumption off the premises or when food or non-alcoholic beverages are not for sale. The maximum penalty for a contravention of the section is a fine of level 3.

For "*refreshment licence,*" see s.9 and Sched. 1.

For the meaning of "*traffick,*" see note to s.90.

### Restriction on sale or supply of liquor in premises subject to entertainment licence

**101.**—(1) The holder of an entertainment licence or his employee or agent shall be guilty of an offence if he trafficks in or supplies any alcoholic liquor for consumption off the premises in respect of which the licence is held.

(2) A licensing board, when granting an entertainment licence, may attach conditions to the licence, including conditions placing restrictions on the permitted hours, in order to secure that the sale or supply of alcoholic liquor is ancillary to the entertainment, and the holder of the licence or his employee or agent shall be guilty of an offence if he contravenes any such condition.

GENERAL NOTE
It is an offence on the part of the holder of an entertainment licence, his employee or agent to sell liquor for consumption off the premises or in contravention of any condition attached to the licence in virtue of subs. (2), which enables a licensing board to attach conditions to an entertainment licence when granting it. The subsection specifically declares that such conditions may include restrictions on the permitted hours to ensure that the supply of liquor is ancillary to the entertainment. The maximum penalty for a contravention of the section is a fine of level 3.

For "*entertainment licence*," see s.9 and Sched. 1.

For the meaning of "*traffick*" see note to s.90; for a consideration of the words "*is ancillary to*," see *Robertson* v. *Mackenzie*, 1975 S.L.T. 222 and *R.* v. *Liverpool Licensing Justices, ex p. Tynan* [1961] 2 All E.R. 363.

## PART VII

### CLUBS

**Register of clubs**

**102.**—(1) The sheriff clerk for each sheriff court district (hereafter in this Part of this Act called "the registrar") shall keep a register of clubs situated within that district in respect of which a certificate of registration has been granted under this Part of this Act.

(2) A sheriff clerk depute may exercise any of the functions of the registrar under this Part of this Act.

(3) There shall be entered in the said register in respect of each club registered therein—

(*a*) the name of the club;

(*b*) the address of the premises in respect of which the certificate of registration has been granted;

(*c*) a statement whether the club is the tenant or the proprietor and occupier of those premises;

(*d*) the name and address of the secretary of the club;

(*e*) the date of the certificate granted to the club; and

(*f*) a statement whether the certificate has been granted for the first time or on renewal.

(4) The registration of a club under this Part of this Act shall not constitute the club licensed premises or authorise any sale of alcoholic liquor therein which would otherwise be illegal.

GENERAL NOTE
A. *Registered clubs—general.* This part of the Act provides the procedure whereby a club may become registered for the purposes of the Act, and may have its certificate of registration renewed triennially. It also specifies the matters for which the club rules must

provide before a certificate of registration may be granted, and the circumstances in which a grant or renewal of a certificate of registration may be used or a current certificate of registration cancelled. A certificate of registration of a club is granted, renewed, refused or cancelled by the sheriff and not by the licensing board, and there is no appeal from his decision, which is final: see note to s.117. The register of clubs in each sheriff court district is kept by the sheriff clerk for that district, and not, as in the case of licensed premises, by the clerk to each licensing board.

It is an offence to sell or supply alcoholic liquor at any time to any person in a club which is not registered under this Part of the Act, or to pay for alcoholic liquor so sold or supplied (s.120(1)), and if alcoholic liquor is kept in the premises of an unregistered club, for sale or supply in these premises, every officer and member of the club is guilty of an offence: s.120(2).

The supply of alcoholic liquor in a registered club to its members, or the consumption or taking away of alcoholic liquor by its members personally for their own consumption (see s.95), is legal, provided it occurs during permitted hours in accordance with the provisions of Part V of the Act. The restriction to permitted hours does not apply if the member is residing in the club premises: s.54(3)(c). S.107(1)(k) specifies the conditions which the club rules must impose for the supply of alcoholic liquor to visitors to the club, and if the rule in this connection is habitually broken (s.108(o)), or if persons who are not members of the club are habitually admitted merely for the purpose of obtaining alcoholic liquor (s.108(l)), renewal of the club's certificate of registration may be refused or the certificate may be cancelled: see ss.108, 109(3).

In a prosecution in relation to a registered club for the supply or consumption or taking from the premises of alcoholic liquor, outwith permitted hours, it is unnecessary to consider whether or not the transaction constitutes a sale, because the supply, consumption and taking from the premises outwith permitted hours are themselves contraventions of s.54(1). If, however, a club or its officials are charged with trafficking in alcoholic liquor or selling spirits by retail without a licence, in contravention of s.90, the prosecutor must prove a sale in order to obtain a conviction. In this connection, when a registered club, which was a members' club, organised an outing, in the course of which excisable liquor was supplied to members by club servants in a marquee, each member paying for the liquor as it was supplied, it was held that no sale to members took place, since the liquor belonged to the members jointly and a conviction for trafficking without a certificate was quashed: *Crossgate British Legion Club* v. *Davidson*, 1954 J.C. 35, following *Humphrey* v. *Tudgay* [1915] 1 K.B. 119. See also *McWilliams* v. *Main* (1902) 4 F.(J.) 54. Prosecutions for trafficking in connection with clubs arose more frequently before the passing of the 1903 Act, which provided for a new category of club, the registered club, and which made it an offence (1903 Act, s.83) to sell or supply or pay for liquor in an unregistered club, for which offence provision is now made by s.120.

Although in *Crossgates British Legion Club* v. *Davidson* (*supra*) it was made an express ground of decision that the club, which was a registered club, was a "members' club," it seems doubtful whether a club can lawfully obtain a certificate of registration if it is *not* a members' club or by virtue of its constitution bearing a close resemblance to a *bona fide* members' club; see *Elgin Indoor Bowling Club, Applicants*, 1989 S.C.C.R. 181 and the editor's Note thereto, where the sheriff granted a licence under the Gaming Act 1968 to a proprietary club, which by virtue of its constitution enjoyed a close resemblance to a bona fide members' club. It is a ground of objection to the grant or renewal of a certificate of registration, and a ground for cancellation of such a certificate, if the supply of alcoholic liquor to the club is not under the control of the members or of the committee of management elected annually by the members (s.108(1)(a)), or if the owner or lessor of the club premises, or the officials, committee of management, manager or a servant, have a personal interest in the purchase by the club, or the sale in the club, of alcoholic liquor, or in the profits therefrom: s.108(m) and (n). The position may perhaps be different in England, where it would appear not to be a ground of objection that the owner or lessor of the premises, or the club manager, has a personal interest in the sale of alcoholic liquor in the club. See, *e.g.* Licensing Act 1953, s.144(1) (now repealed).

B. *Subsections.* (1) The registrar is the sheriff clerk for the sheriff court district where the club is situated. The districts are specified in the Sheriff Court Districts Reorganisation Order 1975 (S.I. 1975 No. 637) (as amended by S.I's 1975 No. 1539, 1977 No. 672, 1978 No. 152, 1978 No. 1926 and 1983 No. 1028). This register, and a copy of the rules of any registered club lodged with the registrar, must at all reasonable times be open to inspection to any person on payment of 20p, and to a chief constable, or constable authorised by him in writing, and to an officer of Customs and Excise, without payment: s.115(1)(2).

(3) Items (a)–(d) of the particulars entered in the register are obtained from the application for the grant or renewal of the certificate of registration lodged with the registrar: see s.103.

(4) As to the meaning of "*licensed premises*," see s.139(1).

## Application for certificate of registration

**103.**—(1) An application for a certificate of registration in respect of any club shall be signed by the chairman, secretary or solicitor of the club, and shall be lodged with the registrar.

(2) There shall be specified in any such application—

(a) the name of the club;

(b) the objects of the club;

(c) the address of the premises occupied by the club.

(3) There shall be lodged along with any such application—

(a) two copies of the rules of the club;

(b) a list containing the name and address of each official and each member of the committee of management or governing body of the club; and

(c) a statement in the form set out in Schedule 6 to this Act certifying that the club is to be or, in the case of an existing club, has been and is to be conducted as a bona fide club and not mainly for the supply of alcoholic liquor.

(4) Any such statement as is referred to in subsection (3)(c) above shall be signed by two members of the licensing board for the area in which the premises occupied by the club are situated, and, if the premises occupied by the club are not owned by it, the statement shall be signed also by the owner of the premises or, if the owner is under a legal disability, by his legal representative:

Provided that any member of a licensing board who has signed the statement may, within 10 days of that signature, withdraw his name therefrom.

(5) Subject to subsection (5A) below, any change—

(a) made in the rules of the club; or

(b) which renders the information contained in the list lodged under subsection (3)(b) above, or as the case may be, the new list lodged under this or the following subsection, inaccurate or incomplete,

shall be intimated to the registrar forthwith; and where intimation is under paragraph (b) of this subsection there shall be lodged therewith a new list containing the name and address of each official and each member of the committee of management or governing body of the club after the change.

(5A) Where a change such as is mentioned in subsection (5)(b) above was made before the date on which section 21 of the Law Reform (Miscellaneous Provisions) (Scotland) Act 1980 came into force and the change was duly intimated to the registrar under the provisions of this Act applying before that date, no further intimation of the change shall be required but a new list containing the name and address of each official and each member of the committee of management or governing body of the club at that date shall forthwith be lodged with the registrar.

(6) If any person in an application under this section or in any of the documents specified in subsection (3), (5) or (5A) above makes any statement which he knows to be false in a material particular, or recklessly makes any statement which is false in a material particular, he shall be guilty of an offence.

(7) If subsection (6) above is contravened as regards any club, every person whose name is, at the time of contravention, contained in the list lodged under subsection (3)(*b*) above, or as the case may be in the new list last lodged under subsection (5) or (5A) above in respect of that club, shall be guilty of an offence under subsection (6) above:

Provided that a person shall not be convicted of such an offence if he proves that the contravention in question took place without his knowledge or consent.

GENERAL NOTE
Amended, 1980, c. 55, s.21.

A. *Application for certificate of registration of a club—general.* The application, with the accompanying documents, must be in complete conformity with the provisions of this section before the sheriff clerk, as registrar, may give notice of it to the persons and bodies mentioned in s.105, which is an essential step towards consideration of it by the sheriff. For the analogous position with regard to an application for the grant of a certificate for licensed premises under the Public Houses Acts Amendment (Scotland) Act 1862, see *Bootland* v. *McFarlane* (1900) 2 F. 1014. An application is incompetent if made before the club is constituted: *Scottish Homosexual Rights Group, Petrs.*, 1981 S.L.T.(Sh.Ct.) 18, because an unconstituted club cannot have a chairman, secretary or solicitor. An application is not duly made, and is invalid, if the statement referred to in subs. (3)(*c*) is signed by persons who have no knowledge of the facts which they purport to certify: *Wellington Athletic Club* v. *Magistrates of Leith* (1904) 12 S.L.T. 570. An application was held not to be invalid because the premises stated to be occupied by the club (see subs. (2)(*c*)) had been purchased under missives which were conditional upon the application being granted: *Bayview Club, Petitioners*, 1954 S.L.T.(Sh.Ct.) 43; but the opposite view was taken, and the application dismissed, where the club which had purchased premises on a similar condition, was not in occupation of any premises at the time of the application, and where the premises named in the application were unsuitable, without alteration, for immediate use as club premises: *Glasgow Rangers Supporters' Club, Petitioners*, 1960 S.L.T.(Sh.Ct.) 27.

The form of the application is not prescribed by the Act, but in practice sheriff clerks provide a printed form of application on request.

B. *Subsections.* (1) As to the form of application, see note A, above. A proposed club cannot have a chairman, secretary or solicitor—see note A. "*Secretary*" includes any officer of the club or other persons performing the duties of a secretary: s.118. If the person signing the application makes any statement in it which he knows to be false in a material particular, or recklessly makes any statement which is false in a material particular, he is guilty of an offence: subs. (6). For an example of an apparent misstatement which was held not to invalidate the application, see note A, above.

(2) As to the position when the premises under (*c*) to be occupied by the club are held under missives which are conditional on the application being granted, see note A, above.

(3)(*a*) The "*rules*" of the club must make provision for the matters specified in s.107. If the rules lodged with the application do not comply with s.107, the application cannot be granted: s.105(6). It was opined in *Scottish Homosexual Rights Group, Petrs.*, that the court should have regard to changes in the rules made between the time of the application and of the hearing, but not to amendments, which are proposed at the time of the hearing to be made in the future—*British Legion (Scotland) Tiree Branch*, 1947 S.L.T.(Sh.Ct.) 65.

(*c*) If the statement is signed by persons who have no knowledge of the facts certified, the application is invalid: see note A, above. As to the offence which may be committed by making a false statement, see subs. (6).

(4) Two members of the licensing board for the area where the club is situated require to sign the statement desiderated by subs. (3)(*c*) and by the proviso to subs. (4) a member can withdraw his name within 10 days of signing. Subs. (4) also contains provisions as to the

requirement of the signature of the owner of the club premises where they are not owned by the club.

(5) and (5A) Subs. (5) was amended and subs. (5A) added by the Law Reform (Miscellaneous Provisions) (Scotland) Act 1980, s.21. The amendment corrected a *causa omissus* and gave effect to the intention of the Act that all members of the governing body of the club should be liable for certain offences, which had been frustrated by the fact that only the secretary's name required to be in the register of clubs. The subsections now provide that a list of members and officials of the committee of management or the governing body of the club should be lodged and kept up-to-date. Any change in the club rules or the list of officials and management committee members lodged in accordance with subs. (3)(*a*) and (*b*) and (5A) must immediately be notified to the registrar.

(6) and (7) In order that the offence mentioned in this section may be committed, the false statement must be known to be false or must be made recklessly. A false statement made innocently, while it would not justify a conviction under this section, may invalidate an application for a certificate of registration. For the position regarding an application for a certificate in respect of licensed premises in this connection, see *Bootland* v. *McFarlane* (1900) 2 F. 1014.

The 1959 Act provided that the offence could be committed by, *inter alios*, the chairman, secretary or solicitor signing the application, and the justices, magistrates or members of the licensing court or court of appeal who sign the certificate as to the bona fides of the club. The position is the same in virtue of subs. (6) under the 1976 Act with the change consequential on the introduction of licensing boards of the substitution of members of the licensing board for justices, etc., and the change consequential on the provisions of subs. (7) whereby every member of the committee of management at the time of the contravention is liable for the offence, unless he proves that the contravention was without his knowledge or consent.

The offence may now be tried in the sheriff or the district court: s.128. The maximum penalty is a fine of level 5 (Sched. 5).

## Application for renewal of certificate of registration

**104.**—(1) Subject to subsection (2) below, an application for the renewal of a certificate of registration granted to a club under this Part of this Act shall be lodged with the registrar by the secretary of the club not later than 21 days before the date of expiry of that certificate.

(2) Notwithstanding subsection (1) above, the sheriff may entertain such an application if it is lodged later than 21 days before the said date, but shall not grant the application unless he is satisfied that the failure to lodge it timeously was due to inadvertence.

(3) The secretary of the club shall lodge, along with such application, a certificate stating either that no changes have been made in the rules of the club or in the list containing the names and addresses of the officials and the members of the committee of management or governing body of the club since the last application was made under this section or section 103 of this Act, as the case may be, or that any such change has already been intimated to the registrar.

(4) Section 103 of this Act shall, with any necessary modifications, apply in respect of an application for the renewal of a certificate of registration as it applies in respect of an application under that section.

GENERAL NOTE

*Application for renewal of certificate of registration.* The *"expiry"* of a certificate is three years from the date of issue: s.106. An application for renewal of the certificate must be lodged by the secretary of the club not later than 21 days before the date of expiry: subs. (1). As to the meaning of *"secretary,"* see s.118. Subs. (2e) gives the sheriff a discretionary power to entertain a late application, provided the application is lodged before the certificate expired (see below), if the failure to lodge timeously was due to inadvertence. It is not competent to invoke subs. (2) if the application is lodged after the certificate has expired: *Royal British Legion Club, Petrs.*, 1984 S.L.T.(Sh.Ct.) 62, following *Chief Constable of Strathclyde* v. *Hamilton and District Bookmakers Club*, 1977 S.L.T.(Sh.Ct.) 78.

When an application for renewal has been made, the certificate of registration remains in force, pending the sheriff's final decision, for a period not exceeding three months from the normal expiry date, and if the sheriff thinks fit, for a further period not exceeding three months (s.106, proviso). An incompetent application, such as a late application after the certificate has expired, does not act to revive retrospectively a certificate which has expired: *Royal British Legion Club, Petrs.*, *supra*.

When cancellation proceedings under the Licensing (Scotland) Act 1913 commenced before an application for renewal was duly made under this section, it was held that the question of cancellation must be disposed of before the renewal application was considered, although before this could be done the normal expiry date of the certificate of registration had passed: *Inch* v. *Buckhaven Burgh Ex-Service Men's Club*, 1953 S.L.T.(Sh.Ct.) 108.

The application for renewal must comply, in respect of the information it contains and the documents which accompany it, with the provisions of s.103.

## Procedure on application for grant or renewal of certificate of registration

**105.**—(1) The applicant shall give intimation of the lodging of an application for the grant of a certificate of registration in respect of a club by—

(a) publishing a notice thereof twice in the seven days immediately following the date of such lodging in a newspaper circulating in the area in which the club is situated;

(b) displaying a notice thereof in a conspicuous place on or near the premises occupied by the club for the period of 21 days immediately following that date.

(2) On an application for the grant or for the renewal of such a certificate being lodged in accordance with the foregoing provisions of this Part of this Act, the registrar shall forthwith give notice of such application—

(a) to the chief constable;

(b) to the council of the district or islands area within which the premises are situated; and

(c) to the fire authority for the area.

(3) Objection to the grant or renewal of a certificate of registration in respect of any club may be made on any of the grounds specified in section 108 of this Act by—

(a) any of the persons to whom notice has been given under subsection (2) above;

(b) any person owning or occupying property in the neighbourhood of the premises occupied by the club;

(c) a community council for the area in which the premises are situated which has been established in accordance with the provisions of the Local Government (Scotland) Act 1973; and

(d) any church which in the opinion of the sheriff represents a significant body of opinion among persons residing in the neighbourhood of those premises.

(4) Any such objections shall be lodged with the registrar by the objector and a copy of the objections shall be sent to the secretary of the club in respect of which the application is made within 21 days of the first publication of the notice in pursuance of subsection (1)(a) above.

(5) Any objections to the renewal of a certificate of registration in respect of any club by any of the persons to whom notice has been given

under subsection (2) above shall be lodged with the registrar and a copy of the objections sent to the secretary of the club concerned within 21 days of the date of the aforesaid notice.

(6) On an application for the grant of a certificate of registration in respect of any club or for the renewal of such a certificate—

(*a*) if no objections to the grant or renewal of such certificate are lodged in accordance with the foregoing provisions of this section, or if all such objections are withdrawn, the sheriff shall, if he is satisfied that the application has been duly made in accordance with the foregoing provisions of this Part of this Act and that the rules of the club are in conformity with the provisions of this Act, grant the application;

(*b*) if such objections are lodged and not withdrawn, the sheriff shall, as soon as may be, hear parties upon the application and objections and may order such enquiry as he thinks fit, and shall thereafter grant or refuse the certificate, and may award expenses against the unsuccessful party.

(7) The sheriff shall, on granting any such application, cause the entries required by section 102 of this Act to be made in the register of clubs and thereupon the registrar shall issue to the applicant a certificate of registration in the form set out in Schedule 6 to this Act.

GENERAL NOTE

A. *General*. This section specifies the procedure which follows the lodging of an application for the grant or renewal of a certificate of registration in conformity with ss.103 and 104.

B. *Subsections*. (1) and (2) *Notice of application*. If the sheriff clerk, as registrar, is satisfied that the application, and the documents which accompany it, comply with the provisions of s.103, and, if the application is for renewal, are lodged timeously in terms of s.104, he must forthwith give notice of the application to the chief constable and to the district council or islands area council for the district or islands area in which club premises are situated, and to the firemaster.

(3) The objectors specified are the same as those specified in connection with licences (for which, see note to s.16(1)). A ward committee is not entitled to object (*Glasgow Fire Service & Salvage Corps Social and Athletic Club, Applicants*, 1968 S.L.T.(Sh.Ct.) 47). In *Free Gardeners* (*East of Scotland*) *Social Club* v. *Chief Constable of Edinburgh*, 1967 S.L.T. (Sh.Ct.) 80, it was held to be an irrelevant objection that adequate police supervision of the premises was impossible.

The grounds of objection are limited to one or more of those specified in s.108.

(4) and (5) Any objector, on lodging objections to an application for a certificate of registration or the renewal of such a certificate must send a copy *to the secretary of the club* within 21 days of the date of the notice of the application. The objector does not comply with the provisions of this subsection if he sends a copy of the objections only to the solicitor who signed the application on behalf of the club. *Chief Constable of Dundee* v. *Dundee and District Railwaymen's Social and Welfare Club*, 1958 S.L.T.(Sh.Ct.) 40.

(6) and (7) *Grant or refusal of application*. If there are no objections, or any objections are withdrawn, the sheriff may not refuse to grant a certificate of registration if the application has been duly made in compliance with s.103, and, if it is an application for renewal, in compliance with s.104, and if the rules of the club are in conformity with s.107. In this respect the sheriff does not have the discretion which is given to a licensing board in relation to the granting or refusing of a licence for licensed premises. When objections are insisted in, the sheriff, after such inquiry as he thinks fit, may refuse the application only if one or more of the grounds of the objection specified in s.108, and founded on the objections lodged by the objector, are established. The sheriff's decision with regard to the grant or renewal of a certificate of registration is final and not subject to appeal except in regard to a procedural interlocutor: s.117(2). Irregular procedure, etc., by the sheriff may

found an action of reduction: see note to s.117. Any undertakings given in respect of a certificate of registration subsist for the currency of the certificate (*United Biscuits (Tollcross) Sports and Social Club, Applicants*, 1973 S.L.T.(Sh.Ct.) 25).

### Currency of certificate of registration

**106.** A certificate of registration shall, subject to the provisions of this Part of this Act, remain in force for a period of three years from the date of issue:

Provided that, where an application for the renewal of such a certificate has been made, that certificate shall remain in force pending the final decision of the sheriff on such application for a period not exceeding three months from the date on which the certificate would otherwise have expired and, if the sheriff thinks fit, for a further period not exceeding three months.

GENERAL NOTE
Where an application for renewal is lodged after the certificate has expired, the certificate is not continued or revived: see note to s.104.

### Club rules qualifying for registration

**107.**—(1) A certificate of registration shall not be granted under this Part of this Act to any club unless the rules of the club provide—

(*a*) that the business and affairs of the club shall be under the management of a committee or governing body who shall be elected for not less than one year by the general body of members and shall be subject in whole or in part or in a specified proportion to annual re-election, or of whom not more than one-third may be non-elected persons from outwith the club and the remainder shall be elected and subject to annual re-election as aforesaid;

(*b*) that no member of the committee or governing body and no manager or servant employed in the club shall have any personal interest in the sale of alcoholic liquor therein or in the profits arising from such sale;

(*c*) that the committee or governing body shall hold periodical meetings;

(*d*) that, unless the club is one to which subsection (4) below applies, all members of the club shall be elected by the whole body of members or by the committee or governing body, with or without specially added members;

(*e*) that, unless the club is one to which subsection (4) below applies, the names and addresses of persons proposed as ordinary members of the club shall be displayed in a conspicuous place in the club premises for at least a week before their election, and that an interval of not less than two weeks shall elapse between the nomination and election of ordinary members;

(*f*) that no alcoholic liquor shall be sold or supplied in the club to any person under 18;

(*g*) that no person under 18 shall be admitted a member of the club unless the club is one which is devoted primarily to some athletic purpose or to which subsection (4) below applies;

(*h*) that no persons shall be allowed to become honorary or temporary members of the club or be relieved of the payment of the regular entrance fee or subscription, except those possessing certain qualifications defined in the rules and subject to conditions and regulations prescribed therein;

(*i*) that there shall be defined subscription payable in advance by members;

(*j*) that correct accounts and books shall be kept showing the financial affairs and intromissions of the club;

(*k*) that a visitor shall not be supplied with alcoholic liquor in the club premises unless on the invitation and in the company of a member and that the member shall, upon the admission of such visitor to the club premises or immediately upon his being supplied with such liquor, enter his own name and the name and address of the visitor in a book which shall be kept for the purpose and which shall show the date of each visit; and

(*l*) that no alcoholic liquor shall be sold or supplied in the club premises for consumption off the premises, except to a member of the club in person for consumption by him or to a person holding a licence or a wholesaler's excise licence for the sale of such liquor:

Provided that this subsection shall not apply to any lodge of Freemasons duly constituted under a charter from the Grand Lodge of Scotland.

(2) Notwithstanding anything in subsection (1) above, the rules of a registered club may provide for the admission to the premises of the club of persons who are members of another club, and for the sale and supply of alcoholic liquor to such persons by or on behalf of the club for consumption on the premises, if—

(*a*) the other club is a registered club whose premises are in the locality and are temporarily closed; or

(*b*) both clubs exist for learned, educational, or political objects of a similar nature; or

(*c*) each of the clubs is primarily a club for persons who are qualified by service or past service, or by any particular service or past service, in Her Majesty's Forces, and are members of an organisation established by Royal Charter, and consists wholly or mainly of such persons; or

(*d*) each of the clubs is primarily a club for persons who carry on the same trade, profession or occupation, and that trade, profession or occupation is the same in the case of either club; or

(*e*) each of the clubs is a working men's club, that is to say, a club which is, as regards its purposes, qualified for registration as a working men's club under the Friendly Societies Act 1974, and is a registered society within the meaning of that Act or of the Industrial and Provident Societies Act 1965; or

(*f*) each of the clubs is one to which subsection (4) below applies.

(3) Notwithstanding anything in this Act, the authority of a licence shall not be required for such a sale of alcoholic liquor as is mentioned in

subsection (2) above and, where the rules of a club provide as aforesaid, alcoholic liquor may be supplied in the premises of the club to such persons as are mentioned in that subsection and their guests for consumption on the premises as it may to members of the club and their guests.

(4) This subsection applies to the students' union of a university, central institution, college of education or a further education college under the management of an education authority, which is recognised and certified as such to the registrar by the Senate or Academic Council of the university or the governing body of the central institution or college of education, or by the education authority, as the case may be; and any expressions used in this subsection which are also used in the Education (Scotland) Act 1962 shall have the same meanings in this subsection as in that Act.

GENERAL NOTE

*Club rules.* Subs. (1) specifies the matters for which the rules of a registered club *must* provide as a statutory minimum. The rules may also, of course, in the club's discretion, deal with other matters, and the detailed working out of the statutory requirements is a matter for the club itself.

Two copies of the rules of the club must be lodged with each application for the grant or renewal of a certificate of registration: s.103(3)(*a*); and the sheriff may not grant or renew such a certificate unless he is satisfied that the club rules are in conformity with this section: s.105(6)(*a*). Changes in the rules made between the time of the application and the hearing may fall to be considered; see note to s.103. If, for any reason, a certificate of registration is granted or renewed, although the club rules do not conform to this section, this would appear to provide a ground for cancelling the certificate of registration if proceedings under s.109 are initiated: see ss.108(*b*), 109(3)(*a*).

If any of the rules of a registered club are habitually broken, the certificate of registration may be cancelled: ss.109(3)(*a*), 108(*o*); or the sheriff may refuse to renew it when application for its annual renewal is made: ss.105(3) and (6)(*b*), 108(*o*).

The proviso to subs. (1) exempts chartered freemasons' lodges. Students' unions which meet the requirements of subs. (4) are exempt from providing for rule (g). For decisions on what constitutes a general body of members of a club, see *Ballieston Miners' Welfare Society* v. *Chief Constable of Lanarkshire*, 1966 S.L.T.(Sh.Ct.) 30, *Archer Golf Club Ptrs.*, 1966 S.L.T.(Sh.Ct.) 10, *Largs Golf Club Ptrs.*, 1966 S.L.T.(Sh.Ct.) 71, and *Oregon and District Working Men's Social Club Ptrs.*, 1966 S.L.T.(Sh.Ct.) 73.

*Sale of liquor in a club to members of other clubs.* Subss. (2) and (3) provide that alcoholic liquor may be sold to non-members of a club without special authority provided the conditions prescribed by those subsections are fulfilled.

## Competent grounds of objection to registration

**108.** The sheriff shall not consider any objection to the grant or renewal of a certificate of registration unless it is made on one or more of the following grounds—

(*a*) that the application made by the club is in any respect specified in such objection not in conformity with the provisions of this Act;

(*b*) that the rules of the club are in any respect specified in such objection not in conformity with the provisions of this Act;

(*c*) that the club has ceased to exist or has less than 25 members;

(*d*) that the premises are, or the situation thereof is, not suitable or convenient for the purposes of a club;

(*e*) that the club occupies premises in respect of which, within the period of 12 months immediately preceding the formation of the club, an order had been made under section 67(3) of this Act or the renewal of a licence under this Act had been refused, or in respect of which at the time when the premises were first occupied by the club an order was in force under section 110 of this Act that they should not be used for the purposes of a club;

(f) that the club is not conducted in good faith as a club, or that it is kept or habitually used for any unlawful purpose or mainly for the supply of alcoholic liquor;

(g) that there has been a failure to intimate to the registrar forthwith any change in the rules of the club or in the list containing the names and addresses of the officials and members of the committee of management or governing body of the club;

(h) that the club is to be used mainly as a drinking club;

(i) that there is frequent drunkenness in the club premises, or that drunken persons are frequently seen to leave the premises;

(j) that the club is or, in the case of an application for the renewal of a certificate of registration, has been, at any time during the currency of the certificate of registration in respect of which the application for renewal is made, conducted in a disorderly manner;

(k) that illegal sales of alcoholic liquor have taken place in the club premises;

(l) that persons who are not members of the club are habitually admitted to the club premises merely for the purpose of obtaining alcoholic liquor;

(m) that the supply of alcoholic liquor to the club is not under the control of the members of the club or of the committee of management or governing body of the club;

(n) that the officials and committee of management or governing body of the club, or the manager, or a servant employed in or by the club, have or will have a personal interest in the purchase by the club or in the sale in the premises of the club of alcoholic liquor or in the profits arising therefrom, or, where the said premises are not owned by the club, that the owner or the immediate lessor of the premises has or will have such a personal interest;

(o) that any of the rules of the club referred to in section 107(1) of this Act are habitually broken;

(p) that persons are habitually admitted or supplied as members of the club without an interval of at least two weeks between their nomination and election as ordinary members, or for a subscription of a nominal amount;

(q) that the officials and committee of management or governing body of the club, or the members of the club, are persons of bad character or persons who follow no lawful occupation and have no means of subsistence;

(r) that the club has been, is or will be used as a resort of persons of bad character;

(s) that alcoholic liquor is sold or supplied for consumption on or off the premises outwith the permitted hours.

GENERAL NOTE

A. *Grounds of objection to registration of club—general.* The only grounds of objection which may be considered by the sheriff to the grant or renewal of a certificate of registration are those specified in this section. The persons who may lodge objections are specified in s.105(3), and the procedure with regard to objections in s.105(4)(5). The grounds of objection specified in this section may also justify the cancellation of a certificate of registration in accordance with the procedure specified in s.109.

B. *Paragraphs.* (*a*) For a case in which an objection to an application was sustained on the ground that the application was not in conformity with the provisions of the Act, see *Wellington Athletic Club* v. *Magistrates of Leith* (1904) 12 S.L.T. 570.

(*b*) As to the statutory requirements regarding the rules of a registered club, see s.107.

(*d*) For an objection that the situation of the premises was unsuitable because they were in a residential area, see *Edinburgh and District Motor Club Ltd.* (1934) 50 Sh.Ct.Rep. 165. In *Scottish Homosexual Rights Group, Petrs.*, 1981 S.L.T.(Sh.Ct.) 18 it was opined that, where works were in progress to alter the premises when the application was lodged, and the work was sufficiently advanced at the date of the hearing to render the premises suitable, the application should not be refused solely on the ground that the work was in progress. In *Dick* v. *Stirling Lawn Tennis and Squash Club*, 1981 S.L.T.(Sh.Ct.) 103, an application was refused, because no modifications had in fact been made and therefore the suitability of the premises at the date of the application fell to be considered. This case highlights the difficulties for a club which proposes extensive modifications or rebuildings, which it would only undertake if registration is guaranteed, but is now required to effect the modification or rebuilding in the hope that its application for registration will then be allowed.

(*h*) This objection, which relates to the *future* use of the club, was sustained when an unregistered club, with large fully-equipped premises, acquired additional small premises half a mile away because the supply of alcohol was prohibited by a clause in the titles of the main premises. The application for registration was in respect only of the additional premises. It was refused on the ground that the additional premises were to be used mainly for drinking: *Shotts Miners' Welfare Society* v. *Chief Constable of Lanarkshire*, Glasgow, January 18, 1960; see also *Dick* v. *Stirling Lawn Tennis and Squash Club, supra.*

(*i*) "*Persons . . . frequently seen to leave the premises*" have been held to include persons who were proved to have come from the club and who were seen in a public street moving away from its vicinity, but who were not actually seen by the witnesses as they were passing from the club premises to the street: *Gordon Highlanders Club* v. *Mason*, 1954 S.L.T.(Sh.Ct.) 45.

(*j*) This subsection was amended by para. 16 of Sched. 8 to the 1990 Act to allow the past conduct of the club during the currency of the certificate to be taken in account upon a renewal application. Prior to amendment it was arguable that only the conduct at the date of application was relevant. A similar amendment has been made to s.109(1) q.v.

(*k*) Illegal sales would include supplying liquor to a member, for consumption outside the club not being for his own consumption, and he not being a person holding a licence for the sale of alcoholic liquor, contrary to s.95(1); or trafficking, contrary to s.90, by selling liquor to non-members where not permitted by s.107(2) and (3).

(*o*) For a case where the rules were habitually broken, see *Madin* v. *M'Lean* (1894) 21 R.(J.) 40; 1 Adam 376.

(*p*) As to the club rule which must provide that an interval of at least two weeks shall elapse between the nomination and election of a member, see s.107(1)(*e*).

(*s*) "*permitted hours*" are defined in s.139(1).

## Cancellation of certificate of registration

**109.**—(1) Any person entitled under section 105(3) of this Act to object to the renewal of the certificate of registration held by a registered club may apply to the sheriff for a finding that the club is being or has been, at any time during the currency of the certificate of registration, so managed or carried on as to give rise to a ground of objection to the renewal of its certificate, being one of the grounds of objection specified in section 108 of this Act; and the sheriff may, if he is satisfied that such ground for objection has been established, make the finding applied for and shall specify therein the grounds for the finding.

(2) Where on an application under subsection (1) above such a finding as is therein mentioned has been made in respect of any club, or where a

conviction has taken place under section 95 of this Act in respect of alcoholic liquor sold or supplied in any club, a certified copy of the application and finding or of the complaint and conviction, as the case may be, shall, within six days from the date of the finding or the conviction, be transmitted by the clerk of the court (unless he is also the registrar) to the registrar.

(3) Where—

(a) such a finding as is mentioned in subsection (1) above has been made in respect of any club; or

(b) a conviction has taken place under section 95 of this Act in respect of alcoholic liquor sold or supplied in any club;

the registrar shall enter such finding or conviction, as the case may be, in the register of clubs and lay the same before the sheriff; and the sheriff may, if he thinks fit, after such further enquiry as he may think necessary, and having regard to the grounds specified in such finding or the magnitude of the offence, as the case may be, cancel the certificate of registration of that club.

(4) Where the certificate of registration of any club has been cancelled under subsection (3) above, that club may apply for renewal of that certificate, but not earlier than 12 months after the date of such cancellation.

(5) The sheriff may, on an application under subsection (1) above, award expenses against the unsuccessful party.

GENERAL NOTE

A. *Cancellation of certificate of registration—general.* This section provides a method whereby a person who has a title to object to the grant or renewal of a club's certificate of registration in terms of s.105(3), may initiate proceedings to have the certificate of registration cancelled during its currency, and without waiting for its normal expiry date, when its renewal could be objected to under s.105.

The proceedings are initiated by summary application to the sheriff. The sheriff may be asked to deal in one and the same process with the finding mentioned in subs. (1), with the cancellation of the certificate of registration mentioned in subs. (3), and also with the disqualification of the premises for use by a registered club under s.110. *Glasgow Corporation* v. *Railwayman's Club* (1915) 31 Sh.Ct.Rep. 220. In such circumstances the earlier practice (see *Glasgow Corporation* v. *Railwayman's Club* (*supra*)) was to defer the question of disqualification of the premises until the normal expiry date of the certificate of registration. This practice has not been uniformly followed in recent years. There are advantages on arriving at a decision on this matter when the evidence is still freshly in mind and when all the parties are represented and in court. The club may apply for renewal after 12 months have elapsed from the date of cancellation (subs. (4)).

The sheriff's decision in cancelling a certificate is final and not subject to appeal; except in regard to a procedural interlocutor, although it might be reviewable by way of reduction: see note to s.117(2).

B. *Subsections.* (1) The procedure prescribed by the section may be initiated by the chief constable, the district or islands council for the area where the club premises are situated, the fire authority, the community council for the area where the club premises are situated, a church representing a significant body of opinion in the neighbourhood of the premises and any person owning or occupying property in the neighbourhood of the club premises (see s.16). It is civil and not criminal procedure, and any doubt on this point which may have been raised by the use of the words "summary complaint" in the 1903 Act, s.85(1), has been removed by the substitution of the words "apply" and "application." The ultimate purpose of the application is to have the certificate of registration cancelled during its currency, instead of waiting until its expiry date and then lodging objections to its renewal. The first step in the procedure is to apply to the sheriff, for a finding that the club is being, or has been at any time during the currency of the certificate of registration, so managed or carried on as to give rise to one or more of the grounds of objection mentioned in s.108. Before making such a finding the sheriff will order intimation of the application to the club, and unless the averments contained therein are at once admitted by the club, will allow the club to lodge answers, and, if the facts are still in dispute, will hear the evidence on both sides.

The sheriff may award expenses against the unsuccessful party: subs. (5).

(2) Where a finding under subs. (1) has been made, or where there has been a conviction of any person in respect of the illegal sale of liquor in a club in contravention of s.95, the clerk of the court which made the finding or the conviction must transmit a certified copy within six days to the sheriff clerk as registrar unless the clerk is the registrar. When the finding is made by the sheriff, he may proceed at once, as part of the original process, to consider the cancellation of the certificate of registration (subs. (3)) and the disqualification of the premises under s.110, provided, of course, that both parties have been heard fully on these matters: see note A, above.

(3) As to the possible procedure when the initial application under subs. (1) is made to the sheriff, see note A, above. The sheriff's decision in cancelling a certificate is final and not subject to appeal, except in regard to a procedural interlocutor, although it might be reviewable by way of reduction perhaps in a judicial review: see note to s.117(2).

(4) Cancellation under subs. (3) affects only the current certificate, which must in any event expire three years after its date of issue (s.106). An application for renewal cannot be made less than 12 months after the date of cancellation. If, of course, the premises have been disqualified under s.110, the certificate of registration cannot be renewed for the same premises until the disqualification terminates. The appropriate application after expiry of disqualification (where the certificate expires during the period of disqualification) is for renewal. A fresh application is not required.

## Disqualification of premises for purposes of club

**110.**—(1) Where the sheriff has refused an application by a club for the renewal of its certificate of registration or where under section 109 of this Act he has cancelled the certificate held by a club, he may, if he thinks fit, order that the premises occupied by that club shall not be occupied and used for the purposes of any registered club.

(2) An order made under subsection (1) above shall be in force for such period as the order shall specify, not exceeding—

(*a*) if the premises have not been subject to a previous order under that subsection, 12 months;

(*b*) if the premises have been subject to any such previous order, five years.

(3) Such an order may, on good cause being shown, be subsequently cancelled or varied by the sheriff.

GENERAL NOTE
*Disqualification of premises for use by registered club.* An order of disqualification under this section may be made by the sheriff, if he thinks fit, when he has refused an application for renewal of a certificate of registration under s.105(6)(*b*), or when he has cancelled a certificate under s.109(3). The basis of either alternative is that one or more of the grounds of objection mentioned in s.109 have been established against the club. Subs. (2) is concerned with the period of disqualification, and subs. (3) with the subsequent variation or cancellation of a period of disqualification. As to possible procedure see s.109 note A.

## Penalties for offences by officials of registered clubs

**111.**—(1) Where a finding has been made under section 109(1) of this Act that a registered club is being so managed or carried on as to give rise to a ground of objection to the renewal of its certificate of registration, then if a ground of objection mentioned in paragraph (*f*), (*i*), (*j*) or (*l*) of section 108 of this Act is specified in such finding, every person whose name is, at the time when the situation which gave rise to the ground of objection mentioned in any of the said paragraphs existed, contained in the list lodged under subsection (3)(*b*) of section 103 of the Act, or as the case may be in the new list last lodged under subsection (5) or (5A) of the said section 103, in respect of that club, shall be guilty of an offence.

(2) A person shall not be convicted of an offence under this section if he proves that the club was managed or carried on as aforesaid without his knowledge or consent and that he exercised all due diligence to prevent the club from being so managed or carried on.

GENERAL NOTE
Amended, 1980, c. 55, s.21(3).
If a finding is made by the sheriff under s.109(1), and the grounds of objection in respect of which the finding is made include one or more of those specified in subs. (1), every person whose name is entered in the register of clubs as an official of the club, or as a member of its committee of management, at the time when the situation which gave rise to the ground of objection existed, is guilty of an offence under this section, unless he proves that the club was managed or carried on as stated in the finding, without his knowledge or consent. For a consideration of *"knowledge"* and *"knowingly,"* see note to s.68; and of *"due diligence,"* see note to s.67. The defence need only be proved on a balance of probabilities—see note to s.83.
The offence may be tried summarily in either the sheriff court or the district court (s.128(1)). The maximum penalty is a fine of level 3 (Sched. 5).

## Persons under 14 not to be allowed in club bars

**112.**—(1) A person under 14 shall not be allowed to be in a bar of a registered club during the permitted hours.

(2) If subsection (1) above is contravened, every person entered in the register of clubs as an official or member of the committee of management or governing body of the club at the time of the contravention shall be guilty of an offence:

Provided that a person shall not be convinced of such an offence if he proves that the contravention in question took place without his knowledge or consent.

(3) No person shall cause any person under 14 to be in a bar of a registered club during the permitted hours, and any person contravening this subsection shall be guilty of an offence.

GENERAL NOTE
*Prohibition on persons under* 14 *years of age in club bars.* A person under 14 is not allowed to be in a club during permitted hours. A breach constitutes an offence on the part of every official and member of the committee of management of the club (subs. (2)). It is a defence for a person accused of such an offence to prove that the contravention occurred without his knowledge or consent (subs. (2), proviso). For a consideration of *"knowledge"* and *"knowingly,"* see note to s.68. The defence need only be proved on a balance of probabilities—see note to s.83. It also constitutes an offence to cause a person under 14 to be present in a bar during permitted hours (subs. (3)).
*"permitted hours"* are defined in s.139(1).
The maximum penalty for a contravention of the section is a fine of level 3 (Sched. 5).

## Persons under 18 not to be employed to serve alcoholic liquor in clubs

**113.**—(1) A person under 18 shall not be employed in a registered club if the purpose, or one of the purposes, of his employment is to serve alcoholic liquor to persons in that club.

(2) If this section is contravened as regards any club, every person whose name is, at the time when the situation which gave rise to the grounds of objection mentioned in any of the said paragraphs existed, contained in the list lodged under subsection (3)(*b*) of section 103 of this Act, or as the case may be in the new list last lodged under subsection (5) or (5A) of the said section 103, in respect of that club, shall be guilty of an offence:

Provided that a person shall not be convicted of an offence under this section if he proves that the contravention in question took place without his knowledge or consent.

(3) For the purpose of this section, a person shall be deemed to be employed in a club where he works notwithstanding that he receives no wages for his work.

(4) Where in any proceedings under this section it is alleged that a person was at any time under 18, and he appears to the court then to have been under that age, for the purposes of the proceedings he shall be deemed to have been then under that age unless the contrary is shown.

GENERAL NOTE

Amended, 1980, c. 55, s.21(2).

*Prohibition of persons under* 18 *years of age serving alcoholic liquor in clubs.* The section makes it an offence on the part of every official or member of the committee of management of a club for the club to employ a person under 18 to serve alcoholic liquor, with the proviso that an accused is not to be convicted of the offence if he proves that the contravention occurred without his knowledge or consent (subss. (1) and (2)). For a consideration of "*knowledge*" and "*knowingly*," see note to s.68. The defence need only be proved on a balance of probabilities—see note to s.83. A person is to be held to be employed even if he receives no wages (sub. (3)). In a prosecution for a contravention of the section, if the person alleged to be under 18 appears to be so to the court, he is to be deemed to be under that age unless the contrary is shown (subs. (4)). *Per contra,* see note to s.68.

"*alcoholic liquor.*" For the meaning, see s.139(1).

The maximum penalty for an offence under the section is a fine of level 3 (Sched. 5).

## Power of police to enter clubs

**114.**—(1) If a justice of the peace or sheriff is satisfied by evidence on oath that there are reasonable grounds for believing—

(*a*) that any registered club is being so managed or carried on as to give rise to a ground of objection to the renewal of its certificate of registration, being one of the grounds of objection specified in section 108 of this Act; or

(*b*) that an offence under this Act has been or is being committed in any registered club;

he may by warrant authorise a constable to enter the premises of such club at any time, if need be by force, and to search the premises and seize any documents relating to the business of the club and to take the names and addresses of any persons found in the premises.

(2) If any person found in the premises of a club refuses to give his name and address on being requested to do so by a constable acting under a warrant granted in pursuance of the foregoing subsection, or gives a false name and address on being so requested, he shall be guilty of an offence.

"*constable*" is defined in s.139(1).

The corresponding provisions for unregistered clubs are contained in s.120. The powers of police officers to enter licensed and unlicensed premises are dealt with in ss.85 and 86 respectively. In *Southern Bowling Club Ltd.* v. *Ross* (1902) 4 F. 405 it was held that the police were entitled to enter a club in disguise for the purpose of detecting whether illegal trafficking in liquor was being carried on therein. The common law does not include the powers, which may be granted under this section, of search, seizure and taking names and addresses.

The offence referred to in subs. (2) may be prosecuted in either the sheriff or the district court (s.128(1)).

### Inspection of register of clubs and of rules and list of members of club

**115.**—(1) The register of clubs and a copy of the rules of any club lodged with the registrar under section 103(3) of this Act shall, at all reasonable times, be open to inspection on a payment of a fee of 20p.

(2) A chief constable or any constable authorised by him in writing or an officer of Customs and Excise shall be entitled to inspect the register of clubs and a copy of the rules of any registered club lodged as aforesaid at all reasonable times without payment.

(3) There shall be kept on the premises of every registered club a copy of a current list containing the names and addresses of every member of the club; and a chief constable or any constable authorised by him in writing shall be entitled to inspect that list at all reasonable times without payment.

### Citation of registered club

**116.** Any citation of a registered club may be validly made in the registered name thereof in accordance with the Citation Amendment (Scotland) Act 1882, or by a copy of the citation being left by an officer of court at the registered address of the club.

GENERAL NOTE
This section can only apply to civil proceedings: Citation Amendment (Scotland) Act 1882 (45 & 46 Vict. c. 77), s.3. It applies to citation only (*i.e.* service of a writ on the club), but in any action the club and its members should be called and designed in accordance with the rules applicable to suing an unincorporated association. In any event, any criminal proceedings will normally concern individual officials, members or servants of the club. The section might perhaps apply if the sheriff ordered intimation to the club of an application for a finding under s.109(1). Nothing in this section has the effect of giving a club a legal *persona*.

### Sheriff's jurisdiction and decision

**117.**—(1) The jurisdiction conferred on the sheriff by this Part of this Act shall not be excluded in relation to any club by reason only of the fact that he is a member of that club.

(2) The decision of the sheriff in dealing with an application for the grant of a certificate of registration or for the renewal of such a certificate or in cancelling such a certificate shall be final.

GENERAL NOTE
*Subsections.* (1) A sheriff's jurisdiction is not excluded by reason only of the fact that he is a member of the club. A sheriff should perhaps be careful in exercising his jurisdiction, if he

is a member of the club, in contentious matters, in case he lays his decision open to reduction on one of the grounds of a breach of natural justice; see note to s.2.

(2) A sheriff's decision on the merits is final, but a procedural interlocutor (*e.g.* treating objections as abandoned) in the course of an application may be subject to review; see *Chief Constable of Strathclyde* v. *Hamilton and District Bookmakers Club*, 1977 S.L.T.(Sh.Ct.) 78; *Edinburgh North Constituency Association S.N.P. Club* v. *Thomas H. Peck Ltd. and Ors.*, 1978 S.L.T.(Sh.Ct.) 76. The sheriff's decision may be liable to reduction perhaps by judicial review—if the sheriff acted *ultra vires*, contrary to natural justice, refused to exercise a jurisdiction or exceed his powers; see D. M. Walker, *Civil Remedies*, p. 187, and see Introduction, para. 6.17. The merits cannot be reviewed in the course of an action of reduction. Reduction or judicial review is competent only in the Court of Session: *Brown* v. *Hamilton District Council*, 1983 S.C. (H.L.) 1.

Any decisions of a sheriff in criminal proceedings, whether or not they concern contraventions of this Act, are subject to appeal in the ordinary way under the Criminal Procedure (Scotland) Act 1975.

### Interpretation of Part VII

**118.** In this Part of this Act, references to the secretary of a club shall include references of any officer of the club or other person performing the duties of a secretary.

## PART VIII

### MISCELLANEOUS, TRANSITIONAL & GENERAL

### Trading hours for off-sale premises and off-sale parts of public houses and hotels

**119.**—(1) The provisions of this Act relating to the permitted hours shall not apply to off-sale premises, but the provisions of this section shall apply.

(2) On granting or transferring a public house or a hotel licence in respect of any premises a licensing board shall, if the applicant so requests and if the board is satisfied—

(a) that a part of the premises (in this section referred to as "the off-sale part") is structurally adapted for the sale and supply of alcoholic liquor for consumption off the premises; and

(b) that there is no internal communication to which customers have access connecting the off-sale part with a part of the premises used, or intended to be used, for the sale and supply of alcoholic liquor for consumption on the premises, or that any such internal communication is capable of being closed to customers;

insert in the licence the following conditions—

(i) a condition that the off-sale part (which shall be specified in the condition) shall not be used for the sale or supply of alcoholic liquor for consumption on the premises;

(ii) a condition that any internal communication to which customers have access connecting the off-sale part with a part of the premises used for the sale and supply of alcoholic liquor for consumption on the premises shall be closed to customers during any time when customers are present in any part of the premises; and

(iii) a condition that no customers shall be permitted to use any internal communication for the purpose of passing from one part of the premises to another part thereof;

and, so long as the licence is subject to the said conditions, the provisions of this Act relating to the permitted hours shall not apply to the off-sale part, but the provisions of this section shall apply.

(3) Off-sale premises and the off-sale part of premises shall not be open for serving of customers with alcoholic liquor earlier than eight o'clock in the morning and shall be closed for the serving of customers with such liquor not later than ten o'clock in the evening; and such premises or the off-sale part of premises shall not be opened for the serving of customers with such liquor on Sundays.

(4) The holder of the licence or his employee or agent shall be guilty of an offence if he contravenes this section or any condition attached to a licence by virtue of subsection (2) above.

GENERAL NOTE

A. *Off-sale part of premises.* This provision enables the holder of an hotel or public-house licence to set aside part of his premises for off-sales only (the part set aside to be known as the off-sale part). The procedure is by request to the licensing board when the licence is being granted or transferred. The board must grant the request if they are satisfied that (i) the part which it is sought to set aside for off-sales is adapted for off-sales; and (ii) there is no internal communication open to customers between the off-sales part and the part used for the supply of liquor for consumption on the premises. (A communication capable of being closed fulfils this condition.) When the request is granted the following conditions are inserted into the licence—(i) that the off-sale part is to be used for off-sales only; (ii) that any communication open to customers between the off-sale part and the part of sale for consumption on the premises shall be closed when customers are present on the premises; and (iii) that customers shall not be permitted to use an internal communication for passing from one part of the premises to another. The permitted hours applicable for the off-sale part are the same as those applicable to premises held under an off-sale licence, for which see subs. (4).

"*granting*" includes grant by way of renewal (s.139(1)).

B. *Trading hours for off-sale premises and off-sale part of premises.* The maximum trading hours for such premises for the sale of alcoholic liquor are 8 a.m. to 10 p.m. with no permitted hours on Sundays (subs. (3)). The restriction of the maximum hours only applies to the sale of liquor and the licence-holder may have his premises open outwith these hours and on Sundays for the sale of other commodities.

"*off-sale premises*" are defined in s.139(1).

C. *Offences.* Subs. (4) makes it an offence for the holder of a licence in respect of premises with an off-sale part, his employee, or his agent to contravene any of the conditions attached to the licence relating to the off-sale part in virtue of subs. (2), and also makes it an offence for the holder of a licence, his employee or his agent to sell alcoholic liquor outwith the prescribed trading hours. The maximum penalty for both offences is a fine of level 3 with both the premises and the holder liable to disqualification. The holder is vicariously liable for both offences (Sched. 5); for consideration of "*vicariously liable*," see note to s.67.

## Liquor in unregistered clubs

**120.**—(1) If any person sells or supplies liquor in the premises of an unregistered club, or authorises the sale or supply of alcoholic liquor in any such premises, to a member or other person, or if any person pays for alcoholic liquor so sold or supplied, he shall be guilty of an offence.

(2) If alcoholic liquor is kept in any such premises for sale or supply in those premises, every officer and member of the club shall be guilty of an offence.

(3) A person shall not be guilty of an offence under subsection (2) above if he proves that the liquor was kept as mentioned in that subsection without his knowledge or consent.

(4) If a justice of the peace is satisfied by evidence on oath that there are reasonable grounds for believing that alcoholic liquor is being sold or supplied in the premises of an unregistered club or is being kept in any such premises for the purpose of being sold or supplied there, he may by warrant authorise a constable to enter those premises at any time, if need be by force, and to search the premises and seize any documents relating to the business of the club and to take the names and addresses of any persons found in the premises.

(5) If a justice of the peace is satisfied by evidence on oath that there are reasonable grounds for believing that alcoholic liquor is being kept in the premises of an unregistered club for the purposes of being sold or supplied there, he may by warrant authorise a constable to seize and remove any such liquor which the constable has reasonable grounds for supposing to be in the premises for the purpose of being sold or supplied there, together with the vessels containing the liquor.

(6) If any of the officers or members of a club from the premises of which any alcoholic liquor has been removed under subsection (5) above is convicted of an offence under subsection (2) above in respect of such liquor or any part thereof, that liquor or such part thereof, as the case may be, and the vessels containing it shall be forfeited and sold and the proceeds thereof paid into the general fund of the district or islands area, as the case may be, in which the said premises are situated.

(7) If any person found in the premises of a club refuses to give his name and address on being requested to do so by a constable acting under a warrant granted in pursuance of subsection (4) above, or gives a false name or address on being so requested, he shall be guilty of an offence.

GENERAL NOTE

A. *Prohibition of selling, supplying or keeping alcoholic liquor in an unregistered club.* For the meaning of "*alcoholic liquor*" and "*constable*," see s.139(1). "*Unregistered club*" means a club in respect of which a certificate of registration under Part VII of the Act is not in force (s.139(1)).

This section makes it an offence (i) for any person to sell or supply alcoholic liquor in the premises of an unregistered club, or to authorise its sale or supply, and for any person to pay for alcoholic liquor in such premises; (ii) to be an officer or member of such a club, if alcoholic liquor is kept in the premises of the club for sale or supply there.

Since the passing of the 1903 Act, which introduced the provision, there has been little need to consider the question of trafficking without a licence in an unregistered club, and the difficulty, which frequently arose in the past in connection therewith as to whether the supply of excisable liquor by a members' club to its members constituted a sale. On this point, see s.102, note A. It should rarely now be necessary to consider a prosecution for trafficking without a certificate in connection with an unregistered club, since any sale or supply to any person in such a club is an offence under this section.

The section also enables a constable, under the authority of a warrant, to enter the premises of an unregistered club, if need be by force, and to search the premises, seize documents and take the names and addresses of any persons found in the premises (subs. (4)), and to seize and remove any liquor, and the vessels containing it, which he has reasonable grounds for supposing to be there to be sold or supplied (subs. (5)). The liquor may in certain circumstances be forfeited (subs. (6)), and any person in the premises refusing to give his name and address, or giving a false name and address, is guilty of an offence.

The offences mentioned in the section may be tried summarily in any court of summary jurisdiction: s.128. The maximum penalty is a fine of level 3 except in the case of the offence enacted in subs. (7) (refusing to give a constable acting under a warrant one's name and address), in which case the maximum fine is one of level 1 (Sched. 5).

171

A club is not entitled to interdict police officers from entering its premises in disguise in order to detect illegal sales: *Southern Club* v. *Ross* (1902) 4 F. 405. Evidence of purchases of liquor by constables in plain clothes is admissible: *Marsh* v. *Johnston*, 1959 S.L.T. (Notes) 28.

B. *Subsections*. (1) The offence is committed by any person who supplies, by any person, such as the owner of the liquor or a member of the committee of management, who authorises him to supply, and by any person who pays for liquor so supplied.

(2) If alcoholic liquor is kept in an unregistered club, it matters not by whom, for sale or supply in its premises, every officer and every member of the club is guilty of the offence mentioned, unless (subs. (3)) he is able to prove that liquor was kept for that purpose without his knowledge or consent; for consideration of "*knowledge*," see note to s.68. The defence need only be proved on a balance of probabilities: see note to s.83. For an examination of a corresponding English provision, see *Hammond* v. *Hanlon* [1935] 1 K.B. 474.

(3) See note (2), above.

(6) The effect of the subsection is that liquor removed from an unregistered club under subs. (5) shall be forfeited and sold if, in a prosecution of officers or members of the club under subs. (2), the court is satisfied beyond reasonable doubt that the liquor was kept in the club for sale or supply, and if at least one of the accused is unable to satisfy the court of the probability that it was so kept without his knowledge or consent.

### Sale or supply of alcoholic liquor in certain theatres

**121.** A theatre erected before January 1, 1904 shall be treated for the purposes of the sale or supply of alcoholic liquor in the theatre as if an entertainment licence were in force in respect of the theatre.

GENERAL NOTE

Theatres erected and licensed as such by the local authority before January 1, 1904, do not require a licence for the sale of alcoholic liquor (s.138(1)(*b*)), and, accordingly, the provisions of Part V as regards permitted hours do not apply to them. The effect of the section is to apply the same conditions as for an entertainment licence to such theatres as regards the sale of and supply of liquor.

For the meaning of "*alcoholic liquor*," see s.139(1). For "*entertainment licence*," see Sched. 1 and note to s.9.

### Proof of trafficking in alcoholic liquor without licence

**122.** It shall be sufficient evidence that a person was trafficking in any alcoholic liquor in any premises or place without holding a licence in that behalf if it is proved—

(*a*) that a person other than the owner or occupier of such premises or place was at the time charged found therein drunk or drinking, or having had drink supplied to him therein; and

(*b*) either that such premises are or such place is, by repute, kept for the illegal sale of alcoholic liquor or that at the time charged such premises or place contained drinking utensils and fittings usually found in licensed premises.

GENERAL NOTE

"*Trafficking*" is defined in s.139(1).

"*Trafficking in alcoholic liquor in any premises or place*" without a licence is made an offence by s.90. As to the meaning of "*premises or place*" in that connection and as to the offence generally, see the notes to that section.

The section provides that proof of (*a*) and (*b*) is evidence which is technically sufficient to establish a contravention of s.90, so that the prosecutor need prove no more than (*a*) and (*b*) in order to secure a conviction, if no other evidence is before the court. For a discussion of how the presumption must be established or may be displaced, see *Macdonald* v. *Skinner*,

1978 S.L.T. (Notes) 52. For a consideration of what is meant by "*drunk*," see note to s.74. The section does not, however, prevent the accused person from leading evidence to show that, despite the inference of guilt arising from (*a*) and (*b*), he was not in fact trafficking in contravention of s.90.

The prosecutor may found upon this section during a trial without having given notice of his intention to do so, and without having mentioned this section in the complaint: *Mann* v. *Cadenhead* (1886) 13 R.(J.) 60.

## Alcoholic liquor in confectionery

**123.**—(1) No provision of this Act as to the sale, supply, purchase, delivery or consumption of alcoholic liquor, except subsection (2) below, and no enactment requiring the authority of a wholesaler's excise licence for the sale or supply of alcoholic liquor, shall have effect in relation to alcoholic liquor in confectionery which—

(*a*) does not contain alcoholic liquor in a proportion greater than 200 millilitres of liquor of a strength of 57 per cent. of ethyl alcohol by volume (at a temperature of 20 degrees Celsius) per kilogramme of the confectionery, and

(*b*) either consists of separate pieces weighing not more than 50 grammes or is designed to be broken into such pieces for the purpose of consumption.

(2) Alcoholic liquor in confectionery shall not be sold to a person under 16, and if any person knowingly contravenes this subsection he shall be guilty of an offence.

GENERAL NOTE

Amended, S.I. 1979 No. 1755.

*Liqueur chocolates*. Liqueur chocolates are exempt from the provision of the Act provided they fulfil the requirements of the section. To qualify for exemption, the confectionery must not contain more than 200 millilitres of liquor of a strength of 57 per cent. of ethyl alcohol by volume (at a temperature of 20 degrees Celsius) per kilogram, and must consist of, or be designed to be broken up into, pieces weighing not more than 50 grammes for consumption. The spirit definition was introduced to conform with EEC Directive No. 76/766/EC (O.J. No. L262, 27.9.1976, p. 149). It is an offence to sell such confectionery to a person under 16, the maximum penalty being a fine of level 3 (Sched. 5).

## Local authority premises

**124.** Subsection (6) of section 91 of the Local Government (Scotland) Act 1973 (certificates not to be granted for sale of liquor in premises provided under that section) shall cease to have effect, and a licensing board may grant any licence in respect of such premises.

## Supply of alcoholic liquor on order by certain officials and others

**125.**—(1) The holder of a licence in respect of any premises may supply alcoholic liquor from those premises during any time when such supply would, apart from this section, be prohibited by or under this Act, on an order stating why the liquor is required and signed—

(*a*) by a constable of or above the rank of inspector or by a constable in charge of a police station; or

(*b*) by the procurator fiscal; or

(*c*) by a medical official; or

(*d*) in the case of sickness, accident or emergency, by a duly qualified medical practitioner.

(2) Any such order shall be sufficient defence in any prosecution in respect of the supply of the alcoholic liquor to which it relates if within 48 hours after the supply of such liquor the order is sent by post to the procurator fiscal together with a note of the description and quantity of the liquor supplied and the name and address of the person to whom the liquor was supplied.

(3) The procurator fiscal shall, not later than seven days before the quarterly meeting of any licensing board having jurisdiction in the district for which he acts or any part thereof, transmit to the clerk of such board a list of orders received by him under subsection (2) above during the current quarter, being orders received from persons holding licences from that board, and the said list shall contain a note of the names and designations of all persons signing such orders.

GENERAL NOTE

"*licence*," "*alcoholic liquor*" and "*constable*" are defined in s.139(1). As to the "time when such supply would be . . . prohibited," see Part V of the Act. As to the quarterly meeting of a licensing board, see s.4(1).

The section is intended to provide for cases of sickness or accident occurring outwith permitted hours. So far as can be ascertained, it has not been used of late.

### Burden of proof in case of drunkenness in licensed premises

**126.** If the holder of a licence in respect of any premises is charged with knowingly permitting drunkenness in those premises, and it is proved that any person was drunk in the premises, it shall lie on the holder of the licence to prove that he and the persons employed by him took all reasonable steps to prevent drunkenness in the premises.

GENERAL NOTE

The "*licence*" referred to in the section includes a seamen's canteen licence in virtue of s.45 as well as any licence as defined in s.139(1).

"*Knowingly permitting drunkenness in.*" S.78(2) makes it an offence for the licence-holder, his employee or agent to permit drunkenness on the premises in respect of which the licence is held.

If in a prosecution on the grounds of knowingly permitting drunkenness in the premises, the prosecutor proves that any person was drunk in the premises, the licence-holder, in order to escape conviction, must then prove that he and his employees took all reasonable steps to prevent drunkenness. For a consideration of (1) "*knowingly*," see note to s.68(2) "*drunk*," see note to s.74. The defence need only be established on a balance of probabilities: see note to s.83.

The onus of proof was held not to lie upon the licence-holder in virtue of this provision, when the only person who was drunk in the premises was one of his employees: *Campbell* v. *Cameron*, 1916 S.C.(J.) 1.

A licence-holder may knowingly permit drunkenness contrary to s.78(2) by allowing drunken persons to remain there. It is not necessary for a conviction that they should have been supplied by him with excisable liquor: *Hope* v. *Warburton* [1982] 2 Q.B. 134. The actual supply of a drunken person is sufficient evidence of the offence: *Edmunds* v. *James* [1892] 1 Q.B. 18. Where a public-house licence-holder entertained two friends after closing hours, and one of them was found drunk in the premises about 3 a.m., it was held that he had not discharged the onus placed upon him by this section of proving that he had taken all reasonable steps to prevent drunkenness, and a conviction for breach of certificate was upheld: *Kessack* v. *Smith* (1905) 7 F.(J.) 75; see also *Lawson* v. *Edminson* [1908] 2 K.B. 952. Where one drunk man and two sober men entered a public-house and the barman supplied the two sober men with a glass of whisky each on condition that they took the other man home, and supplied the drunk man with a bottle of soda water, it was held that drunkenness had not been permitted: *Soutar* v. *Auchinachie*, 1909 S.C.(J.) 16. It has been held that a licence-holder does not permit drunkenness by getting drunk himself: *Warden* v.

*Tye* (1877) 2 C.P.D. 74. It has been held in England that, where one person orders two drinks, it is reasonable to expect the barman to inquire whom the other is for, and if he does not do so, and it is given to a drunken man, then a conviction for permitting drunkenness can be supported: *Radford* v. *Williams* (1913) 30 T.L.R. 109.

## Presumption as to contents of containers

**127.**—(1) For the purposes of any trial in connection with an alleged contravention of any provision of this Act, the following provisions of this section shall apply.

(2) Any liquid found in a container (sealed or open) shall, subject to the provisions of this section, be presumed to conform to the description of the liquid on the container.

(3) An open container which is found to contain—

(*a*) no liquid; or

(*b*) insufficient liquid to permit analysis,

but which when sold or supplied to a person was sealed shall, subject to the provisions of this section, be presumed to have contained at the time of the sale or supply liquid which conformed to the description of the liquid on the container.

(4) Subject to subsection (5) below, in any trial of a person for an offence under this Act, he may rebut the presumption mentioned in subsection (2) or (3) above by showing that, at the time of the sale or supply, the liquid in the container did not conform to the description of the liquid on the container.

(5) A person shall not be entitled to lead evidence for the purpose of rebutting a presumption as mentioned in subsection (4) above unless, not less than seven days before the date of the trial, he has given notice to the prosecutor of his intention to do so.

GENERAL NOTE

*Evidence as to the contents of containers in the prosecution of an offence under the Act.*
Under the rules of evidence applicable to a criminal trial, where a prosecutor seeks to prove the nature of the contents of a container such as a bottle, evidence requires to be led as to the findings of an expert analysis of the contents. Frequently, the container was special to a well-known brand and carried a brand label identifying contents, the nature of which was not challenged by the accused. The purpose of the section is to save the time and expense involved in leading evidence from an analyst where the nature of the contents of a container are a *factum probandum* which is not the matter of an admission by an accused under the provisions of the Criminal Procedure (Scotland) Act 1975, by providing for a presumption as to the contents being as described on the label but, at the same time, protecting the right of an accused person to require that the contents be proved by full legal proof.

The section was amended by s.55(1) of the 1990 Act. The principal effects of the amendment are (1) to allow the presumption to apply to open containers containing no liquid or insufficient liquid to permit analysis, which the prosecution can prove were sold or supplied sealed; (2) to remove the requirement that the prosecution had to give 14 days' notice that they intended to rely on the presumption, which will now apply automatically in any relevant prosecution; and (3) to delete the provision regarding service of notices under this section by recorded delivery and the presumptions arising therefrom as to date of intimation. The defence has to give at least seven clear days' notice before the trial, that they intend to rebut the presumption. The defence will have to prove that they gave seven days' notice, excluding the day of intimation of the notice and the day of the trial; see *Main* v. *City of Glasgow District Licensing Board*, 1987 S.L.T. 305 for a discussion of "at least seven days" and Note to s.16. The rebuttal of the presumption will have to be proved on a balance of probabilities. In *Tudhope* v. *MacDonald*, 1986 S.C.C.R. 32 it was held that, in the absence of any indication of the gravity or strength on the label of a bottle of cider sold to a person under the age of 18 years, it was not sufficient for the Crown to rely on the statutory presumption without leading evidence of the gravity and strength of the liquor. See also *Grieve* v. *Hillary*, 1987 S.C.C.R. 317.

Section 55(2) of the 1990 Act provides that the amended law on presumptions does not apply retrospectively to an offence committed before the commencement of s.55(2) of the 1990 Act, even if the trial commences after the section comes into force.

*Subsections.* (1) The presumption now applies to prosecutions under the Act and to prosecutions under Pt. V of the Criminal Justice (Scotland) Act 1980 [Control of Alcohol at Sporting Events], see s.76 of the 1980 Act, but not to prosecutions for any other crimes or offences.

(2) The primary presumption is that a liquid found in a container shall be presumed to conform to the description of the liquid on the container.

(3) Where an open container is found to contain no liquid or insufficient liquid to permit analysis, which the prosecution can prove was sealed when sold or supplied to a person, it shall be presumed to have contained *at the time of the sale or supply* liquid conform to the description of the liquid on the container.

(4) and (5) provide that the defence may rebut the presumptions set out by ss.(2) and (3) by showing that the container did not contain liquid conform to the description of the liquid on the container, but only if not less than seven days' notice is given [see *supra*] to the prosecutor before the date of the trial of the defences intention to rebut the presumption.

### Trial of offences

**128.**—(1) The following provisions shall have effect in relation to the trial of offences under this Act—

(*a*) all offences shall be tried in a summary manner;

(*b*) all offences other than those referred to in paragraph (*c*) below may be tried in the sheriff court or in the district court;

(*c*) the following offences shall be tried only in the sheriff court, that is to say, any offence under section 2, 7(3), 19(1) or section 36(3) of this Act.

(2) Notwithstanding subsection (1) above, a contravention of any of the provisions of this Act which, if it had been triable on indictment, could competently have been libelled as an additional or alternative charge in the indictment, may be so libelled and may be tried accordingly.

GENERAL NOTE

*Trial of offences.* All offences are to be tried in a summary manner. The section reduces the number of offences which may be tried only in the sheriff court from those specified in the 1959 Act. Prosecutions may be taken in either the sheriff court or the district court with the exception of prosecutions for contraventions of ss.2 (disqualified person acting as a member of a board), 7(3) (clerk or his partner acting as the applicant in proceedings before a board), 19(1) (canvassing of a board member) and 36(3) (failure to comply with a structural alterations order), which must be taken in the sheriff court. Subs. (2) makes provision for the trial of offences under the Act on indictment.

### Conviction of licence-holder to be transmitted to clerk of licensing board

**129.** Where the holder of a licence in respect of any premises is convicted of any offence under this Act in relation to those premises, a certified extract of such conviction shall, within six days after the date of the conviction, be transmitted by the clerk of the court to the clerk of the licensing board within whose jurisdiction such premises are situated.

GENERAL NOTE

The 1959 Act required a conviction for breach of certificate to be notified to the clerk of the licensing court for the area where the premises were situated. The section makes the necessary alterations to the 1959 provision having regard to the substitution of specific offences for breaches of certificate and the introduction of licensing boards.

## Limitation of actions against sheriffs, etc.

**130.** No proceedings against any sheriff, justice of the peace, sheriff clerk, member of a licensing board, clerk of a licensing board, procurator fiscal, constable or other person on account of anything done in the execution of this Act shall lie, unless they are commenced within two months after the cause of such proceedings has arisen.

GENERAL NOTE
See in general D. M. Walker, *Civil Remedies*, Chap. 75; *Boyd* v. *Hislop* (1902) 9 S.L.T. 466.

## Temperance areas

**131.**—(1) Part VIII of the Licensing (Scotland) Act 1959 shall cease to have effect, but notwithstanding that repeal, where immediately before the commencement of this section a limiting resolution or a no-licence resolution was in force in any area, the following provisions of this section shall apply.

(2) The limiting resolution or no-licence resolution shall continue to apply for a period of three years after the commencement of this section and thereafter until the district or islands council concerned with any area or part thereof otherwise resolve.

(3) Before making any resolution as mentioned in subsection (2) above, the district or islands council shall consult with the community council or councils for the area concerned.

(4) Where such a resolution is made in respect of any area, the licensing board for the area may, for a period of five years from the making of the resolution, refuse to grant a licence on the ground that, having regard to the distribution of facilities for the sale and supply of alcoholic liquor in the area, it is inexpedient that the licence applied for should be granted.

(5) Notwithstanding the provisions of this section, where a limiting resolution or a non-licence resolution is in force in any area, the licensing board for the area may, if the board is satisfied that in the special circumstances of the case a licence is reasonably required, grant restaurant or restricted hotel licences for premises situated in the area, and such licences may be granted in addition to the number which the board may grant while a limiting resolution is in force.

(6) Expressions used in this section and in Part VIII of the said Act of 1959 have the same meanings in this section as they have in that Part.

GENERAL NOTE
A. *General.* Clayson (Chap. XII) considered the legislation relating to temperance polls and recommended that it be repealed. The section gives effect to the recommendation and also makes provision for existing areas where, as a result of a poll, there is a resolution limiting the number of licences which may be granted in the area, or a no-licence resolution in force. As regards these areas, the resolutions are to remain in force for a period of three years after the commencement of the section and thereafter until the islands or district council for the area determine otherwise (subs. (2)). Where a council resolve to terminate temperance resolutions, the licensing board for the area may refuse to grant any licences for a further period of five years if the distribution facilities for alcoholic liquor make it inexpedient (subs. (4)). Restricted hotel or restaurant licences may be granted whilst there is a limiting resolution or a no-licence resolution in force (subs. (5)).

B. *Subsections* (1) "*limiting resolution*" and "*no-licence resolution*" have the meanings assigned to them by the 1959 Act in virtue of subs. (6). A limiting resolution reduces the number of licences which may be granted to 75 per cent. of the number at the time the resolution was adopted (1959 Act, ss.199(1) and 108), and a no-licence resolution means that no licences can be granted for the area in which it is in force (1959 Act, ss.199(1) and 110).

(3) "*community council*" means a community council established under Part IV of the Local Government (Scotland) Act 1973.

(4) The Act does not provide for a right of appeal to the sheriff where an application for a grant of a licence is refused on the ground provided for by the subsection.

(5) For the meanings of "*restaurant*" and "*restricted hotel*" licences, see Sched. 1.

## Currency of final licensing certificates

**132.**—(1) Notwithstanding anything in section 58 of the Licensing (Scotland) Act 1959, certificates granted by a licensing court at their last general half-yearly meeting in March 1977 shall have effect in accordance with the provisions of this section.

(2) The chairman of the licensing court at the said meeting shall, in accordance with arrangements made by the licensing court, draw lots in order to determine, in accordance with the provisions of this section, the duration of the certificates granted by the court.

(3) The licensing court shall divide into nine groups or less the respective durations of the certificates which they grant and in respect of which lots are drawn under subsection (2) above, and the durations of the certificates shall, subject to the provisions of this section, be from May 28, 1977 until the quarterly meeting of the licensing board specified as respects each group in the following table:

*Duration of certificates*

| Groups | Quarterly meeting |
|---|---|
| Group 1 | March 1978 |
| Group 2 | June 1978 |
| Group 3 | October 1978 |
| Group 4 | January 1979 |
| Group 5 | March 1979 |
| Group 6 | June 1979 |
| Group 7 | October 1979 |
| Group 8 | January 1980 |
| Group 9 | March 1980 |

(4) As from July 1, 1977, certificates granted in pursuance of this section shall have effect as if they were licences granted under this Act.

(5) Certificates granted in pursuance of this section shall expire on the first day of the appropriate quarterly meeting mentioned in subsection (3) above if no application is made for the renewal of the licence, and where such an application is made, the certificate shall continue to have effect—

    (*a*) until the application for renewal is granted by the licensing board;
       or

(b) if the application for renewal is refused, until the time within which an appeal may be made has elapsed or, if an appeal has been lodged, until the appeal has been abandoned or determined.

GENERAL NOTE

The purpose of the section was to distribute the work of the licensing boards inherited from the former licensing courts evenly throughout their initial quarterly sittings.

## Betting and gaming licences and permits

**133.**—(1) The authority responsible for the grant or renewal of bookmaker's permits, betting agency permits and betting office licences in Scotland under the Betting, Gaming and Lotteries Act 1963 shall be the licensing board for the area concerned, and accordingly for sub-paragraph (b) of paragraph (1) of Schedule 1 to that Act there shall be substituted the following sub-paragraph—

'(b) in any area in Scotland, the licensing board for that area constituted under section 1 of the Licensing (Scotland) Act 1976."

(2) The authority responsible for the grant, renewal, cancellation and transfer of licences in Scotland under the Gaming Act 1968 shall be the licensing board for the area concerned, and accordingly for head (b) of paragraph 1(1) of Schedule 2 to that Act there shall be substituted the following head—

"(b) in any area in Scotland."

(3) The appropriate authority in Scotland for the purposes of Schedule 9 to the Gaming Act 1968 in relation to public houses and hotels shall be the licensing board for the area concerned, and accordingly for sub-paragraph (c) of paragraph 1 of that Schedule there shall be substituted the following sub-paragraph—

"(c) in relation to any premises in Scotland in respect of which a public house licence or a hotel licence is for the time being in force, means the licensing board for the area in which the premises are situated;"

(4) Subsections (4) and (6) to (8) of section 39 of this Act shall apply in relation to appeals under paragraph 24 of Schedule 1 to the Betting, Gaming and Lotteries Act 1963, paragraph 33 or 34 of Schedule 2 and paragraph 15 of Schedule 9 to the Gaming Act 1968 as they apply in relation to appeals under any provision of this Act, and in his decision on any such appeal under the said Acts of 1963 and 1968 the sheriff may include such order as to the expenses of the appeal as he thinks proper.

GENERAL NOTE

The section makes arrangements for the transfer of the functions of licensing courts under the Betting, Gaming and Lotteries Act 1963 and the Gaming Act 1968 to licensing boards.

## Notices, etc.

**134.** Any notice or document required or authorised to be given or serviced under this Act may be served by post.

In terms of s.139(6) introduced by para. 18 of Sched. 8 to the 1990 Act, notices may now be served upon an applicant's agent at the agent's address.

## Orders

**135.** Any power to make an order conferred by any provision of this Act shall include power to make an order varying or revoking any order previously made under that provision.

## Amendment and repeals

**136.**—(1) The enactments mentioned in Schedule 7 to this Act shall have effect subject to the amendments respectively specified in that Schedule, being minor amendments or amendments consequential on the provisions of this Act.

(2) The enactments specified in Schedule 8 to this Act are hereby repealed to the extent specified in the third column of that Schedule.

## Expenses

**137.** There shall be defrayed out of moneys provided by Parliament any increase attributable to the provisions of this Act in the sums payable out of moneys so provided under any other enactment.

## Exemptions and savings

**138.**—(1) Nothing in this Act shall make unlawful—
    (a) trafficking in alcoholic liquor in a canteen held under the authority of a Secretary of State;
    (b) trafficking in alcoholic liquor in a theatre erected before January 1, 1904;
    (c) trafficking, with passengers in an aircraft, or, subject to section 93 of this Act, in a vessel or railway passenger vehicle, in alcoholic liquor for consumption on board the aircraft or vessel or in the railway passenger vehicle, if the aircraft or vessel is employed for the carriage of passengers and is being flown or navigated from a place in the United Kingdom to another such place or from and to the same place in the United Kingdom on the same day, or, as the case may be, if the railway passenger vehicle is a vehicle in which passengers can be supplied with food.

(2) Nothing in this Act shall—
    (a) affect the right of any person to carry on his business during the pendency of an appeal against the refusal of a licensing board to renew his licence;
    (b) save as expressly provided in this Act, prohibit the sale of alcoholic liquor by a wholesaler; or
    (c) affect any penalties recoverable by or on behalf of the Commissioners, or any laws relating to excise.

*Subs.* (1) Both canteens and theatres erected before 1904 are subject to permitted hours, see ss.54 and 121, the theatre having to comply with the conditions of an entertainment licence.

**Interpretation**

**139.**—(1) In this Act, unless the context otherwise requires—

"alcoholic liquor" includes spirits, wine, porter, ale, beer, cider, perry and made-wine, but does not include (*a*) any liquor which is of a strength not exceeding 0·5 per cent. of ethyl alcohol by volume (at a temperature of 20 degrees Celsius); (*b*) perfumes; (*c*) flavouring essences recognised by the Commissioners as not being intended for consumption as or with dutiable alcoholic liquor; (*d*) spirits, wine or made-wine so medicated as to be, in the opinion of the Commissioners, intended for use as a medicine and not as a beverage.

"bar" includes any place exclusively or mainly used for the sale and consumption of alcoholic liquor;

"Commissioners" means Commissioners of Customs and Excise;

"constable" means a constable of a police force maintained under the Police (Scotland) Act 1967;

"contravene" includes fail to comply with, and "contravention" has a corresponding meaning;

"development corporation" has the same meaning as in the New Towns (Scotland) Act 1968;

"enactment" includes any order, rule, regulation or other instrument made under an Act of Parliament;

"fire authority" has the same meaning as in section 38 of the Fire Services Act 1947;

"grant," in relation to a licence, includes a grant by way of renewal, and "granting" and "application" shall be construed accordingly;

"hawking" means trafficking in or about the roads or other places or in or from any boat or other vessel on the water;

"hotel" means—

(*a*) in towns and the suburbs thereof, a house containing at least four apartments set apart exclusively for the sleeping accommodation of travellers;

(*b*) in rural districts and populous places not exceeding 1,000 inhabitants according to the census for the time being last taken, a house containing at least two such apartments;

"licence" means a licence granted under this Act other than under Part III of this Act;

"licence-holder" and "holder of a licence" mean the holder of a licence under this Act other than under Part III of this Act;

"licensed canteen" means a seaman's canteen in respect of which a licence under Part III of this Act is in force;

"licensed premises" means premises in respect of which a licence under this Act is in force other than under Part III of this Act;

"licensing area" means any area for which there is a separate licensing board;

"licensing board" mean a licensing board constituted under section 1 of this Act;

"made-wine" means made-wine within the meaning of section 1 of the Alcoholic Liquor Duties Act 1979;

"new licence" means a licence granted in respect of premises for which, at the time of the application for such grant, either no licence was in force or a licence in a form different from the form of licence so granted was in force;

Provided that a licence granted in respect of premises which have been rebuilt after having been destroyed by fire, tempest or other unforeseen cause, and for which, at the time when they were so destroyed, a licence in the same form as the first-mentioned licence was in force, shall be deemed not to be a new licence;

"off-sale premises" means premises in respect of which an off-sale licence under this Act is in force;

"permitted hours" means the hours during which by virtue of this Act alcoholic liquor may be sold, supplied or consumed in licensed premises;

"prescribed" means prescribed by regulations made under section 37 of this Act;

"public house" includes an inn, ale-house, victualling house or other premises in which alcoholic liquor is sold by retail for consumption either on or off the premises;

"registered club" means a club in respect of which a certificate of registration under Part VII of this Act is in force, and "unregistered club" shall be construed accordingly;

"table meal" means a meal eaten by a person sitting at a table, or at a counter or other structure which serves the purpose of a table and is not used for the service of refreshments for consumption by persons not seated at a table or structure serving the purpose of a table;

"trafficking" means bartering, selling, dealing in, trading in, or exposing or offering for sale, by retail;

"wine" means wine within the meaning of section 1 of the Alcoholic Liquor Duties Act 1979.

(2) References in this Act to a bar counter in any premises shall not include references to a counter in such premises which is bona fide used, or intended to be used,—

(a) as a place at which meals are served to persons sitting thereat and at which alcoholic liquor is supplied to persons taking such meals for consumption by such a person while seated at such counter and as an ancillary to his meal; or

(b) as a place at which alcoholic liquor is dispensed to the holder of a licence in respect of the premises or any servant or agent of his, but to no other person, and is so dispensed in order that it may be supplied to persons frequenting the premises; or

(c) for both of the purposes mentioned in the two foregoing paragraphs;

and for no other purpose.

(3) For the purposes of this Act, a person shall be treated as residing in any premises, notwithstanding that he occupies sleeping accommodation

in a separate building, if he is provided with that accommodation in the course of a business of providing board and lodging for reward at those premises and the building is habitually used for the purpose by way of annex or overflow in connection with those premises and is occupied and managed with those premises.

(4) Unless the context otherwise requires, any reference in this Act to any other enactment is a reference thereto as amended, extended or applied by or under any other enactment, including this Act.

(5) Any requirement under this Act to cause to be published the address of—

(a) an applicant in respect of any competent application made to a licensing board;

(b) an employee or agent of an applicant who is not an individual natural person; or

(c) a person who is to be the holder of a licence under Part III of this Act,

may be satisfied by causing to be published the address of his agent and the clerk of a licensing board shall cause to be published the address of the agent rather than the address of any person mentioned in paragraphs (a) to (c) above if so requested by that person.

(6) Any requirement in this Act to intimate anything to an applicant may be satisfied by so intimating to his agent.

GENERAL NOTE

Amended, 1979, c. 4, Sched. 13; 1981, c. 35, Sched. 19; 1984, c. 54, Sched. 9; 1985, c. 73, s.53; S.I. 1979 No. 1755.

*Subsections.* (1) *"Alcoholic liquor."* The definition was amended by 1985, c. 73, s.53 for the purpose of excluding from the definition of alcoholic liquor, perfumes, flavouring essences and medicines (*e.g.* cough mixture). In order *not* to be alcoholic liquor, liquor has to be at or below *both* levels.

*"Hawking."* See note to s.90. For a definition of *"roads"* see Roads (Scotland) Act 1984, s.151.

*"Hotel."* See *Chief Constable, Northern Constabulary* v. *Lochaber District Licensing Board*, 1985 S.L.T. 410.

*"Licence."* See *Tuzi* v. *Edinburgh District Licensing Board*, 1985 S.L.T. 477.

*"New licence."* See *Kelvinside Community Council* v. *City of Glasgow District Licensing Board*, 1990 S.L.T. 725, where it was held that new licence includes a provisional licence.

*"Permitted hours."* See *Stewart* v. *Dunphy*, 1980 S.L.T. (Notes) 93.

*"Licensed premises."* See *Baljaffray Residents' Association* v. *Milngavie and Bearsden District Council Licensing Board*, 1981 S.L.T.(Sh.Ct.) 106, where it was held that the premises for which a provisional licence had been granted were not "licensed premises."

*"Trafficking."* See *MacDonald* v. *Skinner*, 1978 S.L.T. (Notes) 52.

(5)–(6) This sensible amendment introduced by para. 18 of Sched. 8 to the 1990 Act allows the name and address of the agent to be used in publication of applications or for the service or intimation of anything under the Act. It is sensible because the agent is probably the person who needs timeous intimation of objections or other notices and it allows for confidentiality of the applicant's address. Concern had been expressed that applicants who perhaps had banned undesirable elements from their public-house were at risk by having to reveal their addresses.

**Transitional provisions**

**140.**—(1) Between the time when sections 8, 53, 57, 58, 60 and 131(5) come into force and July 1, 1977, those provisions shall have effect as if the references to a licensing board and to a licence were references to a licensing court and to a certificate.

(2) Any order made under section 5 of the Licensing (Scotland) Act 1962 shall continue to have effect as if made under section 56 of this Act, and, where section 6 or 8 of the said Act of 1962 or section 126 of the Licensing (Scotland) Act 1959 applies to any premises, the corresponding provision of this Act, that is to say, section 57, 58 or 59 of this Act, as the case may be, shall apply to those premises.

(3) Committees for new towns constituted under section 74 of the Licensing (Scotland) Act 1959 shall continue as if constituted under section 47 of this Act.

(4) A certificate of registration granted in respect of any club under Part XI of the said Act of 1959 shall remain in force for a period of three years from the date of issue and shall have effect as if granted under Part VII of this Act.

(5) A special permission granted under section 60 of the said Act of 1959 shall have effect in relation to occasions on or after July 1, 1977 as if that Act were still in force.

(6) Nothing in section 136(2) of this Act shall affect any order, requirement, rule, regulation or byelaw made, direction given or any thing done under any enactment repealed by this Act; but any such order, requirement, rule, regulation, byelaw, direction or thing shall, so far as it has effect immediately before the repeal, continue to have effect, and, so far as it could have been made, given or done under the corresponding provision of this Act, have effect as if it had been made, given or done under that corresponding provision.

(7) Any document referring to an enactment repealed by this Act shall be construed as referring to the corresponding provision of this Act.

(8) The mention of particular matters in this section shall not affect the general application to this Act of section 38 of the Interpretation Act 1889 (which relates to the effect of repeals).

GENERAL NOTE

*Transitional provisions.* The section makes transitional provisions for sections of the Act which came into force before licensing boards took over the functions of licensing courts (subs. (1)), for the continuance of certain orders and applications of sections of the 1959 and 1962 Act to premises (subs. (2)), for the continuance of new town committees constituted under the 1959 Act (subs. (3)), for applying the provisions of the Act to club certificates of registration granted under the 1959 Act (subs. (4)), for the validity of special permissions granted prior to the transfer of functions to licensing boards (subs. (5)), for enactments repealed (subs. (6), (7) and (8)). For the Interpretation Act 1889, s.38, see now the Interpretation Act 1978, ss.16(1) and 17(2)(*a*).

## Short title, extent and commencement

**141.**—(1) This Act may be cited as the Licensing (Scotland) Act 1976 and extends to Scotland only.

(2) Sections 131 and 140(1) of this Act and this section shall come into force on the passing of this Act, and the other provisions of this Act shall come into force on the appointed day, being such day as the Secretary of State may by order made by statutory instrument appoint; and different days may be appointed under this subsection for different provisions of this Act or for different purposes, or for the purposes of the same provision in relation to different cases.

(3) Any reference in this Act to the commencement of any provision thereof shall be construed as a reference to the day when that provision comes into force.

GENERAL NOTE

*Commencement.* For commencement orders see S.I. 1976 No. 2068 and S.I. 1977 Nos. 212 and 718. The whole Act was in force by October 1, 1977.

# SCHEDULES

Section 9                        SCHEDULE 1

## TYPES OF LICENCE

### *Public house licence*

A public house licence is a licence granted in respect of a public house specified therein which authorises the holder thereof to sell by retail alcoholic liquor for consumption on or off the premises.

### *Off-sale licence*

An off-sale licence is a licence granted in respect of premises specified therein which authorises the holder thereof to sell by retail alcoholic liquor for consumption off the premises only.

### *Hotel licence*

A hotel licence is a licence granted in respect of a hotel specified therein which authorises the holder thereof to sell by retail alcoholic liquor for consumption on or off the premises.

### *Restricted hotel licence*

A restricted hotel licence is a licence which—
    (*a*)  is granted in respect of a hotel specified therein which—
        (i)  is structurally adapted and bona fide used, or intended to be used, for the purpose of habitually providing the customary main meal at midday or in the evening or both for the accommodation of persons frequenting the premises of such hotel;
        (ii)  so far as it is used or intended to be used for the purpose of providing meals to persons who are not residing there, is principally used, or intended to be used, for providing the customary main meal at midday or in the evening or both; and
        (iii)  does not contain a bar counter; and
    (*b*)  authorises the holder thereof—
        (i)  to sell by retail or supply alcoholic liquor in the said premises to persons taking table meals there, for consumption by such a person as an ancillary to his meal;
        (ii)  to sell by retail or supply alcoholic liquor in those premises to persons residing there, for consumption on the premises by such a person or by a private friend of such a person who is bona fide entertained by and at the expense of that person;
        (iii)  to supply alcoholic liquor in those premises to any private friends of a person residing there who are bona fide entertained by and at the expense of that person for consumption on the premises by such a friend entertained as aforesaid; and
        (iv)  to sell or supply alcoholic liquor in those premises to persons residing there, for consumption by such a person or by a private friend of such a

person who is bona fide entertained by, and at the expense of, that person as an ancillary to a meal supplied at, but to be consumed off, the premises; or

(v) if the application is made in that behalf, to sell or supply alcoholic liquor only as described in sub-paragraphs (ii) to (iv) above.

*Restaurant licence*

A restaurant licence is a licence granted in respect of premises specified therein which—

(*a*) is granted in respect of premises which—

(i) are structurally adapted and bone fide used, or intended to be used, for the purpose of habitually providing meals for the accommodation of persons frequenting the premises;

(ii) so far as they are used, or intended to be used, for the said purpose, are principally to be used, or intended to be used, for providing the customary main meal at midday or in the evening, or both; and

(iii) do not contain a bar counter; and

(*b*) authorises the holder thereof to sell by retail or supply alcoholic liquor in the said premises to persons taking table meals there, for consumption by such a person as an ancillary to his meal.

*Refreshment licence*

A refreshment licence is a licence granted in respect of premises specified therein which—

(*a*) is granted in respect of premises which—

(i) are structurally adapted and bona fide used or intended to be used for the provision of refreshments including food and non-alcoholic beverages for consumption on the premises; and

(ii) do not contain a bar counter; and

(*b*) authorises the holder thereof to sell by retail or supply alcoholic liquor for consumption on the premises when food and non-alcoholic beverages are also on sale, provided no alcoholic liquor is sold or supplied for consumption off the premises.

*Entertainment licence*

An entertainment licence is a licence granted in respect of premises specified therein, being places of public entertainment such as cinemas, theatres, dance halls and proprietary clubs, which authorises the holder thereof to sell by retail or supply alcoholic liquor to persons frequenting the premises for consumption on the premises as an ancillary to the entertainment provided, subject to such conditions as the licensing board may determine to ensure that such sale or supply is ancillary to the entertainment provided.

**Sections 41 and 43**          SCHEDULE 2

SEAMEN'S CANTEENS

GRANT AND TRANSFER OF LICENCES UNDER PART III OF THIS ACT

PART I

*Applications for grant of licences*

1.—(1) The applicant for the grant of a licence under Part III of this Act shall, not less than five weeks before the hearing of the application, give notice in writing of the application to the chief constable and the clerk of the licensing board and serve both of them with a copy of—

(i) the certificate of the Secretary of State,

   (ii)  the draft rules which it is proposed to make as respects the persons entitled to use the canteen,

   (iii)  a plan of the canteen and particulars of the access to the canteen and of the sanitary accommodation for persons using the canteen.

(2) The clerk of the licensing board shall, not later than three weeks before the hearing of the application, cause to be published notice of the application in one or more newspapers circulating in the licensing area.

(3) A notice under this paragraph shall state the name and address of the person who is to be the holder of the licence, the types of alcoholic liquor it is desired to sell under the licence, and the situation of the canteen.

**2.** Where an applicant has, through inadvertence or misadventure, failed to comply with the foregoing paragraph, the licensing board may, upon such terms as it thinks fit, postpone consideration of the application and, if upon any such postponed consideration it is satisfied that any terms so imposed have been complied with, may deal with the application as if that paragraph had been complied with.

# Part II

## Application for and grant of provisional licences

**3.** The provisions of Part III of this Act relating to the grant of a licence, and the foregoing provisions of this Schedule, shall apply in relation to the grant of a provisional licence subject to the modifications specified in this Part of this Schedule.

**4.**—(1) A notice under paragraph 1 above need not state the name and address of the person who is to be the holder of the licence, and references in that paragraph to the canteen shall be taken as references to the proposed canteen after the construction or conversion has been carried out.

(2) Paragraph (a) of section 41(1) of this Act shall be omitted, and the reference in paragraph (b) of that subsection to the premises shall be taken as a reference to those premises when the construction or conversion has been carried out.

**5.**—(1) A provisional licence shall not come into force until the licensing board has made it final.

(2) The licensing board shall not refuse an application to declare a provisional licence final, except, subject to sub-paragraph (3) below, on either or both of the following grounds—

   (a)  that the canteen had not been constructed or converted in accordance with the plan lodged with the licensing board;

   (b)  that the person to whom the licence is to be granted is disqualified by or under this or any other enactment from holding a licence or is in other respects not a fit and proper person to hold a licence under Part III of this Act.

(3) A licensing board shall declare final a provisional licence notwithstanding that it is not satisfied that the premises have been completed in accordance with the plan thereof lodged with the board, if it is satisfied that the premises have been completed and that the deviations from the said plan are of minor importance and have not materially altered the character of the premises or the facilities for the supply of alcoholic liquor thereat.

(4) An applicant under this paragraph shall give such notices as the licensing board may require.

# Part III

## Application for transfer

**6.**—(1) A person applying to the licensing board for the transfer of a licence under Part III of this Act shall, not less than two weeks before the meeting of the board, give notice in writing to the chief constable.

(2) A notice under this paragraph shall state the name and address of the person to whom the licence is proposed to be transferred and his occupation during the six months preceding the giving of the notice.

**7.** Paragraph 2 above, shall apply in relation to paragraph 6 above as it applies in relation to paragraph 1 above.

**Section 47**                    SCHEDULE 3

[Repealed 1981, c. 23, s.8, Sched. 4.]

**Section 53**                    SCHEDULE 4

SUNDAY OPENING OF PREMISES IN RESPECT OF WHICH A PUBLIC HOUSE
LICENCE OR REFRESHMENT LICENCE IS OR WILL BE IN FORCE AND SUNDAY
RESTRICTION ORDERS RELATING TO LICENSED PREMISES

PART I

*Applications for Sunday opening*

**1.** Applications may be made to a licensing board in accordance with the provisions of this Schedule for permission to open premises on Sundays, and any such application is referred to in this Schedule as "an application for Sunday opening."

**2.** The holder of a public house licence or a refreshment licence in respect of any premises may make an application for Sunday opening of the premises, and any such application shall be in such form as may be prescribed, shall be completed and signed by the applicant or his agent and shall be lodged with the clerk of the licensing board within whose area the premises are situated not later than five weeks before the first day of the meeting of the board at which the application is to be considered.

**3.** The clerk of a licensing board shall, not later than three weeks before the first day of the meeting of the board at which the applications are to be considered, cause to be published in one or more newspapers circulating in the area of the board a list of all competent applications for Sunday opening made to the board under paragraph 2 above.

**4.** The list mentioned in paragraph 3 above shall specify—
  (*a*)  the name, designation and address of the applicant;
  (*b*)  the address of the premises in respect of which the application is made;
  (*c*)  the first day of the meeting of the licensing board at which the application is to be considered.

**5.** Section 10(2)(*b*) and section 10(5) of this Act shall, with any necessary modifications, apply in relation to an application for Sunday opening as they apply in relation to an application for the grant of a new licence.

**6.** It shall be competent for any person mentioned in section 16(1) of this Act to object in relation to any application made under paragraph 2 above, and the provisions of subsections (2) to (4) of that section shall apply in relation to such objections.

**7.** A licensing board shall refuse an application made under paragraph 2 above if it is satisfied that the opening and use on a Sunday of the premises to which the application relates would cause undue disturbance or public nuisance in the locality, but otherwise shall grant the application.

**8.** The consequences of the refusal of an application under paragraph 7 above in respect of any premises is that, except as otherwise provided by this Act there shall be no permitted hours in those premises on a Sunday.

**9.** An applicant may appeal to the sheriff against a decision of a licensing board to refuse an application under paragraph 7 above.

**10.** Any competent objector who appeared at the hearing of any application made under paragraph 2 above may appeal to the sheriff against a decision of the licensing board to grant the application.

**11.** A licensing board shall not within two years of its refusal of an application made under paragraph 2 above in respect of any premises entertain another such application in respect of those premises.

**12, 13, 14.** [Deleted by s.46(8) of the 1990 Act.]

**15.** The grant of an application for Sunday opening under paragraph 2 shall come into effect on the making of the grant except that where there were objections at the hearing the grant shall not come into effect until—
  (*a*)  the time within which an appeal may be made has elapsed, or
  (*b*)  where an appeal has been lodged, the appeal has been abandoned or determined in favour of the applicant for the grant.

**15A.** If an application for renewal of a public house licence or a refreshment licence includes a statement that the applicant intends that the premises should be open for the sale or supply of alcoholic liquor during the permitted hours on a Sunday and if there is currently in force the grant of an application for Sunday opening, that grant shall continue to have effect—

    (*a*)  until the renewal application is granted by the board;

    (*b*)  if the renewal application is refused by the board, or refused in respect of Sunday opening, until the time within which an appeal may be made has elapsed, or if an appeal has been lodged until the appeal has been abandoned or determined.

**16.** The grant of an application for Sunday opening under paragraph 13 above shall come into effect on the renewal of the licence to which the application relates.

**17.** If an application for Sunday opening is made under paragraph 13 above any existing grant of such an application shall continue to have effect—

    (*a*)  until the first mentioned application is granted by the board;

    (*b*)  if the first mentioned application is refused, until the time within which an appeal may be made has elapsed, or if an appeal has been lodged, until the appeal has been abandoned or determined.

**18.** The grant of an application for Sunday opening shall cease to have effect when the licence to which it relates ceases to have effect.

GENERAL NOTE

Section 46 of the 1990 Act requires, despite the amendment of s.45 of that Act, that premises operated under a public house licence or a refreshment licence may only have permitted hours on a Sunday (12.30 p.m. to 2.30 p.m. and 6.30 p.m. to 11 p.m.) where the applicant for the grant, provisional grant or renewal of such a licence has stated the intention that the premises be opened for the sale or supply of alcoholic liquor on a Sunday or where an application for Sunday opening in accordance with Sched. 4 of the 1976 Act has been granted. The existing Sched. 4 procedure continues to have effect until existing licences for Sunday opening are renewed or cease to have effect. Thereafter a new procedure will simplify Sunday opening applications by allowing the applicant simply to state an intention to open on a Sunday on the application for grant, provisional grant or renewal of a public house or refreshment licence. The new provisions allow application for Sunday opening by a person who is not yet a licence-holder, which was not the former position: see *Ginera* v. *City of Glasgow District Licensing Board*, 1982 S.L.T. 136. The statement of intention will also be published and appear on site notices and notices to neighbouring proprietors if the case is a new grant only. The grounds for refusal of permitted hours on a Sunday, introduced by the 1990 Act, that the grant would cause undue disturbance or public nuisance, are the same grounds as those in Sched. 4 to the 1976 Act. Public houses are given the opportunity to apply for occasional or regular extensions of permitted hours on a Sunday for the first time. The application must be for premises to which s.59 of the 1976 Act applies, namely premises structurally adapted and bona fide used for provision of meals or, in the case of premises to which s.59 does not apply, must be for hours in the afternoon and evening only.

Sched. 4 to the 1976 Act continues to have effect until all licences with Sunday opening in force at the commencement of the Act have been renewed or have ceased to have effect. Thereafter a simplification of the procedure is envisaged. However no provision has been made for application at times other than grant or renewal, if an intention to open on Sunday is missed or refused and the licence holder wishes to apply again.

Sched. 4 to the 1976 Act is amended by s.46(8) of the 1990 Act to take account of the new s.10 procedure, namely that an applicant need no longer make a separate application for Sunday opening. Notice does not require to be given in terms of s.10(2)(*b*) and (5) when renewing a Public House or Refreshment Licence in respect of Sunday opening. New subs. (15A) states that where there is already a Sched. 4 grant of Sunday opening, it continues until the renewal of the licence by the board or if renewal is refused, or renewal of Sunday opening refused, until the time has elapsed for the making of an appeal under s.39 of the 1976 Act, or that appeal is determined. Thereafter a statement of intention to open on a Sunday for the sale or supply of alcoholic liquor will suffice.

# PART II

### *Sunday restriction orders*

**19.** Where on a complaint being made to a licensing board by any person mentioned in section 16(1) of this Act, the board is satisfied that the use of licensed premises is the cause of undue disturbance or public nuisance having regard to the way of life in the community in the locality on a Sunday, the board may make an order (in this Part of this Schedule referred to as a "Sunday restriction order"), and the effect of the Sunday restriction order is that there shall be no permitted hours on Sunday for such period as may be specified in the order or that the permitted hours on Sunday shall be reduced by such a time and for such a period as may be so specified.

**20.** The provisions of subsections (4) to (6) of section 31 of this Act shall, with any necessary modifications, apply in relation to a Sunday restriction order as they apply in relation to the suspension of a licence.

**21.** The licensing board may make a Sunday restriction order in relation to individual premises or in relation to a group of premises in respect of which the same type of licence is held.

**22.** Subsections (4) to (8) of section 65 of this Act shall apply in relation to a Sunday restriction order as they apply in relation to a restriction order under that section.

**Section 67**

SCHEDULE 5

[Repealed in Part, 1981, c.23, Sched. 4]

PENALTIES FOR OFFENCES AGAINST PROVISIONS OF THIS ACT

| 1 Provision of this Act creating the offence | 2 Rough description of offence | 3 Whether licence-holder vicariously responsible | 4 Whether licence-holder and premises liable to disqualification | 5 Penalty [see note below] |
|---|---|---|---|---|
| Section 2 | Interested person acting as member of licensing board. | — | — | 5 (£400) |
| Section 7(3) | Clerk of licensing board acting for person in proceedings before board. | — | — | 5 (£400) |
| Section 19(1) | Canvassing member of licensing board. | — | — | 3 (£100) |
| Section 29(2) | Unlawful sale of spirits. | Yes | Yes | 5 (£400) |
| Section 33(4) and (5) | Contravention of condition of occasional licence. | Yes | Yes | 3 (£100) |
| Section 34(3) | Contravention of condition of occasional permission. | — | — | 3 (£100) |
| Section 34(6) | Failure to observance of provisions relating to conduct of licensed premises. | — | — | 3 (£100) |
| Section 36(3) | Failing to comply with order to carry out structural alterations. | — | Yes | 3 (£50 and £5 for every day of default.) |
| Section 38(4) | Contravention of any bye-law or condition attached to licence. | Yes | Yes | 3 (£50) |
| Section 41(1) | Selling unauthorised liquor in canteen. | Yes | Yes | 3 (£100) |
| Section 41(3) | Failure to provide food etc. in canteen. | Yes | Yes | 3 (£100) |
| Section 54(1)(a) | Sale or supply of liquor in licensed premises or canteen or club outwith permitted hours. | Yes | Yes | 3 (£100) |
| Section 54(1)(b) | Consuming liquor in licensed premises or canteen or club outwith permitted hours. | — | — | 3 (£50) |
| Section 57(7) | Failure of club secretary to notify licensing board of alteration to premises with extended afternoon hours. | — | — | 3 (£50) |
| Section 57(8) | Failure to display notice of extended afternoon hours. | — | — | 1 (£20) |

SCHEDULE 5—continued

| 1 Provision of this Act creating the offence | 2 Rough description of offence | 3 Whether licence-holder vicariously responsible | 4 Whether licence-holder and premises liable to disqualification | 5 Penalty [see note below] |
|---|---|---|---|---|
| Section 58(7) | Failure of club secretary to notify licensing board of alterations to premises with extended evening hours. | — | — | 3 (£50) |
| Section 58(8) | Failure to display notice of extended evening hours. | — | — | 1 (£20) |
| Section 59(7) | Failure to display notice in public house of permitted hours on Sunday. | — | — | 1 (£20) |
| Section 64(6) | Contravention of condition of grant of an extension of permitted hours. | Yes | Yes | 3 (£100) |
| Section 68(1) | Selling liquor to, or allowing consumption by persons under 18 in a bar. | Yes | Yes | 3 (£50) |
| Section 68(2) | Purchase of liquor in licensed premises, or consumption of liquor in a bar, by person under 18. | — | — | 3 (£100) |
| Section 68(3) | Acting as agent for person under 18 in purchase of liquor or purchasing liquor for person under 18 or purchasing liquor for person under 18 to consume in a bar. | — | — | 3 (£100) |
| Section 68(5) | Delivering liquor to a person under 18. | Yes | Yes | 3 (£50) |
| Section 69(1) | Permitting person under 14 in a bar or canteen during permitted hours. | Yes | Yes | 3 (£50) |
| Section 69(2) | Bringing person under 14 into a bar during permitted hours. | — | — | 3 (£100) |
| Section 70(1) | Permitting unaccompanied person under 14 in premises with refreshment license during permitted hours. | Yes | Yes | 3 (£50) |
| Section 70(1) | Permitting person under 14 to remain in premises with refreshment license after 8 p.m. | Yes | Yes | 3 (£50) |
| Section 72(1) | Employing person under 18 in bar or canteen during permitted hours. | Yes | Yes | 3 (£100) |

| Section | Offence | | | Penalty |
|---|---|---|---|---|
| Section 73(1) | Employing person under 18 to serve liquor in premises with refreshment licence. | Yes | Yes | 3 (£100) |
| Section 74(1) | Entering licensed premises while drunk | — | — | 1 (£20) |
| Section 74(2) | Being in licensed premises while drunk. | — | — | 1 (£20) |
| Section 75(1) | Procuring liquor in licensed premises for drunken person. | — | — | 3 (£100) |
| Section 75(2) | Aiding a drunken person to obtain liquor. | — | Yes | 3 (£100) |
| Section 76 | Sale or supply of liquor to drunken person. | Yes | Yes | 3 (£50) |
| Section 77 | Licence holder or employee or agent drunk in licensed premises or canteen. | Yes | Yes | 3 (£100) |
| Section 78(1)(a) | Behaving in disorderly manner in licensed premises or canteen. | — | — | 3 (£100) and/or imprisonment for 60 days. |
| Section 78(1)(b) | Using obscene language in licensed premises or canteen. | — | — | 3 (£100) |
| Section 78(2) | Permitting breach of the peace, drunkenness, or riotous or disorderly conduct in licensed premises or canteen. | Yes | Yes | 3 (£50) |
| Section 79(1)(a) or (b) | Refusing to leave licensed premises or canteen. | — | — | 1 (£20) |
| Section 80 | Permitting thieves, prostitutes, etc., or stolen goods in licensed premises. | Yes | Yes | 3 (£100) |
| Section 81 | Permitting unlawful games in licensed premises. | Yes | Yes | 3 (£50) |
| Section 82 | Drinking in premises where liquor sold without a licence. | — | — | 1 (£20) |
| Section 83(1) | Consuming liquor in unlicensed places or public refreshment when public house closed. | — | — | 3 (£50) |
| Section 83(2) | Permitting consumption of liquor outwith permitted hours in unlicensed places of public refreshment. | — | — | 3 (£50) |
| Section 84 | Permitting a constable on duty to remain on the premises or supplying him with liquor. | Yes | Yes | 3 (£50) |
| Section 85 | Refusing to admit a constable to licensed premises or canteen for the execution of his duty. | Yes | Yes | 3 (£50) |
| Section 86 | Refusing to admit a constable or obstructing his entry to unlicensed premises. | — | — | 3 (£50) |

SCHEDULE 5—continued

| 1<br>Provision of this Act creating the offence | 2<br>Rough description of offence | 3<br>Whether licence-holder vicariously responsible | 4<br>Whether licence-holder and premises liable to disqualification | 5<br>Penalty [see note below] |
|---|---|---|---|---|
| Section 87(1)(a) .. .. | Selling or supplying liquor on credit in licensed premises other than hotel or restaurant licensed premises or in club or canteen. | Yes | Yes | 3 (£50) |
| Section 87(1)(b) .. .. | Consuming liquor on credit in licensed premises other than hotel or restaurant licensed premises or in club or canteen. | — | — | 3 (£50) |
| Section 88 .. .. .. | Selling fraudulently adulterated food or drink | Yes | Yes | 3 (£100) |
| Section 89 .. .. .. | Failing to close on order of sheriff or licensing board. | Yes | Yes | 3 (£50) |
| Section 90(a) .. .. | Trafficking in liquor without a licence. | — | — | 5 (£400) |
| Section 90(b) .. .. | Bartering or selling spirits without a licence. | — | — | 5 (£400) |
| Section 90(c) .. .. | Hawking alcoholic liquor. | Yes | Yes | 3 (£100) |
| Section 90A(1) .. .. | Dealing wholesale other than from permitted premises. | Yes | — | 5 |
| Section 90A(2) .. .. | Wholesaler selling liquor to person under 18. | Yes | — | 3 |
| Section 90A(3) .. .. | Wholesaler permitting person under 18 to sell alcohol without approval | Yes | — | 1 |
| Section 91(1)(a) or (b) .. | Delivery of liquor from vehicles without proper entries in day book and invoice. | Yes | Yes | 3 (£100) |
| Section 91(2) .. .. | Carrying or delivering liquor in vehicles without entries in day book and invoice. | Yes | Yes | 3 (£100) |
| Section 91(3) .. .. | Refusing to allow a constable to examine vehicle delivering liquor, or to examine day book and/or invoice. | Yes | Yes | 3 (£100) |

| Section | Offence | | | Penalty |
|---|---|---|---|---|
| Section 92(1) .. .. | Permitting liquor in crates on public service vehicle. | — | — | 3 (£100) for public service vehicle licence-holder. |
| Section 92(2) .. .. | Procuring or attempting to procure contravention of subsection (1). | — | — | 1 (£20) |
| Section 93 .. .. | Sale of liquor on passenger vessels outwith Sunday permitted hours. | — | — | 3 (£100) |
| Section 94(1) .. .. | Wholesaler permitting breach of the peace on the premises. | — | — | 3 (£100) |
| Section 94(1) .. .. | Wholesaler selling liquor to drunk persons, or selling liquor on Sundays. | — | — | 3 (£100) |
| Section 95 .. .. | Sale or supply of liquor for consumption outside registered club by non-members. | — | — | 3 (£100) |
| Section 96(a) .. .. | Sale or supply of liquor in licensed canteens for consumption off the premises. | Yes | Yes | 3 (£100) |
| Section 96(b) .. .. | Taking liquor from licensed canteen for consumption off the premises. | — | — | 3 (£100) |
| Section 97(1) .. .. | Permitting consumption of liquor on off-sale licensed premises. | Yes | Yes | 3 (£100) |
| Section 97(2) .. .. | Consuming liquor on off-sale licensed premises. | — | — | 3 (£50) |
| Section 97(3) .. .. | Taking liquor from off-sale premises for sale. | Yes | Yes | 1 (£10) |
| Section 97(4) .. .. | Selling liquor in open vessels on off-sale licensed premises. | Yes | Yes | 3 (£100) |
| Section 97A .. .. | Permitting person under 18 to sell alcohol without approval | Yes | Yes | 3 (£100) |
| Section 98(1) .. .. | Selling or supplying liquor other than to residents and/or with table meals in premises with restricted hotel licence. | Yes | Yes | 3 (£100) |
| Section 98(2) .. .. | Trafficking in or supplying liquor, except to residents, for consumption off premises subject to restricted hotel licence. | Yes | Yes | 3 (£100) |
| Section 99(a) .. .. | Selling or supplying liquor in premises subject to restaurant licence except with meals. | Yes | Yes | 3 (£100) |

195

SCHEDULE 5—*continued*

| 1<br>Provision of this Act creating the offence | 2<br>Rough description of offence | 3<br>Whether licence-holder vicariously responsible | 4<br>Whether licence-holder and premises liable to disqualification | 5<br>Penalty [see note below] |
|---|---|---|---|---|
| Section 99(*b*) .. : : | Trafficking in or supplying liquor for consumption off premises subject to restaurant licence. | Yes | Yes | 3 (£100) |
| Section 100(*a*) .. : | Trafficking in or selling liquor for consumption off premises subject to refreshments licence. | Yes | Yes | 3 (£50) |
| Section 100(*b*) .. : | Selling liquor in premises subject to refreshment licence when other refreshments are not for sale. | Yes | Yes | 3 (£50) |
| Section 101(1) .. : | Trafficking in or supplying liquor for consumption off premises subject to entertainment licence. | Yes | Yes | 3 (£50) |
| Section 101(2) .. : | Contravention of conditions attached to entertainment licence. | Yes | Yes | 3 (£50) |
| Section 103 .. : : | Making false statement in application for certificate of registration of club. | — | — | 5 (£400) |
| Section 111 .. : | Conducting club in manner giving rise to objections mentioned in paragraph (*f*), (*i*), (*j*) or (*l*) of section 108 of this Act. | — | — | 3 (£100) |
| Section 112(1) .. : | Permitting person under 14 in bar of registered club during permitted hours. | — | — | 3 (£50) |
| Section 112(3) .. : | Causing person under 14 to be in bar of registered club during permitted hours. | — | — | 3 (£50) |
| Section 113 .. : | Employing person under 18 in bar of club to serve liquor. | — | — | 3 (£100) |
| Section 114(2) .. : | Refusing to give name and address or giving false name or address to constable in a registered club. | — | — | 3 (£50) |

196

| Section | Offence | | | Fine |
|---|---|---|---|---|
| Section 119 .. : .. : | Selling liquor on off-sale premises outwith permitted hours or contravening condition of an off-sale licence. | Yes | Yes | 3 (£100) |
| Section 120(1) .. : .. : | Selling or supplying liquor in unregistered club. | Yes | Yes | 3 (£100) |
| Section 120(1) .. : .. : | Paying for liquor supplied in unregistered club. | — | — | 3 (£100) |
| Section 120(2) .. : .. : | Keeping liquor for sale or supply in unregistered club. | — | — | 3 (£100) |
| Section 120(7) .. : .. : | Refusing to give name and address to constable in unregistered club. | — | — | 1 (£20) |
| Section 123(2) .. : .. : | Selling confectionery containing alcoholic liquor to person under 16. | — | — | 3 (£50) |

NOTE: Fixed monetary penalties were transferred into a standard scale of levels by ss. 289E to 289G of the Criminal Procedure (Scotland) Act 1975 introduced by the Criminal Justice Act 1982 (see note to s. 67). In this Schedule in column 5 the appropriate level of fine is given within the originally-enacted fine (where applicable) in parentheses.

197

**Sections 103 and 105**     SCHEDULE 6

FORMS RELATING TO REGISTRATION OF CLUBS

1

*Form of statement to accompany application by club for grant or renewal of certificate of registration*

We, [*here state names and qualifications for making statement*] [*where necessary add* and I,                                    owner of the premises to be occupied [*or* occupied] by the club hereinafter mentioned] hereby certify that to the best of our knowledge and belief the                              club designated in the accompanying application is to be [*or, in the case of an application by an existing club*, has been and is to be] continued as a *bona fide* club, and not mainly for the supply of alcoholic liquor.
[*Signature, date and address of each person certifying, to be here inserted.*]

2

*Form of certificate of registration of clubs to be granted under this Act*

Certificate of Registration

I,                          , sheriff clerk of, registrar of clubs, hereby certify that                              club of [*here insert registered postal address of all premises used by the club*] is registered under the Licensing (Scotland) Act 1976. This certificate shall remain in force until the                    day of                19 ; application for its renewal must be made not later than the-day of                , 19 .
Given under my hand this                      day of, 19 .

*Registrar of Clubs.*

**Section 136**     SCHEDULE 7

[Repealed in part, 1979, c. 4, Sched. 4]

MINOR AND CONSEQUENTIAL AMENDMENT OF ENACTMENTS

*The Burgh Police (Scotland) Act 1892*

1. In section 380(4) (penalties), for the word "exciseable" there shall be substituted the word "alcoholic."
2. In section 440 (brokers not to carry on business as publicans), for the word "exciseable" there shall be substituted the word "alcoholic."

*The Customs and Excise Act 1952*

(Repealed)

*The Finance Act 1967*

5. In section 5(3) (abolition of club licences, etc.), for the word "1959" there shall be substituted the word "1976."

*Countryside (Scotland) Act 1967*

6. In section 78(1) (interpretation), for the definition of "refreshments" there shall be substituted the following definition—
" 'refreshments' includes alcoholic liquor within the meaning of the Licensing (Scotland) Act 1976:."

*The New Towns (Scotland) Act 1968*

7. In section 18(2) (disposal of land by development corporation), for the words "exciseable liquor" there shall be substituted the words "alcoholic liquor."

8. In section 47(1) (interpretation), after the definition of "the Act of 1845" there shall be inserted the following definition—
" 'alcoholic liquor' has the meaning assigned by section 139(1) of the Licensing (Scotland) Act 1976;."

*The Gaming Act 1968*

9. In section 6 (general provisions as to gaming in licensed premises), the following amendments shall be made—
  (*a*)  in subsection (2)(*a*), for the word "certificate," in both places where it occurs, there shall be substituted the word "licence";
  (*b*)  in subsection (3), the words "or certificate" shall be omitted, and for the word "court" there shall be substituted the word "board";
  (*c*)  in subsection (4), for the word "court," in both places where it occurs, there shall be substituted the word "board";
  (*d*)  in subsection (5), for the word "court," in both places where it occurs, there shall be substituted the word "board";
  (*e*)  in subsection (6), for the word "court" there shall be substituted the word "board," and the words "or certificate," in both places where they occur, shall be omitted;
  (*f*)  in subsection (8), for the words after "1964" there shall be substituted the words "and 'hotel licence'; 'public house licence' and 'licensing area' have the same meanings as in the Licensing (Scotland) Act 1976."

10. In section 7(2) (provisions as to persons under 18), the words "or certificate" shall be omitted.

11. In section 8(7) (offences), for the words "subsection (7) of section 14 of the Licensing (Scotland) Act 1962" shall there be substituted the words "Schedule 5 to the Licensing (Scotland) Act 1976," and for the words "the said section 14" there shall be substituted the words "section 67 of the said Act of 1976."

12. In paragraph 23 of Schedule 9 (permits under section 34), for the words from " 'hotel' " onwards there shall be substituted the words " 'public house licence' and 'hotel licence' have the same meanings as in Schedule 1 to the Licensing (Scotland) Act 1976."

SCHEDULE 8

REPEALS

| Chapter | Short Title | Extent of Repeal |
|---|---|---|
| 61 & 62 Vict. c. 60 | The Inebriates Act 1898. | In section 30, the words "the Licensing (Scotland) Act 1959, section 160". |
| 7 & 8 Eliz. 2. c. 51 | The Licensing (Scotland) Act 1959 | The whole Act |
| 10 & 11 Eliz. 2. c. 51 | The Licensing (Scotland) Act 1962 | The whole Act. |
| 10 & 11 Eliz. 2. c. 51 | The Penalties for Drunkenness Act 1962 | In section 1(2), the words "section 152 of the Licensing (Scotland) Act 1959" and the words "sections 153 and 154 of the Licensing (Scotland) Act 1959". |
| 1963 c. 2 | The Betting, Gaming and Lotteries Act 1963 | In Schedule 1, paragraph 24(2). |
| 1967 c. 14. | The Licensing (Certificates in Suspense) (Scotland) Act 1967. | The whole Act. |
| 1967 c. 54 | The Finance Act 1967. | Section 5 (1)(*d*). Schedule 8. |
| 1968 c. 16 | The New Towns (Scotland) Act 1968. | In section 47(1), the definition of "exciseable liquor". |
| 1968 c.65 | The Gaming Act 1968. | In section 6, in subsection (3), the words "or certificate", and, in subsection (6), the words "or certificate", where twice occurring. In section 7(2), the words "or certificate". In Schedule 2, paragraph 33(2) and (3) and paragraph 34(2). In Schedule 9, paragraph 17. |
| 1971 c. 65 | The Licensing (Abolition of State Management) Act 1971. | The whole Act. |
| 1973 c.65 | The Local Government (Scotland) Act 1973. | Section 91(6) Sections 185 and 186 Part I of Schedule 24. |
| 1975 c.20 | The District Courts (Scotland) Act 1975. | Section 10(5) Section 11(8). In section 13(1), the words "or (*b*) a licensing court or court of appeal for that area". Section 13(3) Section 17(2). Section 22. In section 26(1), the definitions of "licensing court" and "court of appeal". In Schedule 1, paragraph 28. |

# Law Reform (Miscellaneous Provisions) (Scotland) Act 1990

## (1990 c. 40)

### PART III

### THE LICENSING (SCOTLAND) ACT 1976

*Times of opening*

An Act, as respects Scotland, to amend the law relating to liquor licensing. [November 1st, 1990]

**Abbreviations**
1959    = The Licensing (Scotland) Act 1959 (7 & 8 Eliz., c. 51).
1962 Act = The Licensing (Scotland) Act 1962 (10 & 11 Eliz. 2, c. 51).
1976 Act = The Licensing (Scotland) Act 1976 (c.66)
1990 Act = The Law Reform (Miscellaneous Provisions) (Scotland) Act 1990 (c.40).

Guest  = The second report of the Guest Committee, 1963 (Cmnd. 2021).
Clayson  = Report of the Departmental Committee on Scottish Licensing Law, Chairman Dr. Clayson (Cmnd. 5354).

## Permitted hours

**45.**—(1) For section 53 of the Licensing (Scotland) Act 1976 (in this Part of this Act referred to as "the principal Act") there shall be substituted the following section— . . . [see s.53 of 1976 Act.]

(2) In section 56 of that Act (permitted hours in certain clubs)— . . . [see s.56 of 1976 Act] and [see subs. 2(*d*) of 1976 Act.].

(3) In subsection (2) of section 57 of that Act (extension of permitted hours in the afternoon in certain premises), . . . [see s.57 of the 1976 Act].

## Sunday opening of licensed premises

**46.**—(1) The amendment by section 45 of this Act of section 53 of the principal Act shall not permit the opening for sale or supply of alcoholic liquor during the permitted hours on a Sunday of premises for which there is in force a public house licence or a refreshment licence unless—

(*a*) the grant, provisional grant or renewal of such licence was in response to an application which stated that it was the intention of the applicant that the premises should be open for the sale or supply of alcoholic liquor during the permitted hours on a Sunday; or

(*b*) before such a licence has been renewed, the licensing board has granted an application for Sunday opening in respect of the premises in accordance with the provisions of Schedule 4 to the principal Act,

and, subject to subsection (8) below, the said Schedule 4 shall continue to have effect until all such licences in force at the commencement of this Act have been renewed or have ceased to have effect.

(2) In section 10 of the principal Act (applications for licences) . . . [see s.10 of 1976 Act.]

(3) In section 12 of that Act (publication of list of applications), . . . [see s.12 of the 1976 Act.]

(4) In section 17 of that Act (grounds for refusal of application) . . . [see s.17 of 1976 Act].

(5) In section 59 (restaurants in public houses to have permitted hours on . . . [see s.59 of 1976 Act.]

(6) In section 60 (other extensions of permitted hours on Sundays), . . . [see s.60 of 1976 Act].

(7) In section 64 (extensions to permitted hours), . . . [see s.64 of 1976 Act.]

(8) In Schedule 4 to the principal Act (provision for Sunday opening of premises with a public house or refreshment licence)— . . . [see Sched. 4 of 1976 Act.]

(9) Expressions used in this section and in the principal Act shall have the same meaning as in the Act.

GENERAL NOTE

This section requires, despite the amendment of s.45, that premises operated under a public house licence or a refreshment licence may only have permitted hours on a Sunday

(12.30 p.m. to 2.30 p.m. and 6.30 p.m. to 11 p.m.) where the applicant for the grant, provisional grant or renewal of such a licence has stated the intention that the premises be opened for the sale or supply of alcoholic liquor on a Sunday or where an application for Sunday opening in accordance with Sched. 4 to the 1976 Act has been granted. The existing Sched. 4 procedure continues to have effect until existing licences for Sunday opening are renewed or cease to have effect. Thereafter a new procedure will simplify Sunday opening applications by allowing the applicant simply to state an intention to open on a Sunday on the application for grant, provisional grant or renewal of a public house or refreshment licence. The new provisions allow application for Sunday opening by a person who is not yet a licence-holder, which was not the former position: see *Ginera* v. *City of Glasgow District Licensing Board*, 1982 S.L.T. 136. The statement of intention will also be published and appear on site notices and notices to neighbouring proprietors if the case is a new grant only. The grounds for refusal of permitted hours on a Sunday, that the grant would cause undue disturbance or public nuisance, are the same grounds as those in Sched. 4 to the 1976 Act. Public Houses are given the opportunity to apply for occasional or regular extensions of permitted hours on a Sunday for the first time. The application must be for premises to which s.59 of the 1976 Act applies, namely premises structurally adapted and bona fide used for provision of meals or, in the case of premises to which s.59 does not apply, must be for hours in the afternoon and evening only; see also para. 12 of Sched. 8 to this Act for regular extension of permitted hours for refreshment licence. S.64 of the 1976 Act is further amended to clarify the position when an extension of hours is granted on a Saturday evening which extends into Sunday mornings. In the past certain Boards have not allowed such an extension to go beyond midnight; however, the sub-section confirms that such an extension is permissible.

### Regular extensions of permitted hours

**47.**—(1) A licensing board shall not grant an application under section 64 of the principal Act for an extension of permitted hours unless it is satisfied by the applicant, taking account of the factors mentioned in subsection (3) of that section—

(*a*) that there is a need in the locality in which the premises in respect of which the application is made are situated for a regular extension of the permitted hours; and

(*b*) that such an extension is likely to be of such benefit to the community as a whole as to outweigh any detriment to that locality.

(2) In determining whether to grant an application for a regular extension to permitted hours in respect of any premises it shall not be a relevant consideration for the licensing board to have regard to whether any application relating to any other premises in its area has, at any time, been granted or refused or the grounds on which any such application has been granted or refused.

(3) Expressions used in this section and in the principal Act shall have the same meaning as in the Act.

GENERAL NOTE

This section extends the criteria to be taken into account by the licensing board when considering an extension of permitted hours in terms of s.64 of the 1976 Act. The wide discretion given to licensing boards in respect of their consideration of occasional and regular extensions has been restricted by the new wording, which states that a Board "shall not" grant an application unless satisfied, by the applicant, having regard to the social circumstances of the locality and to activities taking place in that locality (s.64(3)) that there is a need for an extension of permitted hours *and* that an extension is likely to be of such benefit to the community as a whole as to outweigh any detriment.

*Subsections. (1)*

This places the onus on the applicant to place before the board sufficient material upon which it may be satisfied with regard to the requirements set out in the 1976 Act.

*Subsections. (2)*

This reinforces the requirement that each application for regular extension of permitted hours be considered on its own individual merits, and makes it irrelevant to consider that (1) other premises in the board's area may have been granted or refused extended hours or that (2) the grounds upon which an application in respect of other premises was granted or refused. (For refusal see s.64(8) and Sched. 8, para. 12, to this Act.)

## Restriction orders

**48.**—(1) Section 65 of the principal Act (restriction on the permitted hours) shall be amended in accordance with the following provisions of this section. . . . [see s.65 of 1976 Act].

*Children's certificates*

## Children's certificates

**49.**—(1) The holder of a public house licence or an hotel licence in respect of any premises or an applicant for the grant, provisional grant or renewal of such a licence may apply to the licensing board, in accordance with this section, for the grant of a children's certificate in respect for the premises or any part of parts of the premises specified in the application for the certificate.

(2) A licensing board may grant a certificate (in this section and section 50 of this Act referred to as a "children's certificate") in respect of any premises or, as the case may be, part or parts of any premises if it is satisfied—

    (*a*) that the premises or, as the case may be, the part of parts of the premises constitute an environment in which it is suitable for children to be present; and

    (*b*) that there will be available for sale or supply for consumption in the part of the premises in respect of which the certificate is to apply meals and beverages other than alcoholic liquor within the meaning of the principal Act.

(3) Where a children's certificate is in force in respect of any part of any premises, notwithstanding section 69 of the principal Act, and, subject to the provisions of this section, it shall be lawful for a person under 14 years of age accompanied by a person of not less than 18 years of age to be present in such part at any time when the premises are open to the public between eleven in the morning and eight in the evening for the purpose of the consumption of a meal sold or supplied on the premises.

(4) When granting a children's certificate, the licensing board may attach such conditions to the grant of the certificate, including conditions restricting the hours during which and days on which children may be present in any premises or part of premises to which the certificate relates, as appear to the board to be appropriate.

(5) There shall be displayed at all times in any premises or part of such premises to which a children's certificate applies a notice of the fact that a children's certificate has been granted in respect of such premises or part.

(6) Any person who is the holder of a licence in respect of any premises to which or part of which a children's certificate applies or any employee

or agent of such a person who contravenes this section or any condition attached to a children's certificate shall be guilty of an offence and liable on summary conviction to a fine not exceeding level 3 on the standard scale.

(7) The following provisions of the principal Act shall apply as regards an offence under subsection (6) above—

(*a*) subsections (2) and (3) of section 67, as if an entry relating to that offence appeared respectively in columns 3 and 4 of Schedule 5 to that Act; and

(*b*) section 71.

(8) Schedule 5 to this Act shall have effect as regards the procedure to be followed for the purposes of an application for a children's certificate.

(9) A children's certificate shall be valid—

(*a*) where it is granted at the same time as the grant, provisional grant or renewal of a licence, for the period of the licence;

(*b*) where it is granted at any other time, until the end of the period for which the licence to which it relates has effect in pursuance of section 30 of the principal Act.

(10) Where a licence is transferred in pursuance of section 25 of the principal Act, any children's certificate in respect of the premises or any part of the premises to which the licence relates shall be transferred to the new licence holder subject to the same conditions as were applied to the original grant of the certificate.

(11) Expressions used in this section and section 50 of this Act and in the principal Act shall have the same meaning as in the principal Act.

DEFINITIONS
"bar": s.139(1) of the 1976 Act.

GENERAL NOTE
See also Sched. 1 to the 1976 Act.
This section introduces a Clayson recommendation and permits the holder of a public house or a hotel licence to apply for a children's certificate either in the context of an application for a grant or a provisional grant or renewal of the licence or in terms of the new Sched. 5 procedure in this Act in respect of a suitable part or all of the premises. The grant of a certificate is discretionary: the board needs to be satisfied that the premises or the part to which the application relates constitute an environment in which it is suitable for children to be present and that meals and non-alcoholic beverages will be available. A review of the procedures and requirements adopted by the various boards reveals a diversity of approaches. The requirements, usually monitored by the police or the Environmental Health Department range from the sensible to the ridiculous. They include provisions of baby changing facilities, children's menu, high chairs, non-smoking areas, suitable toilet facilities, non-glass drink vessels, "parking" place for prams and push-chair, for nappy disposal, and heating appliances, open fires, stairs and electrical sockets to be guarded, amusement with prize machines to be covered, switched off or clearly identified with a notice to the effect that persons under 18 must not play, that the certificate apply to the lounge bar and not the public bar, that "nothing shall be done to prevent or dissuade breast-feeding from taking place" and "if the part of the premises under application is a public bar as opposed to a lounge bar, the applicant, as far as possible, ensures that small children are not subjected to offensive language." Bearing in mind that children can be present in premises with a refreshment or restaurant licence without the licence holder requiring to make the sometimes exacting standard imposed by a children's certificate, it would appear that the licence holder applying for a children's certificate for a public house or hotel bar could be at a disadvantage. Where a children's certificate is in force, despite the terms of s.69 of the 1976 Act, children under the age of 14 years are allowed to be present in the bar

if accompanied by a person over 18 years during the hours from 11 a.m. to 8 p.m. or such others as may be specified by the board (see *infra*) for the consumption of a meal sold or supplied on the premises. S.69 of the 1976 Act prohibits persons under 14 to be in the bar of any premises during permitted hours, however, it does not apply where the premises have been considered suitable and granted a children's certificate. The board, in granting a children's certificate, may attach conditions as it sees fit, including conditions restricting the hours during which or days on which children may be allowed on the premises. A notice intimating that a children's certificate is in force must be displayed at all times in the part of the premises to which it relates. Contravention of this section or any condition attached to the certificate is a criminal offence, for which the licence-holder can be vicariously liable, and which can result in disqualification. S.71 of the 1976 Act provides the statutory defence of due diligence. For discussion of vicarious liability and due diligence see paras. 7.3 to 7.8 of the Introduction. The procedure for applying for a children's certificate is set out in Sched. 5 to this Act. The certificate is valid if granted at the same time as the licence, for the period of the licence, or, if granted at any other time, until the end of the validity of the licence in terms of s.30 of the 1976 Act, *i.e.* the balance of its three years. The children's certificate, once granted, will transfer in respect of an application in terms of s.25 of the 1976 Act with the main licence, subject to the same conditions, if any, as attach to the original grant.

### Suspension of children's certificate

**50.**—(1) Where a licensing board considers that the premises or part of the premises to which a children's certificate relates no longer constitute an environment in which it is suitable for children to be present they shall decide whether or not to hold a hearing for the purpose of determining whether to suspend the certificate.

(2) Where the licensing board decides to hold a hearing as mentioned in subsection (1) above—

(a) the clerk of the board shall serve on the holder of the children's certificate, not less than 21 days before the hearing, a notice that the board proposes to hold a hearing, specifying the grounds upon which suspension of the certificate may be made;

(b) the clerk of the board shall give notice of the hearing to the chief constable;

(c) the chief constable may, not less than seven days before the hearing, lodge notice with the clerk of the board that he wishes to be heard in support of suspension of the children's certificate specifying the grounds on which he seeks such suspension, and any such notice shall be intimated by the chief constable to the holder of the licence;

(d) the board shall not order suspension of a children's certificate without hearing the holder thereof unless, after receiving due notice of the hearing, the holder fails to appear.

(3) The period of the suspension of a children's certificate under this section shall be a fixed period not exceeding one year or the unexpired portion of the duration of the certificate, whichever is the less, and the effect of the suspension is that the certificate shall cease to have effect during the period of the suspension.

(4) Where

(a) a children's certificate has been suspended under this section, or further suspended under this subsection; and

(b) it appears to the licensing board that the grounds upon which the suspension or further suspension was made continue to obtain, the licensing board may, not more than one months before the expiry of the period of the suspension or, as the case may be, further suspension, determine that the suspension shall be continued for a further period of not more than one year, and this section shall have effect as regards any such further suspension as it has for the purposes of an initial suspension.

GENERAL NOTE

This section allows the licensing board to decide whether or not to hold a hearing to consider the suspension of a children's certificate when the premises to which the certificate relates no longer constitute an environment suitable for children. The decision to hold a hearing does not need to be made in respect of a complaint, and the terms of the section are similar to the provisions of s.32 of the 1976 Act which gives a licensing board power to make a closure order in respect of premises it considers no longer suitable or convenient for the sale of alcoholic liquor. The procedure for intimation of the hearing is also similar to the terms of s.32 of the 1976 Act, and similarly requires notice to be given to the Chief Constable. Such notice by the Clerk to the Chief Constable should allow the Chief Constable sufficient time to intimate that he wishes to be heard not less than seven days before the hearing. The Chief Constable may give notice not less than seven days before the hearing that he wishes to be heard in support of the suspension and he must specify the grounds on which he seeks suspension. The Chief Constable must intimate that notice, specifying the grounds, to the licence-holder before the hearing. If the licence-holder fails to appear at the hearing, the licensing board may suspend the certificate, but if the licence-holder appears, he must be given the opportunity of being heard. The period of suspension must be fixed and must not exceed one year or the unexpired portion of the duration of the certificate, whichever is less; the effect of suspension is that the certificate ceases to have effect (for discussion of "cease to have effect" see *Argyll Arms* (*McManus*) v. *Lorn*, Mid-Argyll, Kintyre and Islay Divisional Licensing Board, 1988 S.L.T. 290). During the suspension, if the circumstances which led to suspension continue, the licensing board may, not more than one month before the expiry of the suspension, determine that the suspension continue, apparently without need for a further hearing, although natural justice would require a board to give a licence-holder an opportunity to make representations to the board before a decision is made on continuation of the suspension. The further period of suspension must not exceed one year.

## *Transfer of licences*

**Transfer of licences**

NOTE: see further amendment by Licensing (Amendment) (Scotland) Act 1992.

**51.**—(1) In section 5 of the principal Act (arrangements for discharge of functions by licensing boards), . . . [see s.5 of 1976 Act].

(2) In subsection (1) of section 25 of that Act (transfer of licences)— . . . [see s.25 of the 1976 Act].

(5) In section 64 of that Act (occasional and regular extensions of permitted hours), . . . [see s.64 of 1976 Act].

(6) For subsection (7) of that section . . . [see s.25 of 1976 Act].

## *Wholesale selling of alcoholic liquor*

**Wholesale selling of alcoholic liquor**

**52.**—(1) After section 90 of the principal Act there shall be inserted the following section—

**"Wholesale selling of alcoholic liquor**

90A. . . . [see s.90A of the 1976 Act.]

(2) In Schedule 5 to that Act, after the entry relating to section 90(c) there shall be inserted— . . . [see Sched. 5 to the 1976 Act].

## Observations by Chief Constable

**Observations by chief constable in relation to applications**

**53.**—(1) After section 16 of the principal Act (objections in relation to applications), there shall be inserted the following section—

### "Observations by chief constable in relation to applications

16A.— . . . [see s.16A of 1976 Act].

(2) In section 31 of that Act (suspension of licences), after subsection (5) there shall be inserted the following subsection— . . . [see subs. 31(5A) of the 1976 Act].

## Supervision of sales by persons over 18

**Supervision of sales of liquor in off-sale premises by persons 18 or over**

**54.**—(1) After section 97 of the principal Act there shall be inserted the following section—

### "Supervision of sales of liquor in off-sale premises

97A.— . . . [see s.97A of 1976 Act].

(2) In section 71 of that Act (defence of due diligence), [see s.71 of 1976 Act].

(3) In Schedule 5 to that Act, after the entry relating to section 97(4) there shall be inserted— . . . [see Sched. 5 to 1976 Act].

## Presumption as to contents of containers

**Presumption as to contents of containers**

**55.**—(1) In section 127 of the principal Act (presumptions as to the contents of containers) for subsections (2) to (6) there shall be substituted the following subsections— . . . [see s.127 of 1976 Act].

(2) Nothing in this section shall apply to the prosecution of any person for an offence committed before the commencement of this section.

GENERAL NOTE
*Subs. (2)*
   This subsection provides that the amended law on presumptions does not apply retrospectively to an offence committed before the commencement of the section, even if the trial commences after the section comes into force.

**Section 49**                    SCHEDULE 5

### APPLICATIONS FOR CHILDREN'S CERTIFICATES

   1. Applications may be made to a licensing board in accordance with the provisions of this Schedule for a children's certificate within the meaning of section 49 of this Act.
   2. The holder of a public house licence or hotel licence in respect of any premises or the applicant for a new public house or hotel licence or for the renewal of such a licence may make an application for a children's certificate in respect of those premises, and any such application shall be in such form as may be prescribed, shall be completed and signed by the applicant or his agent and shall be lodged with the clerk of the licensing board within whose area the premises are situated not later than five weeks before the first day of the meeting of the board at which the application is to be considered.
   3.—(1) On any application for the grant of a children's certificate in respect of only part of any premises, the licensing board may require a plan of the premises to which the application relates to be produced to it and lodged with the clerk.

(2) A plan produced and lodged in accordance with this paragraph shall be such as will enable the board to ascertain to which part of the premises it is proposed the certificate should relate.

4. A copy of every application made under this Schedule shall be sent by the applicant to the chief constable, and if the chief constable desires to object to the grant of a children's certificate he shall, not later than seven days before the meeting of the licensing board at which the application is to be considered—

(a) lodge with the clerk of the board a written notice of his objection specifying the grounds of his objection to the grant of the certificate; and

(b) intimate such objection and grounds to the applicant,

and the chief constable shall be entitled to appear at the meeting of the licensing board which considers the application and make objection to the grant of the certificate.

5. A licensing board shall not, within two years of its refusal of an application made under paragraph 2 above in respect of any premises, entertain another such application in respect of those premises unless it has made a direction to the contrary in respect of that refusal.

6. An application for a new public house licence or for the renewal of such a licence under section 10 of the principal Act shall state whether the applicant is making an application for a children's certificate.

7. The grant of an application for a children's certificate shall come into effect on the making of the grant or, in the case of such an application made with an application for a new public house or hotel or hotel licence, on the day on which such licence comes into effect.

8. The grant of an application for a children's certificate made at the time of an application for the renewal of a licence shall come into effect on the renewal of the licence to which the application relates.

9. If an application for a children's certificate is made at the same time as an application for the renewal of a licence, any existing grant of such an application for a children's certificate shall continue to have effect until the first mentioned application is granted or, as the case may be, refused by the board.

10. The grant of an application for a children's certificate shall cease to have effect when the licence to which it relates ceases to have effect.

GENERAL NOTE

*Application procedure for a children's certificate*

*Para. 2*
The holder of a public-house or hotel licence may apply. The applicant for a new public-house or hotel licence or the renewal of the same may also apply. Applications are to be made in the form prescribed (sometimes by regulation in terms of s.37 of 1976 Act). The application must be lodged five weeks before the meeting of the board, but does not need to be considered at a quarterly meeting only.

*Para. 3*
Plans may be required of premises to which the application relates. The lodging of plans may be referred to in individual boards' regulations (s.37 of the 1976 Act) and the regulations may require plans to be to a certain scale and that a certain number be lodged. The plans should indicate the parts of premises to which the application relates.

*Para. 4*
A copy of the application should be sent to the Chief Constable by the *applicant*. The Chief Constable may, at least seven clear days before the board's meeting, (a) object by lodging a written notice of objection and he must (b) intimate the grounds of his objection to the applicant.

*Para. 5*
This provision introduces in respect of children's certificates a similar provision to that which applies to the refusal of an application for a new licence (s.14 of the 1976 Act), namely, that a further application in respect of the same premises cannot be made within two years of the refusal of an application unless the board make a direction to the contrary. Unlike the terms of s.14 of the 1976 Act, this provision does not require that the direction be requested and made at the time of the refusal. If not requested at the time of the refusal, the request should probably be made in writing as soon as practicable thereafter.

*Para. 6*

When making an application for a new public-house or hotel licence or renewal of same, the applicant should state whether application is also being made for a children's certificate. (This is similar to the new arrangements for Sunday opening in terms of s.46 of this Act.)

*Para. 7*

This provision stipulates when a children's certificate comes into effect, namely, on the making of the grant of the application, or, in respect of a new public-house or hotel licence when the new licence comes into effect. This clarifies the position as regards application for children's certificates by the holder of a provisional licence and does not follow the decision in *Ginera* v. *City of Glasgow District Licensing Board* 1982 S.L.T. 136.

*Para. 8*

A children's certificate applied for at the same time as the renewal of a licence comes into effect on the renewal of the licence: see s.30(5) of the 1976 Act.

*Para. 9*

An existing grant of a children's certificate remains in effect pending the consideration and grant or refusal of a further application for a children's certificate made at the same time as an application for renewal of a licence: s.30(5) of the 1976 Act.

*Para. 10*

A children's certificate only subsists while the licence to which it relates continues to have effect.

# SCHEDULE 8

## AMENDMENT OF ENACTMENTS

## PART I

## AMENDMENTS TO THE LICENSING (SCOTLAND) ACT 1976

1. The Licensing (Scotland) Act 1976 shall be amended as follows . . . [see 1976 Act for relevant amendments].

GENERAL NOTE

Doubt has been raised whether parts of Sched. 8 have been brought into force effectively. Section 75(3)(*a*) of the 1990 Act brought Part III of the Act into force as at January 1, 1991. It also brought into force "so much of section 74 as relates to those provisions." The difficulty is caused by the words "as relates to those provisions" which refers to Part III (and s.66) of the Act, which suggests the meaning that only the specific paragraphs of Sched. 8 which relate to Part III of the Act are to come into force. Many of the amendments stand alone in that they do not relate to the provisions of Part III of the Act.

None of the statutory instruments which bring parts of the 1990 Act into force (S.I. 1990 No. 2328, 1990 No. 2624, 1991 No. 330, 1991 No. 882, 1991 No. 850, 1991 No. 1252 and 1991 No. 1903) make reference to paragraphs 1 to 18 of Sched. 8, the paragraphs which relate to licensing.

Only paragraph 1 and 13 of Sched. 8 make specific reference to Part III of the 1990 Act, and accordingly it would appear that the remaining provisions have not been brought into force. Clearly the implications are serious, as the remaining paragraphs introduce important changes to the 1976 Act.

Had s.75 referred to so much of s.74 as related to liquor licensing or the Licensing (Scotland) Act 1976 then there would be no room for doubt. The Schedule is entitled "Amendments to the Licensing (Scotland) Act 1976" however this may not be sufficient to overcome the difficulty caused by the use of the words "so much of section 74 as relates to those provisions" which refers to Part III (and s.66) of this Act.

Section 74 when read together with s.75(3)(*a*) only brings "the enactments mentioned in Schedule 8 to this Act" into effect insofar as they "relate to those provisions" namely Part III it would appear. The matter has been raised in the case of *Mount Charlotte Investments plc* v. *Glasgow District Licensing Board*, which has been considered by Sheriff Keane at Glasgow, 1992 G.W.D. 2–87. See The Law Reform (Miscellaneous Provisions) (Scotland) Act 1990 (Commencement No. 9) Order 1991.

A more minor potential confusion is created by the wording of s.51(6) of the 1990 Act, which is read as referring to the preceding section namely s.64 of the 1976 Act, and appears to delete s.64(7) of the 1976 Act, namely the right to object to a regular extension of permitted hours application. This is clearly nonsense, particularly as subs. (6) of s.51 refers to "Sub-section 1(B) above" a clear reference to s.25(1) of the 1976 Act, as amended. The subsection accordingly refers to subs. (7) of s.25 of the 1976 Act which it amends.

# TABLE OF DERIVATIONS AND AMENDMENTS

[*Note*: If a section is not noted it means that it is a new provision in the 1976 Act.]

| Section | Derivation [1959 Act unless otherwise stated] | Amended by | Section | Derivation [1959 Act unless otherwise stated] | Amended by |
|---|---|---|---|---|---|
| 1 | ss. 1 to 9 | 1981, c. 23, Sched. 3 | 40 | s. 65 | |
| 2 | s. 10 | | 41 | s. 66 | |
| 3 | s. 17 | | 42 | s. 67 | |
| 4 | s. 18 | | 43 | s. 68 | |
| (2) | | 1990, s. 51, Sched. 8 | 46 | s. 73 | |
| 5(3) | s. 24(1) | | 47 to 52 | | Repealed: 1981, c. 23, s. 8, Sched. 4 |
| (4) | s. 24(2) | | | | |
| (5) | s. 25 | | | | |
| (7) | s. 22 | | 53 | 1962, s. 4 | 1990, s. 45 |
| (8) | s. 21 | | 54 | ss. 121 & 122 (as amended 1962, ss. 3 & 4) | |
| 6 | ss. 23 & 26 | 1990, s. 8 | | | |
| 7 | s. 28 | | | | |
| 8 | s. 29 | | | | |
| 9 | s. 32 & 1962, s. 1 | | 55 | 1962, s. 2(1) | |
| 10 | s. 34 | 1990, s. 46 | 56 | 1962, s. 5 | 1990, s. 45 |
| 12 | s. 35 | 1990, s. 46 | 56 | 1962, s. 5 | 1990, s. 45 |
| 13 | s. 37 | | 57 | 1962, s. 6 | 1990, s. 45 |
| 15 | s. 46 | | 58 | 1962, s. 7 | |
| 16 | s. 36 | 1990, Sched. 8 | 59 | 1962, s. 8 | 1990, s. 45. Repealed in pt.: 1981, c. 23, Sched. 4 |
| 16A* | 1990, s. 53 | | | | |
| 17 | s. 32(1) | 1990, s. 46, Sched. 8 | | | |
| 18 | 1990, Sched. 8 | | 60 | | 1990, s. 46 |
| 20 | s. 38 | | 61 | s. 128 (as subs. by 1962, s. 9.) | |
| 21 | s. 39 | 1990, Sched. 8 | | | |
| 22 | | Repealed: 1983, c. 28, s. 9, Sched. 10 | | | |
| 23 | ss. 42 & 43 | | 62 | 1962, s. 10 | |
| 24(2) | s. 62(1) | | 63 | s. 130 | 1979, c. 2, Sched. 4 |
| 25 | s. 47 | 1990, s. 51 | 64 | s. 60 | 1980, c. 55, s. 21; 1990, ss. 46, 51 and Sched. 8 |
| 26 | s. 54 & 1962, s. 12 | | | | |
| 27 | s. 55 | | 65 | | 1990, s. 48 |
| 28 | 1962, s. 11 | 1984, c. 54, Sched. 9 | 68 | 1962, s. 14 | |
| 29 | s. 57 | | 69 | s. 143 | 1990, Sched. 8 |
| 30 | s. 58 | | 70 | | 1990, Sched. 8 |
| 33 | s. 60 (part) | 1980, c. 55, s. 21, 1990 Sched. 8 | 71 | | 1990, s. 54 |
| 34 | 1990, Sched. 8 | | 72 | s. 144 | |
| 35 | s. 61 | | 74 | ss. 151 & 152 | |
| 36 | s. 62 | | 75 | s. 156 | |
| 37 | s. 63 | | 78(1) | s. 78(2) | |
| 38 | s. 64 | | 79 | s. 157 | |
| 39 | 1990, Sched. 8 | | 80 | s. 165 | |
| | | | 82 | s. 158 | |
| | | | 83 | s. 162 | |
| | | | 84 | s. 159 | |
| | | | 85 | s. 184 | |

| Section | Derivation [1959 Act unless otherwise stated] | Amended by | Section | Derivation [1959 Act unless otherwise stated] | Amended by |
|---|---|---|---|---|---|
| 86 | s. 185 (part) | | 120 | s. 140 | |
| 87 | s. 150 | | 121 | s. 161 | |
| 89 | s. 188 | | 122 | s. 186 | |
| 90 | ss. 133, 134, & 138 | | 123 | 1962, s. 16 | S.I. 1979 No. 1755 |
| | | | 125 | s. 163 | |
| 90A | 1990, s. 52 | | 126 | s. 187 | |
| 91 | s. 139 | | 127 | | 1990, s. 55 |
| 92 | 1962, s. 22 | 1985, c. 67, Sched. 7 | 128 | s. 189 | |
| 93 | 1962, s.21 | | 129 | s. 192(1) | |
| 94 | | Repealed: 1981, c. 35, Sched. 19 | 130 | s. 195 | |
| | | | 133 | (new provision) | 1985, c. 72, s. 52 |
| 95 | s. 141 | 1980, c. 55, s. 21 | 134 | s. 196 | |
| 96 | s. 142 | | 135 | s. 197 | |
| 97(2) | s. 137 | 1990, Sched. 8 | 138 | s. 198 | 1978, c. 51, Sched. 16 |
| (3) | s. 136 | | 139 | s. 199 | 1979, c. 4, Sched. 3; S.I. 1979 No. 1755; 1984, c. 54, Sched. 9; 1985, c. 73, s. 53; Repealed in pt: 1981, c. 35, Sched. 19; 1990, c. 21, s. 2 and 1990, Sched. 8 |
| 97A | 1990, s. 54 | | | | |
| 102 | s. 168 | | | | |
| 103 | ss. 169 & 178 | 1980, c. 55, s. 21 | | | |
| 104 | s. 170 | | | | |
| 105 | s. 171 | | | | |
| 106 | s. 172 | | | | |
| 107 | s. 173 & 1962, s. 17 | 1980, c. 55, Sched. 2 | 140 | (new provision) | 1980, c. 55, Sched. 2; Repealed in pt: 1980, c. 55, Sched. 3; 1981, c. 23, Sched. 4 |
| 108 | s. 174 | 1990, Sched. 8 | | | |
| 109 | s. 175 | 1990, Sched. 8 | | | |
| 110 | s. 176 | | | | |
| 111 | s. 177 | 1980, c. 55, s. 21 | Sched. 3 | | Repealed: 1981, c. 23, s. 8, Sched. 4 |
| 112 | (new provision) | 1980, c. 55, s. 21 | | | |
| 113 | 1962, s. 19 | 1980, c. 55, s. 21 | Sched. 4 | | 1990, s. 46 |
| 114 | s. 179 | | | | |
| 115 | s. 180 | | Sched. 5 | | 1990, ss. 52, 54. Repealed in pt.: 1981, c. 28, Sched. 4 |
| 116 | s. 180 | | | | |
| 117 | s. 182 | | | | |
| 118 | s. 183 | | | | |
| 119 | 1962, ss. 3(2) & 20 | | Sched. 7 | | 1979, c. 4, Sched. 4 |

# The Law Reform (Miscellaneous Provisions) (Scotland) Act 1990 (Commencement No. 9) Order 1991

(S.I. 1991 No. 2862)

[19th December 1991]

The Secretary of State, in exercise of the powers conferred upon him by section 75(2) of the Law Reform (Miscellaneous Provisions) (Scotland) Act 1990 (c.40) and of all other powers enabling him in that behalf, hereby makes the following Order:

*Citation*

**1.** This Order may be cited as the Law Reform (Miscellaneous Provisions) (Scotland) Act 1990 (Commencement No. 9) Order 1991

*Interpretation*

**2.** In this Order—
"the Act" means the Law Reform (Miscellaneous Provisions) (Scotland) Act 1990.

*Commencement*

**3.** The provisions of the Act which are specified in column 1 of the Schedule to this Order shall, insofar as they are not in force, come into force on 31st December 1991, but, where a particular purpose is specified in column 2 of that Schedule in relation to any such provision, that provision shall come into force on that day only for that purpose.

Schedule

The provisions of the Act which come into force on 31st December 1991

| Column 1 | Column 2 |
| --- | --- |
| Section 74 In Schedule 8, Part I | Only for the purpose of bringing into force Part I of Schedule 8. |

**EXPLANATORY NOTE**

*(This note is not part of the Order)*

This Order appoints 31st December 1991 as the date for the coming into force of the provisions of the Law Reform (Miscellaneous Provisions) (Scotland) Act 1990 which are specified in the Schedule to the Order insofar as these are not already in force. The provisions so specified contain amendments to the Licensing (Scotland) Act 1976 (c.66)

## NOTE AS TO EARLIER COMMENCEMENT ORDERS

*(This note is not part of the order)*

The following provisions of the Act have been brought into force by Commencement Order made the date of this Order:

| Provisions | Date of commencement | S.I. No. |
|---|---|---|
| Sections 63, 72, 74 (partially), 75 and Schedules 8 and 9 (partially) | 1.12.1990 | 1990/2328 |
| Sections 64, 65, 74 (partially) and Schedules 8 and 9 (partially) | 1.1.1991 | 1990/2624 |
| Section 69 | 1.3.1991 | 1991/330 |
| Sections 68, 74 (partially) and Schedule 9 (partially) | 1.4.1991 | 1991/330 |
| Sections 16, 23, 34 (partially), 35, 44, 73 (partially), 74 (partially), and Schedules 1 (partially), 3, 4, and 8 (partially) | 1.4.1991 | 1991/822 |
| Sections 61 and 62 and Schedules 6 and 8 (partially) | 1.4.1991 | 1991/850 |
| Sections 24, 30, 33, 34 (partially), 74 (partially) and Schedules 8 (partially) and 9 (partially) | 3.6.1991 | 1991/1252 |
| Sections 74 (partially) and Schedule 9 (partially) | 15.8.1991 | 1991/1252 |
| Sections 74 (partially), and Schedules 8 (partially) and 9 (partially) | 26.8.1991 | 1991/1903 |
| Sections 17 (partially), 18 (partially), 38, 39, 40, 41, 42, 56 (partially), 57 (partially), 58 (partially), 59 (partially), 60, 74 (partially), and Schedules 8 (partially) and 9 (partially) | 30.9.1991 | 1991/2151 |

# Licensing (Scotland) (Amendment) Act 1992

(1992 c. 18)

AN

ACT

TO

Amend the provisions of the Licensing (Scotland) Act 1976 relating to the transfer of licences; and for connected purposes.

Be it enacted by the Queen's most Excellent Majesty, by and with the advice and consent of the Lords Spiritual and Temporal, and Commons, in this present Parliament assembled, and by the authority of the same, as follows:—

*Amendment of section 25 of 1976 Act*

**1.**—(1) Section 25 of the Licensing (Scotland) Act 1976 (transfer of licences) shall be amended as follows—

(*a*) in subsection (1), the word "temporarily" shall cease to have effect;

(*b*) for subsections (1A) to (1C) there shall be substituted the following subsections—

"(1A) At any time, a licensing board may make such a transfer on a temporary basis and the licence so transferred shall have effect until the appropriate meeting of the board, which shall be—

(*a*) the next meeting of the board; or

(*b*) where the temporary transfer has been made within the period of 6 weeks before the first day of the next meeting, the next following meeting of the board.

(1B) At the appropriate meeting and on an application for a permanent transfer, the licensing board shall make a decision on the permanent transfer of the licence transferred temporarily under subsection (1A) above.

(1C) Where a board refuses to make a permanent transfer of a licence which has been temporarily transferred under subsection (1A) above, the licence so transferred shall have effect until the time within which an appeal may be made has elapsed or, if an appeal has been lodged, until the appeal has been abandoned or determined.";

(*c*) in subsection (7), after the word "subsection" there shall be inserted the words "(1) or".

(2) In section 19(1) of that Act (prohibition of canvassing board members), for the words "or permanent transfer" there shall be substituted the words ", permanent transfer, temporary transfer under section 25(1A) of this Act or confirmation of transfer under subsection (4) of that section".

(3) In section 51 of the Law Reform (Miscellaneous Provisions) (Scotland) Act 1990 (amendment of section 25 of the Licensing (Scotland) Act 1976 paragraph (a) of subsection (2) and subsection (3) shall cease to have effect.

*Citation, extent and commencement*

**2.**—(1) This Act, which extends to Scotland only, may be cited as the Licensing (Amendment) (Scotland) Act 1992.

(2) The provisions of section 1 of this Act shall come into force on such day as the Secretary of State may appoint by order made by statutory instrument, and such an order may contain such incidental and transitional provisions and savings as appear to him to be necessary or expedient.

217

# Act of Sederunt (Appeals under the Licensing (Scotland) Act 1976) 1977

(S.I. 1977 No. 1622)

[6th October 1977]

The Lords of Council and Session under and by virtue of the powers conferred upon them by section 32 of the Sheriff Courts (Scotland) Act 1971 and by section 39(9) of the Licensing (Scotland) Act 1976 and of all other powers enabling them in that behalf, do hereby enact and declare—

*Citation, commencement and interpretation*

**1.**—(1) This Act of Sederunt may be cited as the Act of Sederunt (Appeals under the Licensing (Scotland) Act 1976) 1977 and shall come into operation on 29th October 1977.

(2) In this Act of Sederunt—

> (*a*) "the 1976 Act" means the Licensing (Scotland) Act 1976; and
> (*b*) the Interpretation Act [1978] shall apply to the interpretation of this Act of Sederunt as it applies to the interpretation of an Act of Parliament.

*Appeals procedure*

**2.** Any appeal to the sheriff under section 39 of the 1976 Act against a decision of a licensing board shall be made by way of initial writ under the Sheriff Courts (Scotland) Acts 1907 and 1913 and such appeals shall be disposed of as a summary application as defined in the said Acts.

¹**3.** At the same time as the initial writ is lodged with the sheriff clerk or as soon as may be thereafter, the appellant shall serve a copy of the initial writ—

> (*a*) on the clerk of the licensing board; and
> (*b*) if he was the applicant at the hearing before the licensing board, on all other parties who appeared (whether personally or by means of a representative) at the hearing; and
> (*c*) if he was an objector at that hearing, on the applicant.

GENERAL NOTE
¹ As substituted by S.I. 1979 No. 1520.

**4.** Where the appellant has received a statement of reasons for its decision from the licensing board he shall lodge a copy thereof with the sheriff clerk.

**5.** Where an appeal is made to the sheriff against a decision of a licensing board and that board has given as reasons for its decision one or more of the statutory grounds of refusal, the sheriff may, at any time prior to pronouncing a final interlocutor request the licensing board to give their reasons for finding such ground or grounds of refusal to be established.

GENERAL NOTE

Para. 3. See Note to s.39 regarding service of Initial writ. In an appeal against a suspension under s.31 the complainer is treated as "the applicant" and the licence holder as the "objector" for the purpose of service under this para.; *Perfect Swivel Ltd.* v. *City of Dundee District Licensing Board*, Ct. of Session, 4 March 1992, unreported. Para. 5. See *Augustus Barnett Ltd.* v. *Bute and Cowal District Licensing Board*, 1991 S.L.T. 572; Introduction at para. 3.27; Notes to ss.18 and 39.

# INDEX